# INTERIOR DESIGN

## *Illustrated*

# INTERIOR DESIGN
## *Illustrated*

### Second Edition

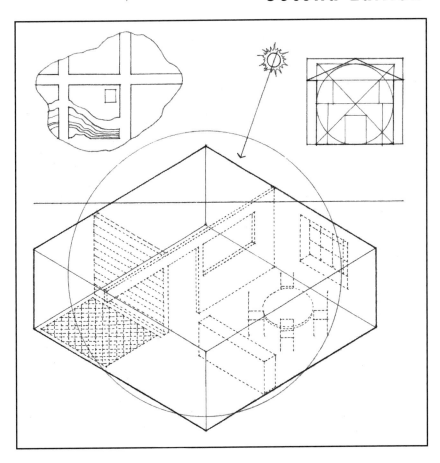

Francis D. K. Ching • Corky Binggeli

John Wiley & Sons, Inc.

Library of Congress Cataloging-in-Publication Data:

Ching, Frank, 1943–
  Interior design illustrated / Francis D.K. Ching, Corky Binggeli.— 2nd ed.
     p. cm.
  Includes bibliographical references and index.
  ISBN 0-471-47376-6 (pbk.)
  1. Interior architecture. 2. Space (Architecture) 3. Interior decoration—History—21st century. I. Binggeli, Corky. II. Title.
  NA2850.C45 2004
   729—dc22
  2004017256

Printed in the United States of America.

10  9  8  7  6  5  4  3

# CONTENTS

**Preface**................................................................ vii

**1  Interior Space**.......................................... 1

**2  Interior Design**...................................... 35

**3  A Design Vocabulary**....................... 81

**4  Interior Building Elements**............ 145

**5  Interior Environmental Systems**........ 213

**6  Lighting and Acoustics**.................. 233

**7  Finish Materials**.......................... 273

**8  Furnishings**................................ 303

**Bibliography**................................. 335

**Index**............................................ 337

# PREFACE

We spend the majority of our lives indoors, in the interior spaces created by the structures and shells of buildings. These interior spaces provide the context for much of what we do and give substance and life to the architecture that houses them. This introductory text is a visual study of the nature and design of these interior settings.

The first edition of this primer introduced students of interior design to the fundamental elements that make up our interior environments. It outlined the characteristics of each element and presented the choices we have in selecting and arranging them into design patterns. This second edition continues to emphasize these basic elements and principles of design and how design relationships determine the functional, structural, and aesthetic qualities of interior spaces.

While this second edition retains the organizational scheme of the first edition, three additional chapters allow interior building elements and environmental systems to be discussed more thoroughly. This exploration of the ways and means of developing interior settings begins with the space itself, for it is the prime material with which the interior designer works.

**Chapter 1—Interior Space** proceeds from a general discussion of architectural space to the particular characteristics of interior space in three dimensions and introduces the essential components of a building.

**Chapter 2—Interior Design** outlines a method for translating programmatic needs and requirements into three-dimensional design decisions.

**Chapter 3—A Design Vocabulary** explores the fundamental elements and principles of visual design and applies each of them to the unique field of interior design.

**Chapter 4—Interior Building Elements** describes the major categories of interior elements and discusses how each affects the functional and aesthetic development of interior spaces.

**Chapter 5—Interior Environmental Systems** outlines the environmental control systems that must be integrated with a building's structure and the layout of the interior spaces.

**Chapter 6—Lighting and Acoustics** addresses the lively and ever-present interaction of light and sound with the interior environment.

**Chapter 7—Finish Materials** introduces the palette used by interior designers to modify the architectural elements of interior spaces.

**Chapter 8—Furnishings** discusses basic types of movable components and their interplay within the built environment.

Since interior design is to a great extent a visual art, drawings are used extensively to convey information, express ideas, and outline possibilities. Some of the illustrations are quite abstract; others are more specific and particular. All of them, however, should be viewed essentially as diagrams that serve to demonstrate design principles or to clarify the relationships existing among the elements of a design.

Professional interior designers enhance the function and quality of interior spaces for the purpose of protecting the health, safety, and welfare of the public and increasing productivity and improving the quality of life. The field of interior design encompasses both visual and functional design, as well as basic knowledge of building materials, construction, and technology. This introduction to interior design is therefore broad in scope. The intent, nevertheless, is to treat the subject with clarity, make it as accessible as possible, and stimulate further in-depth study and research.

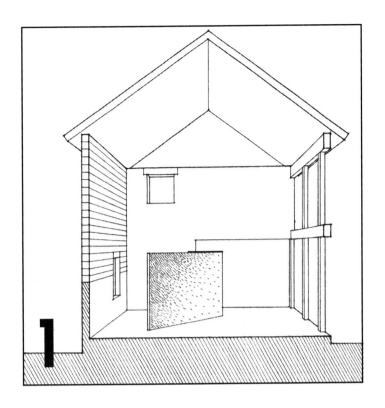

# Interior Space

Space is a prime ingredient in the designer's palette and the quintessential element in interior design. Through the volume of space we not only move, we see forms, hear sounds, feel gentle breezes and the warmth of the sun, and smell the fragrances of flowers in bloom. Space inherits the sensual and aesthetic characteristics of the elements in its field.

Space is not a material substance like stone or wood. It is an inherently formless and diffuse vapor. Universal space has no definition. Once an element is placed in its field, however, a visual relationship is established. As other elements are introduced into the field, multiple relationships are established between the space and the elements as well as among the elements themselves. Space is thus formed by our perception of these relationships.

## SPACE

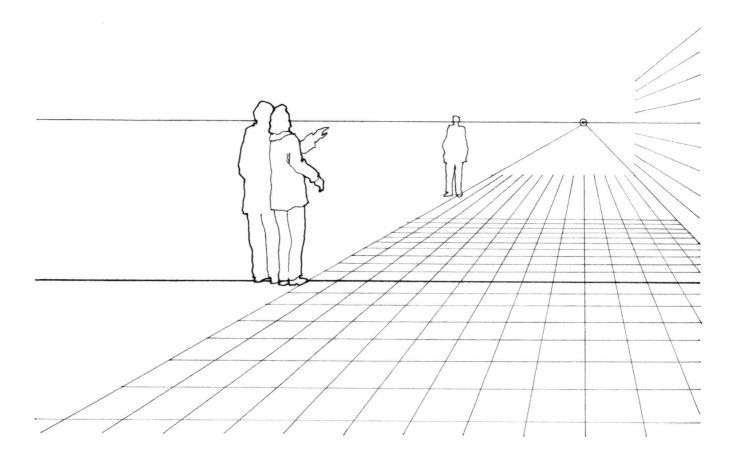

The geometric elements—point, line, plane, and volume—can be arranged to articulate and define space. In architecture, these fundamental elements become linear columns and beams and planar walls, floors, and roofs.

- A column marks a point in space and makes it visible in three dimensions.
- Two columns define a spatial membrane through which we can pass.
- Supporting a beam, the columns delineate the edges of a transparent plane.
- A wall, an opaque plane, marks off a portion of amorphous space and separates here from there.
- A floor defines a field of space with territorial boundaries.
- A roof provides shelter for the volume of space beneath it.

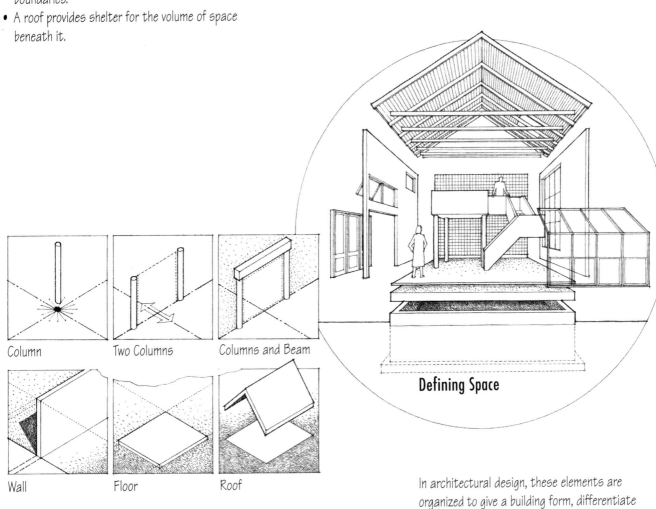

Column

Two Columns

Columns and Beam

Wall

Floor

Roof

**Defining Space**

In architectural design, these elements are organized to give a building form, differentiate between inside and outside, and define the boundaries of interior space.

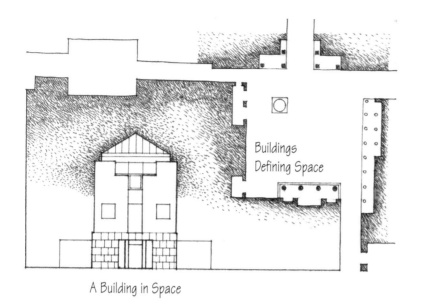

Buildings
Defining Space

A Building in Space

A building's form, scale, and spatial organization are the designer's response to a number of conditions—functional planning requirements, technological aspects of structure and construction, economic realities, expressive qualities of image and style. In addition, the architecture of a building should address the physical context of its site and the exterior space.

A building can be related to its site in several ways. It can merge with its setting or dominate it. It can surround and capture a portion of exterior space. One of its faces can be made to address a feature of its site or define an edge of exterior space. In each case, due consideration should be given to the potential relationship between interior and exterior space, as defined by the nature of a building's exterior walls.

## Buildings

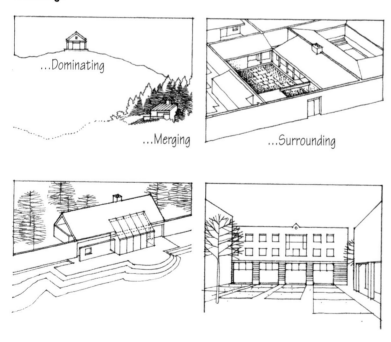

...Dominating

...Merging

...Surrounding

...Fronting

...Defining an Edge

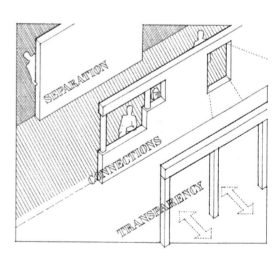

## Exterior Walls

A building's exterior walls constitute the interface between our interior and exterior environments. In defining both interior and exterior space, they determine the character of each. They may be thick and heavy and express a clear distinction between a controlled interior environment and the exterior space from which it is isolated. They may be thin, or even transparent, and attempt to merge inside and outside.

Windows and doorways, the openings that penetrate a building's exterior walls, are the spatial transitions between exterior and interior space. Their scale, character, and composition often tell us something about the nature of the interior spaces that lie between them.

Special transitional spaces, belonging to both the outside world and the inside, can be used to mediate between the two environments. A familiar example in residential architecture is the porch. Cultural and climatic variations of this theme include the veranda, lanai, and arcaded gallery.

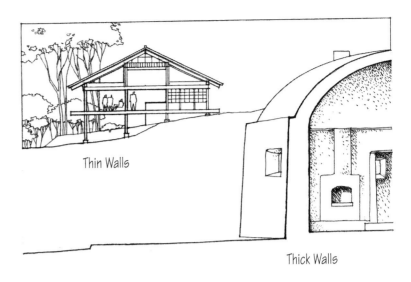

Thin Walls

Thick Walls

**Spatial Transitions**

Entrances mark the transition from here to there.

Upon entering a building, we sense shelter and enclosure. This perception is due to the bounding floor, walls, and ceiling planes of interior space. These are the architectural elements that define the physical limits of rooms. They enclose space, articulate its boundaries, and separate it from adjoining interior spaces and the outside.

Floors, walls, and ceilings do more than mark off a simple quantity of space. Their form, configuration, and pattern of window and door openings also imbue the defined space with certain spatial or architectural qualities. We use terms such as *grand hall*, *loft space*, *sun room*, and *alcove* not simply to describe how large or small a space is but also to characterize its scale and proportion, its quality of light, the nature of its enclosing surfaces, and how it relates to adjacent spaces.

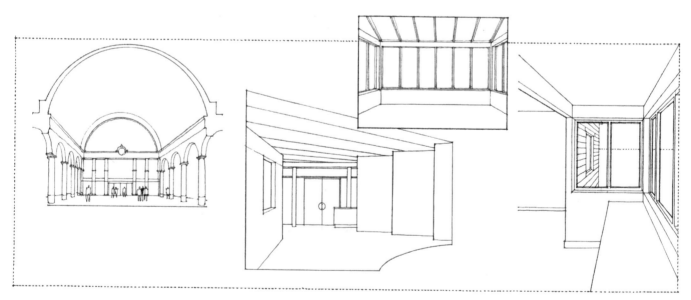

**Spatial Qualities**    Form   •   Scale   •   Light   •   Outlook

Interior design necessarily goes beyond the architectural definition of space. In planning the layout, furnishing, and enrichment of a space, the interior designer should be acutely aware of its architectural character as well as its potential for modification and enhancement. The design of interior spaces requires, therefore, an understanding of how they are formed by the building systems of structure and enclosure. With this understanding, the interior designer can effectively elect to work with, continue, or even offer a counterpoint to the essential qualities of an architectural space.

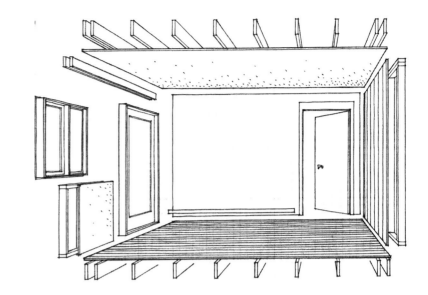

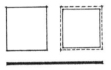

Continuation

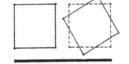

Contrast

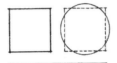

Counterpoint

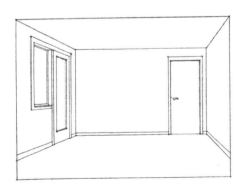

The basic shell

...modified architecturally

...or through interior design

## Interior Space

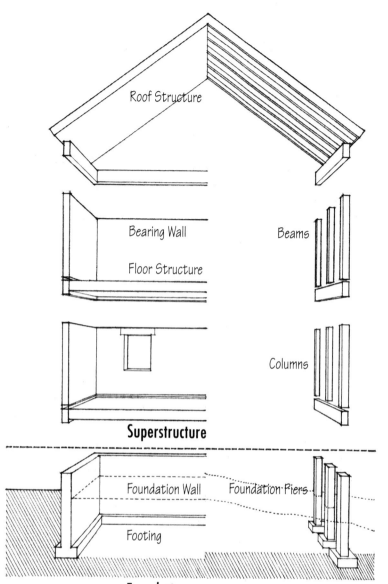

Roof Structure

Bearing Wall

Beams

Floor Structure

Columns

**Superstructure**

Foundation Wall          Foundation Piers

Footing

**Foundation**

Buildings typically consist of physical systems of structure, enclosure, and mechanical equipment.

## Structural System

- The superstructure is the vertical extension of the foundation system and consists of the columns, beams, and load-bearing walls that support the floor and roof structures.
- The foundation system is the substructure that forms the base of a building, anchors it firmly to the ground, and supports the building elements and spaces above.

These systems must work together to support the following types of loads:

**Dead Loads:** How a building is constructed determines its dead load, which is a static vertical load comprising the weight of its structural and nonstructural components, including any equipment permanently attached to the structure.

**Live Loads:** How a building is used determines its live load, which is a movable or moving load comprising the weight of its occupants and any mobile equipment and furnishings. In cold climates, collected snow and water impose an additional live load on a building.

**Dynamic Loads:** Where a building is located determines its potential loading from the dynamic forces of wind and earthquake.

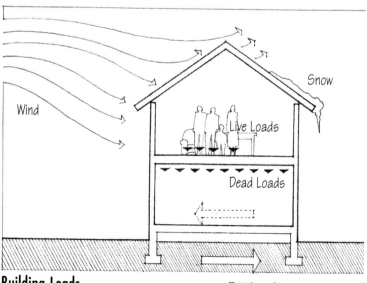

Wind

Snow

Live Loads

Dead Loads

**Building Loads**

Earthquake

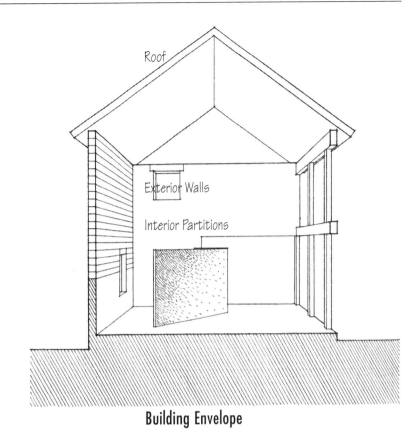

## Enclosure System
- The building envelope consists of exterior walls, windows, doors, and roof, which protect and shelter interior spaces from the exterior environment.
- Interior walls, partitions, and ceilings subdivide and define interior space. Many of these components are nonstructural in nature and carry no loads other than their own weight.

## Mechanical Systems
- Mechanical systems provide essential services to a building, such as the heating, ventilation, and air-conditioning of interior spaces. Plumbing systems supply water suitable for consumption and firefighting and dispose of sanitary waste. Electrical systems control and safely distribute power for lighting, equipment, security, communication, and vertical transportation.

**Building Envelope**

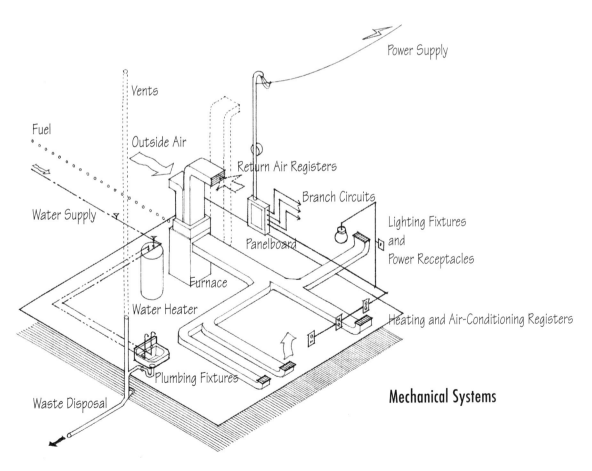

**Mechanical Systems**

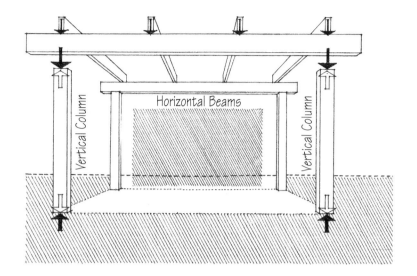

A building's structural system is formed according to the geometry of its materials and how they react to the forces applied to them. This structural form and geometry, in turn, influence the dimensions, proportion, and arrangement of the interior spaces within the building volume.

The two basic linear structural elements are the column and the beam. A column is a vertical support that transmits compressive forces downward along its shaft. The thicker a column is in relation to its height, the greater its load-bearing capacity and its ability to resist buckling resulting from off-center loading or lateral forces.

A beam is a horizontal member that transmits forces perpendicular to itself along its length to its supports. A beam is subject to bending and deflection, which results in an internal combination of compressive and tensile stresses. These stresses are proportionally greater along the upper and lower regions of a beam's cross-section. Increasing depth and placing material where stresses are greatest optimizes a beam's performance.

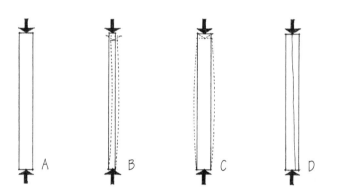

A. Columns are subject to compression.
B. Slender columns are susceptible to buckling.
C. Thick columns may compress, or
D. In the case of timber or concrete, they may split or fracture.

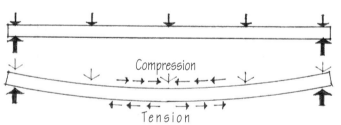

Beams are subject to bending.

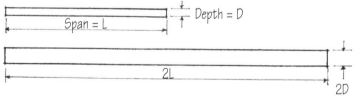

Increasing a beam's depth enables it to span greater distances.

Columns mark points in space and provide a measure for its horizontal divisions. Beams make structural and visual connections across the space between their supports. Together, columns and beams form a skeletal framework around interconnected volumes of space.

While a linear structural system may suggest a grid layout of repetitive spaces, floor, walls, and ceiling planes are necessary for the support and enclosure of interior space. Floor and ceiling planes, which define the vertical limits of space, may consist of planar slabs or a hierarchical arrangement of girders (large, primary beams) and beams and joists (a series of smaller, parallel beams). Walls and partitions need not be load-bearing and do not have to be aligned with the columns of a structural frame except when serving as shear walls and providing for lateral stability. They are free to define the horizontal dimensions of space according to need, desire, or circumstance.

Linear structural systems are cumulative by nature and eminently flexible. They allow for growth, change, and the adaptation of individual spaces to their specific uses.

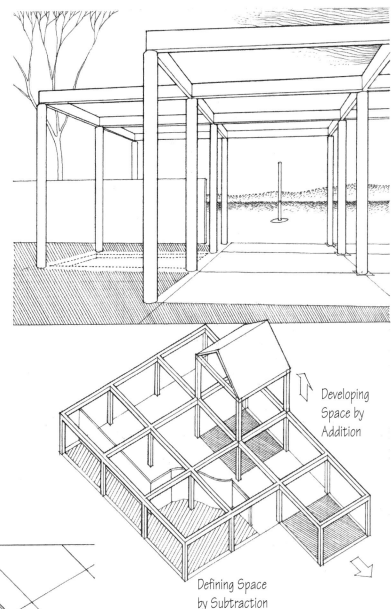

Developing Space by Addition

Defining Space by Subtraction

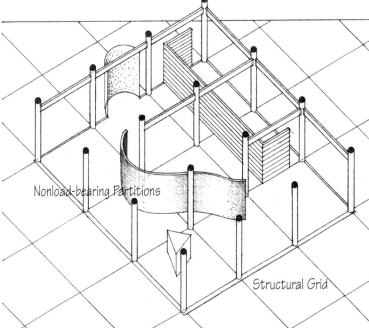

Nonload-bearing Partitions

Structural Grid

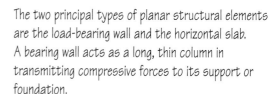

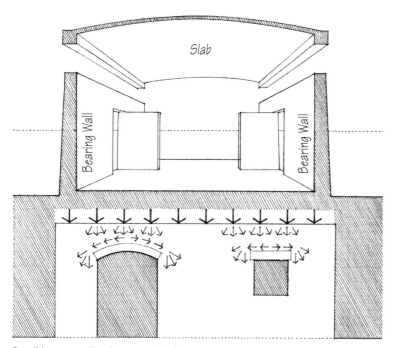

The two principal types of planar structural elements are the load-bearing wall and the horizontal slab. A bearing wall acts as a long, thin column in transmitting compressive forces to its support or foundation.

Small beams or lintels are required to span openings in bearing walls.

Window and door openings within a bearing wall tend to weaken its structural integrity. Any opening must be spanned by an arch or a short beam called a lintel to support the wall load above and allow compressive stresses to flow around the opening to adjacent sections of the wall.

A common pattern for bearing walls is a parallel layout spanned by floor joists and roof rafters or by horizontal slabs. For lateral stability, pilasters and cross walls are often used to help brace bearing walls.

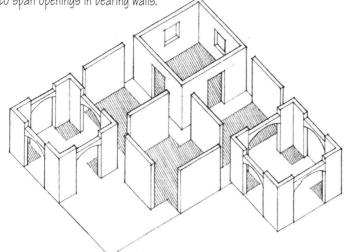

While linear structural elements outline the edges of spatial volumes, planar elements such as the bearing wall define the physical limits of space. They provide a real sense of enclosure and serve as barriers against the elements.

Varying degrees of spatial enclosure are possible with walls, depending on the size and location of openings within their planes.

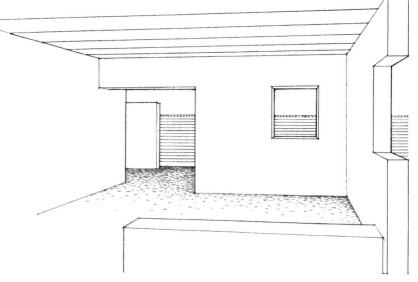

A slab is a horizontal, rigid, usually monolithic plate. A common example is a reinforced concrete slab. A slab is able to support both concentrated and distributed loads because the resulting stresses can fan out across the plane of the slab and take various paths to the slab supports.

When supported along two edges, a slab can be considered a wide, shallow beam extending in one direction. Supported along four sides, a slab becomes a two-way structural element. For greater efficiency and reduced weight, a slab can be modified in section to incorporate ribs.

When integrally connected with reinforced concrete columns, flat slabs can be supported without beams. They form horizontal layers of space punctuated only by the shafts of the supporting columns.

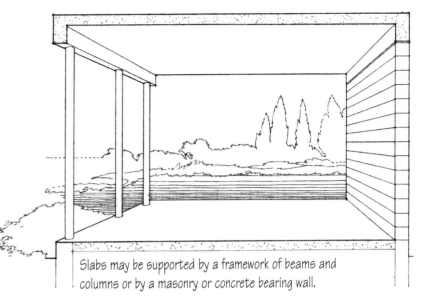

Slabs may be supported by a framework of beams and columns or by a masonry or concrete bearing wall.

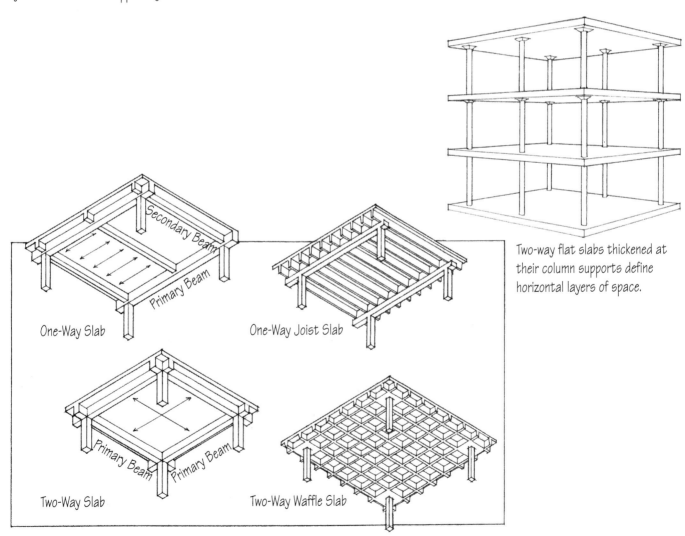

Two-way flat slabs thickened at their column supports define horizontal layers of space.

Secondary Beam

Primary Beam

One-Way Slab

One-Way Joist Slab

Primary Beam

Primary Beam

Two-Way Slab

Two-Way Waffle Slab

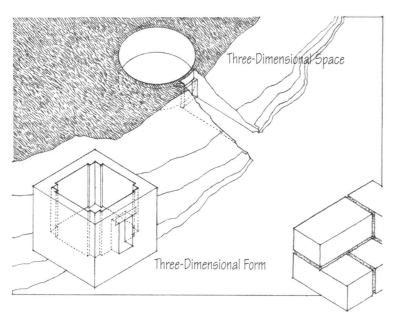

A volumetric structural system consists of a three-dimensional mass. The mass of the material occupies the void of space. Out of the mass is carved the volume of interior space. Because of the efficiency of engineering methods and the strength of modern building materials, pure volumetric structural systems are quite rare today. At a small scale, however, stone and clay masonry units can be seen to be volumetric structural elements. At a larger scale, any building that encloses interior space can be viewed as a three-dimensional structure that must have strength in width, length, and depth.

Three-Dimensional Space

Three-Dimensional Form

Three-Dimensional Material

Composite systems combine linear, planar, and volumetric elements into three-dimensional compositions of form and space.

Most structural systems are in fact composites of linear, planar, and volumetric elements. No one system is superior to all others in all situations. For the structural designer, each presents advantages and disadvantages, depending on the size, location, and intended use of a building. An interior designer should be aware of the character of the interior spaces each system defines.

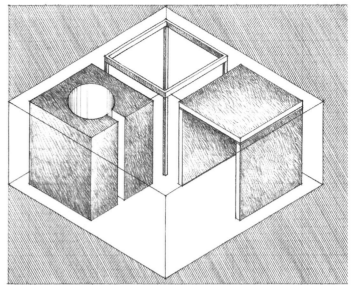

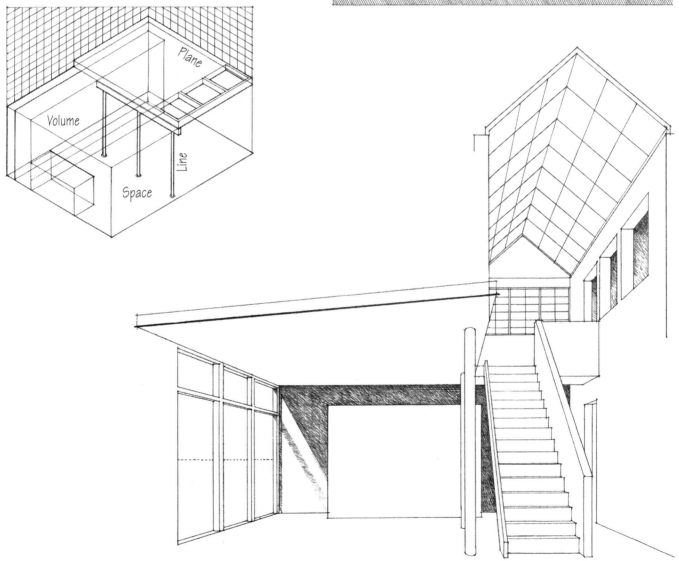

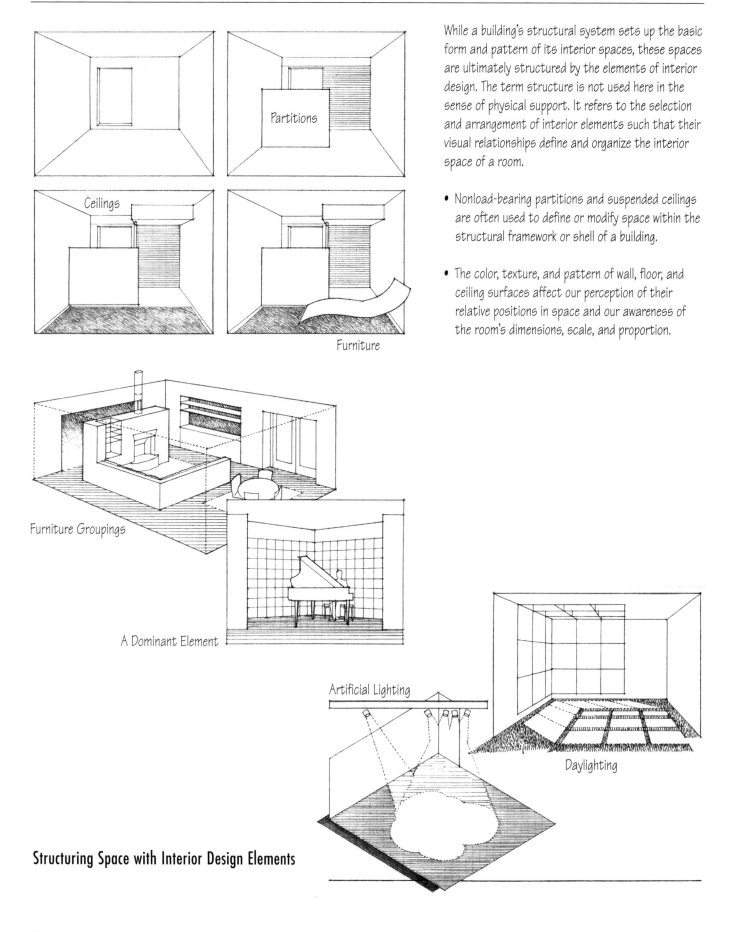

Partitions

Ceilings

Furniture

Furniture Groupings

A Dominant Element

Artificial Lighting

Daylighting

While a building's structural system sets up the basic form and pattern of its interior spaces, these spaces are ultimately structured by the elements of interior design. The term structure is not used here in the sense of physical support. It refers to the selection and arrangement of interior elements such that their visual relationships define and organize the interior space of a room.

• Nonload-bearing partitions and suspended ceilings are often used to define or modify space within the structural framework or shell of a building.

• The color, texture, and pattern of wall, floor, and ceiling surfaces affect our perception of their relative positions in space and our awareness of the room's dimensions, scale, and proportion.

**Structuring Space with Interior Design Elements**

- Within a large space, the form and arrangement of furnishings can divide areas, provide a sense of enclosure, and define spatial patterns.

- Lighting, and the light-and-dark patterns it creates, can call our attention to one area of a room, de-emphasize others, and thereby create divisions of space.

- Even the acoustic nature of a room's surfaces can affect the apparent boundaries of a space. Soft, absorbent surfaces muffle sounds and can diminish our awareness of the physical dimensions of a room. Hard surfaces that reflect sounds within a room help to define its physical boundaries. Echoes can suggest a large volume.

- Finally, space is structured by how we use it. The nature of our activities and the rituals we develop in performing them influence how we plan, arrange, and organize interior space.

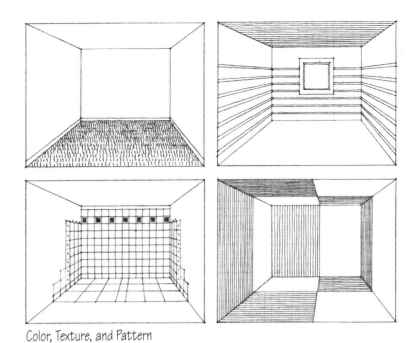

Color, Texture, and Pattern

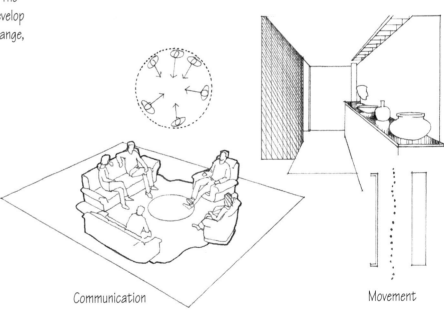

Communication

Movement

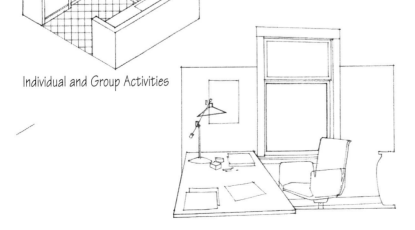

Individual and Group Activities

Interior spaces are formed first by a building's structural system, further defined by wall and ceiling planes, and related to other spaces by windows and doorways. Every building has a recognizable pattern of these elements and systems. Each pattern has an inherent geometry that molds or carves out a volume of space into its likeness.

It is useful to be able to read this figure-ground relationship between the form of space-defining elements and that of the space defined. Either the structure or the space can dominate this relationship. Even as one appears to dominate, we should be able to perceive the other as an equal partner in the relationship.

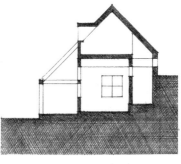

It is equally useful to see this alternating figure-ground relationship occurring as interior design elements, such as tables and chairs, are introduced and arranged within an interior space.

When a chair is placed in a room, it not only occupies space, it also creates a spatial relationship between itself and the surrounding enclosure. We should see more than the form of the chair. We should also recognize the form of the space surrounding the chair after it has filled some of the void.

As more elements are introduced into the pattern, the spatial relationships multiply. The elements begin to organize into sets or groups, each of which not only occupies space but also defines and articulates the spatial form.

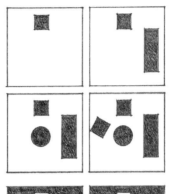

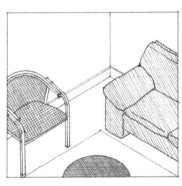

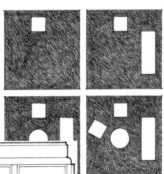

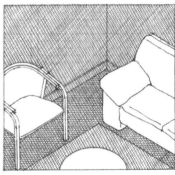

The dimensions of interior space, like spatial form, are directly related to the nature of a building's structural system—the strength of its materials and the size and spacing of its members. The dimensions of space, in turn, determine a room's proportion and scale and influence how it is used.

One horizontal dimension of space, its *width*, has traditionally been limited by the materials and techniques used to span it. Today, given the necessary economic resources, almost any architectural structure is technically possible. Wood or steel beams and concrete slabs can span up to 30 feet (9 m). Wood or steel trusses can span even farther, up to 100 feet (30 m) or more. Longer roof spans are possible with space frames and a variety of curved structures, such as domes, suspension systems, and membranes supported by air pressure.

While the width of an interior space may be limited by structural necessity, it should be established by the requirements of those who use the space and their need to set boundaries for themselves and their activities.

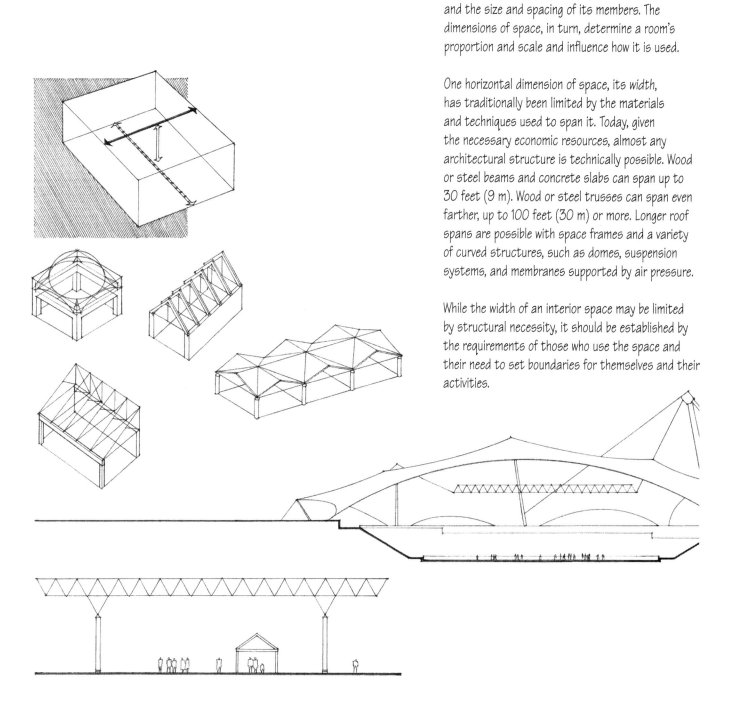

The other horizontal dimension of space, its *length*, is limited by desire and circumstance. Together with width, the length of a space determines the proportion of a room's plan shape.

A square room, where the length of the space equals its width, is static in quality and often formal in character. The equality of the four sides focuses on the room's center. This centrality can be enhanced or emphasized by covering the space with a pyramidal or dome structure.

To de-emphasize the centrality of a square room, the form of the ceiling can be made asymmetrical or one or more of the wall planes can be treated differently from the others.

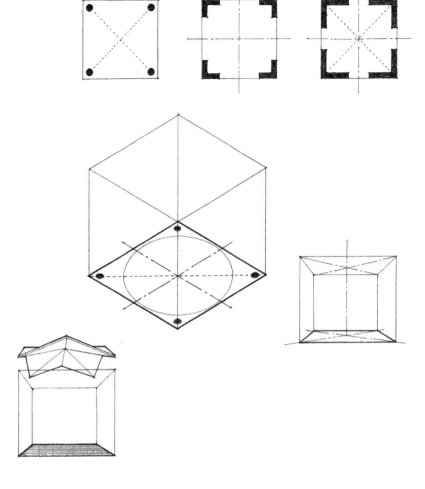

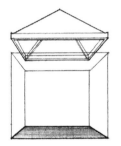

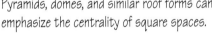

Pyramids, domes, and similar roof forms can emphasize the centrality of square spaces.

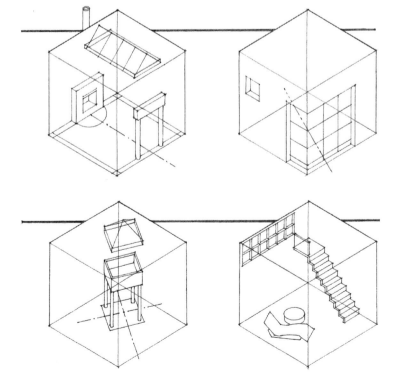

The placement of architectural elements, such as windows and stairways, can de-emphasize the centrality of square spaces.

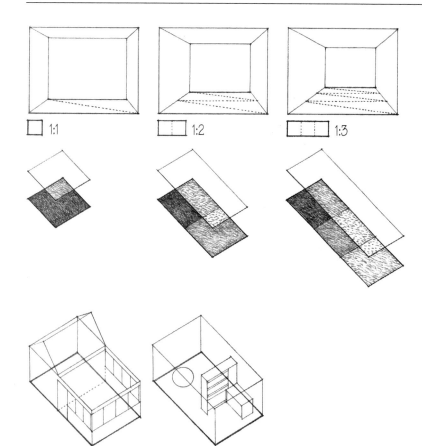

☐ 1:1          ☐ 1:2          ☐ 1:3

Square rooms are rare and distinctive. More often, a room will have a length greater than its width. A rectangular space, normally spanned across its width, is eminently flexible. Its character and usefulness are determined not only by its proportion of width to length but also by the configuration of its ceiling, the pattern of its windows and doorways, and its relationship to adjacent spaces.

When the length of a space is greater than twice its width, it tends to dominate and control the room's layout and use. Given sufficient width, the space can be divided into a number of separate but related areas.

A space whose length greatly exceeds its width encourages movement along its long dimension. This characteristic of linear spaces makes them suitable for use as gallery spaces or as connectors of other spaces.

Horizontal dimensions alone do not determine the ultimate qualities and usefulness of a space. They only suggest opportunities for development.

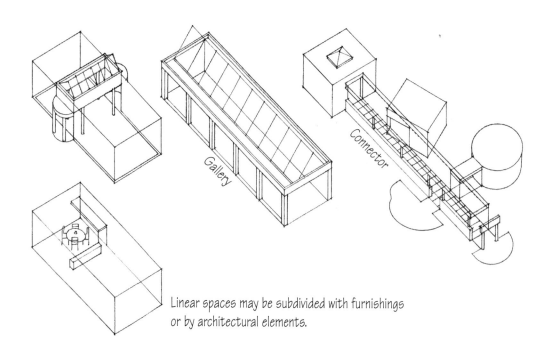

Gallery

Connector

Linear spaces may be subdivided with furnishings or by architectural elements.

Both square and rectangular spaces can be altered by addition or subtraction or by merging with adjacent spaces. These modifications can be used to create an alcove space or to reflect an adjoining circumstance or site feature.

Extension          Addition          Subtraction          Merging

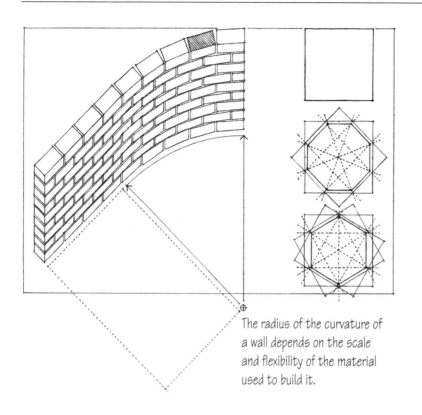

The radius of the curvature of a wall depends on the scale and flexibility of the material used to build it.

The nature of building materials and the techniques used to assemble them establish rectangular spaces as the norm. Curvilinear spaces are exceptional and usually reserved for special circumstances.

The simplest curvilinear space is a circular one. It is compact and self-centering. While focusing in on its center, a circular space also relates to the surrounding space equally in all directions. It has no front, back, or sides, unless defined by other elements.

An elliptical space is more dynamic, having two centers and unequal axes.

Other curvilinear spaces can be seen as transformations of circular or elliptical spaces that have been combined in an overlapping manner.

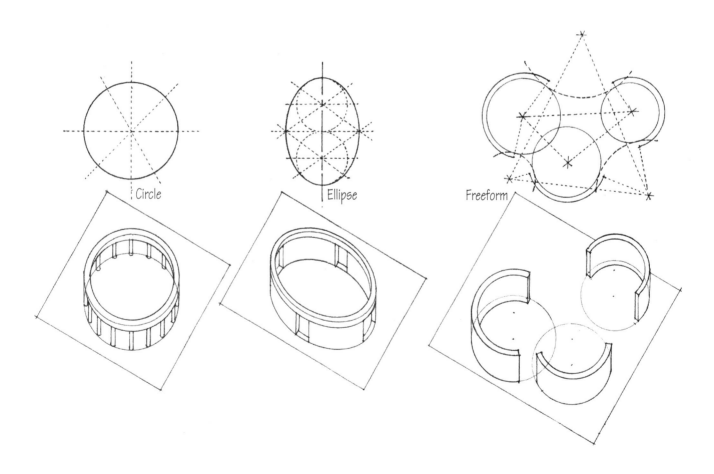

Circle

Ellipse

Freeform

Within a rectilinear context, a curvilinear space is highly visible. Its contrasting geometry can be used to express the importance or uniqueness of its function. It can define a freestanding volume within a larger space. It can serve as a central space about which other rooms are gathered. It can articulate the edge of a space and reflect an exterior condition of the building site.

Curved walls are dynamic and visually active, leading our eyes along their curvature. The concave aspect of a curved wall encloses and focuses space inward, while its convex aspect pushes space outward.

An important consideration when dealing with a curvilinear space is the integration of furniture and other interior elements into its volume. One way of resolving conflicting geometries is to arrange interior forms as freestanding objects within the curvilinear space. Another is to integrate the form of built-in furniture and fixtures with the curved boundaries of the space.

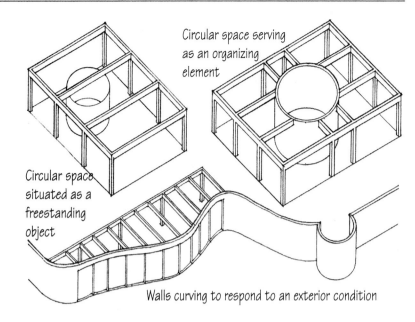

Circular space serving as an organizing element

Circular space situated as a freestanding object

Walls curving to respond to an exterior condition

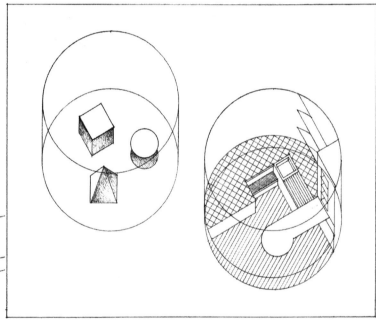

Furnishings may be placed as freestanding objects within a curvilinear space or be integrated within the curved forms.

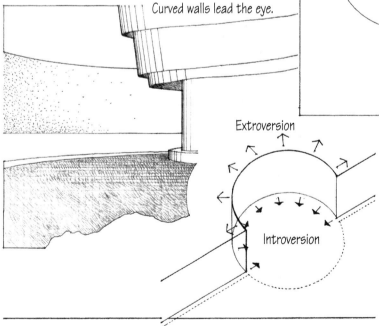

Curved walls lead the eye.

Extroversion

Introversion

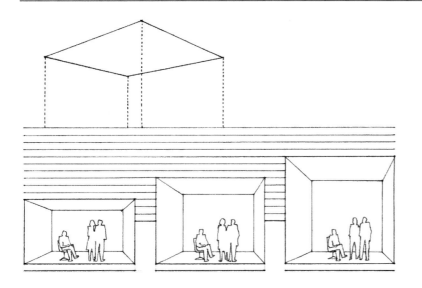

The third dimension of interior space, its *height*, is established by the ceiling plane. This vertical dimension is as influential as the horizontal dimensions of space in forming the spatial quality of a room.

While our perception of a room's horizontal dimensions is often distorted by the foreshortening of perspective, we can more accurately sense the relationship between the height of a space and our own body height. A measurable change in the height of a ceiling seems to have a greater effect on our impression of a space than a similar change in its width or length.

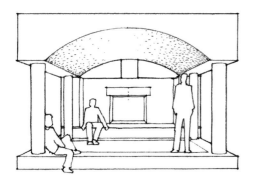

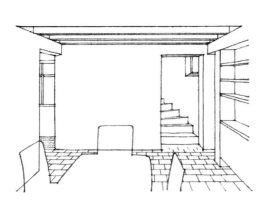

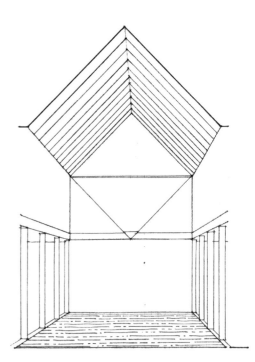

Varying the ceiling height can have a powerful effect on the perceived scale of a space.

High ceilings are often associated with feelings of loftiness or grandeur. Low ceilings often connote cave-like coziness and intimacy. Our perception of the scale of a space, however, is affected not by the height of the ceiling alone but by its relationship to the width and length of the space.

A ceiling defined by a floor plane above is typically flat. A ceiling created by a roof structure can reflect its form and the manner in which it spans the space. Shed, gable, and vaulted ceiling forms give direction to space, while domed and pyramidal ceilings emphasize the center of a space.

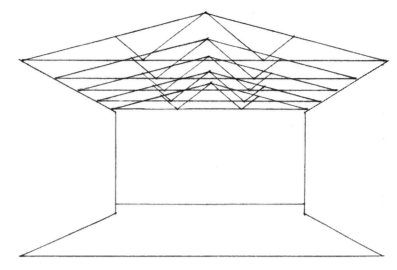

The roof structure can sometimes be left exposed, giving texture, pattern, and depth to the ceiling plane.

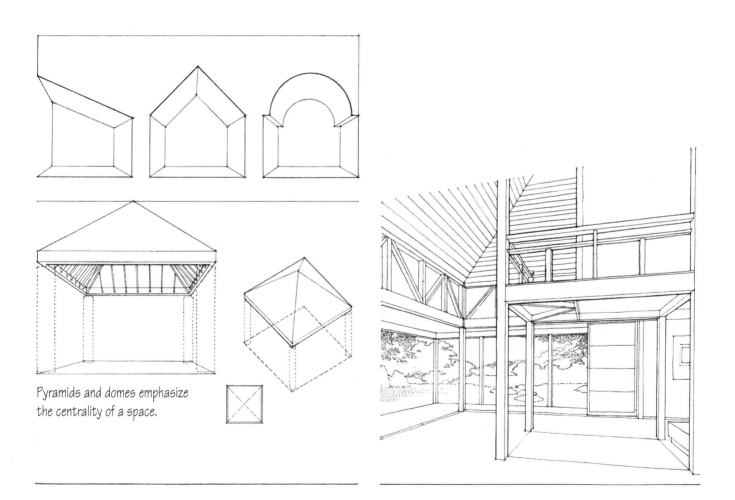

Pyramids and domes emphasize the centrality of a space.

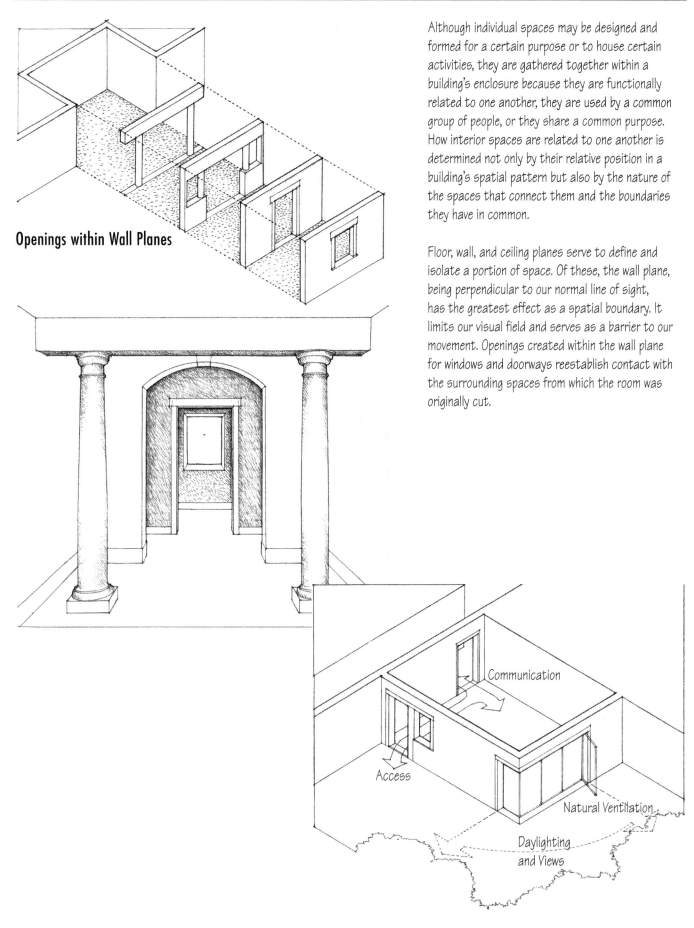

**Openings within Wall Planes**

Although individual spaces may be designed and formed for a certain purpose or to house certain activities, they are gathered together within a building's enclosure because they are functionally related to one another, they are used by a common group of people, or they share a common purpose. How interior spaces are related to one another is determined not only by their relative position in a building's spatial pattern but also by the nature of the spaces that connect them and the boundaries they have in common.

Floor, wall, and ceiling planes serve to define and isolate a portion of space. Of these, the wall plane, being perpendicular to our normal line of sight, has the greatest effect as a spatial boundary. It limits our visual field and serves as a barrier to our movement. Openings created within the wall plane for windows and doorways reestablish contact with the surrounding spaces from which the room was originally cut.

Communication

Access

Natural Ventilation

Daylighting and Views

Doorways provide physical access from one space to another. When closed, they shut a room off from adjacent spaces. When open, they establish visual, spatial, and acoustical links between spaces. Large open doorways erode the integrity of a room's enclosure and strengthen its connection with adjacent spaces or the outdoors.

The thickness of the wall separating two spaces is exposed at a doorway. This depth determines the degree of separation we sense as we pass through the doorway from one space to another. The scale and treatment of the doorway itself can also provide a visual clue to the nature of the space being entered.

The number and location of doorways along a room's perimeter affects our pattern of movement within the space and how we may arrange its furnishings and organize our activities.

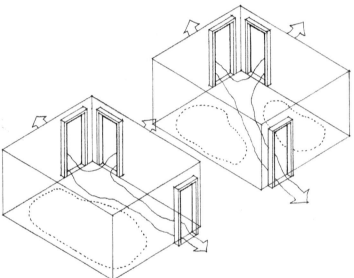

Doorway locations affect our patterns of movement and activities within a room.

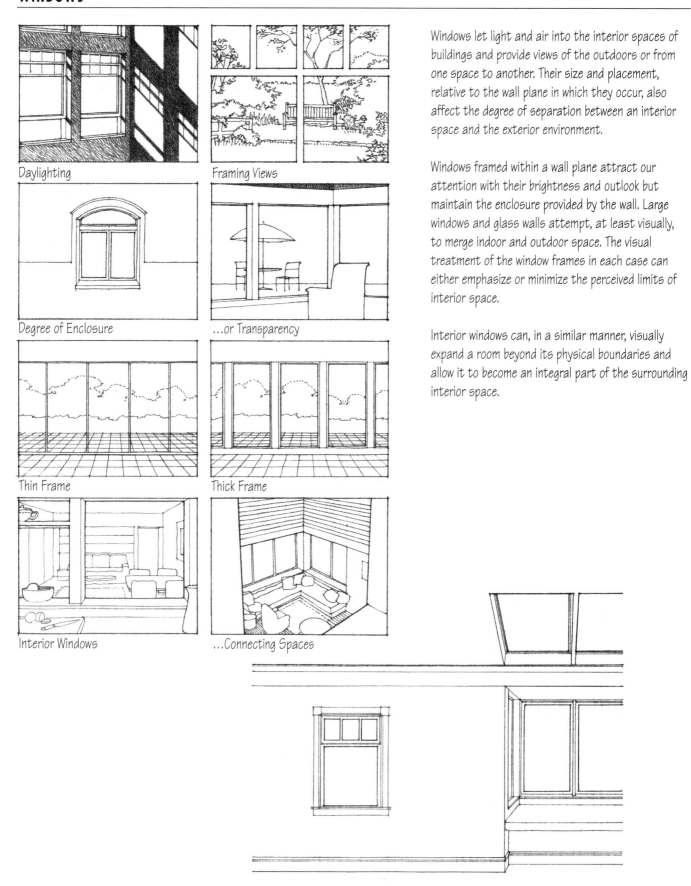

Daylighting

Framing Views

Degree of Enclosure

...or Transparency

Thin Frame

Thick Frame

Interior Windows

...Connecting Spaces

Windows let light and air into the interior spaces of buildings and provide views of the outdoors or from one space to another. Their size and placement, relative to the wall plane in which they occur, also affect the degree of separation between an interior space and the exterior environment.

Windows framed within a wall plane attract our attention with their brightness and outlook but maintain the enclosure provided by the wall. Large windows and glass walls attempt, at least visually, to merge indoor and outdoor space. The visual treatment of the window frames in each case can either emphasize or minimize the perceived limits of interior space.

Interior windows can, in a similar manner, visually expand a room beyond its physical boundaries and allow it to become an integral part of the surrounding interior space.

Stairways are also important forms of spatial transitions between rooms. An exterior set of steps leading to a building's entrance can serve to separate private domain from public passage and enhance the act of entry into a transitional space like a porch or terrace.

Interior stairways connect the various levels of a building. The manner in which they perform this function shapes our movement in space—how we approach a stairway, the pace and style of our ascent and descent, and what we have an opportunity to do along the way. Wide, shallow steps can serve as an invitation, while a narrow, steep stairway can lead to more private places. Landings that interrupt a flight of steps can allow a stairway to change direction and give us room for pause, rest, and outlook.

The space a stairway occupies can be considerable, but its form can be fit into an interior in several ways. It can fill and provide a focus for a space, run along one of its edges, or wrap around a room. It can be woven into the boundaries of a space or be extended into a series of terraces.

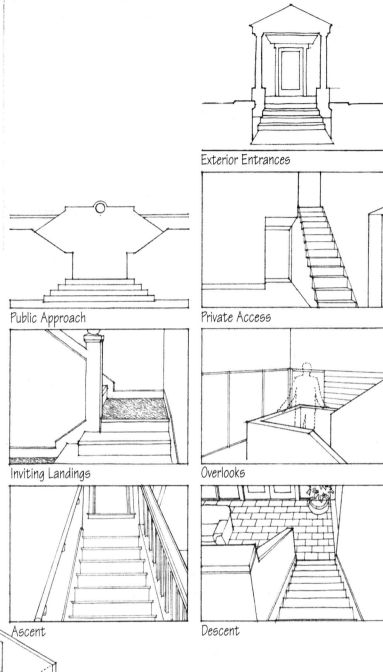

Exterior Entrances

Public Approach

Private Access

Inviting Landings

Overlooks

Ascent

Descent

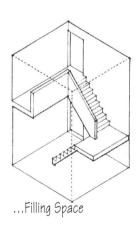

...Filling Space

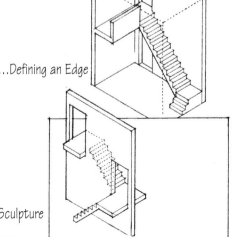

...Defining an Edge

**Stairways**  ...as Sculpture

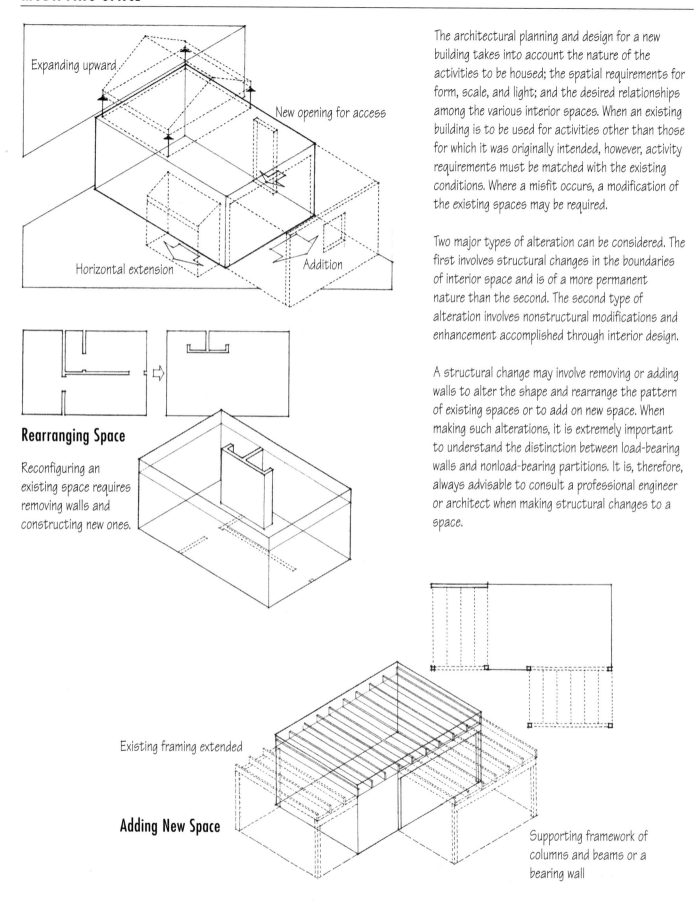

Expanding upward

New opening for access

Horizontal extension

Addition

### Rearranging Space

Reconfiguring an existing space requires removing walls and constructing new ones.

### Adding New Space

Existing framing extended

Supporting framework of columns and beams or a bearing wall

The architectural planning and design for a new building takes into account the nature of the activities to be housed; the spatial requirements for form, scale, and light; and the desired relationships among the various interior spaces. When an existing building is to be used for activities other than those for which it was originally intended, however, activity requirements must be matched with the existing conditions. Where a misfit occurs, a modification of the existing spaces may be required.

Two major types of alteration can be considered. The first involves structural changes in the boundaries of interior space and is of a more permanent nature than the second. The second type of alteration involves nonstructural modifications and enhancement accomplished through interior design.

A structural change may involve removing or adding walls to alter the shape and rearrange the pattern of existing spaces or to add on new space. When making such alterations, it is extremely important to understand the distinction between load-bearing walls and nonload-bearing partitions. It is, therefore, always advisable to consult a professional engineer or architect when making structural changes to a space.

Within the boundaries of space, the existing pattern of openings can also be altered. Windows may be enlarged or added for better daylighting or to take advantage of a view. A doorway may be moved or added for better access to a room or to improve the movement paths within the space. A large doorway may be created to merge two adjacent spaces. Any new or enlarged opening in a load-bearing wall requires a lintel or header sized to carry the wall load above the opening.

To add a stairway, daylight a space with skylights, or create a vertical relationship between two levels of space, structural changes in the floor or ceiling plane are required. Alterations in these horizontal structures of a building require that the edges of any new openings be reinforced and supported by a system of beams, columns, posts, or bearing walls.

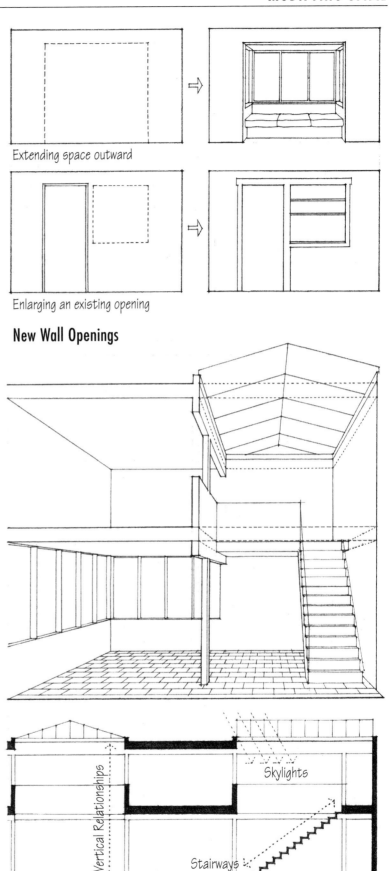

Extending space outward

Enlarging an existing opening

### New Wall Openings

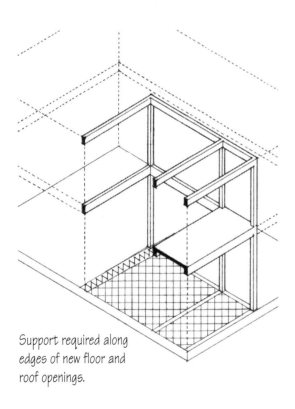

Support required along edges of new floor and roof openings.

Vertical Relationships

Skylights

Stairways

**Vertical Expansion**

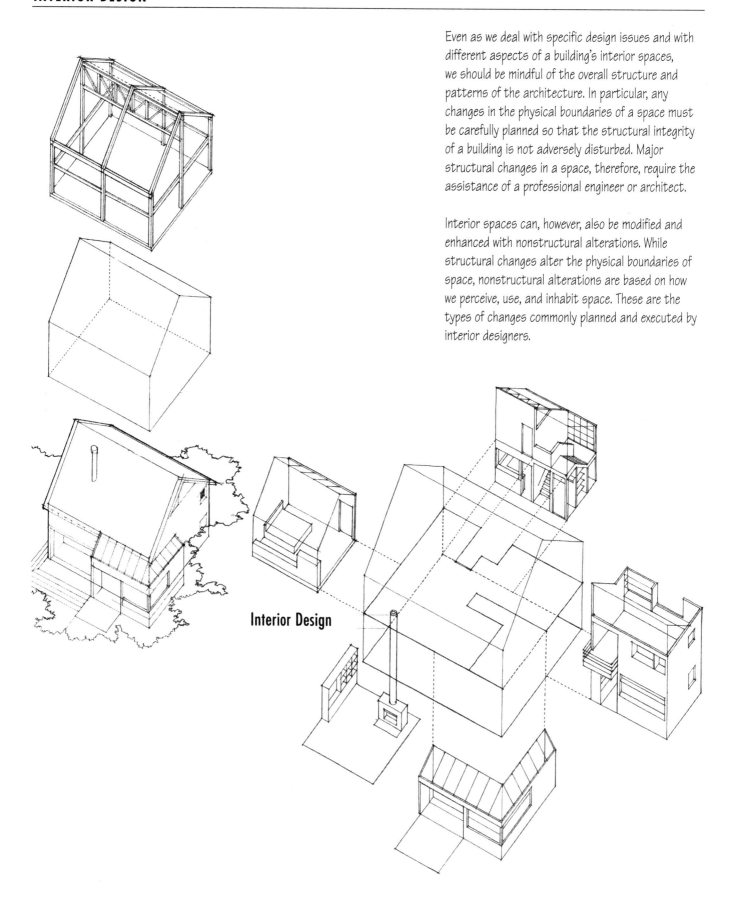

Even as we deal with specific design issues and with different aspects of a building's interior spaces, we should be mindful of the overall structure and patterns of the architecture. In particular, any changes in the physical boundaries of a space must be carefully planned so that the structural integrity of a building is not adversely disturbed. Major structural changes in a space, therefore, require the assistance of a professional engineer or architect.

Interior spaces can, however, also be modified and enhanced with nonstructural alterations. While structural changes alter the physical boundaries of space, nonstructural alterations are based on how we perceive, use, and inhabit space. These are the types of changes commonly planned and executed by interior designers.

Interior Design

# Interior Design

Interior design is the planning, layout, and design of the interior spaces within buildings. These physical settings satisfy our basic need for shelter and protection; they set the stage for and influence the shape of our activities; they nurture our aspirations and express the ideas that accompany our actions; they affect our outlook, mood, and personality. The purpose of interior design, therefore, is the functional improvement, aesthetic enrichment, and psychological enhancement of interior spaces.

# THE PLANNING LAYOUT & DESIGN

# OF THE PARTS

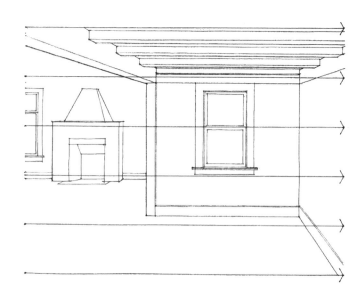

**The Architectural Context**

**Interior Elements**

The purpose of any design is to organize its parts into a coherent whole to achieve certain goals. In interior design, selected elements are arranged into three-dimensional patterns according to functional, aesthetic, and behavioral guidelines. The relationships among the elements established by these patterns ultimately determine the visual qualities and functional fitness of an interior space and influence how we perceive and use it.

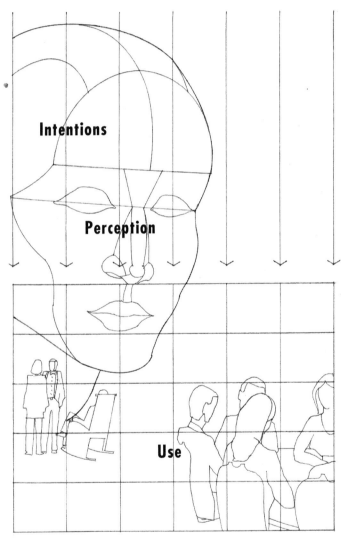

**Intentions**

**Perception**

**Use**

# INTO A WHOLE

**The Interior Environment**

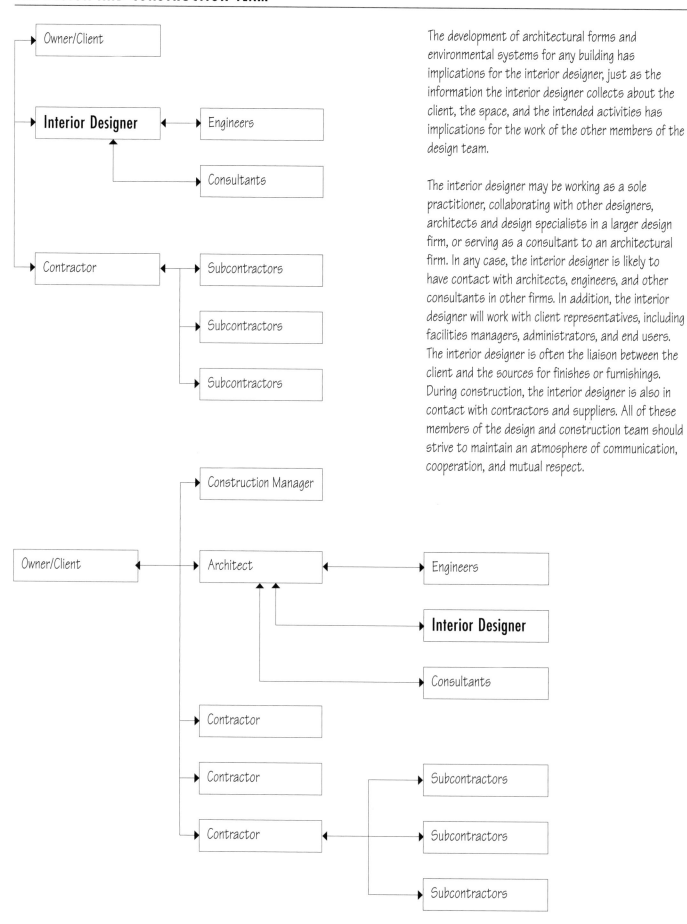

The development of architectural forms and environmental systems for any building has implications for the interior designer, just as the information the interior designer collects about the client, the space, and the intended activities has implications for the work of the other members of the design team.

The interior designer may be working as a sole practitioner, collaborating with other designers, architects and design specialists in a larger design firm, or serving as a consultant to an architectural firm. In any case, the interior designer is likely to have contact with architects, engineers, and other consultants in other firms. In addition, the interior designer will work with client representatives, including facilities managers, administrators, and end users. The interior designer is often the liaison between the client and the sources for finishes or furnishings. During construction, the interior designer is also in contact with contractors and suppliers. All of these members of the design and construction team should strive to maintain an atmosphere of communication, cooperation, and mutual respect.

We determine which elements to use and how to arrange them into patterns through the process of design. Although presented as a linear series of steps, the design process is more often a cyclical, iterative one in which a sequence of careful analysis, synthesis, and evaluation of available information, insights, and possible solutions is repeated until a successful fit between what exists and what is desired is achieved.

The design problem is first defined. The ability to define and understand the nature of the design problem adequately is an essential part of the solution. This definition should specify how the design solution will perform and what goals and objectives will be met.

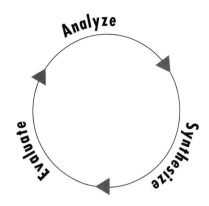

## PROBLEM STATEMENT

[ ] **Identify client needs.**
- Who, what, when, where, how, why?

[ ] **Set preliminary goals.**
- Functional requirements
- Aesthetic image and style
- Psychological stimulus and meaning

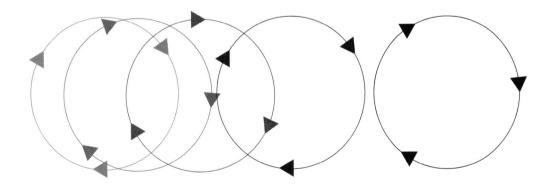

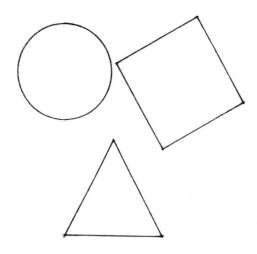

An analysis of the problem requires that it be broken down into parts, issues clarified, and values assigned to the various aspects of the problem. Analysis also involves gathering relevant information that would help us understand the nature of the problem and develop appropriate responses. From the outset, it is worthwhile knowing what limitations will help shape the design solution. Any givens—what can change and what cannot be altered—should be determined. Any financial, legal, or technical constraints that will impinge on the design solution should be noted.

Through the design process, a clearer understanding of the problem should emerge. New information may develop that could alter our perception of the problem and its solution. The analysis of a problem, therefore, often continues throughout the design process.

## PROGRAMMING

[ ] **What exists?**
- Collect and analyze relevant information.
- Document physical/cultural context.
- Describe existing elements.

[ ] **What's desired?**
- Identify user needs and preferences.
- Clarify goals.
- Develop matrices, charts, and adjacency diagrams.

[ ] **What's possible?**
- What can be altered...what cannot?
- What can be controlled...what cannot?
- What is allowed...what is prohibited?
- Define limits: time, economic, legal, and technical.

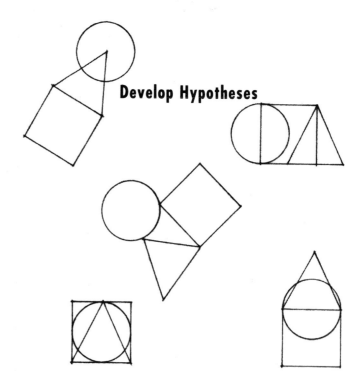

**Develop Hypotheses**

From the analysis of the problem and its parts, we can begin to formulate possible solutions. This requires synthesizing—bringing together and integrating—responses to the various issues and aspects of the problem into coherent solutions. Design requires rational thought based on knowledge and gained through experience and research. Also playing equal roles in the design process are intuition and imagination, which add the creative dimension to the otherwise rational design process.

There are several approaches one can take to generate ideas and also synthesize possible design solutions:

• Isolate one or more key issues of value or importance and develop solutions around them.
• Study analogous situations that could serve as models for developing possible solutions.
• Develop ideal solutions for parts of the problem, which could be integrated into whole solutions and tempered by the reality of what exists.

## CONCEPT DEVELOPMENT

[ ] **Brainstorm ideas.**
• Diagram major functional and spatial relationships.
• Assign values to key issues or elements.
• Search for ways to combine several good ideas into a single better one.
• Manipulate the parts to see how a change might affect the whole.
• Look at the situation from different points of view.

[ ] **Draft a concept statement.**
• Verbalize the principal design ideas in a concise manner.

[ ] **Develop schematic designs.**
• Establish major functional and spatial relationships.
• Show relative sizes and shapes of important features.
• Develop several alternatives for comparative study.

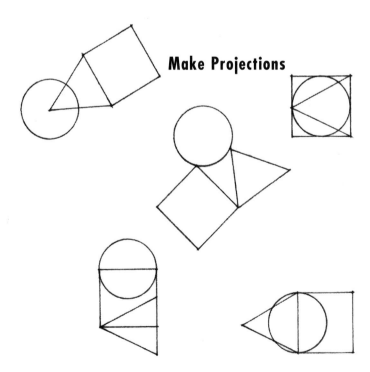

**Make Projections**

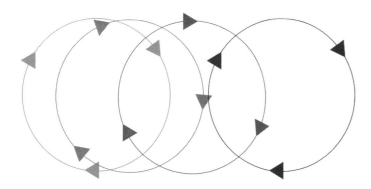

Design requires a critical view of alternatives and careful weighing of the strengths and weaknesses of each proposal until the best possible fit between problem and solution is achieved. Given a range of possible solutions, each must be evaluated according to the criteria set forth in the problem statement and further clarified in the problem analysis. Successive explorations of the problem and the evaluation of alternative solutions should help narrow the choices for design development. While the initial stages of the design process encourage divergent thinking about the problem, this latter phase requires a convergent focus on a specific design solution.

## COMPARE ALTERNATIVES

[ ] Compare each alternative with design goals.
[ ] Weigh the benefits and strengths against the costs and liabilities of each alternative.
[ ] Rank alternatives in terms of suitability and effectiveness.

## MAKE DESIGN DECISIONS

[ ] Combine best design elements into the final design.
  • Draw preliminary plans.
  • Construct scale drawings.
  • Show important interior architectural details (e.g., walls, windows, built-in elements).
  • Show furniture if appropriate.

[ ] Make preliminary material selections.
  • Develop alternative color and finish schemes.
  • Collect material samples.

[ ] Make preliminary furniture and lighting selections.

[ ] Prepare presentation to client for feedback and preliminary approval.

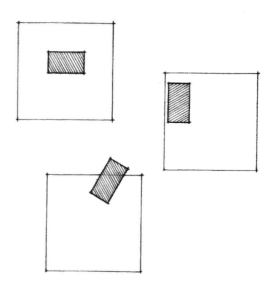

### Test and Refine Ideas

Once a final decision has been made, the design proposal is developed, refined, and prepared for implementation. This includes the production of construction drawings and specifications and other services related to purchasing, construction, and supervision.

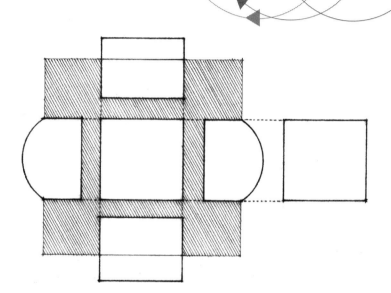

## DEVELOP AND REFINE DESIGN

[ ] Develop plans, elevations, sections, and details.
[ ] Develop specifications for interior finish materials, furnishings, and lighting.

## IMPLEMENT DESIGN

[ ] Prepare construction drawings.
[ ] Finalize specifications for interior finish material, furnishings, and lighting.

## REEVALUATE COMPLETED DESIGN

[ ] Design reviews
[ ] Coordination with architect, engineers, and consultants
[ ] Client feedback
[ ] Postoccupancy evaluation

No design process is complete until a design solution that has been implemented is evaluated for its effectiveness in solving a given problem. This critical appraisal of a completed design can build up our knowledge base, sharpen our intuition, and provide valuable lessons that may be applied in future work.

One of the idiosyncrasies of the design process is that it does not always lead simply and inevitably to a single, obvious, correct answer. In fact, there is often more than one solution to a design problem. How then can we judge whether a design is good or bad?

A design may be good in the judgment of the designer, the client, or the people who experience and use the design, for any of several reasons:

- A design may be good because it functions well— it works.
- A design may be good because it is affordable— it is economical, efficient, and durable.
- A design may be good because it looks good— it is aesthetically pleasing.
- A design may be good because it recreates a feeling remembered from another time and place— it carries meaning.

At times, we may judge a design to be good because we feel it follows current design trends or because of the impression it will make on others—it is in fashion or it enhances our status.

As these reasons suggest, there are several meanings that can be conveyed by a design. Some operate at a level generally understood and accepted by the general public. Others are more readily discerned by specific groups of people. Successful designs usually operate at more than one level of meaning and thus appeal to a wide range of people.

A good design, therefore, should be understandable to its audience. Knowing why something was done helps to make a design comprehensible. If a design does not express an idea, communicate a meaning, or elicit a response, either it will be ignored or it will appear to be a bad design.

In defining and analyzing a design problem, one also develops goals and criteria by which the effectiveness of a solution can be measured. Regardless of the nature of the interior design problem being addressed, there are several criteria with which we should be concerned.

## Function and Purpose
First, the intended function of the design must be satisfied and its purpose fulfilled.

## Utility and Economy
Second, a design should exhibit utility, honesty, and economy in its selection and use of materials.

## Form and Style
Third, the design should be aesthetically pleasing to the eye and our other senses.

## Image and Meaning
Fourth, the design should project an image and promote associations that carry meaning for the people who use and experience it.

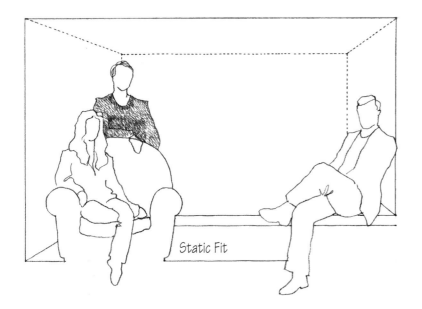

Static Fit

The interior spaces of buildings are designed as places for human movement, activity, and repose. There should be, therefore, a fit between the form and dimensions of interior space and our own body dimensions. This fit can be a static one as when we sit in a chair, lean against a railing, or nestle within an alcove.

There can also be a dynamic fit as when we enter a building's foyer, walk up a stairway, or move through the rooms and halls of a building.

A third type of fit is how space accommodates our need to maintain appropriate social distances and to control our personal space.

In addition to these physical and psychological dimensions, space also has tactile, auditory, olfactory, and thermal characteristics that influence how we feel and what we do within it.

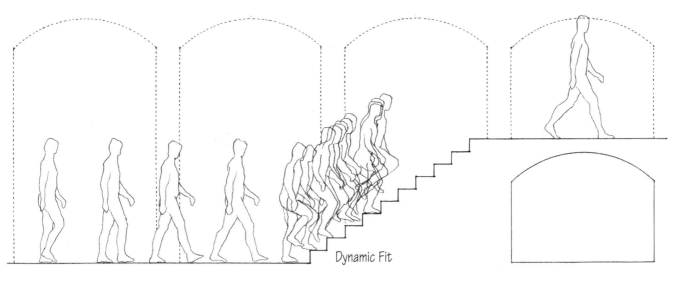

Dynamic Fit

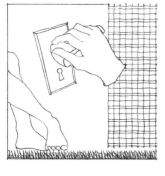

Touch

Hearing

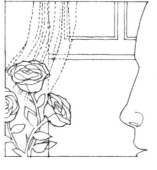

Smell

Heat

Our body dimensions, and the way we move through and perceive space, are prime determinants of architectural and interior design. In the following section, basic human dimensions are illustrated for standing, walking, sitting, ascending or descending stairs, lying down, reaching, and viewing. Dimensional guidelines are also given for group activities, such as dining or conversing.

There is a difference between the structural dimensions of our bodies and those dimensional requirements that result from how we reach for something on a shelf, sit down at a table, walk down a set of stairs, or interact with other people. These are functional dimensions that vary according to the nature of the activity engaged in and the social situation.

Caution should always be exercised whenever you use any set of dimensional tables or illustrations such as those on the following pages. These are based on typical or average measurements that may have to be modified to satisfy specific user needs. Variations from the norm will always exist due to the differences between men and women, among various age and genetic groups, even from one individual to the next.

Most people will experience different physical ranges and abilities as they grow and age and with changes in weight, height, and physical fitness. These changes over time affect how an interior environment will fit or accommodate the user.

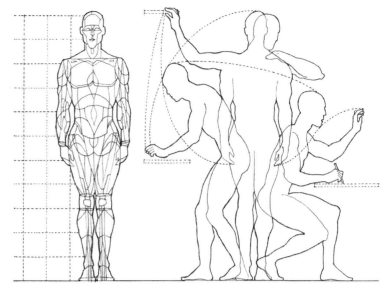

Structural Dimensions          Functional Dimensions

Individual Variations and Abilities

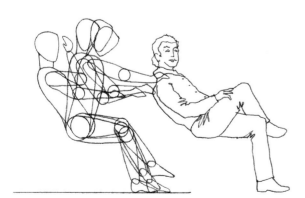

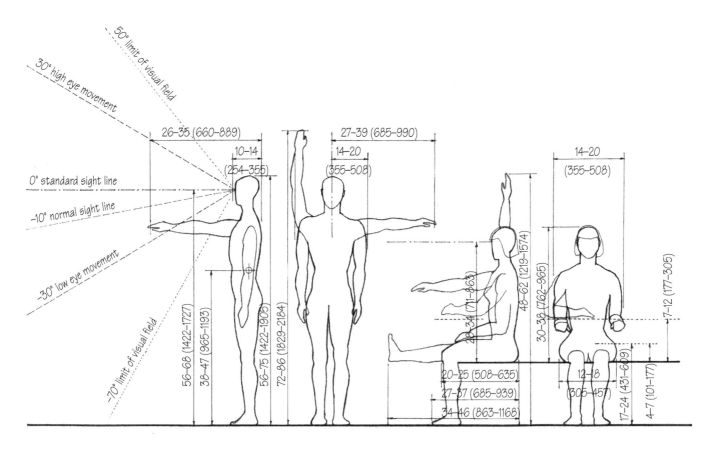

50° limit of visual field

30° high eye movement

0° standard sight line

−10° normal sight line

−30° low eye movement

−70° limit of visual field

26–35 (660–889)

10–14 (254–355)

27–39 (685–990)

14–20 (355–508)

14–20 (355–508)

56–68 (1422–1727)

38–47 (965–1193)

56–75 (1422–1905)

72–86 (1829–2184)

28–34 (711–863)

48–62 (1219–1574)

30–38 (762–965)

7–12 (177–305)

20–25 (508–635)

27–37 (685–939)

34–46 (863–1168)

12–18 (305–457)

17–24 (431–609)

4–7 (101–177)

- Unless otherwise specified, dimensions are in inches, with their metric equivalents in millimeters (shown in parentheses).

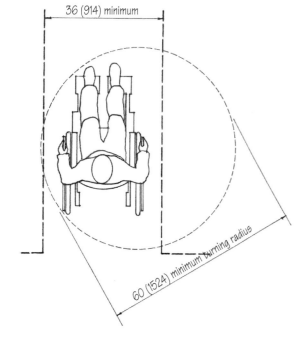

36 (914) minimum

60 (1524) minimum turning radius

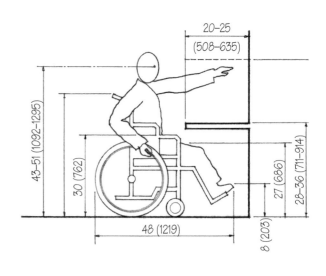

20–25 (508–635)

43–51 (1092–1295)

30 (762)

27 (686)

28–36 (711–914)

48 (1219)

8 (203)

Human beings share with animals a perception of the appropriate uses of the space around their bodies, which varies between groups and cultures and among individuals within a group. This is a person's defensible or territorial space. Others are allowed to penetrate these areas only for short periods of time. The presence of other people, objects, and the immediate environment can expand or contract our sense of personal space. The invasion of an individual's personal space can affect the person's feelings and reactions to everything around them.

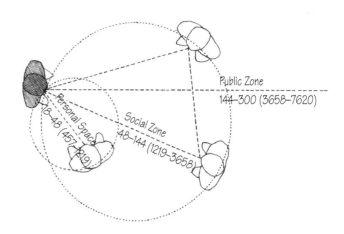

## Intimate Zone

- Allows physical contact; invasion by a stranger can result in discomfort.

## Personal Space

- Allows friends to come close and possibly penetrate inner limit briefly; conversation at low voice levels is possible.

## Social Zone

- Appropriate for informal, social, and business transactions; communication occurs at normal to raised voice levels.

## Public Zone

- Acceptable for formal behavior and hierarchical relationships; louder voice levels with clearer enunciation are required for communication.

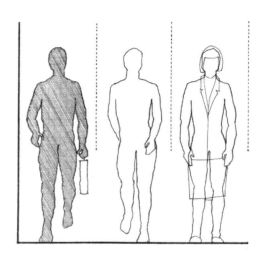

Space for movement varies from 30–36 (762–914) for a single person to 72–96 (1829–2438) for three people walking abreast.

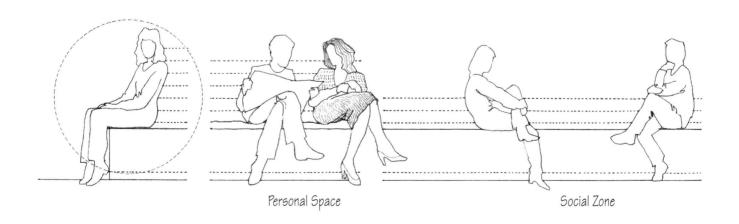

Personal Space                Social Zone

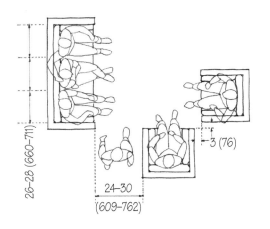

26–28 (660–711)

24–30
(609–762)

3 (76)

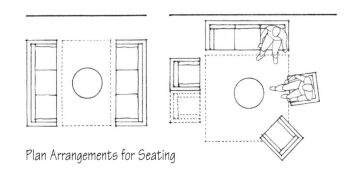

Plan Arrangements for Seating

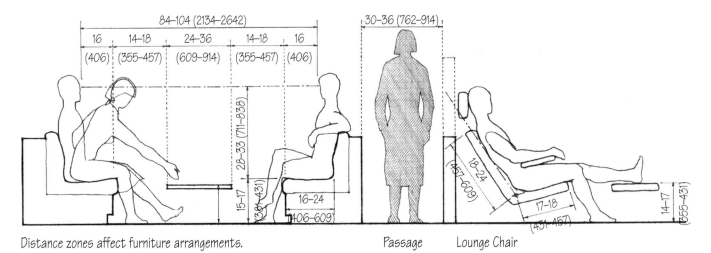

84–104 (2134–2642)

| 16 (406) | 14–18 (355–457) | 24–36 (609–914) | 14–18 (355–457) | 16 (406) |

28–33 (711–838)

15–17 (381–431)

16–24 (406–609)

30–36 (762–914)

18–24 (457–609)

17–18 (431–457)

14–17 (355–431)

Distance zones affect furniture arrangements.

Passage     Lounge Chair

• Unless otherwise specified, dimensions are in
  inches, with their metric equivalents in millimeters
  (shown in parentheses).

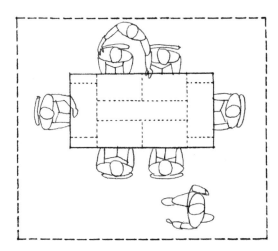

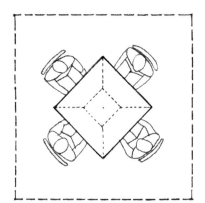

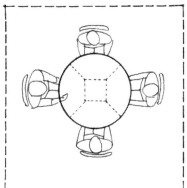

Plan Arrangements for Dining Tables

## Seating

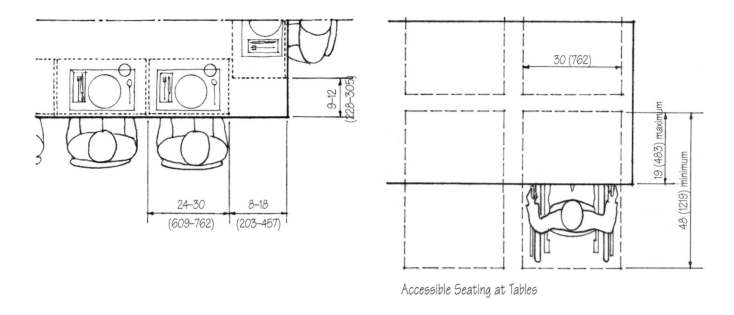

9–12 (228–305)

24–30 (609–762)  8–18 (203–457)

30 (762)

19 (483) maximum

48 (1219) minimum

Accessible Seating at Tables

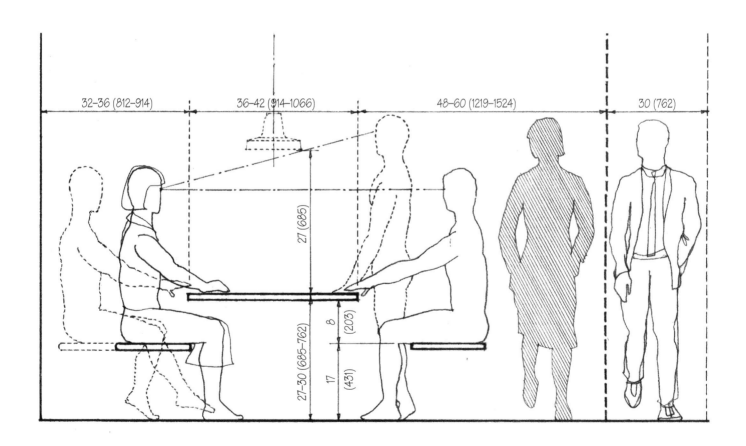

32–36 (812–914)  36–42 (914–1066)  48–60 (1219–1524)  30 (762)

27 (685)

8 (203)

27–30 (685–762)

17 (431)

**Dining**

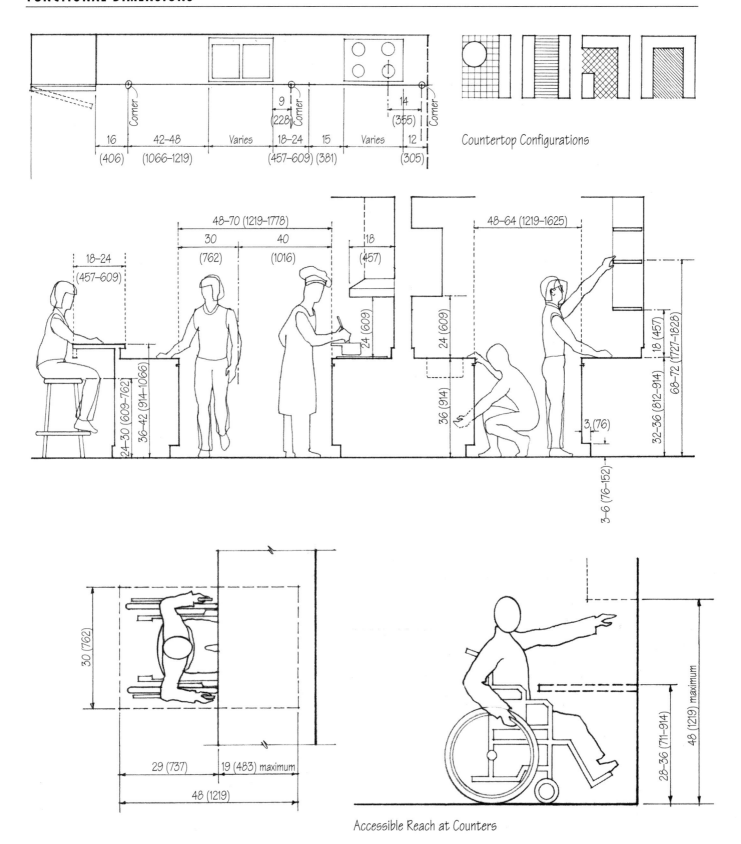

Countertop Configurations

Accessible Reach at Counters

## Kitchen Layouts

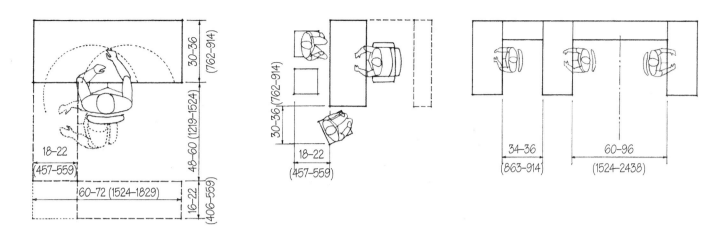

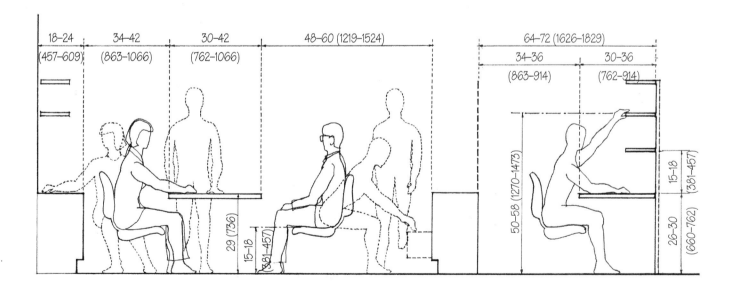

## Work Stations

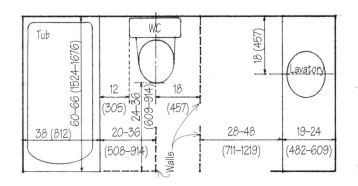

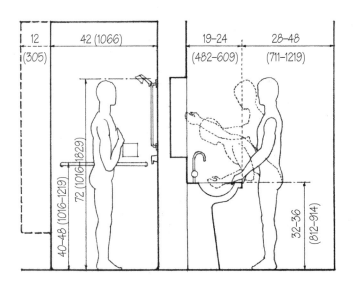

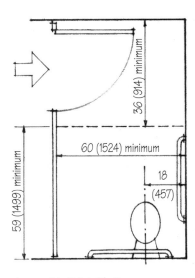

Accessible Toilet Stall

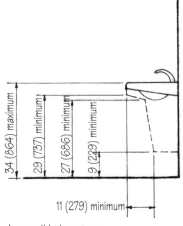

Accessible Lavatory

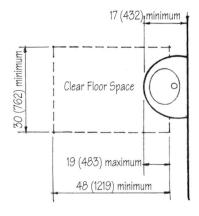

Accessible Lavatory

## Bathing

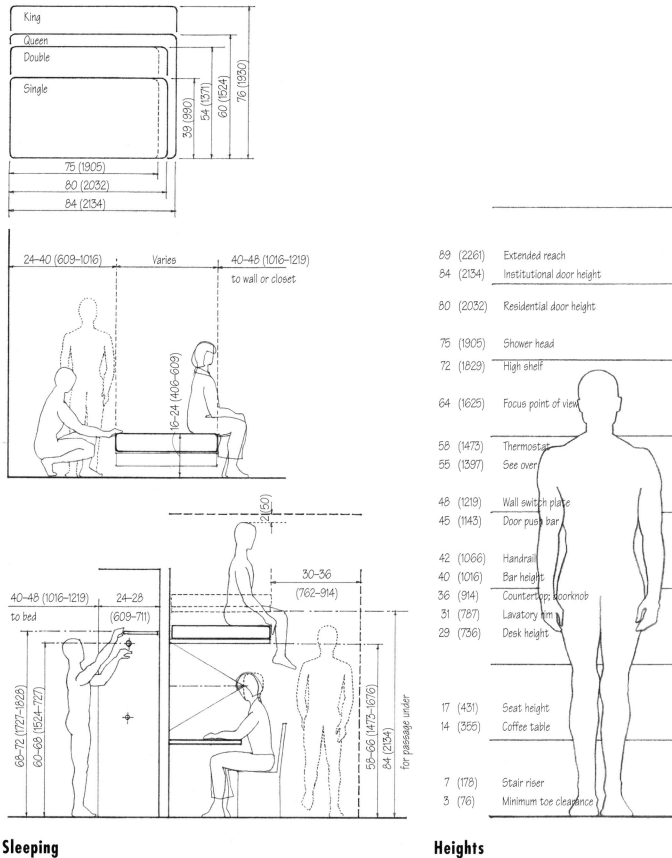

King

Queen

Double

Single

39 (990)
54 (1371)
60 (1524)
76 (1930)

75 (1905)
80 (2032)
84 (2134)

24–40 (609–1016)    Varies    40–48 (1016–1219)
to wall or closet

16–24 (406–609)

2 (50)

30–36
(762–914)

40–48 (1016–1219)    24–28
to bed    (609–711)

68–72 (1727–1828)
60–68 (1524–727)

58–66 (1473–1676)
84 (2134)
for passage under

| | | |
|---|---|---|
| 89 | (2261) | Extended reach |
| 84 | (2134) | Institutional door height |
| 80 | (2032) | Residential door height |
| 75 | (1905) | Shower head |
| 72 | (1829) | High shelf |
| 64 | (1625) | Focus point of view |
| 58 | (1473) | Thermostat |
| 55 | (1397) | See over |
| 48 | (1219) | Wall switch plate |
| 45 | (1143) | Door push bar |
| 42 | (1066) | Handrail |
| 40 | (1016) | Bar height |
| 36 | (914) | Countertop; doorknob |
| 31 | (787) | Lavatory rim |
| 29 | (736) | Desk height |
| 17 | (431) | Seat height |
| 14 | (355) | Coffee table |
| 7 | (178) | Stair riser |
| 3 | (76) | Minimum toe clearance |

## Sleeping

## Heights

A prime criterion for judging the success of an interior design is whether it is functional. Function is the most fundamental level of design. We design to improve the functioning of interior spaces and make our tasks and activities within them more convenient, comfortable and pleasurable. The proper functioning of a design is, of course, directly related to the purposes of those who inhabit and use it, as well as to their physical dimensions and abilities.

To help understand, and ultimately to fulfill, the function and purpose of an interior space, it is necessary to analyze carefully the user and activity requirements for that space. The following outline can help the designer program these requirements, translate these needs into forms and patterns, and integrate them into the spatial context.

## USER REQUIREMENTS

[ ] **Identify Users**
- Individuals
- User groups
- User characteristics
- Age groups

[ ] **Identify Needs**
- Specific individual needs and abilities
- Group needs and abilities

[ ] **Establish Territorial Requirements**
- Personal space
- Privacy
- Interaction
- Access
- Security

[ ] **Determine Preferences**
- Favored objects
- Favorite colors
- Special places
- Special interests

[ ] **Research Environmental Concerns**

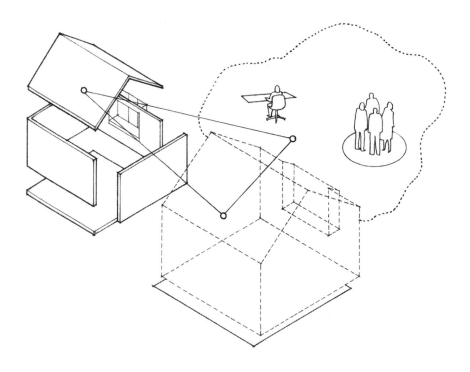

## ACTIVITY REQUIREMENTS

[ ]  **Identify Primary and Secondary Activities**
- Name and function of primary activity
- Names and functions of secondary or related activities

[ ]  **Analyze Nature of the Activities**
- Active or passive
- Noisy or quiet
- Public, small group, or private
- Compatibility of activities if space is to be used for more than one activity
- How often is the space to be used?
- What times of day or night?

[ ]  **Determine Requirements for**
- Privacy and enclosure
- Access
- Americans with Disabilities Act (ADA) accessibility guidelines
- Flexibility
- Light
- Acoustic quality
- Security
- Maintenance and durability

## FURNISHING REQUIREMENTS

[ ]  **Determine Furnishing and Equipment Requirements for Each Activity**
Number, type, and style of:
- Seating
- Tables
- Work surfaces
- Storage and display units
- Accessories

[ ]  **Identify Other Special Equipment Required**
- Lighting
- Electrical
- Mechanical
- Plumbing
- Data and communications

[ ]  **Establish Quality Requirements of Furnishings**
- Comfort
- Safety
- Variety
- Flexibility
- Style
- Durability
- Maintenance

[ ]  **Develop Possible Arrangements**
- Functional groupings
- Tailored arrangements
- Flexible arrangements

## Space Planning

The form of a building's structure and enclosure affects the character of the spaces within. Space planning involves the efficient and productive use of these spaces, fitting living patterns to the architectural patterns of space.

The term space planning is often used to refer to the specific task of planning and designing large-scale spaces for commercial and retail businesses. In this narrow sense, space planners program client needs, study user activities, and analyze spatial requirements. The results of such planning are then used in the architectural design of new construction or for negotiating the leasing of existing commercial spaces.

## SPACE ANALYSIS

[ ]  Document Existing or Proposed Space
- Measure and draw base plan, sections, and interior elevations
- Photograph existing space

[ ]  Analyze Space
- Orientation and site conditions of space
- Form, scale, and proportion of space
- Doorway locations, points of access, and the circulation paths they suggest
- Windows and the light, views, and ventilation they afford
- Wall, floor, and ceiling materials
- Significant architectural details
- Location of plumbing, electrical, and mechanical fixtures and outlets
- Possible architectural modifications
- Elements for possible reuse, including finishes and furnishings

## DIMENSIONAL REQUIREMENTS

[ ]  Determine Required Dimensions for Space and Furniture Groupings
- Each functional grouping of furniture
- Access to and movement within and between activity areas
- Number of people served
- Appropriate social distances and interaction

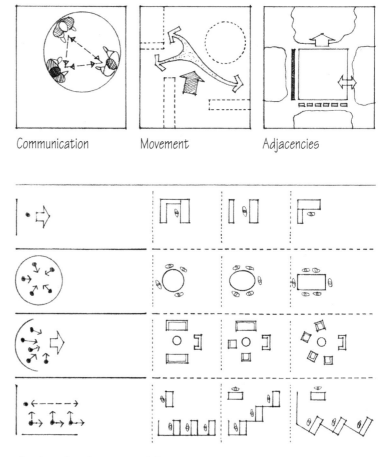

Communication          Movement          Adjacencies

Furniture Requirements and Arrangements

In a broader sense, all interior designers are involved in the planning and layout of interior spaces whether small or large, residential or commercial. Once a design program has been outlined and developed from an analysis of the client's or users' needs, the design task is to allocate properly the available or desired interior spaces for the various required activities.

Area requirements can be estimated from an analysis of the number of people served, the furnishings and equipment they require, and the nature of the activity that will go on in each space. These area requirements can then be translated into rough blocks of space and related to each other and to the architectural context in a functional and aesthetic manner.

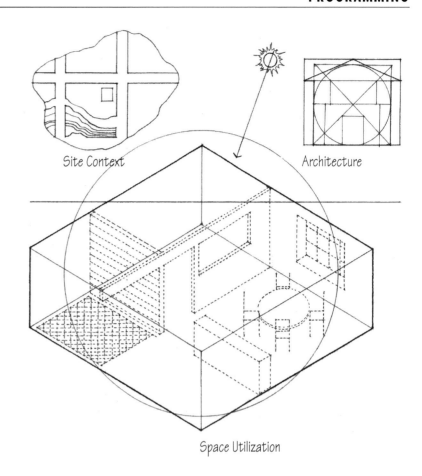

Site Context

Architecture

Space Utilization

## Analysis of User Requirements + Existing or Proposed Spaces......Integration

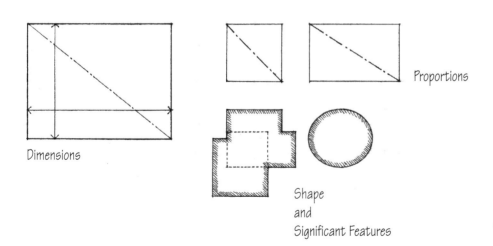

Dimensions

Proportions

Shape
and
Significant Features

# DESIRED QUALITIES

[ ] **Determine qualities appropriate to spatial context and compatible with client's or users' needs or wishes.**
- Feeling, mood, or atmosphere
- Image and style
- Degree of spatial enclosure
- Comfort and security
- Quality of light
- Focus and orientation of space
- Color and tone
- Textures
- Acoustical environment
- Thermal environment
- Flexibility and projected length of use

# DESIRED RELATIONSHIPS - - - - - - - - - →

[ ] **Desired relationships between**
- Related activity areas
- Activity areas and space for movement
- Room and adjacent spaces
- Room and the outside

[ ] **Desired zoning of activities**
- Organization of activities into groups or sets according to compatibility and use

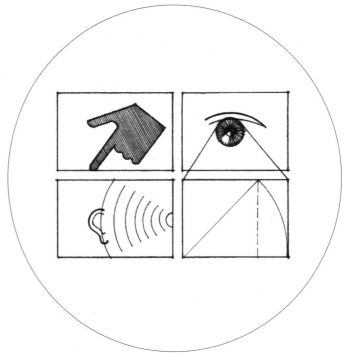

Whether collaborating on the design of a new building or planning the remodeling of an existing structure, the interior designer strives for a proper fit between the demands of activities and the architectural nature of the spaces that house them.

Certain activities may need to be closely related or adjacent to each other, while others may be more distant or isolated for privacy. Some activities may require easy accessibility, while others may need controlled entries and exits. Some activities may require daylighting or natural ventilation, while others may not need to be located near exterior windows. Some activities may have specific spatial requirements, while others may be more flexible or be able to share a common space.

• Which activities should be closely related?

• Which activities can be isolated by enclosure or distance?

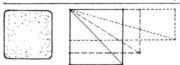

• What degree of accessibility is required?

• Are there specific proportional requirements?

• Do activity relationships suggest a spatial pattern?

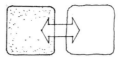

• Can any activities share the same space?

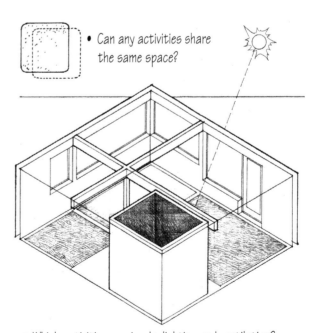

• Which activities require daylighting and ventilation?

As interior areas are organized on the basis of the considerations discussed on pages 58–61, along with considerations of the building site and adjacent structures, the architect will begin to develop the shape and form of a new building.

Whether a space is situated within an existing structure or is contemplated in a newly designed building, it usually provides clues for the interior designer as to how it can best be utilized. The entries into a space may define a pattern of movement that divides the area into certain zones. Some zones may be more readily accessible than others. Some may be large enough to accommodate group activities, while others are not. Some may have access to exterior windows or skylights for daylighting or ventilation; others may be internalized. Some may include a natural center of interest, such as a view window or a fireplace.

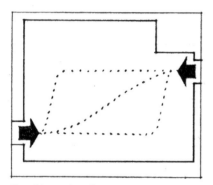

Possible paths of movement

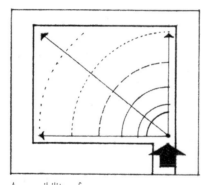

Accessibility of zones

External outlooks

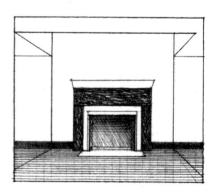

Internal focus

The zoning of a space may be suggested by the shape of its enclosure or by the architecture. Doorways suggest paths of movement and establish the accessibility of certain zones. The daylighting afforded by windows or skylights should influence the placement of activities. An external outlook or an internal focus might suggest how a space could be organized.

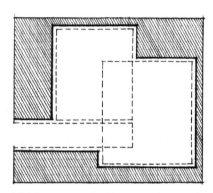

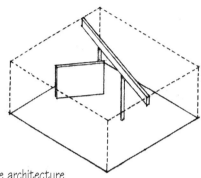

Divisions suggested by room shape or by the architecture

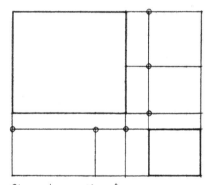

Size and proportion of zones

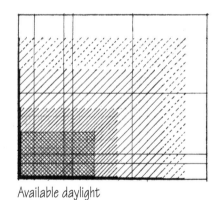

Available daylight

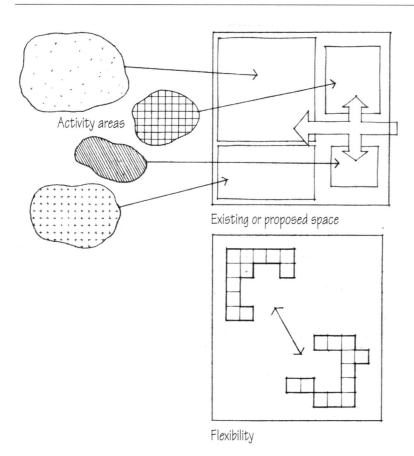

Activity areas

Existing or proposed space

Flexibility

From the preceding activity and space analyses, one can begin to match the space requirements of each activity to the characteristics of the available spaces. The design task then shifts to selecting and arranging furnishings, finishes, and lighting into three-dimensional patterns within the given spatial boundaries. These arrangements of shapes and forms in space should respond both to functional and aesthetic criteria.

## Function

- Activity-specific grouping of furniture
- Workable dimensions and clearances
- Appropriate social distances
- Suitable visual and acoustical privacy
- Adequate flexibility or adaptability
- Appropriate lighting and other electrical or mechanical services

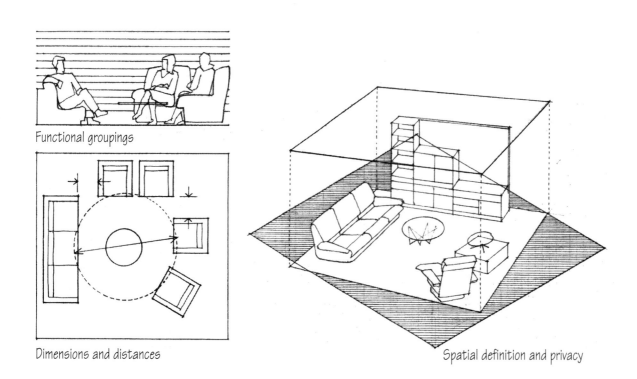

Functional groupings

Dimensions and distances

Spatial definition and privacy

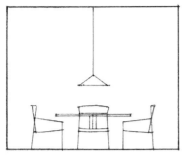

Scalar relationship to space

## Aesthetics

- Appropriate scale to space function
- Visual grouping: unity with variety
- Figure-ground reading
- Three-dimensional composition: rhythm, harmony, balance
- Appropriate orientation toward light, view, or an internal focus
- Shape, color, texture, and pattern

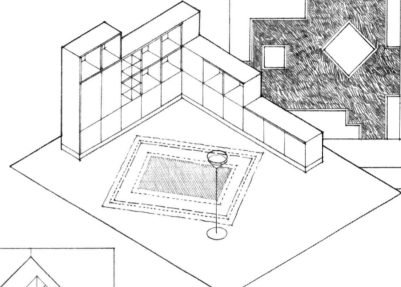

Figure-ground patterns

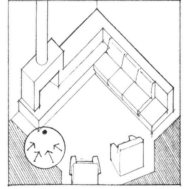

Grouping and orientation

Objects in space or merging with space

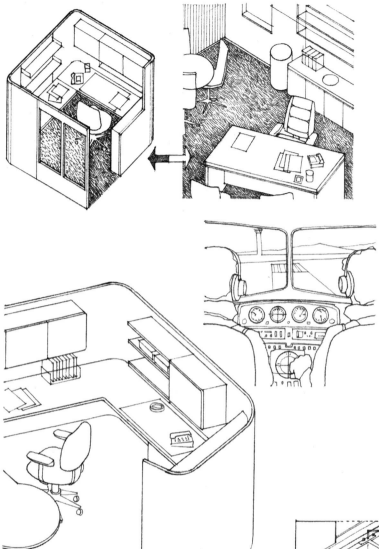

## Tight Fit

Plan arrangements can be generally classified into two broad categories, according to how each uses the available space—tight fit and loose fit. The first exhibits a close correspondence between furniture and equipment. This may be particularly appropriate when space is at a premium or when functional efficiency is important. Because a tight-fit arrangement may not be readily adaptable to other uses, it is important that it is laid out with great care for its intended use.

A tight-fit arrangement usually employs modular or unit furniture components that can be combined in a number of ways to form integrated, often multifunctional, structures. Such structures utilize space efficiently and leave a maximum amount of floor area around them. A tailored arrangement of modular furniture can also be used to define a space within a larger volume for greater privacy or intimacy.

Carried to an extreme, a tight-fit arrangement can be built in place and become a permanent extension of a room's architecture. Like modular and unit arrangements, built-in furniture utilizes space efficiently; conveys an orderly, unified appearance; and mitigates visual clutter in a space.

Tight-fit or tailored arrangements require careful study and analysis of functional relationships.

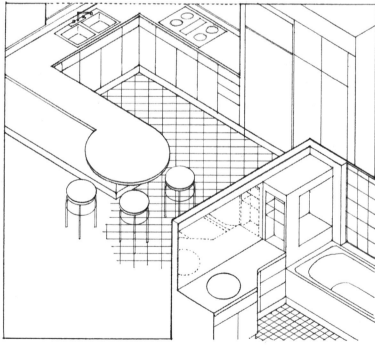

# Loose Fit

A second, more common type of plan arrangement exhibits a looser fit between function and space. Loose-fit arrangements are desirable for the flexibility and diversity they afford.

Most rooms with a loose-fit arrangement can accommodate a variety of uses, especially if the furniture used can be easily moved and rearranged. This inherent flexibility in adapting to changes in use or circumstance makes a loose fit arrangement the more common method for laying out furniture in a space. It also offers the opportunity for a greater mix of furniture types, sizes, and styles to be selected over time to suit almost any design situation.

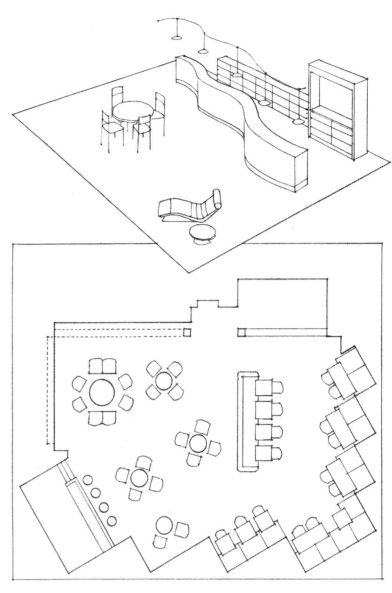

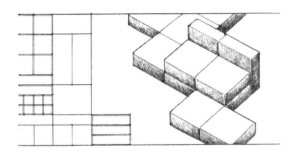

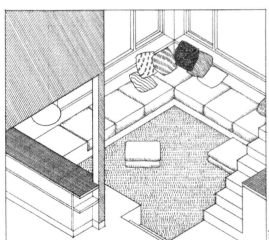

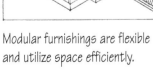

Modular furnishings are flexible and utilize space efficiently.

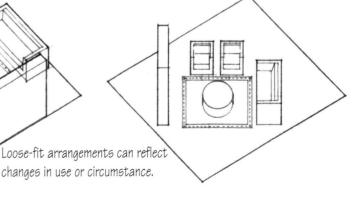

Loose-fit arrangements can reflect changes in use or circumstance.

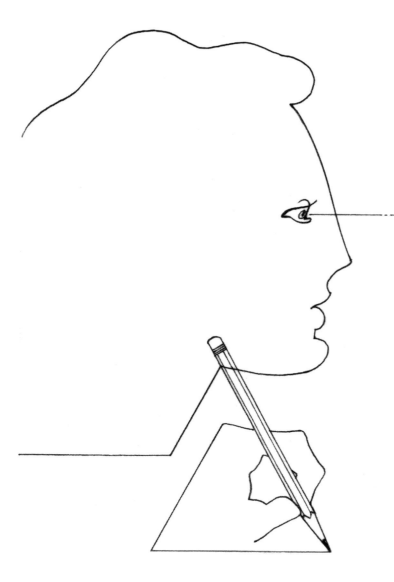

Designers use drawings in many ways. The presentation drawings executed at the end of a design project are used to persuade the client, peers, or the general public of the merits of a design proposal. Construction or working drawings are required to provide graphic instructions for the production or building of a project. But designers use both the process and products of drawing in other ways as well. In design, the role of drawing expands to include recording what exists, working out ideas, and speculating and planning for the future. Throughout the design process, we use drawings to guide the development of an idea from concept to proposal to constructed reality.

Whether executed with a pen or pencil on paper or executed with a computer and graphic or Computer-Aided-Design (CAD) software, the graphic representation of design ideas is particularly useful in the early stages of the design process. Drawing a design idea out on paper enables us to explore and clarify it in much the same way as we form and order a thought by putting it into words. Making design ideas concrete and visible enables us to act on them. We can analyze them, see them in a new light, combine them in new ways, and transform them into new ideas.

Although the use of computers can speed up the process of redrawing a base plan or moving repeating elements, many interior designers find that they can concentrate on the synthesis of design ideas more easily with paper and a pen or pencil, without the distraction and restraints of operating the computer software. The grids on the following pages can be used as base drawings by laying tracing paper over them and sketching the possibilities you envision. Remember that loose sketches can evolve into explorations of alternative design schemes. Analyze your ideas, synthesize the good ones, and evaluate the results. Then refine them into preliminary designs for further evaluation and development.

The central task of architectural drawing is representing three-dimensional forms, constructions, and spatial environments on a two-dimensional surface. Three distinct types of drawing systems have evolved over time to accomplish this mission: *multiview, paraline,* and *perspective* drawings. These visual systems of representation constitute a formal graphic language that is governed by a consistent set of principles.

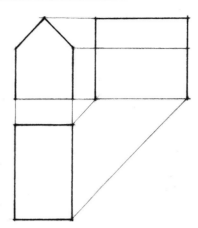

## Multiview Drawings
- Plans, sections, and elevations
- A related series of orthographic projections

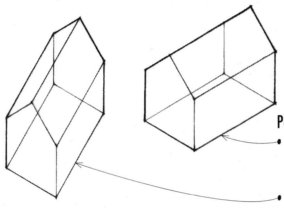

## Paraline Drawings
- Axonometric projections, including isometrics, dimetrics, and trimetrics

- Oblique projections, including elevation obliques and plan obliques

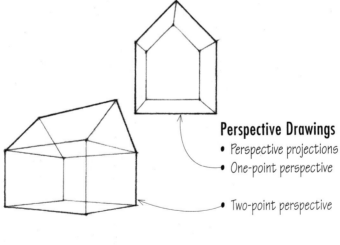

## Perspective Drawings
- Perspective projections
- One-point perspective

- Two-point perspective

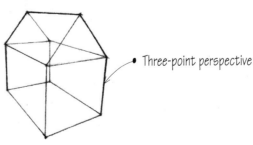

- Three-point perspective

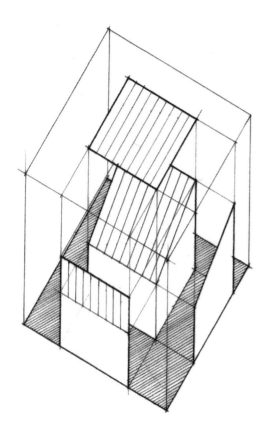

Multiview drawings comprise the drawing types we know as plans, elevations, and sections. Each is an orthographic projection of a particular aspect of an object or construction. In orthographic projection, parallel projectors meet the picture plane at right angles. Therefore, the orthographic projection of any feature or element that is parallel to the picture plane remains true in size, shape, and configuration. This gives rise to the principal advantage of multiview drawings—the ability to precisely locate points, gauge the length and slope of lines, and describe the shape and extent of planes.

A single multiview drawing can only reveal partial information about an object or construction. There is an inherent ambiguity of depth as the third dimension is flattened onto the picture plane. Whatever depth we read in a solitary plan, section, or elevation must be implied by such graphic depth cues as hierarchical line weights and contrasting tonal values. While a sense of depth can be inferred, it can be known with certainty only by looking at additional views. We, therefore, require a series of distinct but related views to describe fully the three-dimensional nature of a form or composition—hence the term multiview.

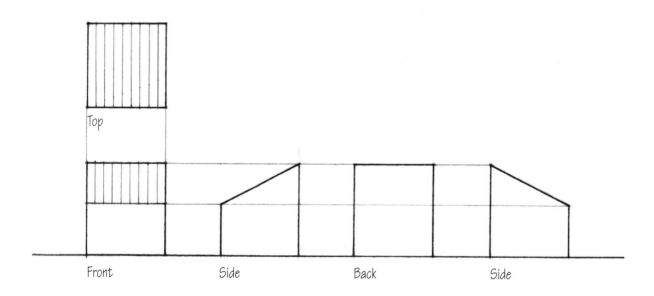

A plan is an orthographic projection of an object, structure, or composition on a horizontal plane.

A floor plan represents a section through a building or portion of a building after a horizontal slice is made, usually at about four feet above the floor, and the upper part removed.

- Profile the thicknesses of walls and columns that are cut through.
- Note the locations and sizes of doors and windows.

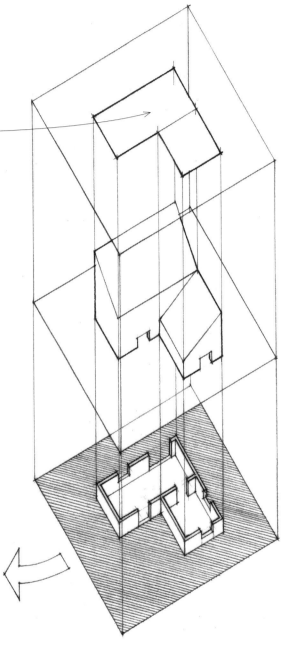

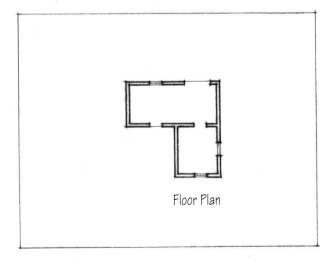

Floor Plan

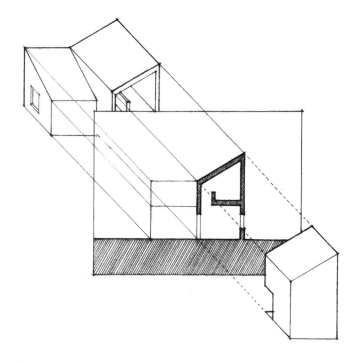

A section is an orthographic projection of an object or structure as it would appear if cut through by a vertical plane to show its internal configuration.

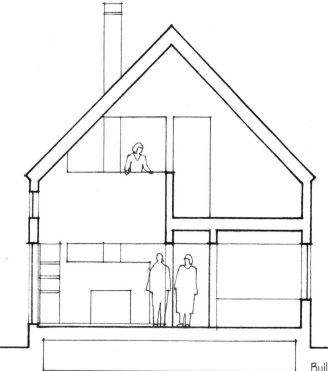

A building section shows the relationship between the floors, walls, and roof structure of a building and reveals the vertical dimensions, shape, and scale of the spaces defined by these elements.

• Profile the floor, wall, and ceiling elements that are cut through in a section drawing.

• Draw the elevations of elements seen beyond the plane of the section cut.

• Draw people as this helps to establish the scale of the space.

Building Section

Interior elevations are orthographic projections of the significant interior walls of a building. While normally included in the drawing of building sections, they may stand alone to study and present highly detailed spaces, such as kitchens, bathrooms, and stairways. In this case, instead of profiling the section cut, we emphasize instead the boundary line of the interior wall surfaces.

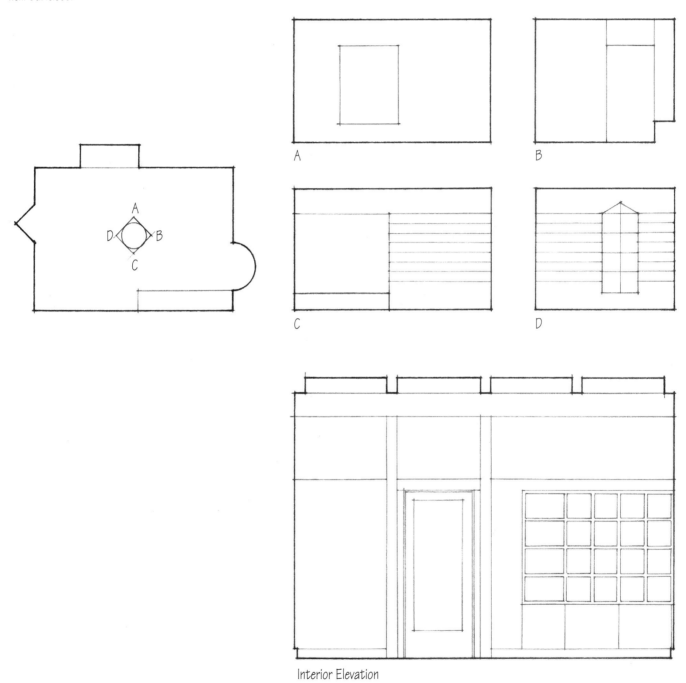

Interior Elevation

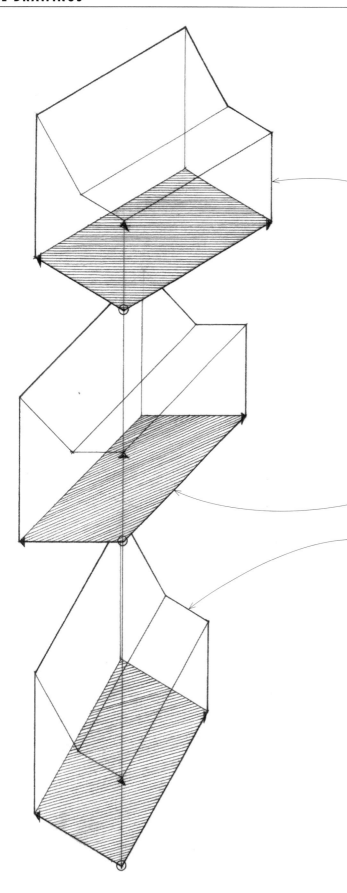

Paraline drawings convey the three-dimensional nature of a form or construction in a single pictorial view. They include a subset of orthographic projections known as axonometric projection, the most common of which is the isometric projection, as well as the entire class of oblique projections.

## Axonometric Projections

- Isometrics—The three principal axes make equal angles with the picture plane.
- Dimetrics—Two of the three principal axes make equal angles with the picture plane.
- Trimetrics—The three principal axes make unequal angles with the picture plane.

## Oblique Projections

- Elevation obliques—A principal vertical face is oriented parallel to the picture plane.
- Plan obliques—A principal horizontal face is oriented parallel to the picture plane.

In all paraline drawings—both axonometrics and obliques:
- Parallel lines in the subject remain parallel in the drawn view.
- All measurements parallel to any of the three principal axes can be made and drawn to scale.

Isometrics are axonometric projections of an object or structure inclined to the picture plane in such a way that the three principal axes are equally foreshortened.

- The three principal axes appear 120° apart on the picture plane.
- In a true isometric projection, these three axes are equally foreshortened to 0.816 of their true length.
- It is common practice, however, to construct an isometric drawing by laying out all axial lines—lines parallel to any of the principal axes—to their true length and drawn to the same scale.

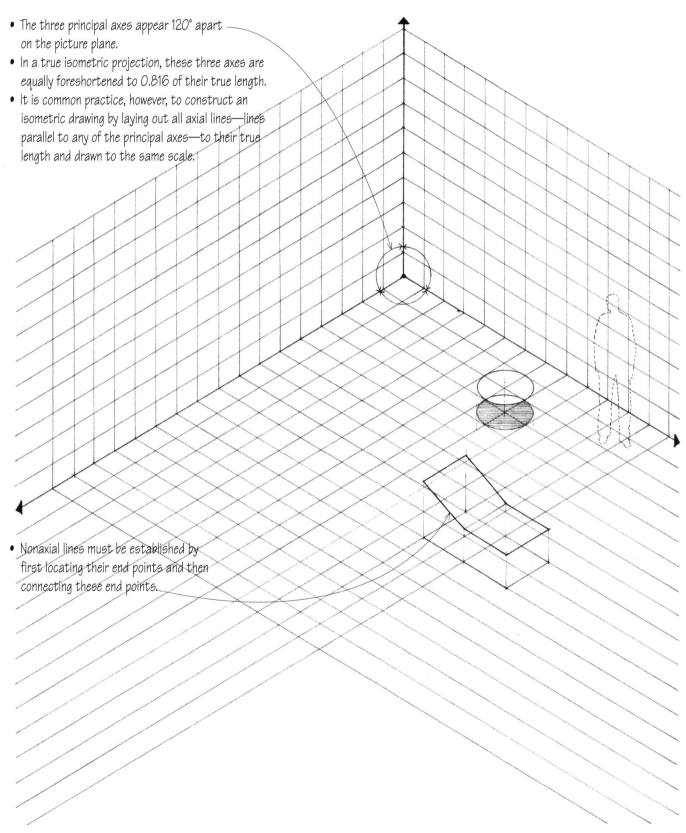

- Nonaxial lines must be established by first locating their end points and then connecting these end points.

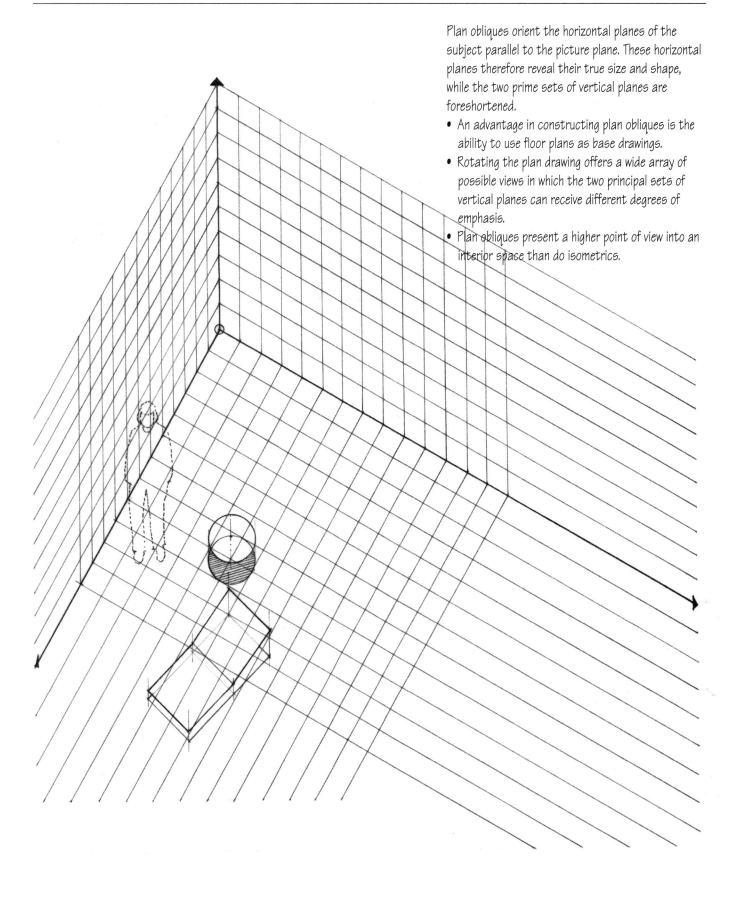

Plan obliques orient the horizontal planes of the subject parallel to the picture plane. These horizontal planes therefore reveal their true size and shape, while the two prime sets of vertical planes are foreshortened.

- An advantage in constructing plan obliques is the ability to use floor plans as base drawings.
- Rotating the plan drawing offers a wide array of possible views in which the two principal sets of vertical planes can receive different degrees of emphasis.
- Plan obliques present a higher point of view into an interior space than do isometrics.

Perspective projection portrays a three-dimensional form or construction by projecting all of its points to a picture plane (PP) through the use of straight lines that converge at a fixed point, representing a single eye of the observer. While we normally see through both eyes in what is termed binocular vision, perspective projection assumes we view a three-dimensional subject or scene through a single eye, which we call the station point (SP).

Multiview and paraline drawings utilize parallel projectors and the projected size of an element remains the same regardless of its distance from the picture plane. The converging projectors or sightlines in a perspective drawing, however, alter the apparent size of a line or plane according to its distance from the picture plane and the observer. In other words, converging sightlines reduce the size of distant objects.

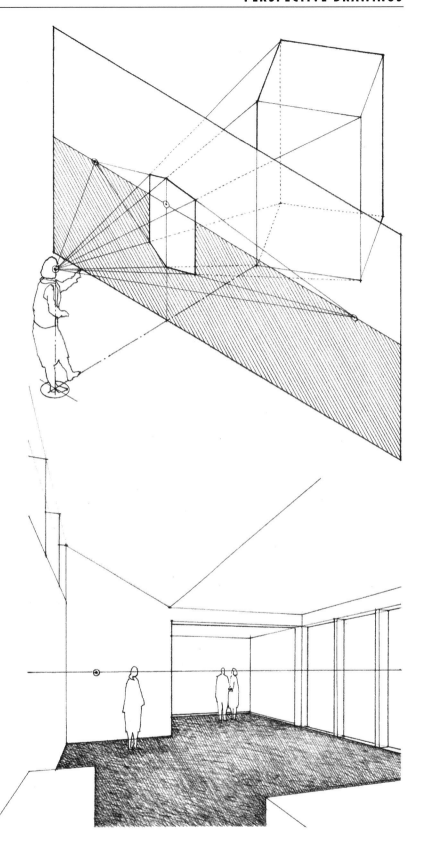

The primary use of perspective drawings in design is to convey an experiential view of space and spatial relationships.

3D computer modeling programs, while following the mathematical principles of perspective, can easily create distorted perspective views. Keeping the central portion of a subject or scene within a reasonable 60° cone of vision is therefore critical to avoiding such distortion.

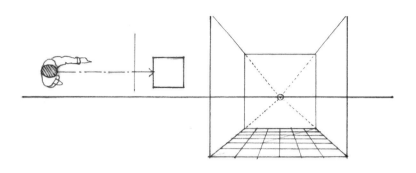

If we view a cube with our central axis of vision (CAV) perpendicular to one of its faces, all of the cube's vertical lines are parallel with the picture plane and remain vertical. Horizontal lines that are parallel to the PP and perpendicular to the CAV also remain horizontal. Lines parallel to the CAV, however, will appear to converge at a single point on the horizon line (HL), the center of vision (C).

One-point perspectives are particularly effective in depicting interior spaces because the display of three bounding faces provides a clear sense of enclosure.

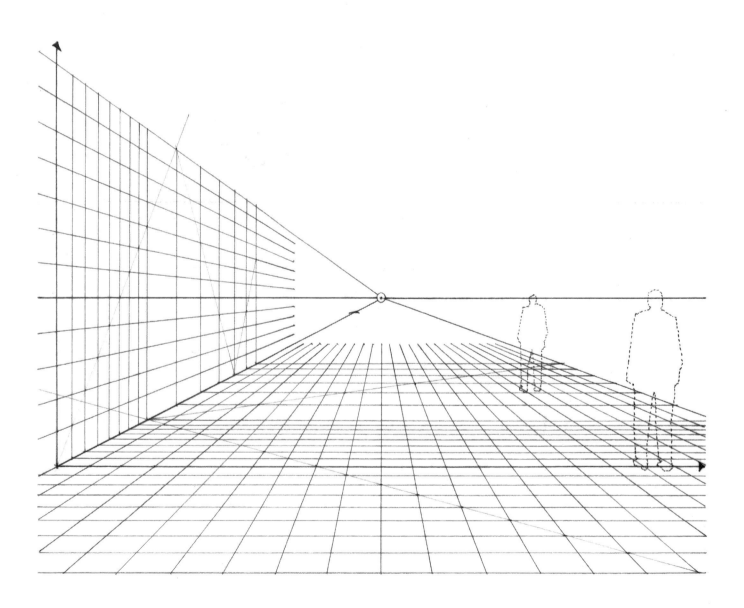

If we shift our view of a cube so that we view it obliquely, but keep our CAV horizontal, then the cube's vertical lines will remain vertical. The two sets of horizontal lines, however, are now oblique to the PP and will appear to converge, one set to the left and the other to the right. These are the two points referred to in two-point perspective.

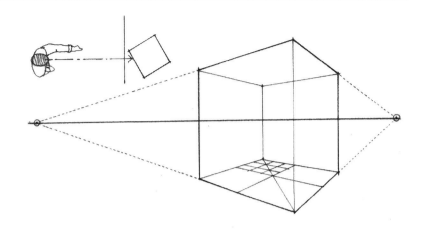

The pictorial effect of a two-point perspective varies with the observer's angle of view. In depicting interior spaces, a two-point perspective is most effective when the angle of view approaches that of a one-point perspective. Any perspective view that displays three bounding faces of a spatial volume provides the clear sense of enclosure inherent in interior spaces.

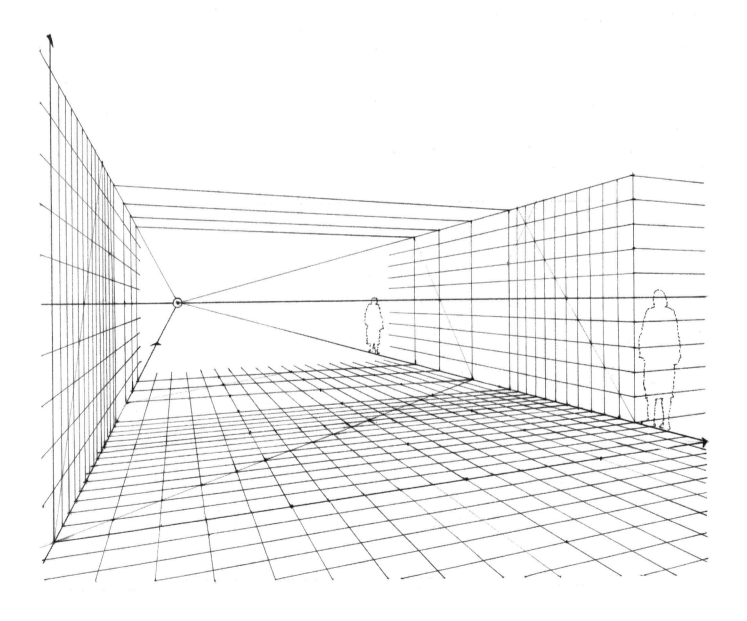

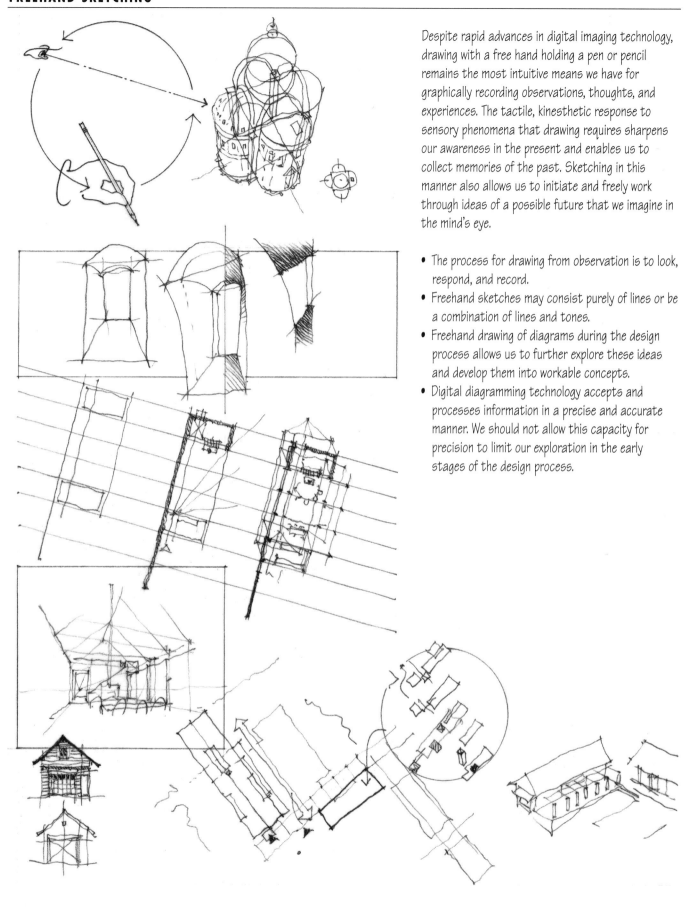

Despite rapid advances in digital imaging technology, drawing with a free hand holding a pen or pencil remains the most intuitive means we have for graphically recording observations, thoughts, and experiences. The tactile, kinesthetic response to sensory phenomena that drawing requires sharpens our awareness in the present and enables us to collect memories of the past. Sketching in this manner also allows us to initiate and freely work through ideas of a possible future that we imagine in the mind's eye.

- The process for drawing from observation is to look, respond, and record.
- Freehand sketches may consist purely of lines or be a combination of lines and tones.
- Freehand drawing of diagrams during the design process allows us to further explore these ideas and develop them into workable concepts.
- Digital diagramming technology accepts and processes information in a precise and accurate manner. We should not allow this capacity for precision to limit our exploration in the early stages of the design process.

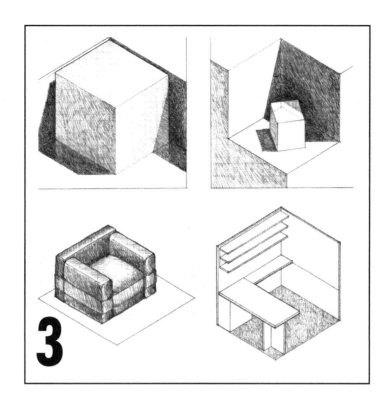

**3**

# A Design
# Vocabulary

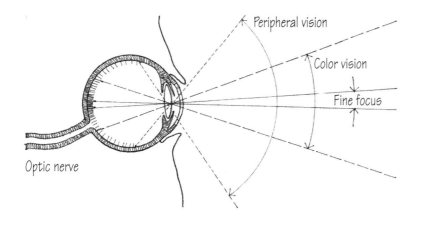

Peripheral vision

Color vision

Fine focus

Optic nerve

Our ability to focus on and perceive detail is restricted to a fairly narrow cone of vision. In surveying our visual field, our eyes continually move, scan, focus, and refocus to discover visual information. To make sense of what we see, the brain interprets the visual data gathered by our eyes and assembles the information into visual patterns that we can recognize and understand.

The normal process of perception is utilitarian and geared toward recognition. When we see a chair, we recognize it to be a chair if its form and configuration fit a pattern established by chairs we have seen and used in the past. If we look carefully, however, we would also be able to perceive the chair's specific shape, size, proportion, color, texture, and material. This ability to see beyond recognition and utility is extremely important to designers. We must continually strive to see and be conscious of the specific visual characteristics of things and how they relate and interact to form the aesthetic quality of our visual environments.

**A Design Vocabulary**

Form

Shape

Color

Texture

Light

Proportion

Scale

Balance

Harmony

Unity and Variety

Rhythm

Emphasis

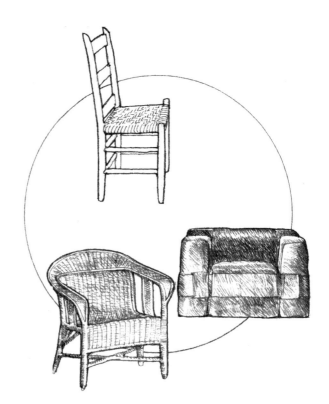

Our perception of the visual shape, size, color, and texture of things is affected by the optical environment in which we see them and the relationships we can discern between them and their visual setting. If our visual field were undifferentiated, we would see nothingness. As a perceptible change in tonal value, color, and texture occurred, however, we would begin to discern an object or figure as differentiated from its background. To read the lines, shapes, and forms of objects in our field of vision, therefore, we must first perceive contrast between them and their background.

Figure-Ground Relationships

Visual Contrast

Those elements that appear to stand out from or in front of their background are called figures. In addition to tonal value contrast, what distinguishes a figure from its background are its shape and size relative to its field. While a figure shares a common border with its background, it has a more distinct and recognizable shape that makes it appear as an object. Figures are sometimes referred to as positive elements—having a positive shape—while backgrounds are described as negative or neutral elements—lacking a clear or discernible shape.

Figures are most discernible when surrounded by a generous amount of space or background. When the size of a figure is such that it crowds its background, the background can develop its own distinct shape and interact with the shape of the figure. At times, an ambiguous figure-ground relationship can occur wherein elements in a composition can be seen alternately, but not simultaneously, as both figure and ground.

Our visual world is, in reality, a composite image constructed from a continuous array of figure-ground relationships. In interior design, these relationships can be seen to exist at several scales, depending on one's point of view.

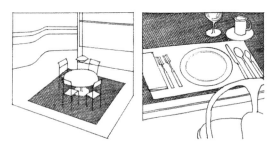

The point is the generator of all form. As a point moves, it leaves a trace of a line—the first dimension. As the line shifts in direction, it defines a plane—a two-dimensional element. The plane, extended in a direction oblique or perpendicular to its surface, forms a three-dimensional volume.

Point, line, plane, and volume. These are the primary elements of form. All visible forms are, in reality, three-dimensional. In describing form, these primary elements differ according to their relative dimensions of length, width, and depth—a matter of proportion and scale.

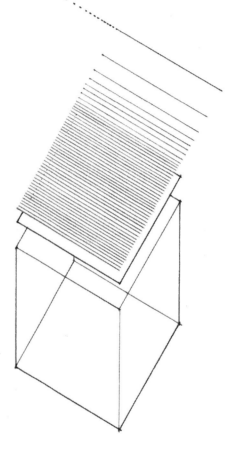

**Point**

**Line**

**Plane**

**Volume**

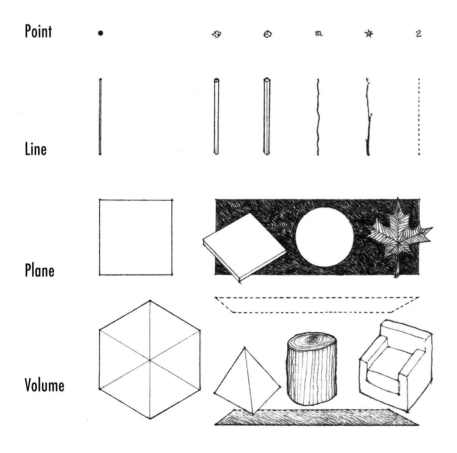

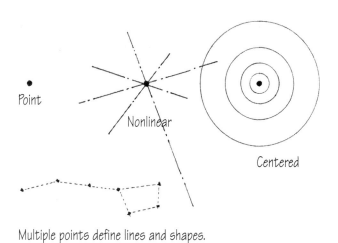

Point

Nonlinear

Centered

Multiple points define lines and shapes.

Relatively small shapes can read as points.

A point marks a location in space. Conceptually, it has no length, width, or depth. It is, therefore, static and directionless. As the prime generator of form, a point can mark the ends of a line, the intersection of two lines, or the corner where the lines of a plane or volume meet.

As a visible form, a point is most commonly manifested as a dot, a circular shape that is small relative to its field. Other shapes can also be seen as point-forms if sufficiently small, compact, and nondirectional.

When at the center of a field or space, a point is stable and at rest and capable of organizing other elements about itself. When moved off-center, it retains its self-centering quality but becomes more dynamic. Visual tension is created between the point and its field. Point-generated forms, such as the circle and the sphere, share this self-centering quality of the point.

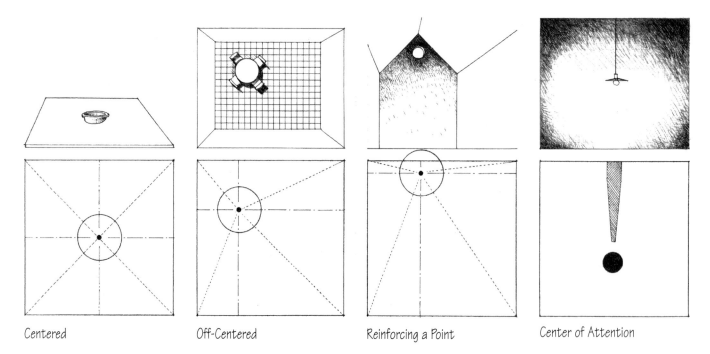

Centered

Off-Centered

Reinforcing a Point

Center of Attention

Point-generated forms, such as the circle and the sphere, are self-centering.

A point extended becomes a line. Conceptually, a line has only one dimension, length. In reality, a line's length visually dominates whatever thickness it must have to be visible. Unlike a point, which is static and directionless, a line is capable of expressing movement, direction, and growth.

As visible forms, lines may vary in weight and character. Whether bold or delicate, taut or limp, graceful or jagged, a line's visual character is due to our perception of its length-to-width ratio, its contour, and its degree of continuity.

A line can also be implied by two points. Carried further, the simple repetition of similar elements, if continuous enough, can define a line with significant textural qualities.

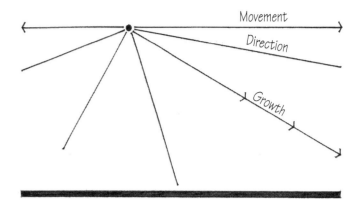

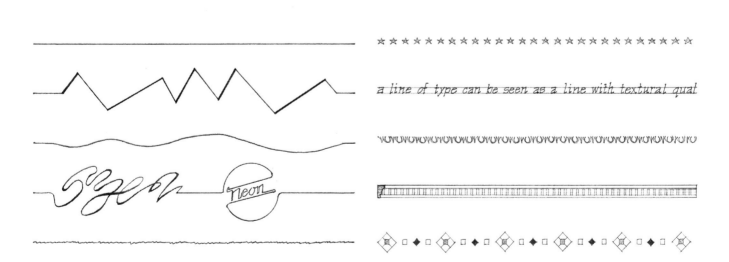

Lines varying in weight, contour, and texture

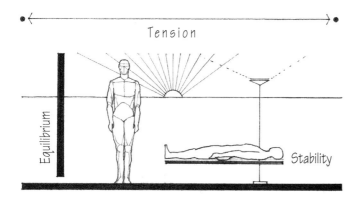

A straight line represents the tension that exists between two points. An important characteristic of a straight line is its direction. A horizontal line can represent stability, repose, or the plane upon which we stand or move. In contrast to this, a vertical line can express a state of equilibrium with the force of gravity.

Diagonal lines, deviations from the horizontal and the vertical, can be seen as rising or falling. In either case, they imply movement and are visually active and dynamic.

A curved line represents movement deflected by lateral forces. Curved lines tend to express gentle movement. Depending on their orientation, they can be uplifting or represent solidity and attachment to the earth. Small curves can express playfulness, energy, or patterns of biological growth.

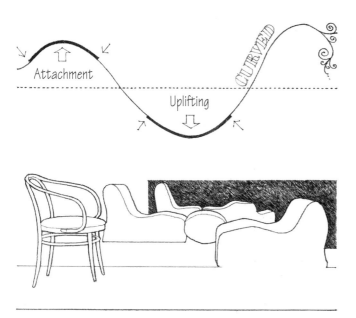

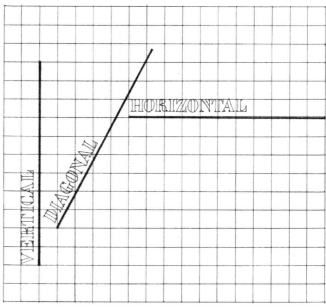

Line is an essential element in the formation of any visual construction. Without lines, we would not be able to define shape—that characteristic by which we generally recognize things. Lines describe the edges of a shape and separate it from the space around it. In addition, the contours of these lines imbue the shape with their expressive qualities.

In addition to describing shape, lines can articulate the edges of planes and the corners of volumes. These lines can be expressed either by the absence of material—reveals and recessed joints—or by the application of trim.

Lines can also be used to create texture and patterns on the surfaces of forms.

Lines defining shapes

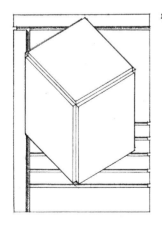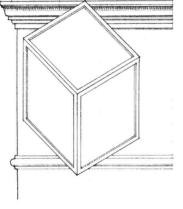

Lines articulating edges

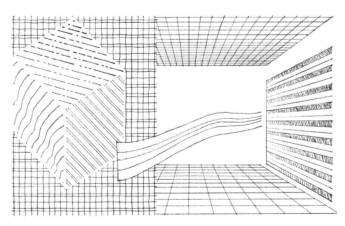

Lines creating textures and patterns

Linear forms have traditionally been used to provide vertical support, span and express movement across space, and define the edges of spatial volumes. This structural role of linear elements can be seen at the scale of both architecture and interior space and furnishings.

Within the design process itself, lines are used simply as regulating devices to express relationships and establish patterns among design elements.

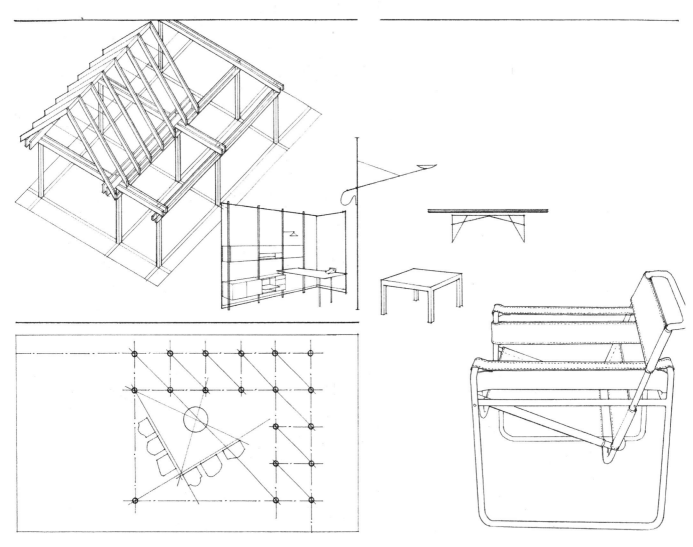

We often use lines to regulate relationships in drawing and design.

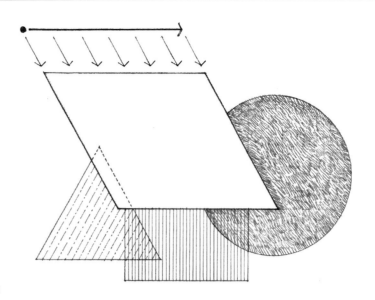

A line shifted in a direction other than its intrinsic direction defines a plane. Conceptually, a plane has two dimensions—width and length—but no depth. In reality, a plane's width and length dominate whatever thickness it must have to be visible.

Shape is the primary characteristic of a plane. It is described by the contour of the lines defining the edges of the plane. Since our perceptions of a plane's shape can be distorted by perspective, we see the true shape of a plane only when we view it frontally.

In addition to shape, planar forms have significant surface qualities of material, color, texture, and pattern. These visual characteristics affect a plane's:

• Visual weight and stability
• Perceived size, proportion, and position in space
• Light reflectivity
• Tactile qualities
• Acoustic properties

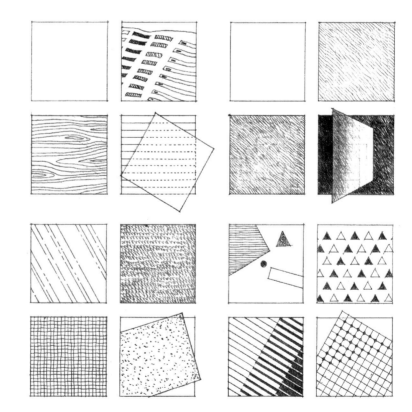

Material and Color

Texture and Pattern

Surface Characteristics of Planar Elements

Planar forms are fundamental elements of architecture and interior design. Floor, wall, and ceiling or roof planes serve to enclose and define three-dimensional volumes of space. Their specific visual characteristics and their relationships in space determine the form and character of the space they define. Within these spaces, furnishings and other interior design elements can also be seen to consist of planar forms.

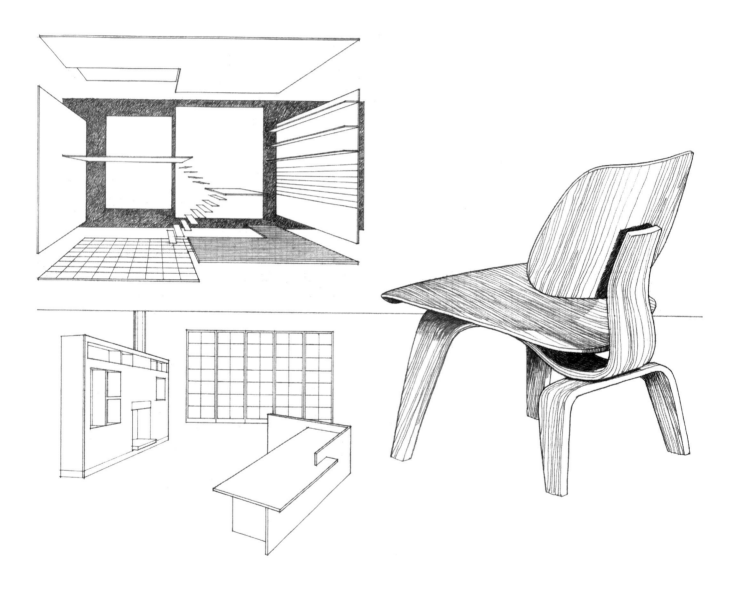

Shape is the primary means by which we distinguish one form from another. It may refer to the contour of a line, the outline of a plane, or the boundary of a three-dimensional mass. In each case, shape is defined by the specific configuration of the lines or planes that separate a form from its background or surrounding space.

There are several broad categories of shapes. Natural shapes represent the images and forms of our natural world. These shapes may be abstracted, usually through a process of simplification, and still retain the essential characteristics of their natural sources.

Nonobjective shapes make no obvious reference to a specific object or to a particular subject matter. Some nonobjective shapes may result from a process, such as calligraphy, and carry meaning as symbols. Others may be geometric and elicit responses based on their purely visual qualities.

Geometric shapes dominate the built environment of both architecture and interior design. There are two separate and distinct types of geometric shapes—rectilinear and curvilinear. In their most regular form, curvilinear shapes are circular while rectilinear shapes include the series of polygons that can be inscribed within a circle. Of these, the most significant geometric shapes are the circle, the triangle, and the square. Extended into the third dimension, these primary shapes generate the sphere, the cylinder, the cone, the pyramid, and the cube.

Natural Shapes

Nonobjective Shapes

Geometric Shapes

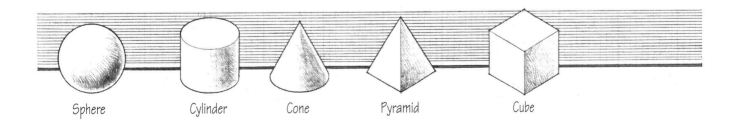

Sphere     Cylinder     Cone     Pyramid     Cube

The circle is a compact, introverted shape that has its centerpoint as its natural focus. It represents unity, continuity, and economy of form.

A circular shape is normally stable and self-centering in its environment. When associated with other lines and shapes, however, a circle can appear to have motion.

Other curvilinear lines and shapes can be seen to be fragments or combinations of circular shapes. Whether regular or irregular, curvilinear shapes are capable of expressing softness of form, fluidity of movement, or the nature of biological growth.

The triangle represents stability. Triangular shapes and patterns are often used in structural systems since their configuration cannot be altered without bending or breaking one of their sides.

From a purely visual point of view, a triangular shape is also stable when resting on one of its sides. When tipped to stand on one of its points, however, the triangular shape becomes dynamic. It can exist in a precarious state of balance or imply motion as it tends to fall over onto one of its sides.

The dynamic quality of a triangular shape is also due to the angular relationships of its three sides. Because these angles can vary, triangles are more flexible than squares and rectangles. In addition, triangles can be conveniently combined to form any number of square, rectangular, and other polygonal shapes.

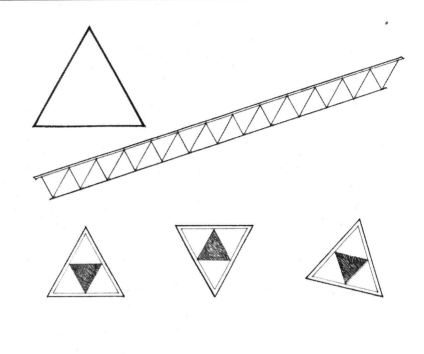

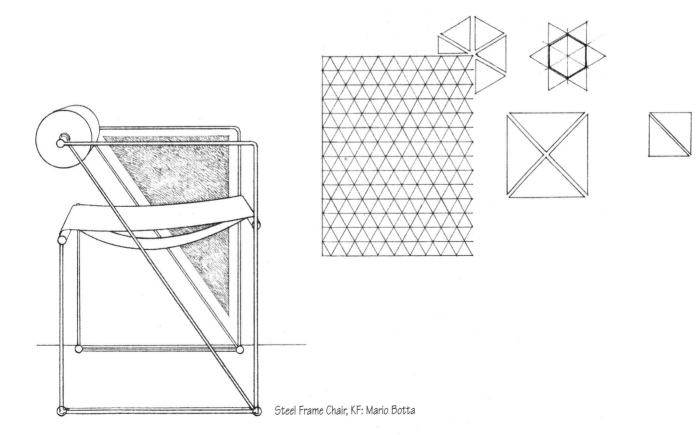

Steel Frame Chair, KF: Mario Botta

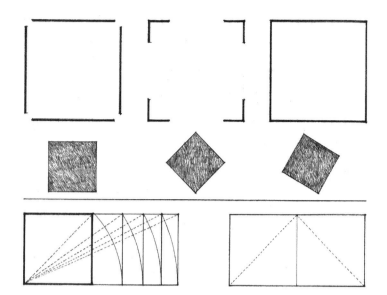

The square represents the pure and the rational. The equality of its four sides and its four right angles contributes to its regularity and visual clarity.

A square shape has no preferred or dominant direction. Like the triangle, the square is a stable, tranquil figure when resting on one of its sides, but becomes dynamic when standing on one of its corners.

All other rectangles can be considered to be variations of the square with the addition of width or length. While the clarity and stability of rectangular shapes can lead to visual monotony, variety can be introduced by varying their size, proportion, color, texture, placement, or orientation.

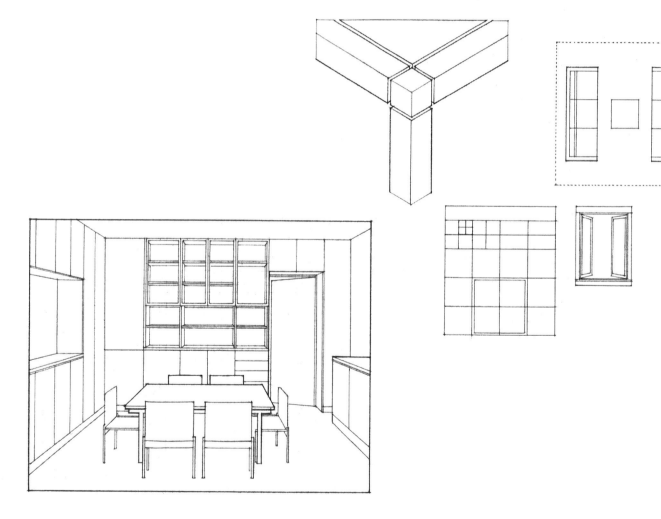

Texture is the specific quality of a surface that results from its three-dimensional structure. Texture is most often used to describe the relative smoothness or roughness of a surface. It can also be used to describe the characteristic surface qualities of familiar materials, such as the roughness of stone, the grain of wood, and the weave of a fabric.

There are two basic types of texture. Tactile texture is real and can be felt by touch; *visual* texture is seen by the eye. All tactile textures provide visual texture as well. Visual texture, on the other hand, may be illusory or real.

Our senses of sight and touch are closely intertwined. As our eyes read the visual texture of a surface, we often respond to its apparent tactile quality without actually touching it. We base these physical reactions to the textural qualities of surfaces on previous associations with similar materials.

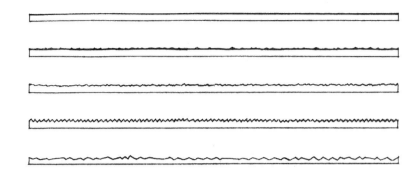

Texture refers to the three-dimensional structure of a surface.

Physical Texture

Visual Texture

Material Texture

Texture is intertwined with our senses of sight and touch.

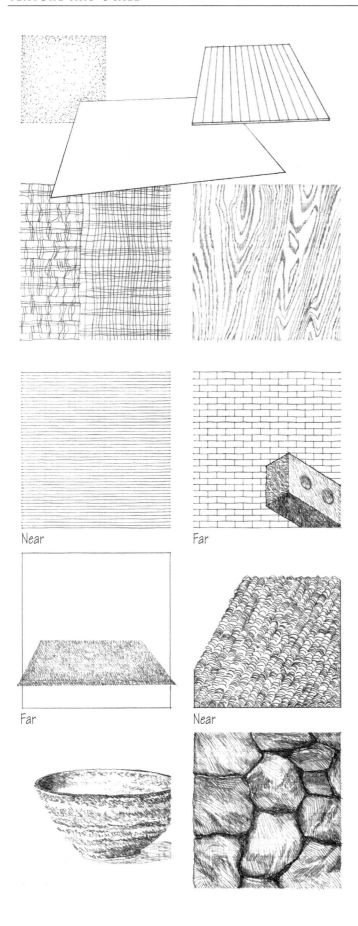

Near

Far

Far

Near

Scale, viewing distance, and light are important modifying factors in our perception of texture and the surfaces they articulate.

All materials have some degree of texture. But the finer the scale of a textural pattern, the smoother it will appear to be. Even coarse textures, when seen from a distance, can appear to be relatively smooth. Only upon closer viewing would the texture's coarseness become evident.

The relative scale of a texture can affect the apparent shape and position of a plane in space. Textures with a directional grain can accentuate a plane's length or width. Coarse textures can make a plane appear closer, reduce its scale, and increase its visual weight. In general, textures tend to visually fill the space in which they exist.

Light influences our perception of texture and, in turn, is affected by the texture it illuminates. Direct light falling across a surface with physical texture will enhance its visual texture. Diffused lighting deemphasizes physical texture and can even obscure its three-dimensional structure.

Smooth, shiny surfaces reflect light brilliantly, appear sharply in focus, and attract our attention. Surfaces with a matte or medium-rough texture absorb and diffuse light unevenly and, therefore, appear less bright than similarly colored but smoother surfaces. Very rough surfaces, when illuminated with direct lighting, cast distinct shadow patterns of light and dark.

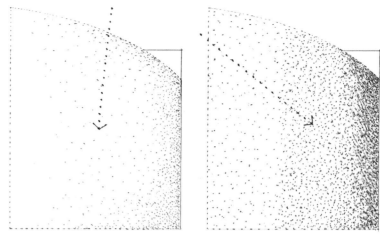

Lighting direction affects our reading of texture.

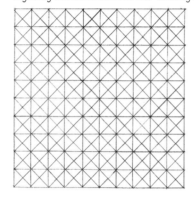

Shiny surfaces reflect.     Matte surfaces diffuse.

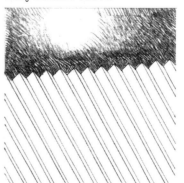

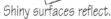

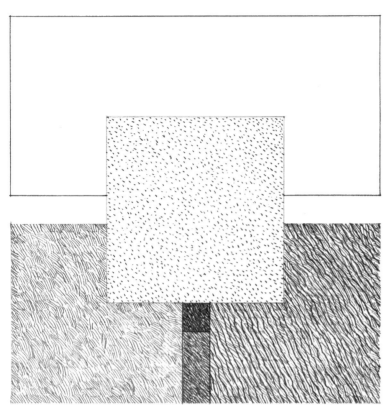

Contrast influences how strong or subtle a texture will appear to be. A texture seen against a uniformly smooth background will appear more obvious than when placed in juxtaposition with a similar texture. When seen against a coarser background, the texture will appear to be finer and reduced in scale.

Finally, texture is a factor in the maintenance of the materials and surfaces of a space. Smooth surfaces show dirt and wear but are relatively easy to clean, while rough surfaces may conceal dirt but are difficult to maintain.

Contrast affects the apparent strength or subtlety of adjacent textures.

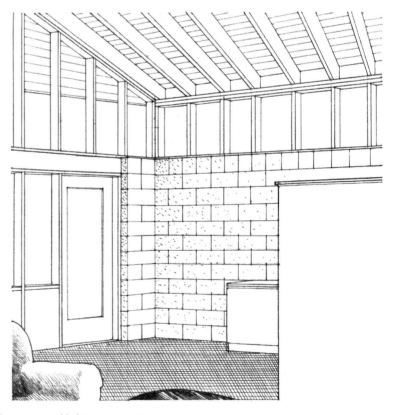

Texture can also result from the manner in which materials are assembled in construction.

Texture and pattern are closely related design elements. Pattern is the decorative design or ornamentation of a surface that is almost always based on the repetition of a motif—a distinctive and recurring shape, form, or color in a design. The repetitive nature of a pattern often gives the ornamented surface a textural quality as well. When the elements that create a pattern become so small that they lose their individual identity and blend into a tone, they become more texture than pattern.

A pattern may be structural or applied. A structural pattern results from the intrinsic nature of a material and the way it is processed, fabricated, or assembled. An applied pattern is added to a surface after it is structurally complete.

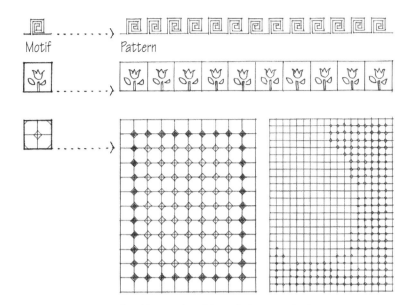

Motif        Pattern

A pattern reduced in scale becomes texture.

Structural Patterns

Applied Patterns

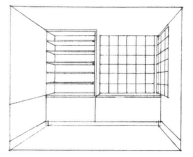

Minimal Texture

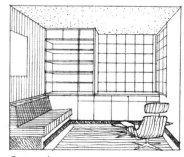

Textured

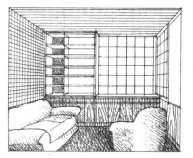

Texture Filling Space

Competing Textures

Texture is an intrinsic characteristic of the materials we use to define, furnish, and embellish interior space. How we combine and compose differing textures is just as important as the composition of color and light and should suit the desired character and use of a space.

The scale of a textural pattern should be related to the scale of a space and its major surfaces, as well as to the size of secondary elements within the space. Since texture tends to fill space visually, any textures used in a small room should be subtle or used sparingly. In a large room, texture can be used to reduce the scale of the space or to define a more intimate area within it.

A room with little textural variation can be bland. Combinations of hard and soft, even and uneven, and shiny and dull textures can be used to create variety and interest. In the selection and distribution of textures, moderation should be exercised and attention paid to their ordering and sequence. Harmony among contrasting textures can be sustained if they share a common trait, such as degree of light reflectance or visual weight.

A plane extended in a direction other than along its surface forms a volume. Conceptually and in reality a volume exists in three dimensions.

Form is the term we use to describe the contour and overall structure of a volume. The specific form of a volume is determined by the shapes and interrelationships of the lines and planes that describe the boundaries of the volume.

As the three-dimensional element of architectural and interior design, a volume can be either solid (space displaced by the mass of a building or building element) or a void (space contained and defined by wall, floor, and ceiling or roof planes). It is important to perceive this duality of containment versus displacement, especially when reading orthographic plans, elevations, and sections.

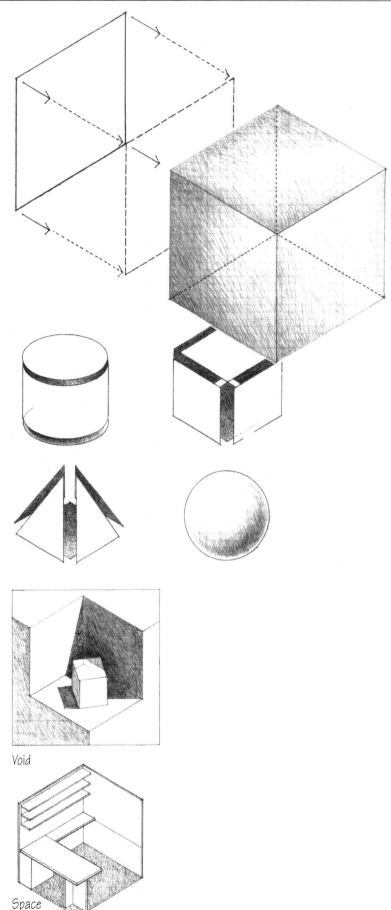

Solid

Void

Mass

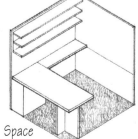

Space

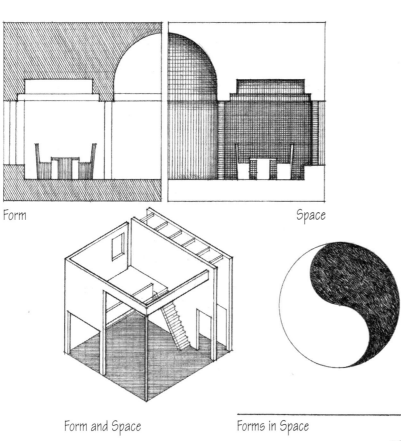

Form

Space

The duality of solid forms and spatial voids represents the essential unity of opposites that shapes the reality of architecture and interior design. Visible forms give space dimension, scale, color, and texture while space reveals the forms. This symbiotic relationship between form and space can be seen at several scales in interior design.

Form and Space

Forms in Space

Color is, like shape and texture, an inherent visual property of all form. We are surrounded by color in our environmental settings. The colors we attribute to objects, however, find their source in the light that illuminates and reveals form and space. Without light, color does not exist.

The science of physics deals with color as a property of light. Within the spectrum of visible light, color is determined by wavelength; starting at the longest wavelength with red, we proceed through the spectrum of orange, yellow, green, blue, indigo, and violet to arrive at the shortest visible wavelengths. When these colored lights are present in a light source in approximately equal quantities, they combine to produce white light—light that is apparently colorless.

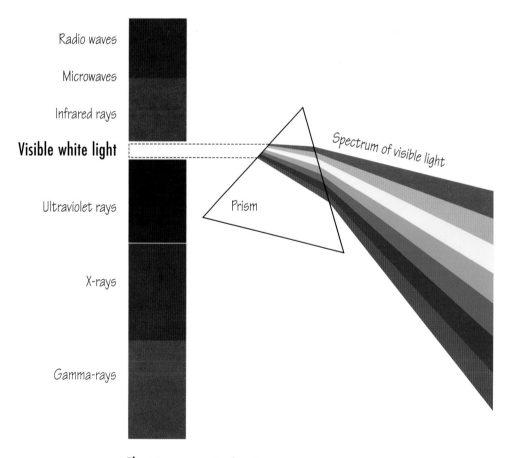

Radio waves

Microwaves

Infrared rays

**Visible white light**

Spectrum of visible light

Ultraviolet rays

Prism

X-rays

Gamma-rays

**Electrico-magnetic Spectrum**

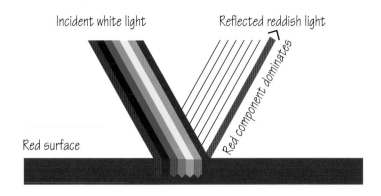

When white light falls on an opaque object, selective absorption occurs. The surface of the object absorbs certain wavelengths of light and reflects others. Our eyes apprehend the color of the reflected light as the color of the object.

White light, such as noon sunlight, is composed of the entire spectrum of colored lights. Some light sources, such as fluorescent lamps or light reflected off a colored wall, may not be well balanced and may lack part of the spectrum. This lack of certain colors would make a surface illuminated by such light appear to also lack those colors.

Which wavelengths or bands of light are absorbed and which are reflected as object color is determined by the pigmentation of a surface. A red surface appears red because it absorbs most of the blue and green light falling on it and reflects the red part of the spectrum; a blue surface absorbs the reds. Similarly, a black surface absorbs the entire spectrum; a white surface reflects all of it.

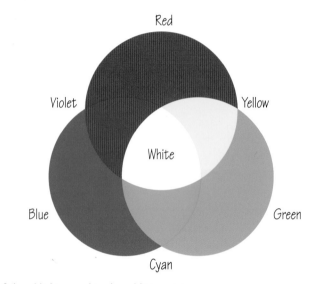

Colored lights combine by additive mixing.

A surface has the natural pigmentation of its material. This coloration can be altered with the application of paints, stains, or dyes that contain color pigments. While colored light is additive in nature, color pigments are subtractive. Each pigment absorbs certain proportions of white light. When pigments are mixed, their absorptions combine to subtract various colors of the spectrum. The colors that remain determine the hue, value, and intensity of the mixed pigment.

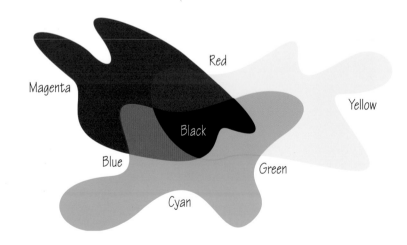

Pigment colors combine by subtractive mixing.

Color has three dimensions:

## Hue
The attribute by which we recognize and describe a color, such as red or yellow.

## Value
The degree of lightness or darkness of a color in relation to white and black.

## Saturation
The brilliance or dullness of a color; this depends on the amount of hue in a color.

All of these attributes of color are necessarily interrelated. Each principal hue has a normal value. Pure yellow, for example, is lighter in value than pure blue. If white, black, or a complementary hue is added to a color to lighten or darken its value, its saturation will also be diminished. It is difficult to adjust one attribute of a color without simultaneously altering the other two.

A number of color systems attempt to organize colors and their attributes into a visible order. The simplest type, such as the Brewster or Prang color wheel, organizes color pigments into primary, secondary, and tertiary hues.

The primary hues are red, yellow, and blue. The secondary hues are orange, green, and violet. The tertiary hues are red-orange, yellow-orange, yellow-green, blue-green, blue-violet, and red-violet.

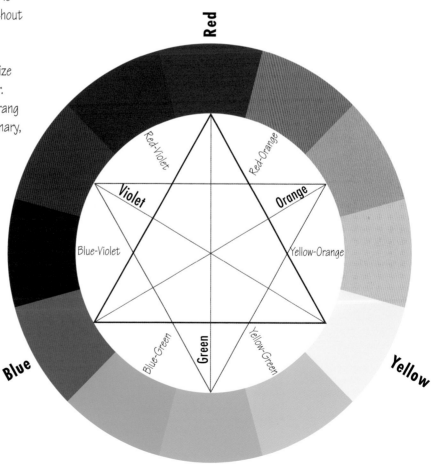

A more comprehensive system for the accurate specification and description of color is the Munsell system, developed by Albert H. Munsell. The system arranges colors into three orderly scales of uniform visual steps according to their attributes of hue, value, and chroma (intensity).

The Munsell system is based on five principal hues and five intermediate hues. These ten major hues are arranged horizontally in a circle.

Extending vertically through the center of the hue circle is a scale of neutral gray values, graded in ten equal visual steps from black to white.

Radiating out from the vertical scale of values are equal steps of chroma or intensity. The number of steps will vary according to the attainable saturation of each color's hue and value.

With this system, a specific color can be identified with the following notation: Hue Value/Chroma, or H V/C. For example, 5R 5/14 would indicate a pure red at middle value and maximum chroma.

While the ability to accurately communicate the hue, value, and intensity of a specific color without an actual sample is important in science, commerce, and industry, color names and notations cannot adequately describe the visual sensation of color. Actual color samples, seen in the color of the light in which they will be used, are essential in the design of a color scheme.

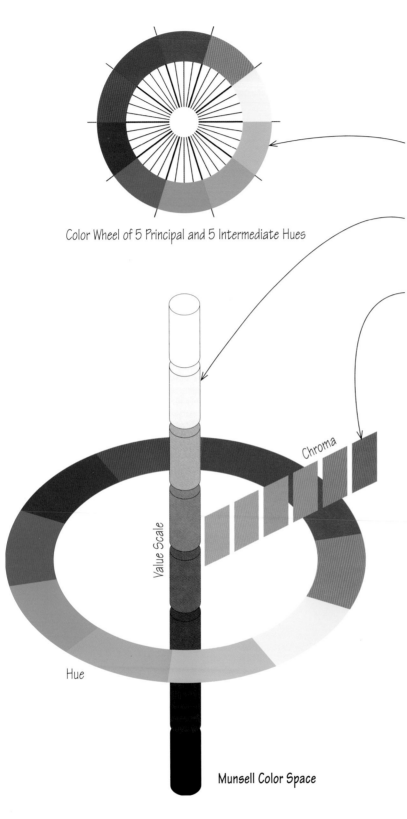

Color Wheel of 5 Principal and 5 Intermediate Hues

Value Scale

Chroma

Hue

Munsell Color Space

With the advent of color computer monitors and printers, the need for a universal language of color communication has become even more pressing. Interior designers often must indicate a color to be used uniformly in paints, textiles, graphic design materials, and other media.

Commission Internationale l'Eclairage (CIE) standards are based on the precise measurement of light waves reflected by a surface, factored by sensitivity curves that have been measured for the human eye. Although cumbersome to use, CIE standards are specified by most American furniture manufacturers.

Color maps, such as the color space developed by Munsell and described on the previous page, allow color communication between any two individuals with the same map.

Systems like Pantone® for architecture and interiors provide the interior designer with a way to specify, communicate, and manage color choices for a wide variety of materials, both online and offline.

Electronic color analyzers to identify color data from samples and color viewing lights that simulate varied lighting conditions are also available.

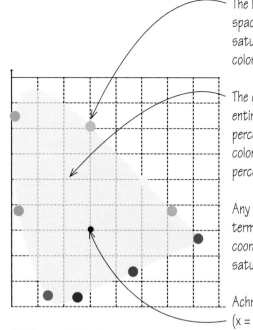

The boundary of the color space represents the maximum saturation of the spectral colors.

The color space contains the entire range of human color perception, i.e., all of the colors of the visible spectrum perceivable by the human eye.

Any color can be expressed in terms of the two chromaticity coordinates for hue and saturation, x and y.

Achromatic point $(x = 1/2; y = 1/3)$

**CIE Chromaticity Diagram**

A Sampling of Pantone® Color Swatches

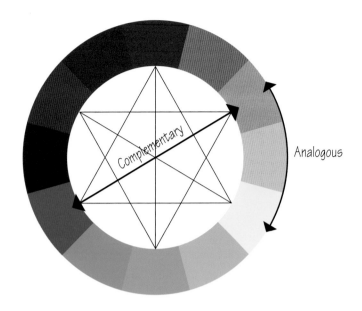

Object colorants, such as paints and dyes, are means to modify the color of the illuminating light, which we interpret to be the color of the object. In mixing the pigments of paints and dyes, each of the attributes of color can be altered.

The hue of a color can be changed by mixing it with other hues. When neighboring or analogous hues on the color wheel are mixed, harmonious and closely related hues are created. In contrast to this, mixing complementary hues, hues directly opposite of each other on the color wheel, produces neutral hues.

The value of a color can be raised by adding white and lowered by adding black. Lightening a hue's normal value by adding white creates a tint of that hue; darkening the hue's normal value with black creates a shade of the hue. A normally high-value color, such as yellow, is capable of more shades than tints, while a low-value color, such a red, is able to have more tints than shades.

The intensity of a color can be strengthened by adding more of the dominant hue. It can be lowered by mixing gray with the color or by adding to the color its complementary hue. Hues that are grayed or neutralized in this manner are often called tones.

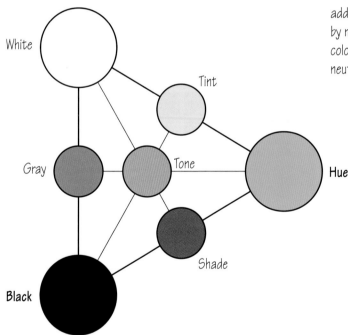

Apparent changes in an object's color can also result from the effects of light and from the juxtaposition of surrounding or background colors. These factors are especially important to the interior designer, who must carefully consider how the colors of elements in an interior space interact and how they are rendered by the light illuminating them.

Light of a particular hue, other than white, is rarely used for general illumination. Not all sources of white light, however, are spectrally well balanced. Incandescent bulbs cast a warm glow, while many fluorescent lamps cast a cool light. Daylight, too, can be warm or cool, depending on the time of day and the direction from which it comes. Even the color of a large reflecting surface can tint the light within an interior space.

Warm light tends to accentuate warm colors and neutralize cool hues, while cool light intensifies cool colors and weakens warm hues. If light is tinted with a particular hue, it will raise the intensity of colors of that hue and neutralize colors of a complementary hue.

The apparent value of a color can also be altered by the amount of light used to illuminate it. Lowering the amount of illumination will darken a color's value and neutralize its hue. Raising the lighting level will lighten the color's value and enhance its intensity. High levels of illumination, however, can also tend to make colors appear less saturated or washed out.

Since the natural fluctuations of light in an interior setting alter colors in often subtle ways, it is always best to test colors in the environment in which they are to be viewed, under both daylight and nighttime conditions.

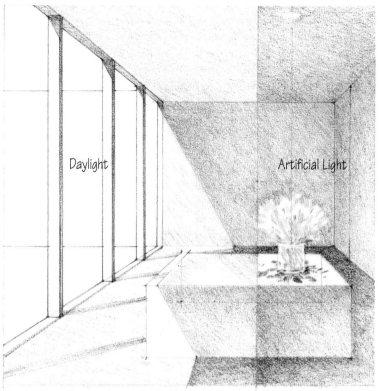

Daylight       Artificial Light

Conditions affecting the rendition of colors in an interior space

Strong Illumination     Medium Illumination     Low Illumination

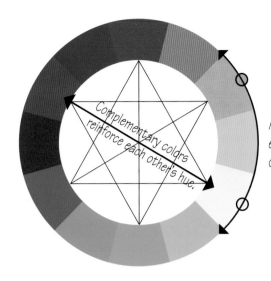

Analogous colors push each other toward the other's complement.

While mixing two complementary color pigments results in a neutralized or grayed hue, placing them next to each other can produce the opposite effect. In the phenomenon known as simultaneous contrast, the eye tends to generate a color's complementary hue and project it as an afterimage on adjacent colors. Thus two complementary colors placed side by side tend to heighten each other's saturation and brilliance without an apparent change in hue.

When the two colors are not complementary, each will tint the other with its own complement and shift it toward that hue. The result is that the two colors are pushed farther apart in hue.

Simultaneous contrast in hue is most easily perceived when two colors are fairly uniform in value. If one color is much lighter or darker than the other, the effects of contrasting values become more noticeable.

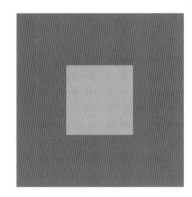
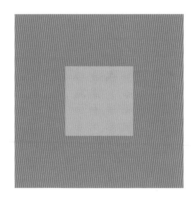

**Simultaneous Contrast**

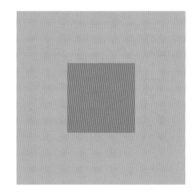

Complementary Colors

Analogous Colors; Contrasting Values

Analogous Colors; Similar Values

Simultaneous contrast also affects the apparent value of a color, which can be made to appear lighter or darker according to the value of its background color. A light color will tend to deepen a dark color while a dark color will tend to brighten a light color.

Both black and white have a visible effect on colors when brought into contact with them. Surrounding colors with black tends to make them richer and more vibrant, while outlining with white often has the opposite effect. A large area of white will reflect light onto adjacent colors, while thin white lines tend to spread and tint the hues they separate.

The effects of contrasting hues and values depend on areas large enough to be perceived as separate colors. If the areas are small and closely spaced, the eye does not have enough time to adjust to their differences and mixes the colors optically. The effects of optical mixing are often used in the weaving of textiles to create an impression of many hues and values with a limited number of colored yarns or threads.

Contrasting values alter perceived values.

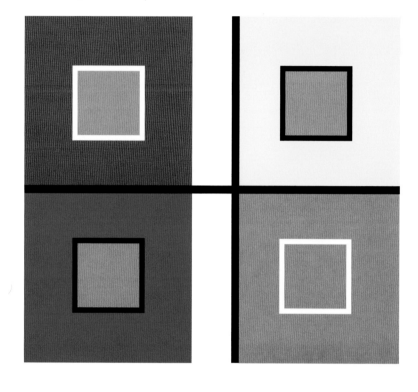

Effect of outlining colors with white or black.

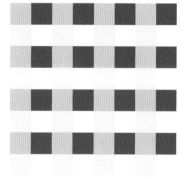 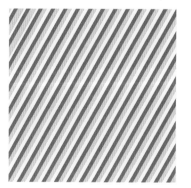

Optical mixing occurs when dots or strokes of colors merge to produce more luminous hues.

In addition to how colors interact and alter one another's attributes, it is important to note how color might affect our perception of form and the dimensions and qualities of interior space.

Colors are often divided into warm and cool categories. Reds, oranges, and yellows are considered to be warm colors that advance. Blues, greens, and violets are cooler and tend to recede. Neutrals, such as grays, may be either warm (brownish) or cool (bluish).

The warmth or coolness of a color's hue, along with its relative value and degree of saturation, determines the visual force with which it attracts our attention, brings an object into focus, and creates space. The following generalizations summarize some of these effects of color.

Warm hues and high intensities are said to be visually active and stimulating, while cool hues and low intensities are more subdued and relaxing. Light values tend to be cheerful, middle values undemanding, and dark values somber.

Bright, saturated colors and any strong contrasts attract our attention. Grayed hues and middle values are less forceful. Contrasting values in particular make us aware of shapes and forms. Contrasting hues and saturations can also define shape; but if they are too similar in value, the definition they afford will be less distinct.

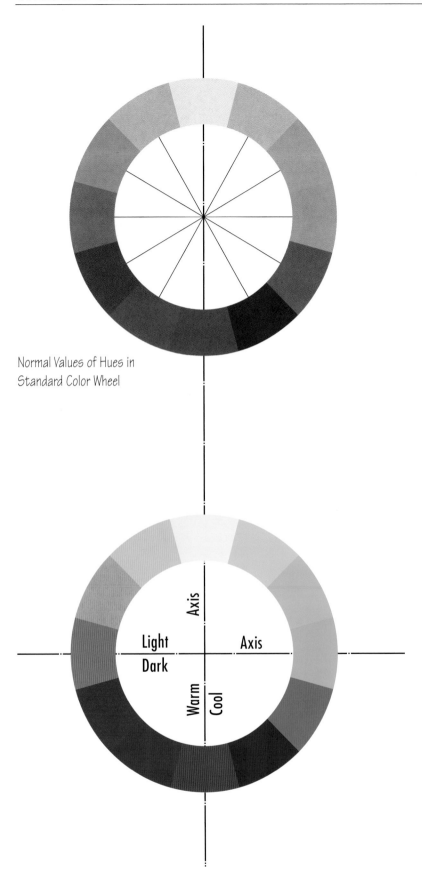

Normal Values of Hues in Standard Color Wheel

Value contrast aids in our perception of shape.

Deep, cool colors appear to contract. Light, warm colors tend to expand and increase the apparent size of an object, especially when seen against a dark background.

When used on an enclosing plane of a space, light values, cool hues, and grayed colors appear to recede and increase apparent distance. They can therefore be used to enhance the spaciousness of a room and increase its apparent width, length, or ceiling height.

Warm hues appear to advance. Dark values and saturated colors suggest nearness. These traits can be used to diminish the scale of a space or, in an illusionary way, shorten a room's dimensions.

We should acknowledge here that our emotional reactions to color vary with our personal experiences and cultural associations. In addition, favored color combinations are subject to fashion trends, with certain color palettes closely tied to specific times or places.

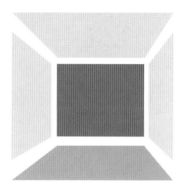

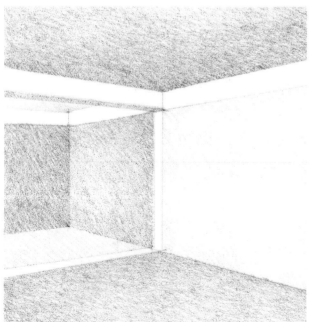

The effect of color on spatial boundaries

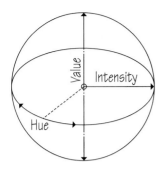

Although each of us may have favorite colors and a distinct dislike of others, there is no such thing as a good or bad color. Some colors are simply in or out of fashion at a given time; others may be appropriate or inappropriate given a specific color scheme. The suitability of a color depends ultimately on how and where it is used and how it fits into the palette of a color scheme.

If colors are like the notes of a musical scale, then color schemes are like musical chords, structuring color groups according to certain visual relationships among their attributes of hue, value, and intensity. The following color schemes are based on the hue relationships within a color group.

There are two broad categories of hue schemes, related and contrasting. Related hue schemes, based on either a single hue or a series of analogous hues, promote harmony and unity. Variety can be introduced by varying value and intensity, including small amounts of other hues as accents, or bringing shape, form, and texture into play.

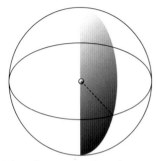

Monochromatic color schemes vary the value of a single hue.

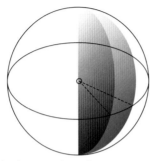

Analogous color schemes use two or more hues from the same quarter of the color wheel.

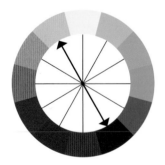

Complementary color schemes use two hues on opposite sides of the color wheel.

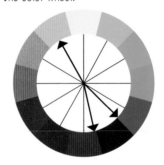

Split complementary color schemes combine one hue with the two hues adjacent to its complement.

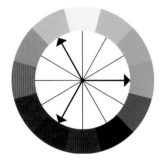

Triadic color schemes use colors located at three equidistant points on the color wheel.

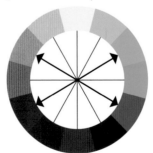

Contrasting hue schemes, based on complementary or triadic color combinations, are inherently more rich and varied since they always include both warm and cool hues.

Hue schemes merely outline the approaches one can take in organizing a combination of hues. In designing a color scheme, other color relationships must also be considered.

The color triangle developed by Faber Birren illustrates how modified colors—tints, tones, and shades—might be related in a harmonious sequence. The triangle is based on the three basic elements, pure color, white, and black. They combine to create the secondary forms of tint, shade, gray, and tone. Any of the bold-line paths illustrated to the right define a harmonious sequence since each involves a series of visually related elements.

Ultimately, whether a color scheme is lively and exuberant or restful and quiet will depend on the chromatic and tonal values of the hues chosen. Large intervals between the colors and values will create lively contrasts and dramatic effects. Small intervals will result in more subtle contrasts and patterns.

Small Intervals

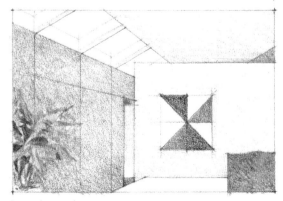

Large Intervals

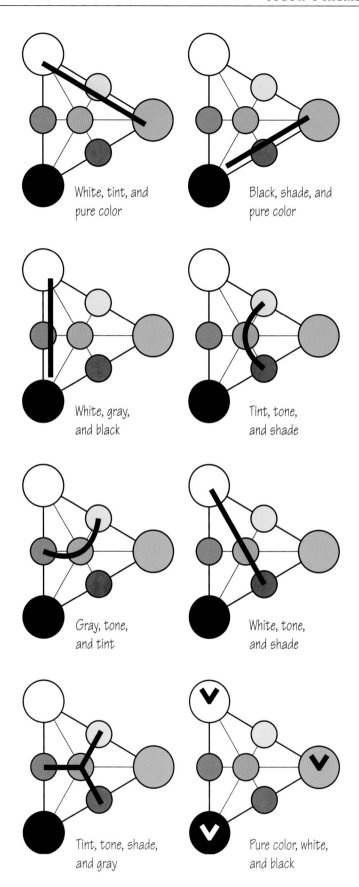

White, tint, and pure color

Black, shade, and pure color

White, gray, and black

Tint, tone, and shade

Gray, tone, and tint

White, tone, and shade

Tint, tone, shade, and gray

Pure color, white, and black

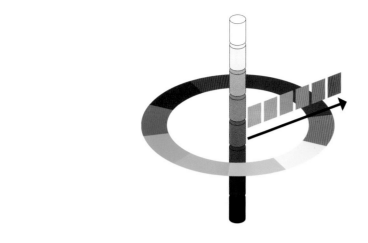

In developing a color scheme for an interior space, one must consider carefully the chromatic and tonal key to be established and the distribution of the colors. The scheme must not only satisfy the purpose and use of the space but also take into account its architectural character.

Decisions must be made regarding the major planes of an interior space and how color might be used to modify their apparent size, shape, scale, and distance. Which elements will form the background, middle ground, and foreground? Are there architectural or structural features that should be accentuated or undesirable elements to be minimized?

Usually, the largest surfaces of a room—its floor, walls, and ceiling—have the most neutralized values. Against this background, secondary elements such as large pieces of furniture or area rugs can have greater chromatic intensity. Finally, accent pieces, accessories, and other small-scale elements can have the strongest chroma for balance and to create interest.

Neutralized color schemes are the most flexible. For a more dramatic effect, the main areas of a room can be given the more intense values while secondary elements have lesser intensity. Large areas of intense color should be used with caution, particularly in a small room. They reduce the apparent distance and can be visually demanding.

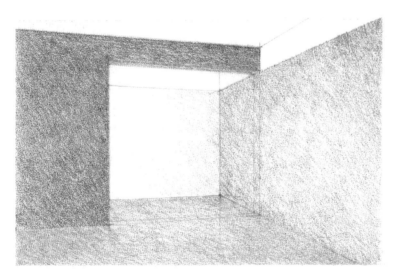

Large areas of intense color can be both dramatic and visually demanding.

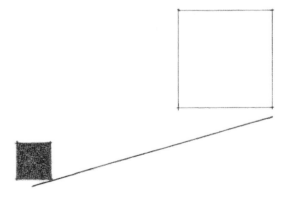

Balance large neutral areas with smaller areas of stronger intensity.

Of equal importance to chromatic distribution is tonal distribution, the pattern of lights and darks in a space. It is generally best to use varying amounts of light and dark values with a range of middle values to serve as transitional tones. Avoid using equal amounts of light and dark unless a fragmented effect is desired.

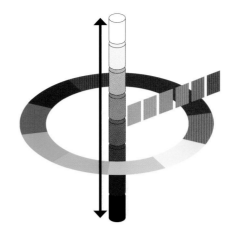

Typically, large areas of light value are offset by smaller areas of medium and dark values. This use of light values is particularly appropriate when the efficient use of available light is important. Dark color schemes can absorb much of the light within a space, resulting in a significant loss of illumination.

Another way of distributing values is to follow the pattern of nature. In this tonal sequence, the floor plane has the darkest value, surrounding walls are in the middle to light range, and the ceiling above is fairly light.

Of course, the distribution of values and their degree of contrast will also depend on the size, shape, and scale of the space. Because light values tend to recede while dark values advance, their placement can modify our perception of these spatial dimensions.

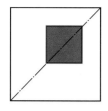 **Proportion**

 **Scale**

 **Balance**

 **Harmony**

 **Unity and Variety**

 **Rhythm**

**Emphasis**

Interior design involves the selection of interior design elements and their arrangement within a spatial enclosure to satisfy certain functional and aesthetic needs and wishes. This arrangement of elements in a space includes the act of making patterns. No one single part or element in a space stands alone. In a design pattern, all of the parts, elements, or pieces depend on one another for their visual impact, function, and meaning.

We are concerned here with the visual relationships established among the interior design elements in a space. The following design principles are not intended to be hard and fast rules but rather guidelines to the possible ways design elements can be arranged into recognizable patterns. Ultimately, we must learn to judge the appropriateness of a pattern, its visual role in a space, and its meaning to the users of the space. These principles, however, can help develop and maintain a sense of visual order among the design elements of a space while accommodating their intended use and function.

### ▶ Arranging Design Patterns

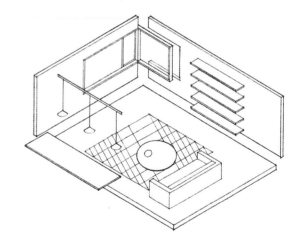

Proportion refers to the relationship of one part to another or to the whole, or between one object and another. This relationship may be one of magnitude, quantity, or degree.

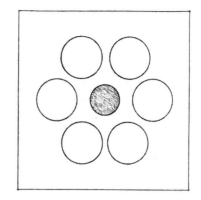

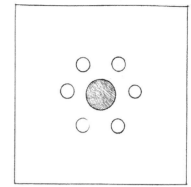

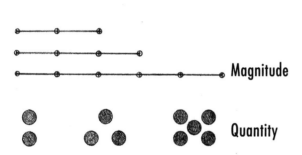 **Magnitude**

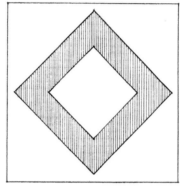

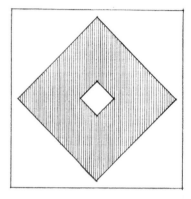

   **Quantity**

The apparent size of an object is influenced by the relative sizes of other objects in its environment.

**Degree**

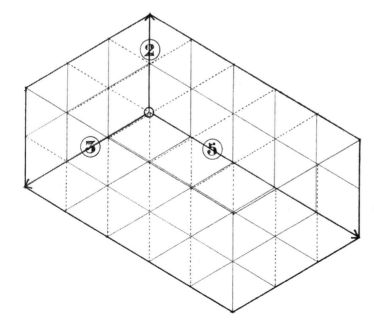

When dealing with forms in space, one must consider proportion in three dimensions.

Ratio      A:B      $A / B$

Proportion    A:B:C      $A / B = B / C$

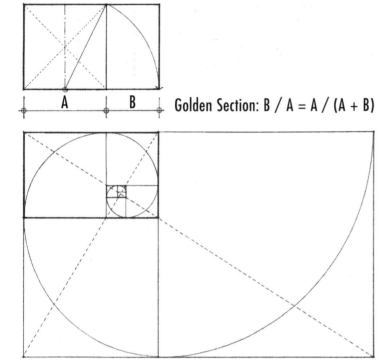

A       B      Golden Section: $B / A = A / (A + B)$

In the course of history, a number of mathematical or geometric methods have been developed to determine the ideal proportion of things. These proportioning systems go beyond functional and technical determinants in an attempt to establish a measure of beauty—an aesthetic rationale for the dimensional relationships among the parts and elements of a visual construction.

According to Euclid, the ancient Greek mathematician, a ratio refers to the quantitative comparison of two similar things, while proportion refers to the equality of ratios. Underlying any proportioning system, therefore, is a characteristic ratio, a permanent quality that is transmitted from one ratio to another.

Perhaps the most familiar proportioning system is the golden section established by the ancient Greeks. It defines the unique relationship between two unequal parts of a whole in which the ratio between the smaller and greater parts is equal to the ratio between the greater part and the whole.

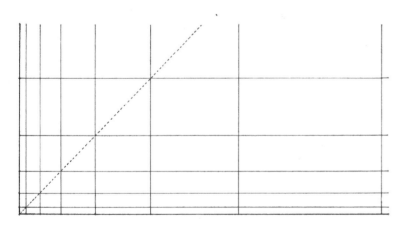

**1, 1, 2, 3, 5, 8, 13, 21, 34, 55...**

The Fibonacci series is a progression of whole numbers in which each term is the sum of the preceding two. The ratio between two consecutive terms approximates the golden section.

Although often defined in mathematical terms, a proportioning system establishes a consistent set of visual relationships among the parts of a composition. It can be a useful design tool in promoting unity and harmony. Our perception of the physical dimensions of things is, however, often imprecise. The foreshortening of perspective, viewing distance, even cultural bias, can distort our perception.

The matter of proportion is still primarily one of critical visual judgment. In this respect, significant differences in the relative dimensions of things are important. Ultimately, a proportion will appear to be correct for a given situation when we sense that neither too little nor too much of an element or characteristic is present.

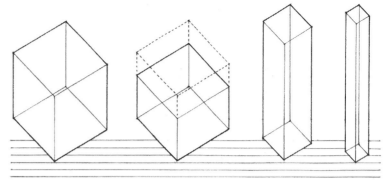

Significant differences in proportion

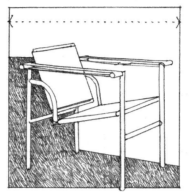
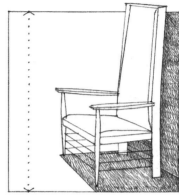

Pieces of furniture that differ significantly in their proportions

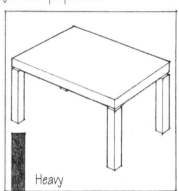

Thin

Heavy

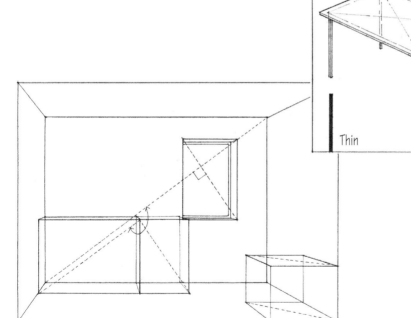

Diagonals that are parallel or perpendicular to each other indicate that the rectangles they bisect have similar proportions.

In interior design, we are concerned with the proportional relationships between the parts of a design element, between several design elements, and between the elements and the spatial form and enclosure.

## Proportional Differences

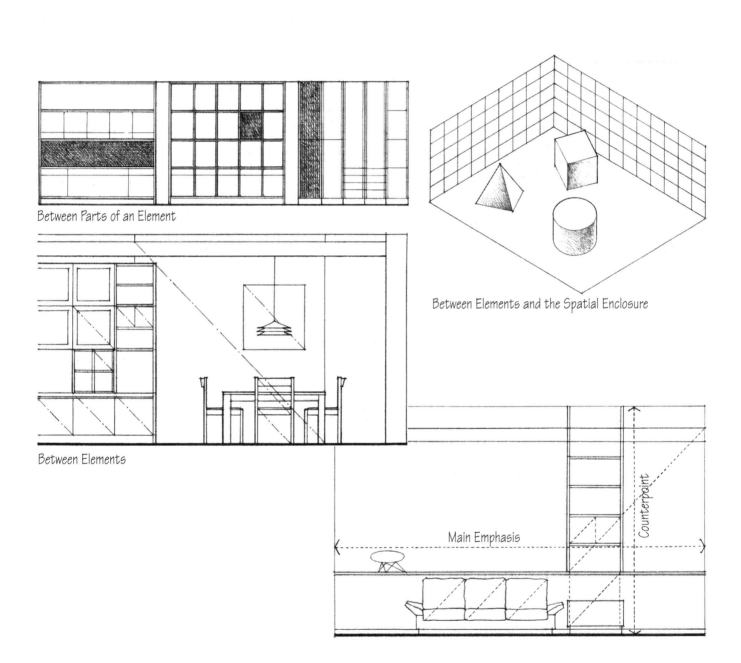

Between Parts of an Element

Between Elements and the Spatial Enclosure

Between Elements

Main Emphasis

Counterpoint

The design principle of scale is related to proportion. Both proportion and scale deal with the relative sizes of things. If there is a difference, proportion pertains to the relationships between the parts of a composition, while scale refers specifically to the size of something, relative to some known standard or recognized constant.

Mechanical scale is the calculation of something's physical size according to a standard system of measurement. For example, we can say that a table is, according to the U.S. Customary System, 3 feet wide, 6 feet long, and 29 inches high. If we are familiar with this system and with objects of similar size, we can visualize how big is the table. Using the International Metric System, the same table would measure 914 mm wide, 1829 mm long, and 737 mm high.

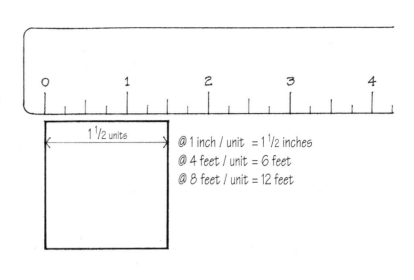

1 ¹/₂ units

@ 1 inch / unit  = 1 ¹/₂ inches
@ 4 feet / unit = 6 feet
@ 8 feet / unit = 12 feet

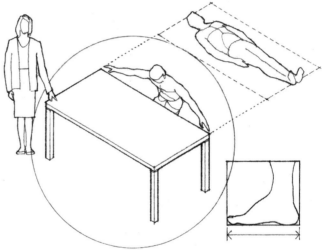

Our bodies can serve as a system of measurement.

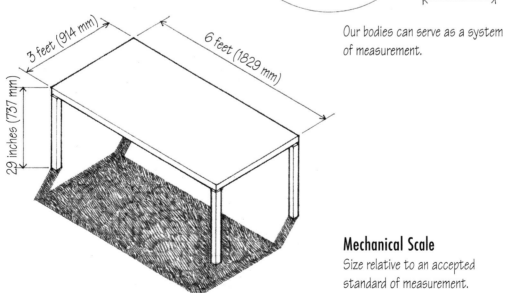

3 feet (914 mm)
6 feet (1829 mm)
29 inches (737 mm)

## Mechanical Scale
Size relative to an accepted standard of measurement.

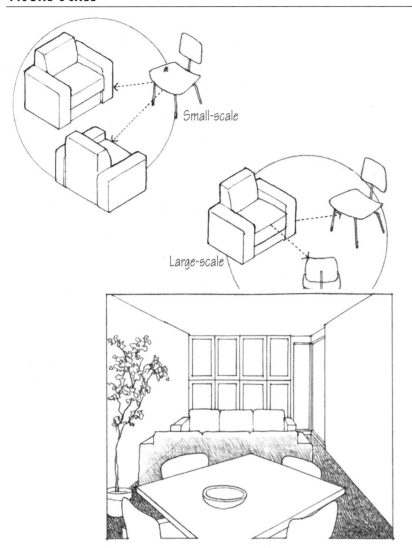

Small-scale

Large-scale

Visual scale refers to the size something appears to have when measured against other things around it. Thus, an object's scale is often a judgment we make based on the relative or known sizes of other nearby or surrounding elements. For example, the aforementioned table can appear to be in-scale or out-of-scale with a room, depending on the relative size and proportions of the space.

We can refer to something as being small-scale if we are measuring it against other things that are generally much larger in size. Similarly, an object can be considered to be large-scale if it is grouped with relatively small items or if it appears to be larger than what is considered normal or average in size.

Small-scale space or large-scale furniture

## Visual Scale
Size relative to other objects in the environment or to the surrounding space

Human scale refers to the feeling of bigness something gives us. If the dimensions of an interior space or the sizes of elements within it make us feel small, we can say they lack human scale. If, on the other hand, the space does not dwarf us or if the elements offer a comfortable fit with our dimensional requirements of reach, clearance, or movement, we can say they are human in scale.

Most of the elements we use to ascertain human scale are those whose dimensions we have become accustomed to through contact and use. These include doorways, stairs, tables, counters, and various types of seating. These elements can be used to humanize a space that would otherwise lack human scale.

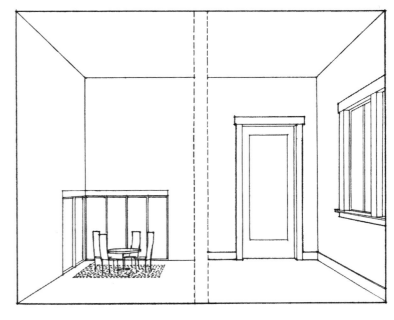

We can judge the scale of a space by the relative size of the interior elements within it.

We often use doorways, window sills, tables and chairs to discern human scale because we have become accustomed to their dimensions.

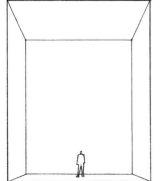  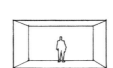

## Human Scale
The feeling of smallness or bigness a space or an interior element gives us.

127

The issue of scale in an interior space is not limited to one set of relationships. Interior elements can be related simultaneously to the whole space, to each other, and to those people who use the space. It is not unusual for some elements to have a normal, orderly scale relationship but have an exceptional scale when compared to other elements. Unusually scaled elements can be used to attract attention or create and emphasize a focal point.

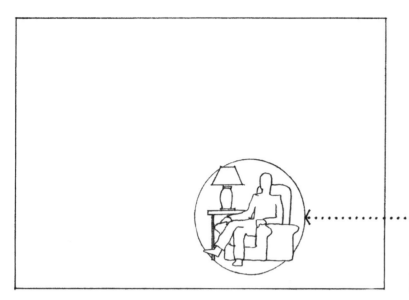

A set of scale relationships can exist within a larger context.

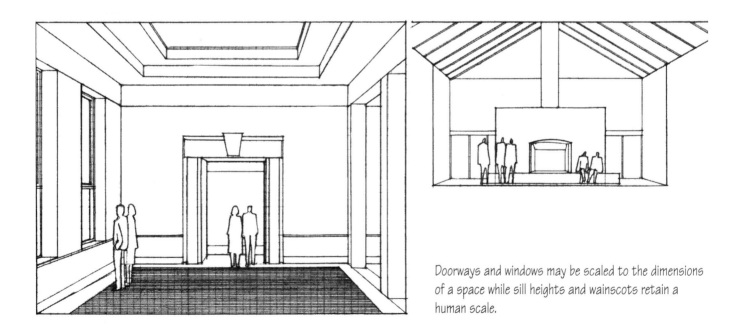

Doorways and windows may be scaled to the dimensions of a space while sill heights and wainscots retain a human scale.

Interior spaces—and their elements of enclosure, furnishings, lighting, and accessories—often include a mix of shapes, sizes, colors, and textures. How these elements are organized is a response to functional needs and aesthetic desires. At the same time, these elements should be arranged to achieve visual balance—a state of equilibrium among the visual forces projected by the elements.

Each element in the ensemble of interior space has specific characteristics of shape, form, size, color, and texture. These characteristics, along with the factors of location and orientation, determine the visual weight of each element and how much attention each will attract in the overall pattern of space.

Characteristics that will enhance or increase the visual weight of an element—and attract our attention—are:

• Irregular or contrasting shapes
• Bright colors and contrasting textures
• Large dimensions and unusual proportions
• Elaborate details

Interiors: a mix of shapes, colors, and textures

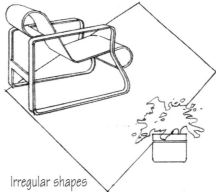 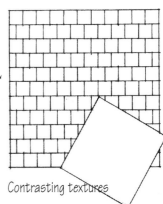

Attracting attention with…

Irregular shapes

Contrasting textures

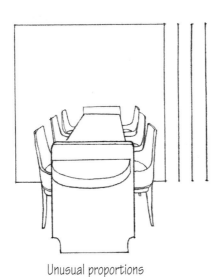 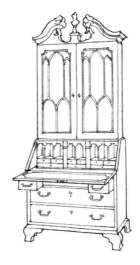

Unusual proportions

Elaborate details

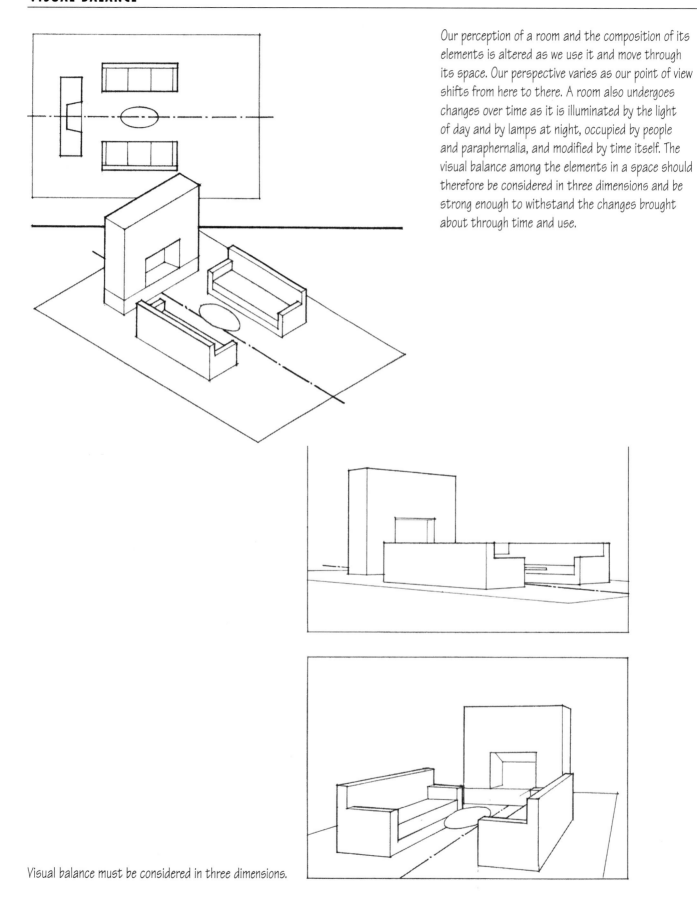

Our perception of a room and the composition of its elements is altered as we use it and move through its space. Our perspective varies as our point of view shifts from here to there. A room also undergoes changes over time as it is illuminated by the light of day and by lamps at night, occupied by people and paraphernalia, and modified by time itself. The visual balance among the elements in a space should therefore be considered in three dimensions and be strong enough to withstand the changes brought about through time and use.

Visual balance must be considered in three dimensions.

There are three types of visual balance: symmetrical, radial, and asymmetrical. *Symmetrical balance* results from the arrangement of identical elements, corresponding in shape, size, and relative position, about a common line or axis. It is also known as axial or bilateral symmetry.

Symmetrical balance most often results in a quiet, reposed, and stable equilibrium that is readily apparent, especially when oriented on a vertical plane. Depending on its spatial relationships, a symmetrical arrangement can either emphasize its central area or focus attention on the terminations of its axis.

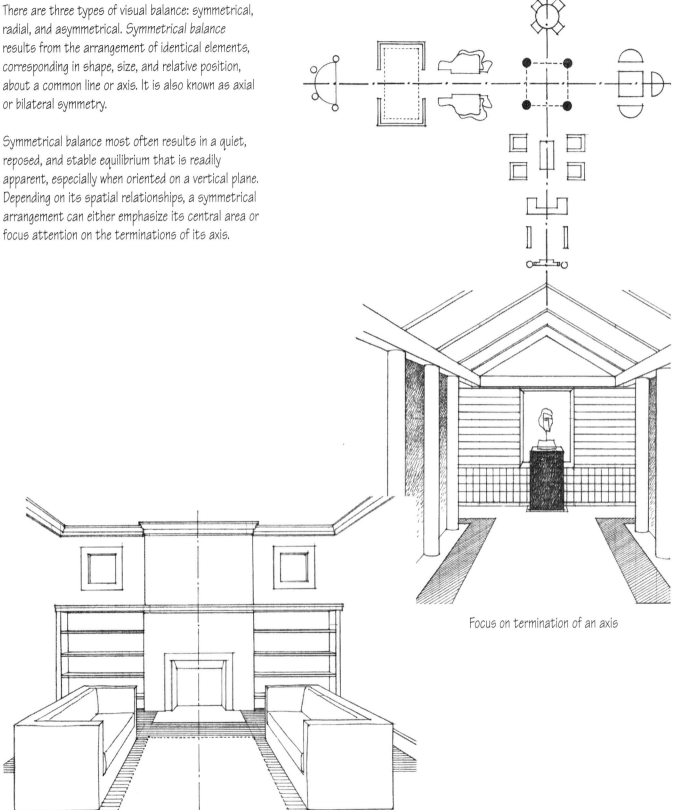

Focus on termination of an axis

Focus on the middle ground

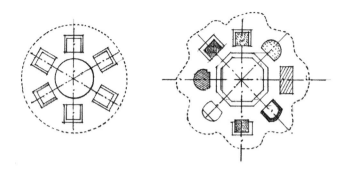

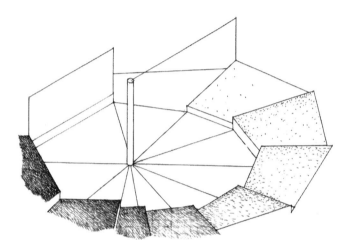

Symmetry is a simple yet powerful device to establish visual order. If carried far enough, it can impose a strict formality on an interior space. Total symmetry, however, is often undesirable or difficult to achieve because of function or circumstance.

It is often possible or desirable to arrange one or more parts of a space in a symmetrical manner and produce local symmetry. Symmetrical groupings within a space are easily recognized and have a quality of wholeness that can serve to simplify or organize the room's composition.

The second type of balance, radial balance, results from the arrangement of elements about a center point. It produces a centralized composition that stresses the middle ground as a focal point. The elements can focus inward toward the center, face outward form the center, or simply be placed about a central element.

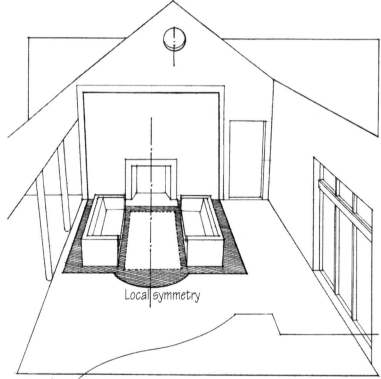

Local symmetry

Asymmetry is recognized as the lack of correspondence in size, shape, color, or relative position among the elements of a composition. While a symmetrical composition requires the use of pairs of identical elements, an asymmetrical composition incorporates dissimilar elements.

To achieve an *occult* or *optical balance*, an asymmetrical composition must take into account the visual weight or force of each of its elements and employ the principle of leverage in their arrangement. Elements that are visually forceful and attract our attention—unusual shapes, bright colors, dark values, variegated textures—must be counterbalanced by less forceful elements that are larger or placed farther away from the center of the composition.

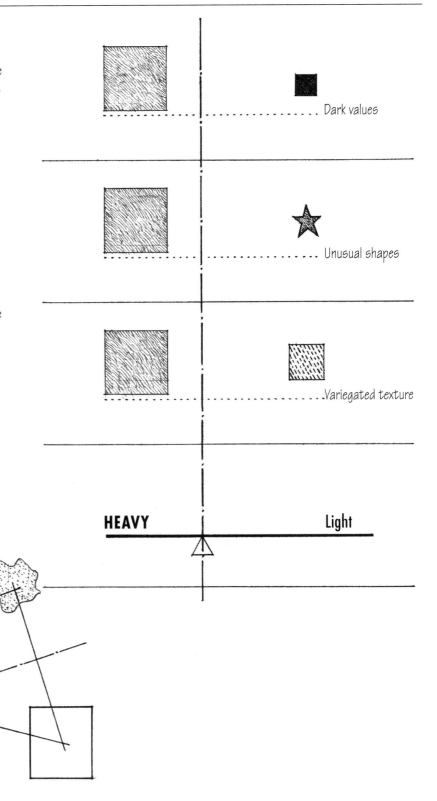

Dark values

Unusual shapes

Variegated texture

HEAVY · · · Light

Asymmetrical balance is not as obvious as symmetry and is often more visually active and dynamic. It is capable of expressing movement, change, even exuberance. It is also more flexible than symmetry and can adapt more readily to varying conditions of function, space, and circumstance.

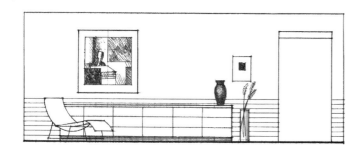

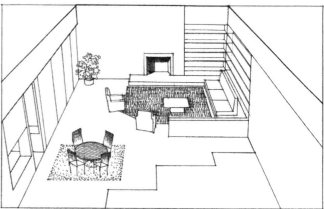

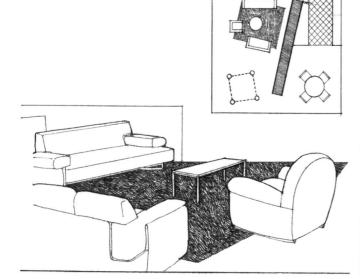

Harmony can be defined as consonance or the pleasing agreement of parts or combination of parts in a composition. While balance achieves unity through the careful arrangement of both similar and dissimilar elements, the principle of harmony involves the careful selection of elements that share a common trait or characteristic, such as shape, color, texture, or material. It is the repetition of a common trait that produces unity and visual harmony among the elements in an interior setting.

## Sharing a Common Trait

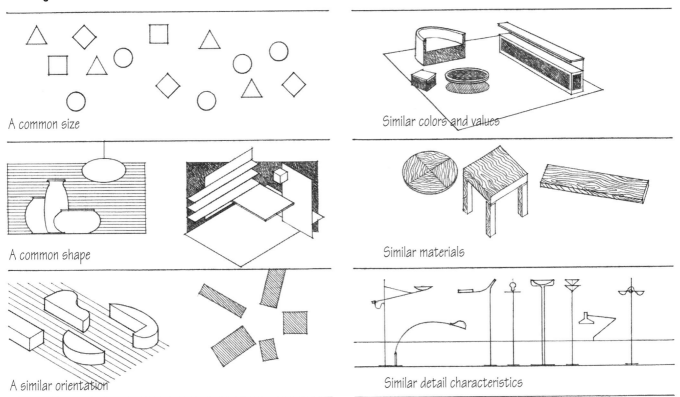

A common size

Similar colors and values

A common shape

Similar materials

A similar orientation

Similar detail characteristics

Harmony, when carried too far in the use of elements with similar traits, can result in a unified but uninteresting composition. Variety, on the other hand, when carried to an extreme for the sake of interest, can result in visual chaos. It is the careful and artistic tension between order and disorder—between unity and variety—that enlivens harmony and creates interest in an interior setting.

## Introducing Variety

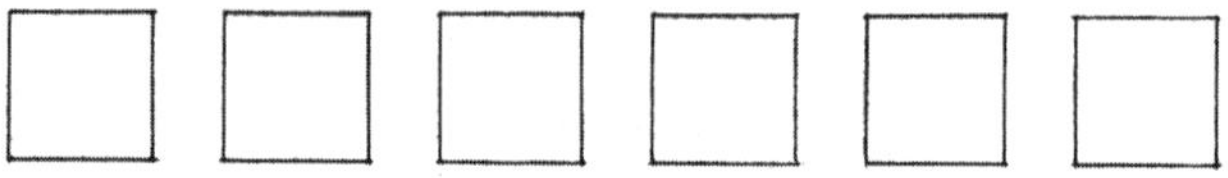

Given a set of identical shapes, variety can be introduced by:

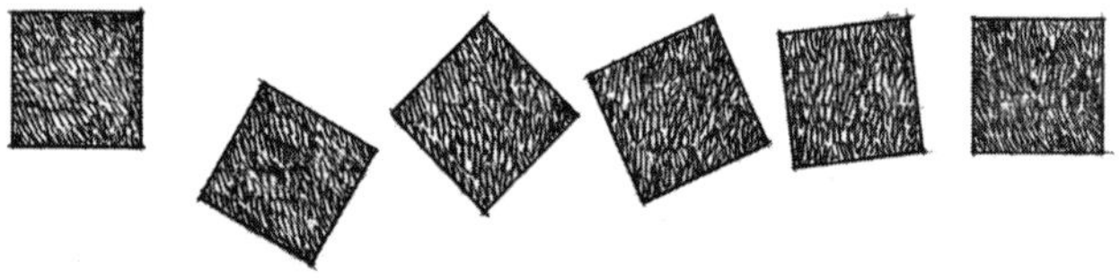

Varying orientation

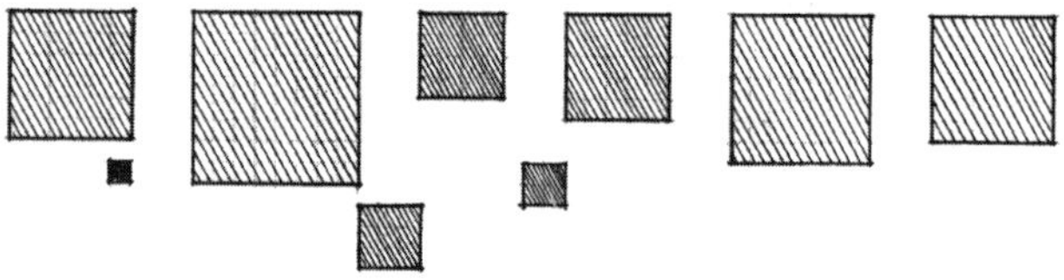

Varying size

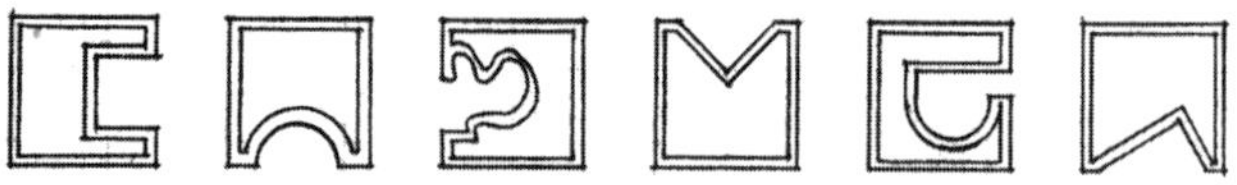

Varying color

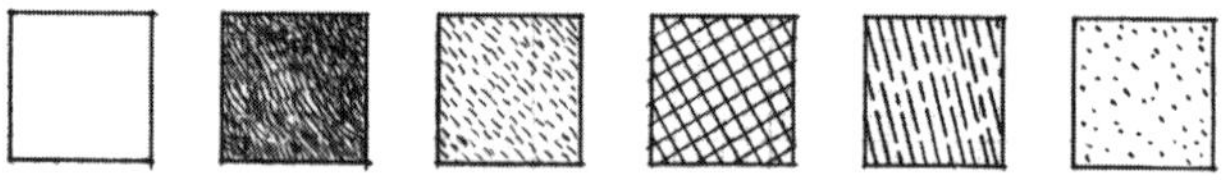

Varying texture

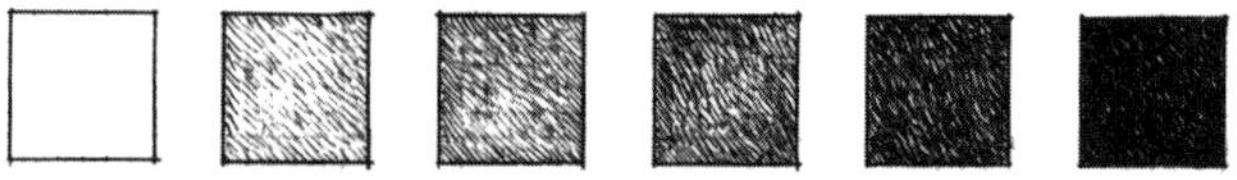

Varying detail characteristics

It is important to note that the principles of balance and harmony, in promoting unity, do not exclude the pursuit of variety and interest. Rather, the means for achieving balance and harmony are intended to include in their patterns the presence of dissimilar elements and characteristics.

For example, asymmetrical balance produces equilibrium among elements that differ in size, shape, color, or texture. The harmony produced by elements that share a common characteristic permits the same elements to also have a variety of unique, individual traits.

Another method for organizing a number of dissimilar elements is simply to arrange them in close proximity to one another. We tend to read such a grouping as an entity to the exclusion of other elements farther away. To further reinforce the visual unity of the composition, continuity of line or contour can be established among the elements' shapes.

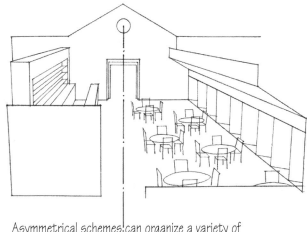

Asymmetrical schemes can organize a variety of shapes, colors, and textures into their layouts.

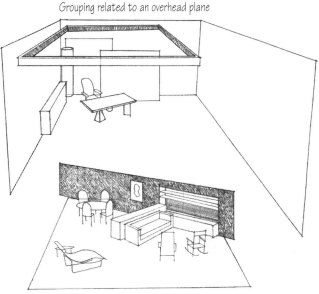

Grouping related to an overhead plane

Foreground elements organized by a common backdrop

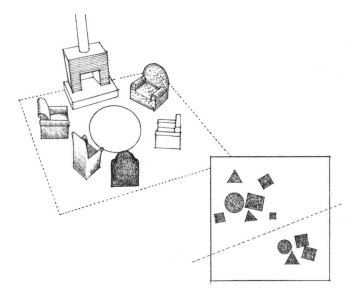

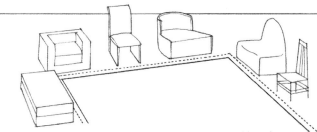

Dissimilar elements can be organized by grouping them in close proximity or by relating them to a common line or plane.

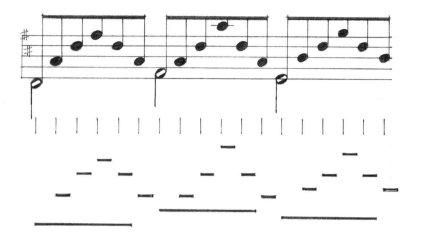

The design principle of rhythm is based on the repetition of elements in space and time. This repetition not only creates visual unity but also induces a rhythmic continuity of movement that a viewer's eyes and mind can follow along a path, within a composition, or around a space.

The simplest form of repetition consists of the regular spacing of identical elements along a linear path. While this pattern can be quite monotonous, it can also be useful in establishing a background rhythm for foreground elements or in defining a textured line, border, or trim.

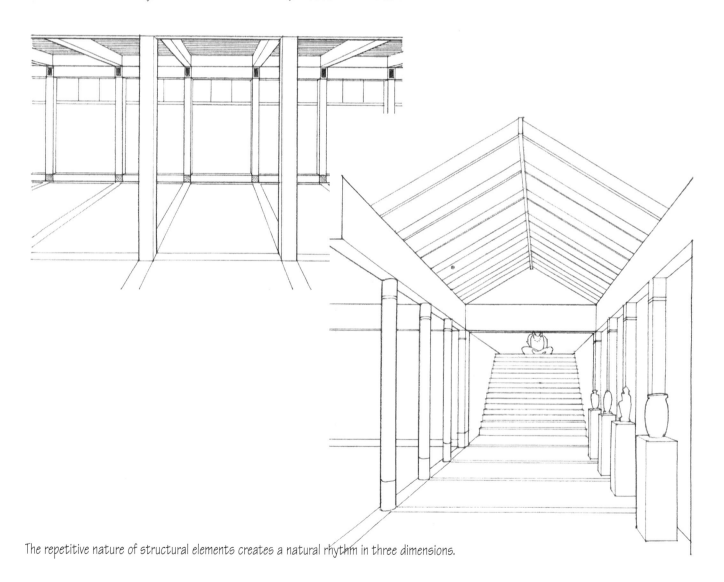

The repetitive nature of structural elements creates a natural rhythm in three dimensions.

More intricate patterns of rhythm can be produced by taking into account the tendency for elements to be visually related by their proximity to one another or their sharing of a common trait.

The spacing of the recurring elements, and thus the pace of the visual rhythm, can be varied to create sets and subsets and to emphasize certain points in the pattern. The resulting rhythm may be graceful and flowing or crisp and sharp. The contour of the rhythmic pattern and the shape of the individual elements can further reinforce the nature of the sequence.

While the recurring elements must, for continuity, share a common trait, they can also vary in shape, detail, color, or texture. These differences, whether subtle or distinct, create visual interest and can introduce other levels of complexity. An alternating rhythm can be superimposed over a more regular one or the variations can be progressively graded in size or color value to give direction to the sequence.

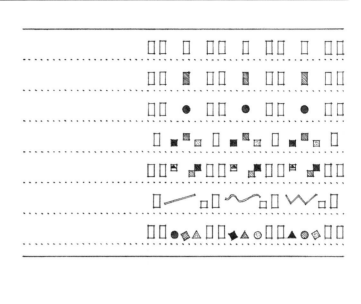

Detail variations in rhythm

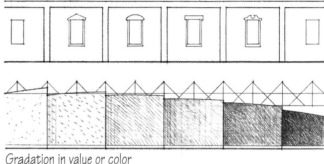

Gradation in value or color

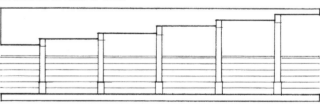

Gradation in size

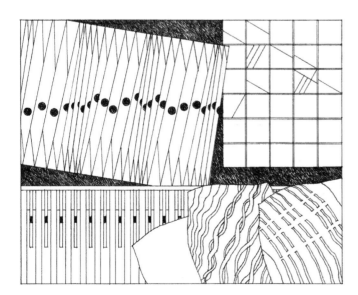

Rhythm existing at the detail level

139

Visual rhythm is most easily recognized when the repetition forms a linear pattern. Within an interior space, however, nonlinear sequences of shape, color, and texture can provide subtler rhythms that may not be immediately obvious to the eye.

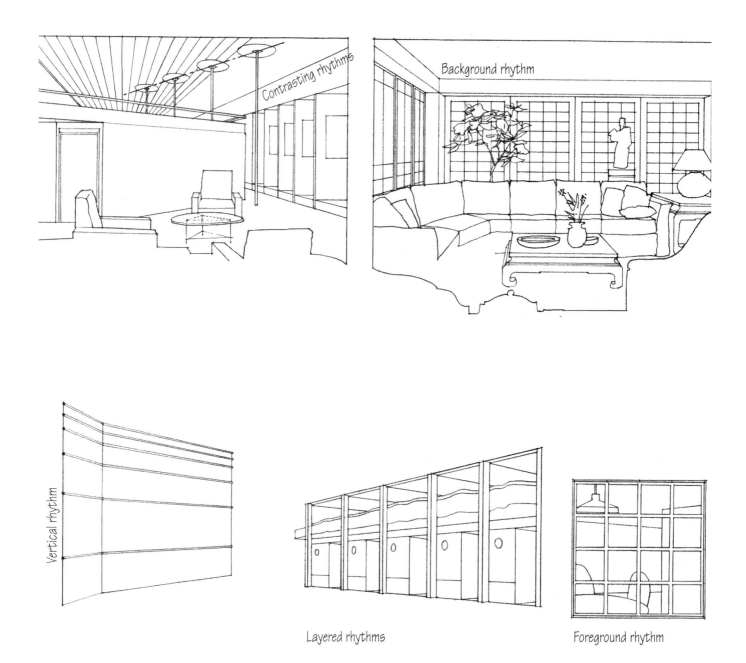

Contrasting rhythms

Background rhythm

Vertical rhythm

Layered rhythms

Foreground rhythm

Rhythm may refer to the movement of our bodies as we advance through a sequence of spaces. Rhythm incorporates the fundamental notion of repetition as a device to organize forms and spaces in architecture. Beams and columns repeat themselves to form repetitive structural bays and modules of space. Spaces often recur to accommodate similar or repetitive functional requirements in the building program.

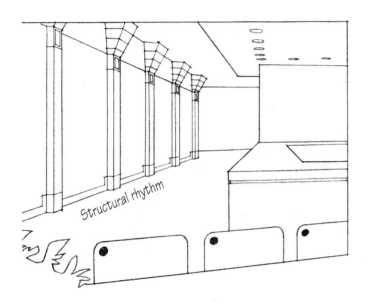

Structural rhythm

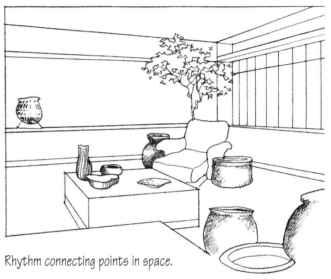

Rhythm connecting points in space.

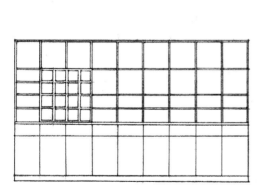

Vertical and horizontal rhythms

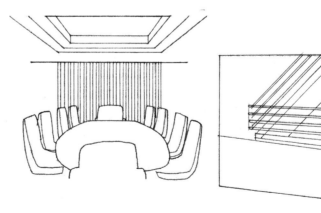

The manner in which stairways and railings express movement naturally results in rhythmic patterns.

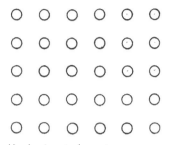

No dominant elements...
no emphasis

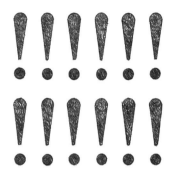

Too many dominant elements...
no emphasis

The principle of emphasis assumes the coexistence of dominant and subordinate elements in the composition of an interior setting. A design without any dominant elements would be bland and monotonous. If there are too many assertive elements, the design would be cluttered and chaotic, detracting from what may be important. Each part of a design should be given proper significance according to its degree of importance in the overall scheme.

An important element or feature can be given visual emphasis by endowing it with significant size, a unique shape, or a contrasting color, value, or texture. In each case, a discernible contrast must be established between the dominant element or feature and the subordinate aspects of the space. Such contrast would attract our attention by interrupting the normal pattern of the composition.

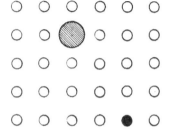

Points of emphasis can be created by a perceptible contrast in size, shape, color, or tonal value.

Exceptional size

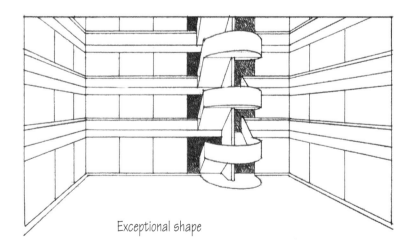

Exceptional shape

An element or feature can also be visually emphasized by its strategic position and orientation in a space. It can be centered within the space or serve as the centerpiece of a symmetrical organization. In an asymmetric composition, it can be offset or isolated from the rest of the elements. It can be the termination of a linear sequence or a path of movement.

To further enhance its visual importance, an element can be oriented to contrast with the normal geometry of the space and the other elements within it. It can be lit in a special manner. The lines of secondary and subordinate elements can be arranged to focus our attention on the significant element or feature.

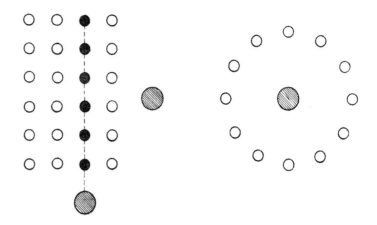

Points of emphasis can also be created by the strategic positioning of important elements.

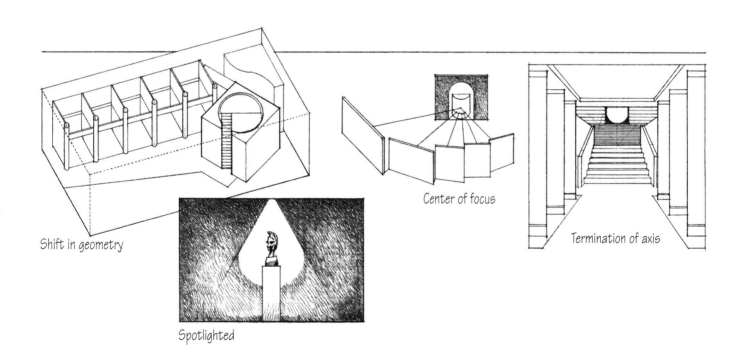

Shift in geometry

Spotlighted

Center of focus

Termination of axis

Just as there may be varying degrees of importance among the elements in an interior setting, there can also be varying degrees of emphasis given to them. Once the significant elements or features are established, then a strategy for orchestrating the subordinate elements must be devised to enhance the dominant ones.

A room's focal points should be created with some subtlety and restraint. They should not be so visually dominant that they cease to be integral parts of the overall design. Secondary points of emphasis—visual accents—can often help knit together dominant and subordinate elements. Following the principle of harmony, related shapes, colors, and values can also help retain unity of design.

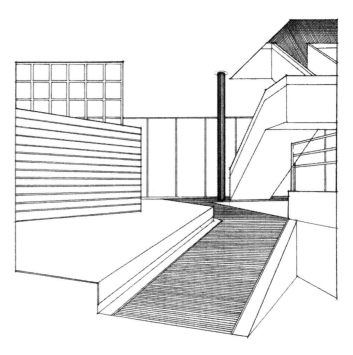

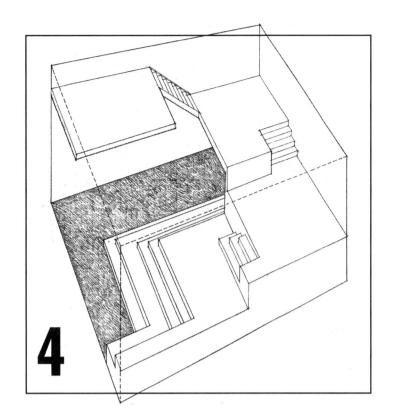

# Interior Building Elements

Interior spaces within buildings are defined by the architectural components of structure and enclosure, such as columns, walls, floors, and roofs. These elements give a building its form, demarcate a portion of infinite space and set up a pattern of interior spaces. This chapter outlines the major elements of interior design with which we develop, modify, and enhance these interior spaces and make them habitable, that is, functionally fit, aesthetically pleasing, and psychologically satisfying for our activities.

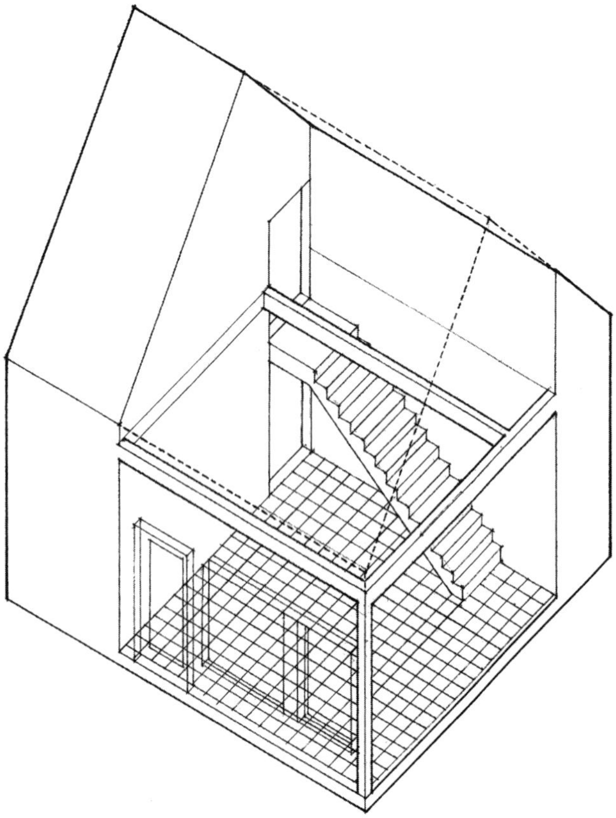

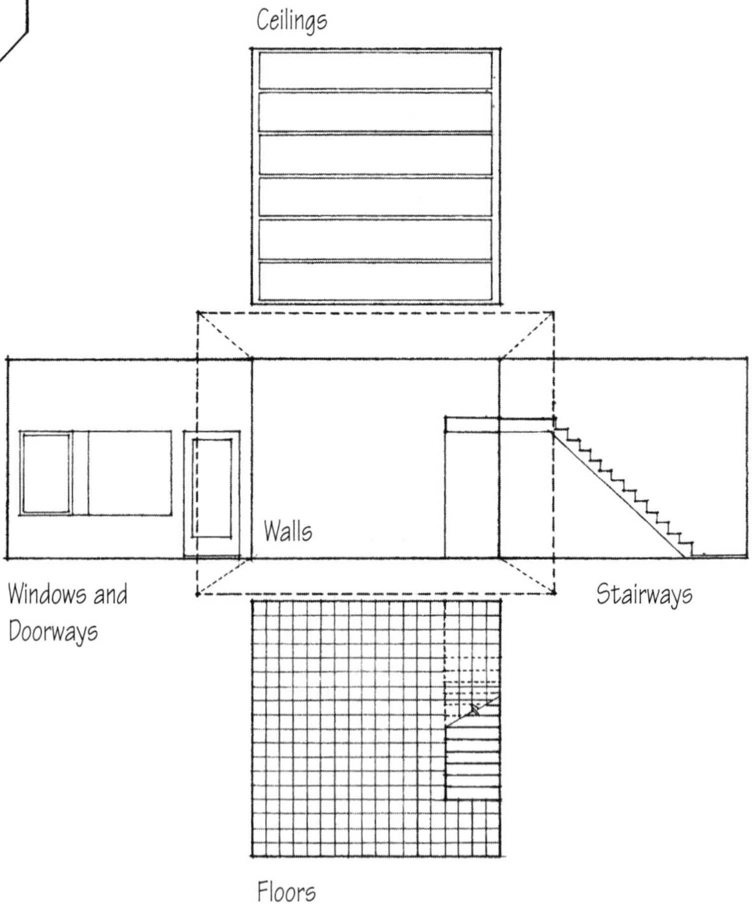

# INTERIOR BUILDING ELEMENTS

Ceilings

Walls

Windows and
Doorways

Stairways

Floors

These design elements, and the choices they represent, are the interior designer's palette. The manner in which we select and manipulate these elements into a spatial, visual, and sensory pattern will affect not only the function and use of a space but also its expressive qualities of form and style.

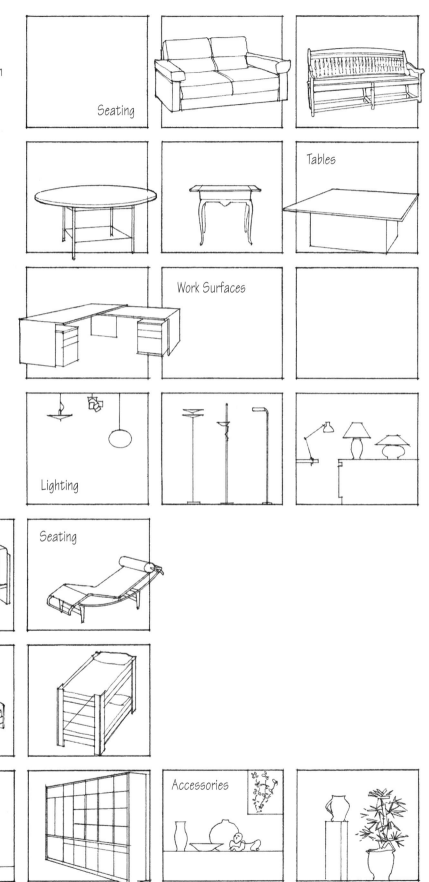

Seating

Tables

Work Surfaces

Lighting

Seating

Beds

Storage

Accessories

Floors are the flat, level base planes of interior space. As the platforms that support our interior activities and furnishings, they must be structured to carry the resulting loads safely. Their surfaces must be durable enough to withstand continual use and wear.

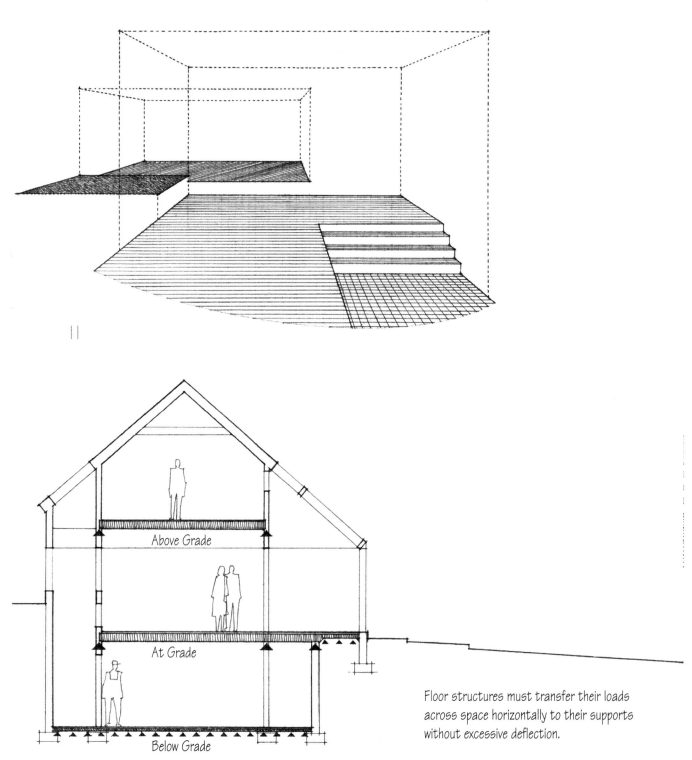

Above Grade

At Grade

Below Grade

Floor structures must transfer their loads across space horizontally to their supports without excessive deflection.

A floor may be constructed of a series of parallel beams or joists overlaid with a subfloor—a structural material such as plywood sheathing, concrete planks or steel decking capable of spanning the beams or joists. The subfloor and beams or joists are secured so that they act together as a structural unit in resisting stresses and transferring loads to their supports.

A floor may also consist of a monolithic, steel-reinforced concrete slab capable of extending in one or two directions. The form of a slab's underside often reflects the manner in which it extends across space and transfers its loads. Instead of being cast monolithically in place, a slab can also be precast as planks.

Whether a floor structure is a monolithic slab or a framed assembly, its surface must be smooth, level, and dense enough to receive the finish flooring material. To compensate for any roughness or unevenness, a layer of underlayment or a cement topping may be required for some flooring materials.

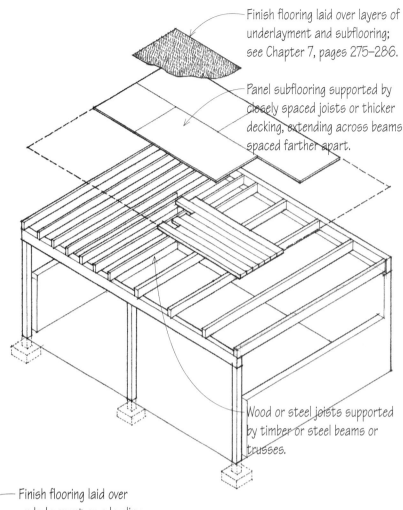

Finish flooring laid over layers of underlayment and subflooring; see Chapter 7, pages 275–286.

Panel subflooring supported by closely spaced joists or thicker decking, extending across beams spaced farther apart.

Wood or steel joists supported by timber or steel beams or trusses.

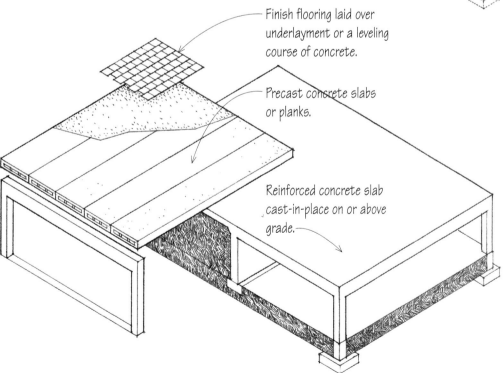

Finish flooring laid over underlayment or a leveling course of concrete.

Precast concrete slabs or planks.

Reinforced concrete slab cast-in-place on or above grade.

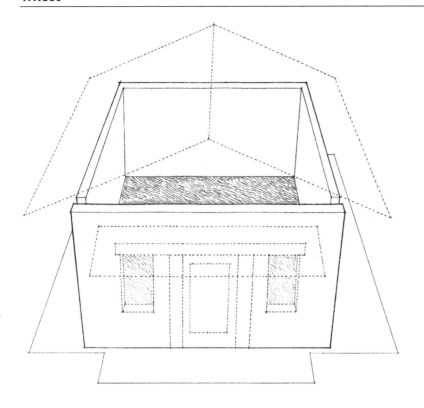

Walls are essential architectural elements of any building. They have traditionally served as structural supports for above-grade floors, ceilings, and roofs. They form the facades of buildings. They enclose, separate, and protect the interior spaces they create.

The exterior walls of a building must control the passage of air, heat, moisture, water vapor, and sound. The exterior skin, whether applied to or integral with the wall structure, must also be able to withstand the effects of sun, wind, and rain.

Interior walls subdivide the interior spaces of a building, provide privacy for these spaces, and control the passage of sound, heat, and light from one space to the next.

Both exterior and interior walls may be load-bearing structures of homogeneous or composite construction designed to support imposed loads from floors and roofs. They may also consist of a framework of columns and beams with nonstructural panels attached to or filling in between them.

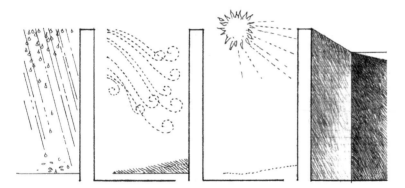

Exterior walls control the passage of air, heat, moisture, water vapor, and sound.

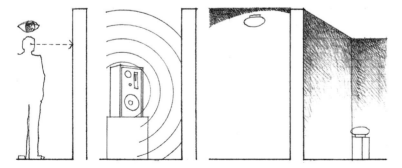

Interior walls control the passage of sound, heat, and light.

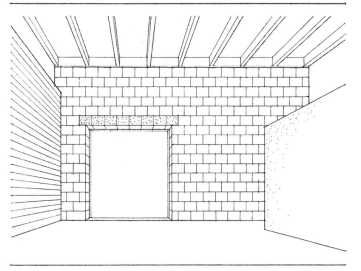

Load-bearing walls define the physical boundaries of space.

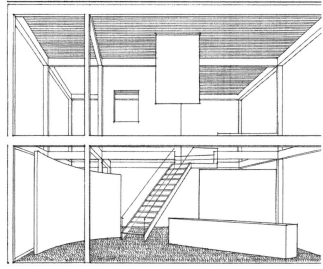

Columns and beams imply the edges of interior space.

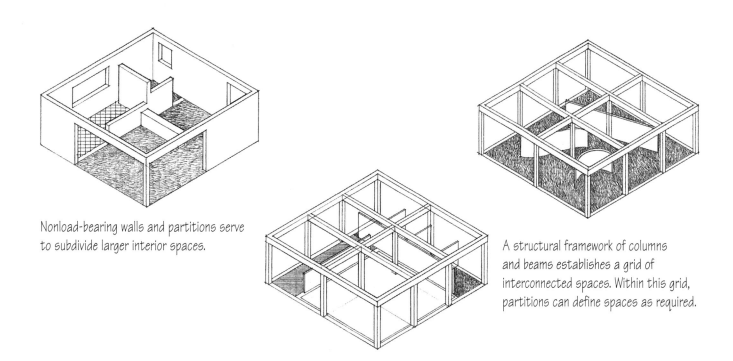

Nonload-bearing walls and partitions serve to subdivide larger interior spaces.

A structural framework of columns and beams establishes a grid of interconnected spaces. Within this grid, partitions can define spaces as required.

Stud-framed walls may be constructed of wood or metal studs tied together by sole and top plates. Onto this frame are laid one or more layers of a sheet material, such as plywood or gypsum board, which stiffens the plane of the wall.

The sheet material may serve as the finish of interior walls, but more often, it serves as a support for a separate layer of finish material. Exterior cladding of siding, shingles, or stucco must be weather-resistant. Interior wall finishes do not have to withstand climatic elements and can therefore be selected from a wide range of materials.

Stud-framed walls are flexible in form due to the workability of the relatively small pieces and the various means of fastening available.

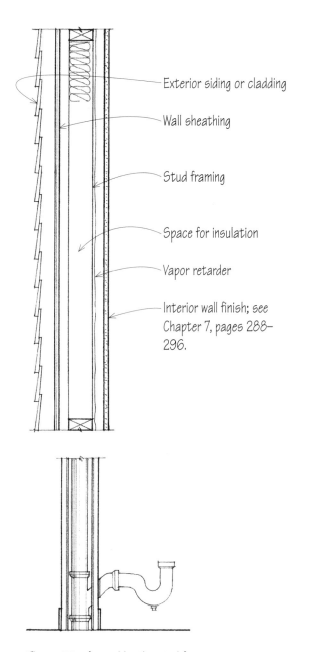

Exterior siding or cladding

Wall sheathing

Stud framing

Space for insulation

Vapor retarder

Interior wall finish; see Chapter 7, pages 288–296.

The cavities formed by the stud frame can accommodate thermal and acoustic insulation, vapor retarders, and the distribution of mechanical and electrical services and outlets.

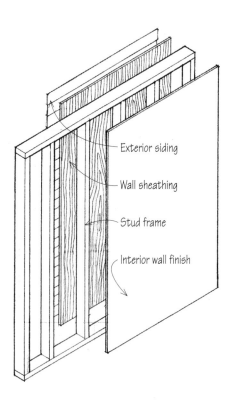

Exterior siding

Wall sheathing

Stud frame

Interior wall finish

Concrete and masonry walls are typically load-bearing and qualify as noncombustible construction. They forcefully define the physical boundaries of space and are more difficult to alter than framed walls.

Concrete and masonry walls are usually thicker than stud-framed walls because they depend on their mass for their strength and stability. Cavities are often used to accommodate thermal insulation and deter the passage of moisture and water vapor.

Concrete and masonry walls may be left exposed. The attractive color and texture of stone and brick are, of course, almost always left exposed as the finish wall surface. Even concrete and concrete masonry walls can now be constructed with attractive colors and textures. If a separate finish is desired, an intermediate layer of supporting lath or furring may be required.

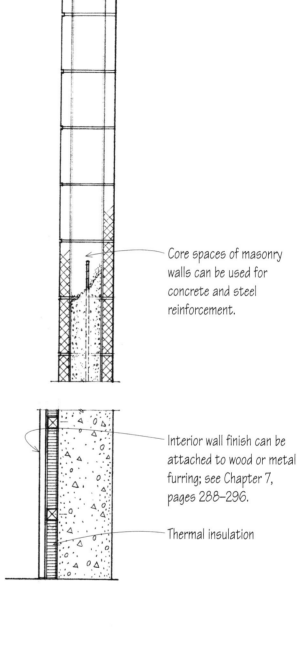

Core spaces of masonry walls can be used for concrete and steel reinforcement.

Interior wall finish can be attached to wood or metal furring; see Chapter 7, pages 288–296.

Thermal insulation

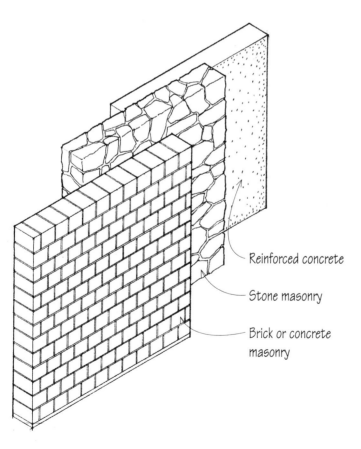

Reinforced concrete

Stone masonry

Brick or concrete masonry

The pattern of load-bearing walls should be coordinated with the spans of floor and roof structures they support. At the same time, this structural pattern will begin to dictate the possible sizes, shapes and layouts of interior spaces.

When the size and shape requirements of interior spaces and the activities they house do not or would not correspond well with a firm pattern of structural walls, a structural framework of columns and beams can be used. Nonstructural walls and partitions could then freely define and enclose interior spaces as required. This is often done in commercial, multistory, and other buildings where flexibility in the layout of spaces is desirable.

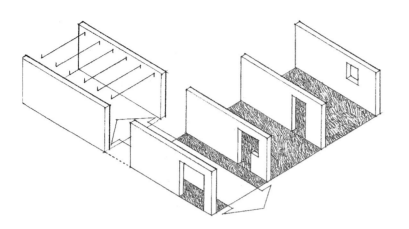

It makes sense to lay out load-bearing walls in a parallel series to support one-way floor and roof structures.

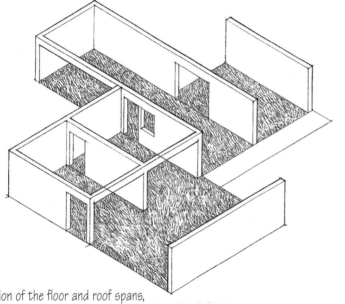

Changing the direction of the floor and roof spans, or using two-way systems, can lead to more complex spatial relationships.

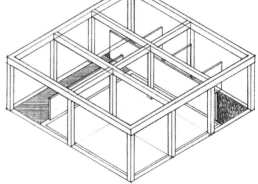

While a column-and-beam structural system suggests a succession of interconnected volumes, the spaces themselves can be organized in harmony with or as a counterpoint to the grid of the structural framework.

Nonstructural walls need only support themselves and any attachments. They therefore offer more possibilities than do load-bearing walls in shaping and enclosing space.

A nonstructural wall can stop short of the ceiling or adjacent walls and allow the flow of air and light from one space to the next. Spatial continuity between two areas can be reinforced while some degree of visual, but not necessarily acoustical, privacy is maintained.

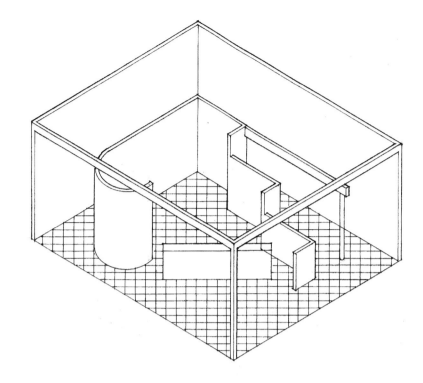

Nonbearing walls or partitions most commonly are supported by the floor system. They can also be secured to columns or bearing wall structures, or they can be hung from the ceiling or roof structure overhead. Whether freestanding on the floor or hung from above, nonbearing walls should be stabilized against lateral forces.

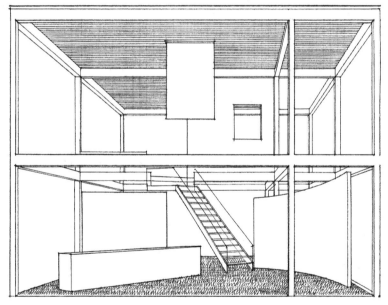

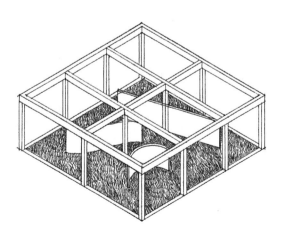

Nonbearing partitions may be attached to or fill in the spaces in the structural frame. An example of exterior nonload-bearing walls are the metal or glass curtain-wall systems often used in commerical and institutional buildings.

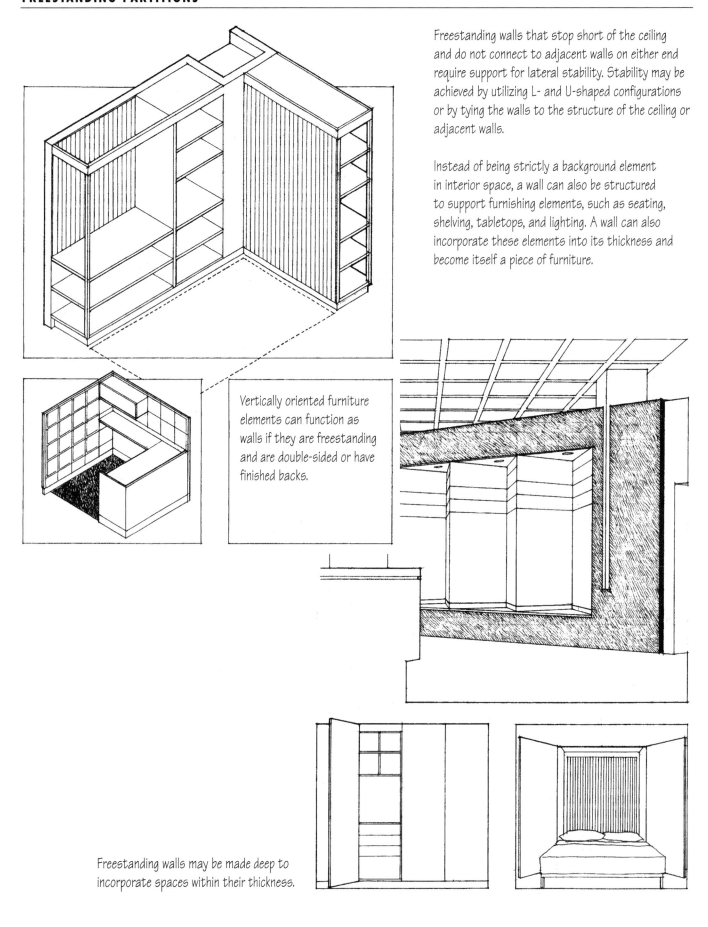

Freestanding walls that stop short of the ceiling and do not connect to adjacent walls on either end require support for lateral stability. Stability may be achieved by utilizing L- and U-shaped configurations or by tying the walls to the structure of the ceiling or adjacent walls.

Instead of being strictly a background element in interior space, a wall can also be structured to support furnishing elements, such as seating, shelving, tabletops, and lighting. A wall can also incorporate these elements into its thickness and become itself a piece of furniture.

Vertically oriented furniture elements can function as walls if they are freestanding and are double-sided or have finished backs.

Freestanding walls may be made deep to incorporate spaces within their thickness.

Walls are the primary elements with which we define interior space. Together with the floor and ceiling planes that complete the enclosure, walls govern the size and shape of a room. They can also be seen as barriers that limit our movement. They separate one space from the next and provide the occupants of a space with visual and acoustical privacy.

Rectilinear space defined by flat, rectangular walls is clearly the norm. Wall planes can also be curved, with the amount of curvature being determined in part by the materials and method of construction. The concave aspect of a curved wall encloses while its convex side expands space.

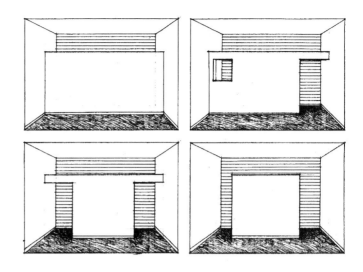

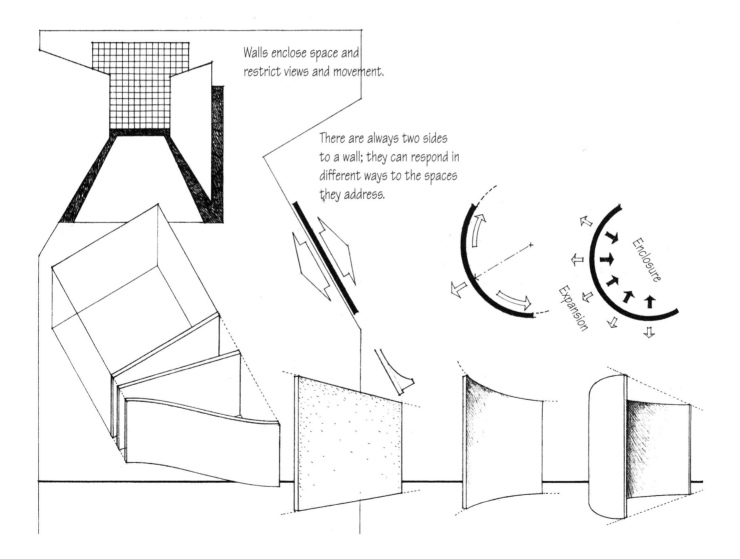

Walls enclose space and restrict views and movement.

There are always two sides to a wall; they can respond in different ways to the spaces they address.

Enclosure

Expansion

Openings within or between wall planes allow for continuity and our physical movement between spaces, as well as the passage of light, heat, and sound. As they increase in size, the openings also begin to erode the sense of enclosure the walls provide and visually expand the space to include adjacent spaces. Views seen through the openings become part of the enclosed space. Enlarging the openings further would result ultimately in an implied separation of space defined by a framework of columns and beams.

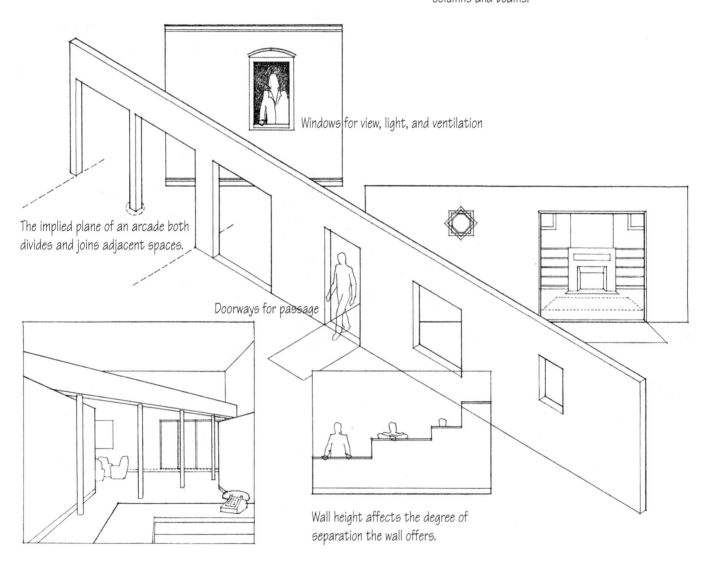

Windows for view, light, and ventilation

The implied plane of an arcade both divides and joins adjacent spaces.

Doorways for passage

Wall height affects the degree of separation the wall offers.

A wall can be visually differentiated from either the adjoining wall or ceiling plane by a change of color, texture, or material. The distinction can be made clearer with either trimwork or a reveal.

Trimwork, such as base and crown moldings, serves to conceal the unfinished construction joints and gaps between materials and to embellish architectural surfaces. Trim moldings can be simple or complex, depending on their profile and finish. Much of their impact depends on their scale, color, and the shadow lines cast by their profile.

A reveal is a continuous recess that visually separates the meeting of two planes and articulates their edges by the shadow lines they create. When two planes meet in this manner, their surfaces must have finished or trimmed edges when exposed to our view.

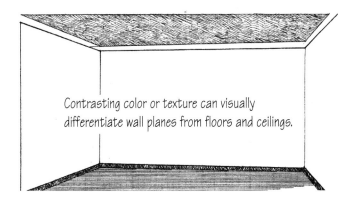

Contrasting color or texture can visually differentiate wall planes from floors and ceilings.

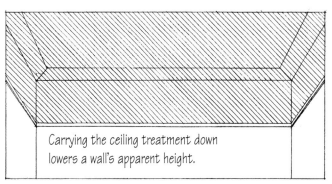

Carrying the ceiling treatment down lowers a wall's apparent height.

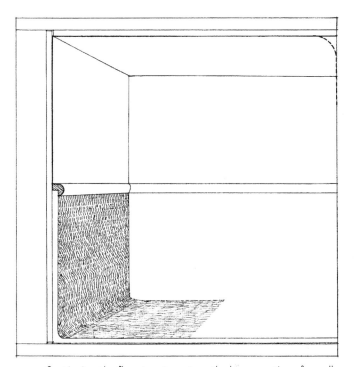

Continuing the floor treatment up the lower portion of a wall can visually enlarge the floor area while reducing the apparent wall height. Continuing the ceiling treatment down a portion of a wall can similarly reduce the vertical scale of the wall.

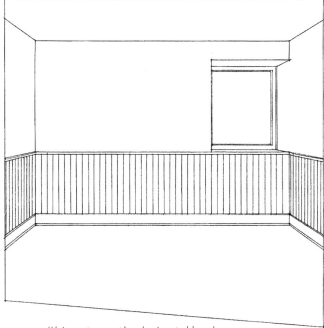

Wainscots or other horizontal bands can reduce the vertical scale of a room's walls.

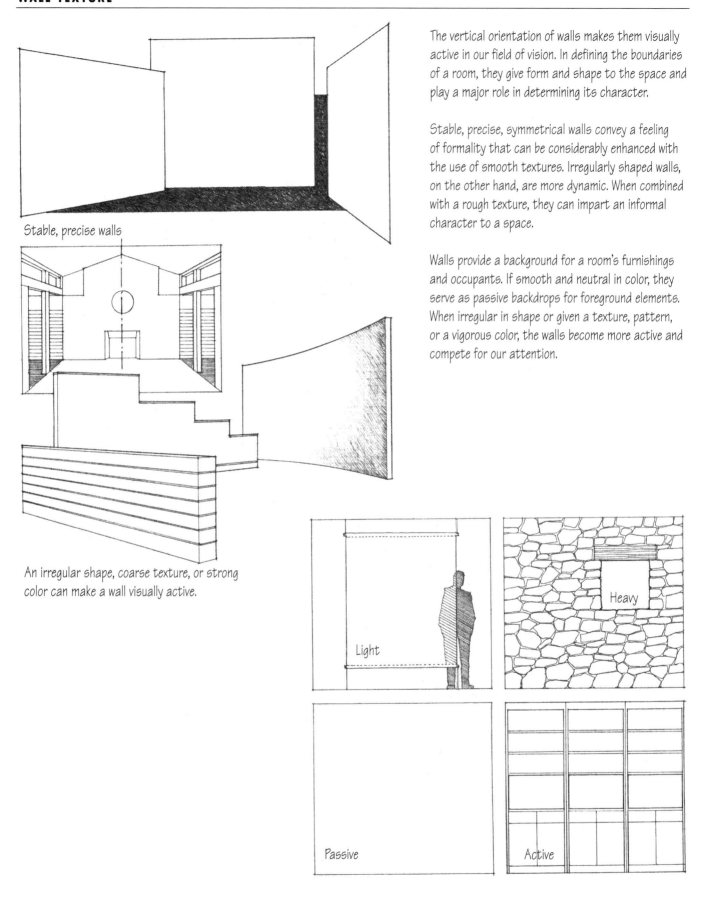

Stable, precise walls

An irregular shape, coarse texture, or strong color can make a wall visually active.

Light

Heavy

Passive

Active

The vertical orientation of walls makes them visually active in our field of vision. In defining the boundaries of a room, they give form and shape to the space and play a major role in determining its character.

Stable, precise, symmetrical walls convey a feeling of formality that can be considerably enhanced with the use of smooth textures. Irregularly shaped walls, on the other hand, are more dynamic. When combined with a rough texture, they can impart an informal character to a space.

Walls provide a background for a room's furnishings and occupants. If smooth and neutral in color, they serve as passive backdrops for foreground elements. When irregular in shape or given a texture, pattern, or a vigorous color, the walls become more active and compete for our attention.

Light-colored walls reflect light effectively and serve as efficient backdrops for elements placed in front of them. Light, warm colors on a wall exude warmth, while light, cool colors increase a room's spaciousness.

Dark-colored walls absorb light, make a room more difficult to illuminate, and convey an enclosed, intimate feeling.

A wall's texture also affects how much light it will reflect or absorb. Smooth walls reflect more light than textured ones, which tend to diffuse the light striking their surfaces. In a similar manner, smooth, hard wall surfaces will reflect more sound back into a space than porous or soft-textured walls.

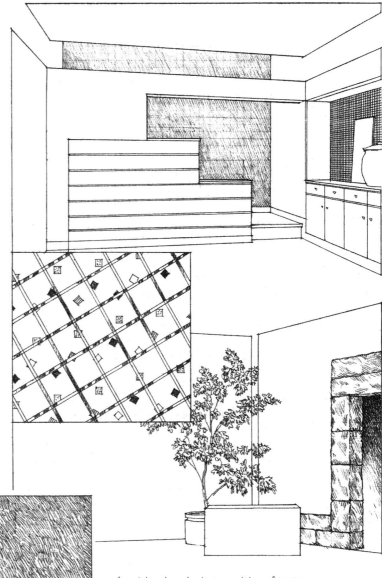

As with color, the juxtaposition of textures enhances both the coarse and the smooth.

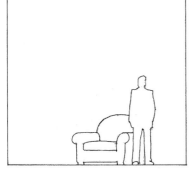

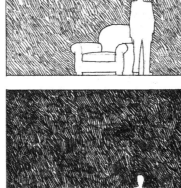

Color, texture, and pattern can be used to differentiate one wall plane from the next and to articulate the form of the space.

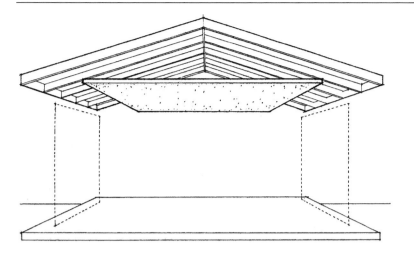

The third major architectural element of interior space is the ceiling. Although out of our reach and not used in the way of floors and walls, the ceiling plays an important visual role in shaping interior space and limiting its vertical dimension. It is the sheltering element of interior design, offering both physical and psychological protection for those beneath its canopy.

Ceilings are formed by the undersides of floor and roof structures. The ceiling material can be attached directly to the structural frame or be suspended from it. In some cases, the overhead structure can be left exposed and serve as the ceiling.

Ceiling suspended from a roof or floor structure

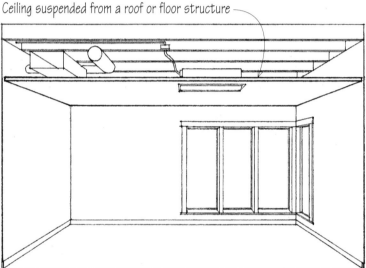

Ceiling defined by an exposed roof structure

Ceiling formed by material attached to the underside of a roof structure

Ceiling formed by an overhead floor structure

Instead of being surfaced with a smooth, planar material, a ceiling can consist of or express the structural pattern of the floor or roof above. Linear structural members or materials can create parallel, grid, or radial patterns. Any ceiling pattern will tend to attract our attention and appear to be lower than it is because of its visual weight. Since linear patterns direct the eye, they can also emphasize that dimension of space to which they are parallel.

Exposed floor and roof structures provide a ceiling with texture, pattern, depth, and direction. These characteristics attract our attention and are best displayed in contrast to smoother wall planes.

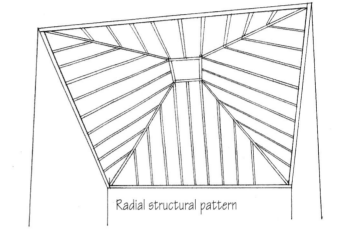

Radial structural pattern

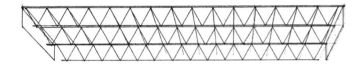

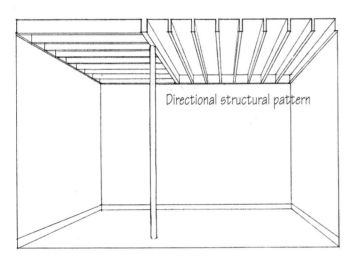

Directional structural pattern

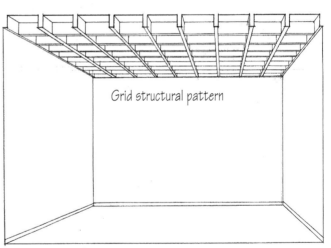

Grid structural pattern

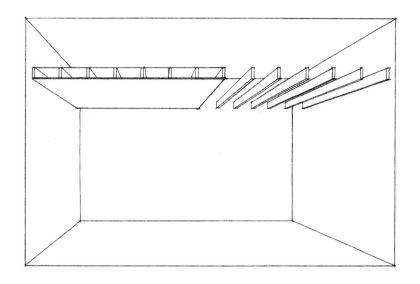

In a room with a high ceiling, all or a portion of the ceiling can be dropped to lower the scale of the space, or to differentiate an area from the space around it. Because a dropped ceiling is usually suspended from the floor or roof structure above, its form can either echo or contrast with the shape and geometry of the space.

The effect of a suspended ceiling can be created with open framing or with nonstructural elements, such as fabric or a series of suspended lighting fixtures.

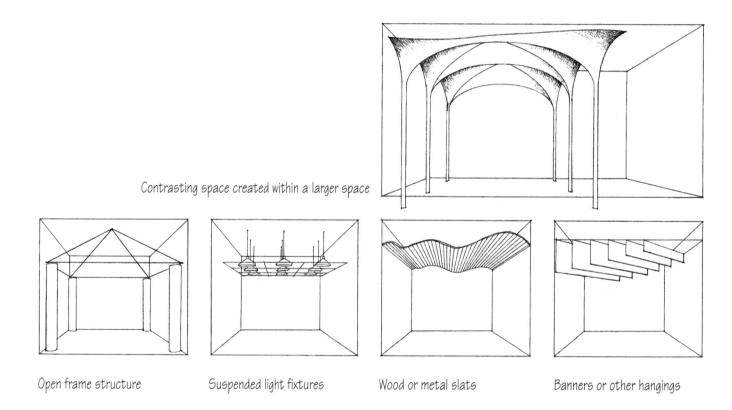

Contrasting space created within a larger space

Open frame structure

Suspended light fixtures

Wood or metal slats

Banners or other hangings

In commercial spaces, a suspended ceiling system is often used to provide a concealed space for mechanical ductwork, electrical conduit, and plumbing lines. Light fixtures, air-conditioning registers, sprinkler heads, fire detection devices, and sound systems can be integrated with the grid of modular ceiling tiles or panels. The ceiling membrane can be fire-rated and provide fire protection for the supporting overhead structure.

The typical suspended ceiling system consists of modular acoustical tiles supported by a metal grid suspended from the overhead floor or roof structure. The grid may be exposed, using lay-in tiles, or be concealed, using tiles with tongue-and-groove or kerfed edges.

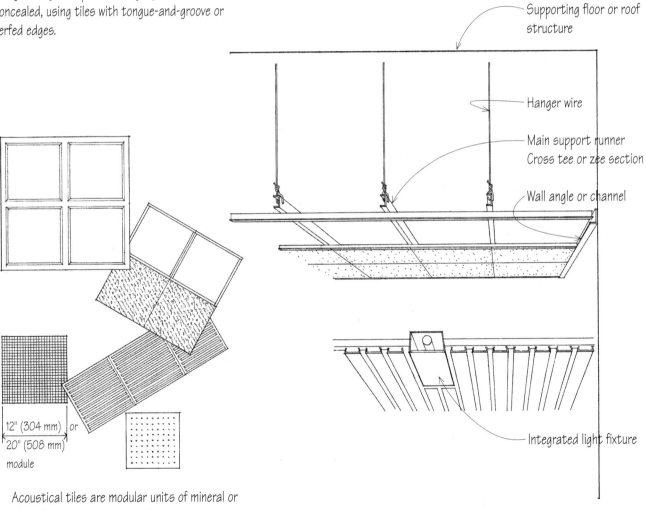

Supporting floor or roof structure

Hanger wire

Main support runner
Cross tee or zee section

Wall angle or channel

Integrated light fixture

12" (304 mm) or 20" (508 mm) module

Acoustical tiles are modular units of mineral or glass fiber. Some may have aluminum or ceramic faces. The tiles are usually removable for access to the ceiling space. See Chapter 7, page 299.

The height of a ceiling has a major impact on the scale of a space. While a ceiling's height should be considered relative to a room's other dimensions and to its occupancy and use, some generalizations can still be made about the vertical dimension of space.

High ceilings tend to give space an open, airy, lofty feel. They can also provide an air of dignity or formality, especially when regular in shape and form. Instead of merely hovering over a space, they can soar.

Low ceilings, on the other hand, emphasize their sheltering quality and tend to create intimate, cozy spaces.

Changing the ceiling height within a space, or from one space to the next, helps to define spatial boundaries and to differentiate between adjacent areas. Each ceiling height emphasizes, by contrast, the lowness or height of the other.

High ceilings can, by comparison, diminish the apparent width of a space.

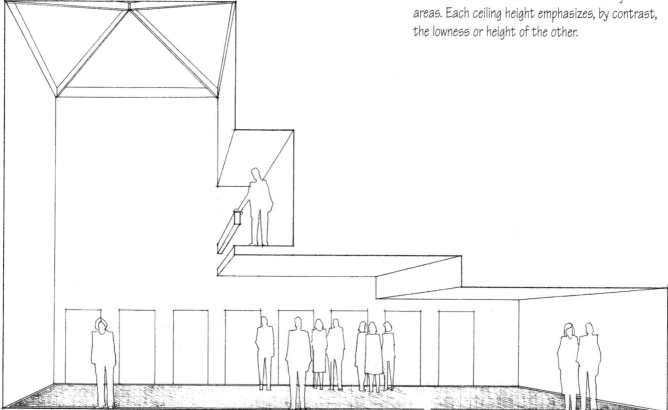

The normal height of a ceiling should be in proportion to a room's horizontal dimensions and its use.

When a flat ceiling is formed by a floor above, its height is fixed by the floor-to-floor height and the depth of the floor construction. Given this dimension, the apparent height of a ceiling can be altered in several ways.

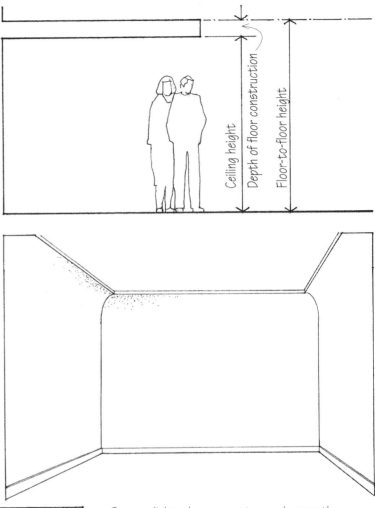

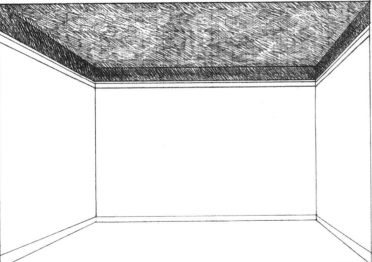

Because light values appear to recede, smooth, light-colored ceilings that reflect light convey a feeling of spaciousness. Carrying the wall material or finish onto the ceiling plane can also make a ceiling appear higher than it is, especially when a cove is used to make the transition between wall and ceiling.

The apparent height of a ceiling can be lowered by using a dark, bright color that contrasts with the wall color or by carrying the ceiling material or finish down onto the walls.

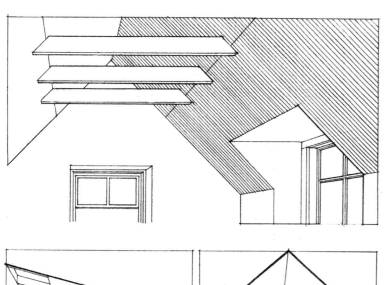

Ceilings supported by a floor structure above are normally flat. When created by a roof structure, however, a ceiling can take on other forms that reflect the shape of the structure, add visual interest, and give direction to the space.

A single slope or shed form may lead the eye up toward the ridge or down toward the eave line, depending on the location of the daylighting sources within the room.

Gabled ceilings expand space upward toward the ridgeline. Depending on the direction of any exposed structural elements, the gabled form may direct our attention to the height of the ridge or to its length.

A pyramid ceiling directs the eye upward to its peak, a focus that can be accentuated further with an illuminating skylight.

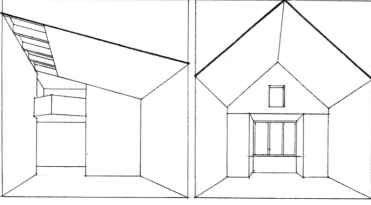

Single-slope Ceiling

Gabled Ceiling

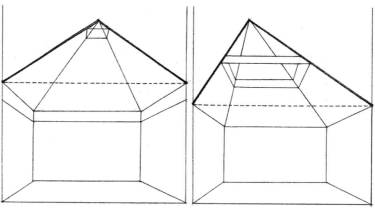

Pyramid Ceiling

Off-center Pyramid

A coved ceiling uses a curved surface to soften its meeting with the surrounding wall planes. The resulting merger of vertical and horizontal surfaces gives the enclosed space a plastic, moldable quality.

Increasing the scale of the cove further leads to vaulted and domed ceiling forms. A vaulted ceiling directs our eyes upward and along its length. A dome is a centralized form that expands space upward and focuses our attention on the space beneath its center.

Freeform ceilings contrast with the planar quality of walls and floors and, therefore, attract our attention. Whether curvilinear or angular in nature, they are decorative and can often dominate the other elements of interior space.

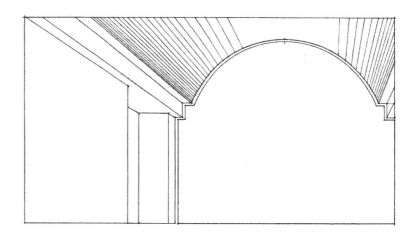

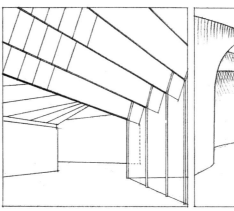

Freeform Ceiling

Freeform Ceiling

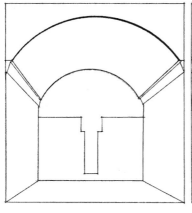

Vaulted Ceiling

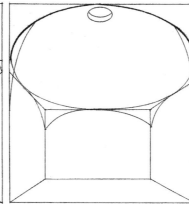

Domed Ceiling

As a functional element, a ceiling affects the illumination of space, its acoustical quality, and the amount of energy required to heat or cool a space.

The height and surface qualities of a ceiling affect the light level within a space. Fixtures mounted on a high ceiling must cast their light a greater distance to achieve the same level of illumination as fewer fixtures suspended from the ceiling.

Because it is not usually encumbered with elements that can block the illumination from light sources, the ceiling plane can be a efficient reflector of light when smooth and light-colored. When directly lit from below or the side, the ceiling surface itself can become a broad surface of soft illumination.

See Chapter 6, pages 242–245 for more information on daylighting.

The intensity of light diminishes according to the square of the distance from its source.

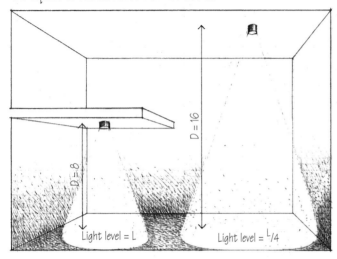

Light level = L      Light level = $^L/4$

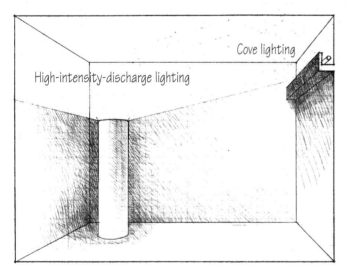

High-intensity-discharge lighting

Cove lighting

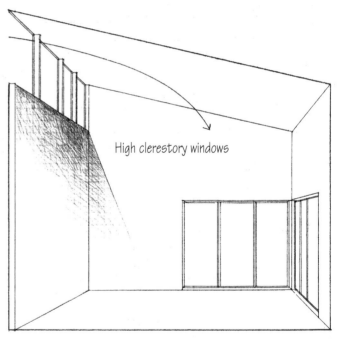

High clerestory windows

Light-colored ceilings can become sources of illumination when lit by broad sources of light.

Because the ceiling represents the largest unused surface of a room, its form and texture can have a significant impact on the room's acoustics. The smooth, hard surfaces of most ceiling materials reflect airborne sound within a space. In most situations, this is acceptable since other elements and surfaces in a space can employ sound-absorbing materials. In offices, stores, and restaurants, where additional sound-absorbing surfaces may be required to reduce the reflection of noise from numerous sources, acoustical ceilings can be employed.

Undesirable flutter within a space results when repeated echoes traverse back and forth between two nonabsorbing parallel planes, such as a hard, flat ceiling opposite a hard-surface floor. Concave domes and vaults focus reflected sound and can intensify echoes and flutter. A remedy for flutter is to add absorbing surfaces. Another is to slope the ceiling plane or use one with a multifaceted surface.

Warm air rises while cooler air descends. Thus a high ceiling allows the warmer air in a room to rise and cooler air to settle at floor level. This pattern of air movement makes a high-ceilinged space more comfortable in warm weather but also more difficult to heat in cold weather. Conversely, a low-ceilinged space traps warm air and is easier to heat in cold weather but can be uncomfortably warm in hot weather.

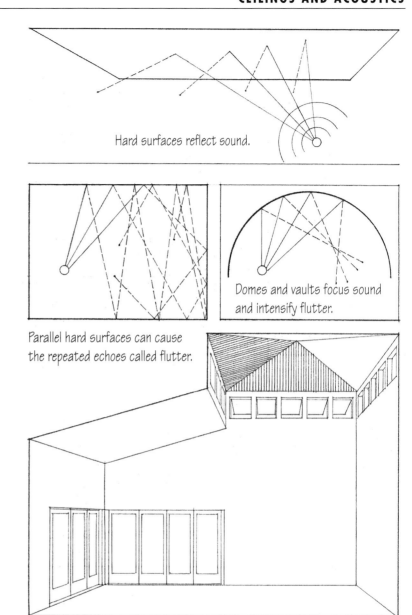

Hard surfaces reflect sound.

Domes and vaults focus sound and intensify flutter.

Parallel hard surfaces can cause the repeated echoes called flutter.

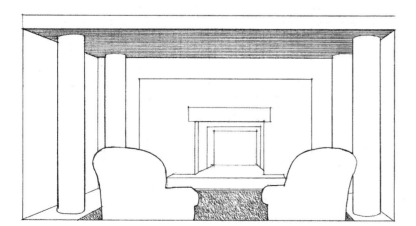

Windows and doorways interrupt the wall planes that give a building its form and interior spaces their definition. They are the transitional elements of architectural and interior design that link, both visually and physically, one space to another and inside to outside.

The size, shape, and placement of windows affect the visual integrity of a wall surface and the sense of enclosure it provides. A window can be seen as a bright area within a wall or a dark plane at night, an opening framed by a wall, or a void separating two wall planes. It can also be enlarged to the point where it becomes the physical wall plane—a transparent window wall that visually unites an interior space with the outdoors or an adjacent interior space.

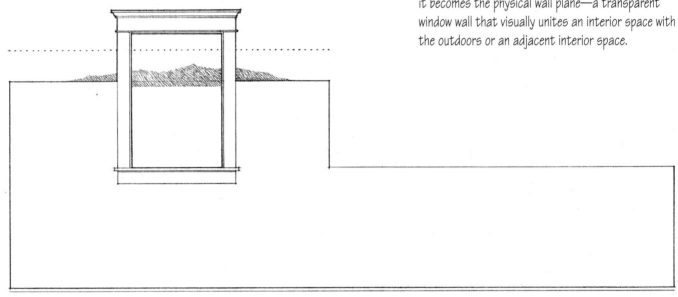

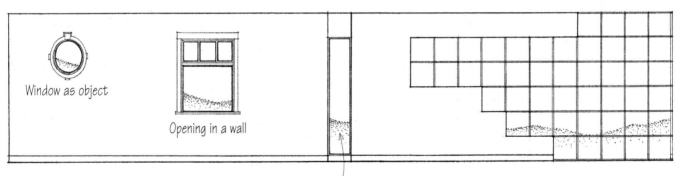

Window as object

Opening in a wall

Window separating two planes

Window framing a view beyond

The scale of a window is related not only to the surrounding wall plane but also to our own dimensions. We are accustomed to a window head height slightly above our height and to a sill height that corresponds to our waistline. When a large window is used to expand visually a space, broaden its outlook, or complement its scale, the window can be subdivided into smaller units to maintain a human scale.

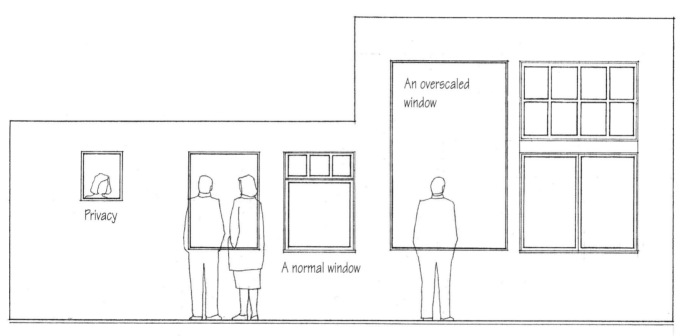

Privacy

A normal window

An overscaled window

Varying the scale of window openings

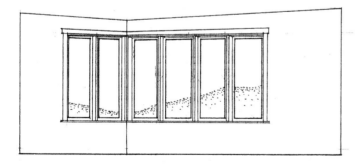

The design and placement of windows in a building is called fenestration.

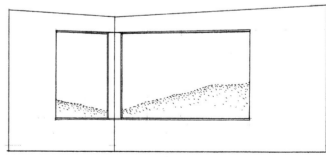

The fenestration pattern and window trim details affect the sense of enclosure provided by the walls of a room.

Windows can be categorized into two major groups: *fixed* and *ventilating*. While both groups provide interior spaces with light and views, fixed windows do not allow for the passage of air as do ventilating windows. Fixed windows can never be opened; ventilating windows can be opened and closed. It would seem then that the decision to use fixed windows should be a carefully considered one.

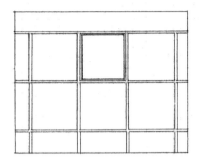
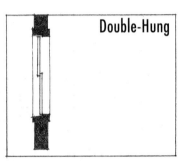

### Fixed

Glazing refers to the panes or sheets of glass set in the frame of a window.

- Frame and glazing are stationary.
- Glazing refers to the panes or sheets of glass set in the frame of a window.
- No ventilation possible.
- Hardware or screens not required.
- Flexible size and shape, depending on maximum glazing size available.

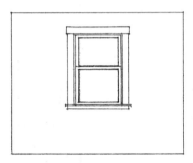

### Double-Hung

- Two sashes travel vertically in separate tracks or grooves and are held in the desired position by friction or a balancing device.
- No rain protection.
- Can be weatherproofed effectively.
- May be screened on outside.
- 50% ventilation.
- Difficult to paint and clean without pivoting sash.

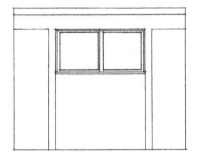
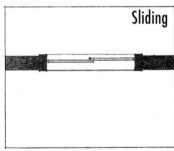

### Sliding

- May consist of (A) two sashes of which one slides horizontally (50% ventilation) or (B) three sashes, of which the middle is fixed while the other two slide (66% ventilation).
- No rain protection.
- Screened on exterior.
- Sliding patio doors are similar to large sliding windows.

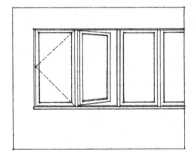
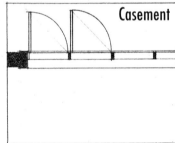

### Casement

- Operating sash is side-hinged and usually swings outward.
- 100% ventilation; can direct or deflect breezes.
- No rain protection; projecting sash can be an obstruction; Roto-hardware or friction hardware used for stability of sash when open.

Building codes regulate the minimum size of window openings that provide natural lighting and ventilation for habitable spaces, as well as the size of operable windows that serve as an emergency exit from residential sleeping spaces.

- Similar to casements but hinged at top (awning) or bottom (hopper).
- 100% ventilation.
- Both types provide draft-free ventilation; awning windows also provide some rain protection.
- May be difficult to weatherproof.
- Requires space for swing of sash.

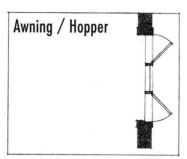
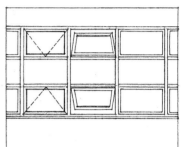

**Awning / Hopper**

- Similar in principle to awning windows except that a series of narrow opaque or translucent strips are used.
- Able to direct flow of incoming air.
- Difficult to clean and weatherproof.
- Used in warm climates where ventilation is required along with privacy.

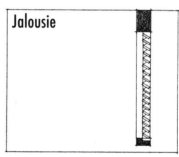
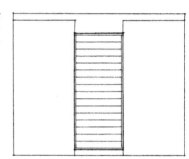

**Jalousie**

- Bay windows use a combination of fixed and operable windows and skylights to project a portion of interior space outward into the surrounding landscape.

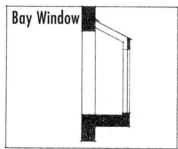
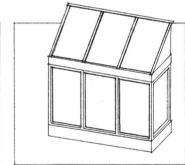

**Bay Window**

- Skylights may consist of fixed or ventilating units.
- Safety glazing with wired, laminated, heat-strengthened, or fully tempered glass or with acrylic or polycarbonate plastic required.
- Skylights provide daylighting without interfering with furniture arrangement and while maintaining privacy or blocking unwanted view.
- Ventilating skylights can be effective cooling mechanisms, allowing rising hot air to escape in warm weather.

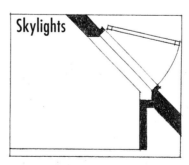
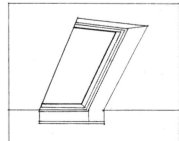

**Skylights**

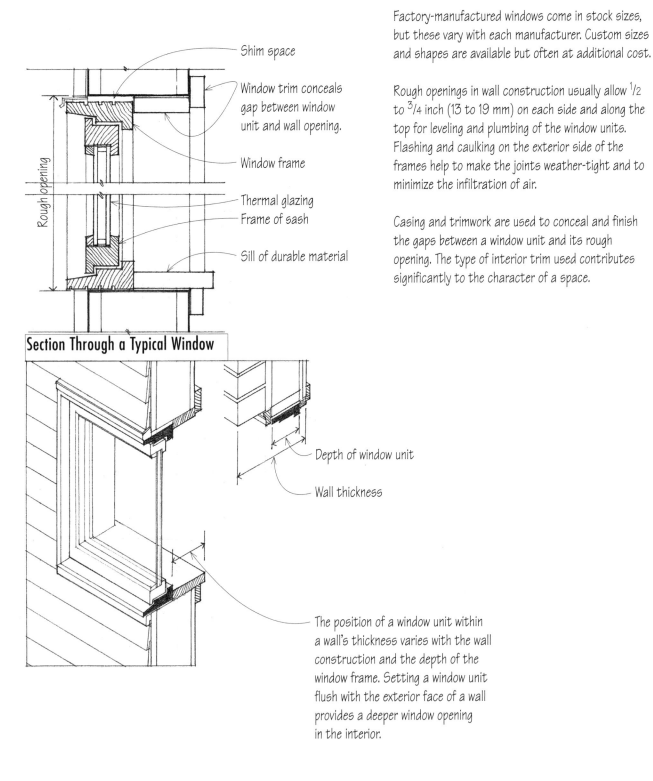

Shim space

Window trim conceals gap between window unit and wall opening.

Window frame

Thermal glazing
Frame of sash

Sill of durable material

Rough opening

**Section Through a Typical Window**

Depth of window unit

Wall thickness

The position of a window unit within a wall's thickness varies with the wall construction and the depth of the window frame. Setting a window unit flush with the exterior face of a wall provides a deeper window opening in the interior.

Factory-manufactured windows come in stock sizes, but these vary with each manufacturer. Custom sizes and shapes are available but often at additional cost.

Rough openings in wall construction usually allow $1/2$ to $3/4$ inch (13 to 19 mm) on each side and along the top for leveling and plumbing of the window units. Flashing and caulking on the exterior side of the frames help to make the joints weather-tight and to minimize the infiltration of air.

Casing and trimwork are used to conceal and finish the gaps between a window unit and its rough opening. The type of interior trim used contributes significantly to the character of a space.

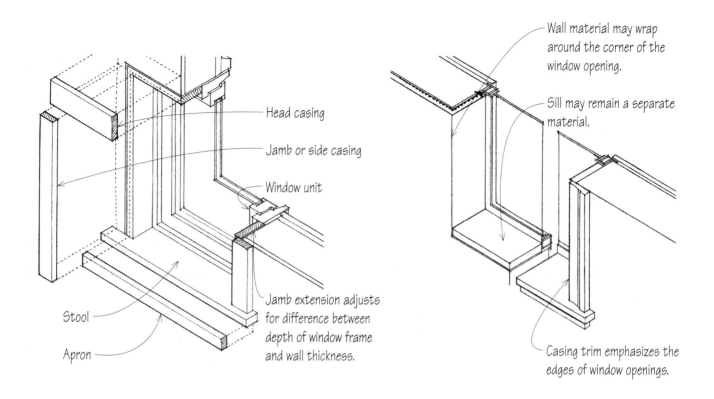

Head casing

Jamb or side casing

Window unit

Jamb extension adjusts for difference between depth of window frame and wall thickness.

Stool

Apron

Wall material may wrap around the corner of the window opening.

Sill may remain a separate material.

Casing trim emphasizes the edges of window openings.

## Interior Window Trim

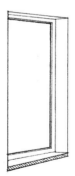

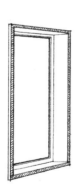

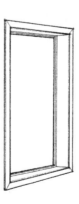

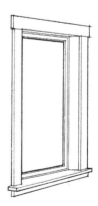

**Minimal Trim:**
Wall material wraps around corner of window opening.

**Light Trim:**
Only edge thickness of window trim is exposed.

**Medium Trim:**
Narrow casing trim wraps around entire window opening.

**Heavy Trim:**
Head, jamb, and sill are differentiated.

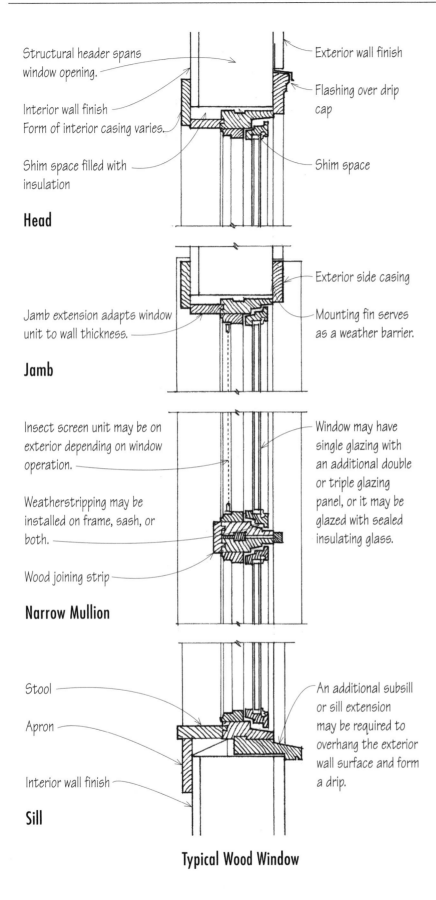

Structural header spans window opening.

Interior wall finish

Form of interior casing varies.

Shim space filled with insulation

Exterior wall finish

Flashing over drip cap

Shim space

**Head**

Jamb extension adapts window unit to wall thickness.

Exterior side casing

Mounting fin serves as a weather barrier.

**Jamb**

Insect screen unit may be on exterior depending on window operation.

Weatherstripping may be installed on frame, sash, or both.

Wood joining strip

Window may have single glazing with an additional double or triple glazing panel, or it may be glazed with sealed insulating glass.

**Narrow Mullion**

Stool

Apron

Interior wall finish

An additional subsill or sill extension may be required to overhang the exterior wall surface and form a drip.

**Sill**

**Typical Wood Window**

Most windows used today are prefabricated units with frames of wood or metal. Wood frames are generally constructed of kiln-dried, clear, straight-grain wood. They are usually treated in the factory with water-repellant preservatives. The exterior of the frame may be ordered unfinished, stained, primed for painting, or clad with vinyl or with acrylic-coated aluminum for reduced maintenance. The interior of the frame is usually ordered unfinished.

Metal frames are stronger and therefore usually thinner in profile than wood frames. Aluminum and steel are the most common types, although stainless steel and bronze windows are also available. Aluminum frames may have a natural, mill finish or be anodized for additional protection and color. Because aluminum is an efficient conductor of heat, moisture can condense on the inner face of metal sashes in cold weather unless a thermal break is built into their construction. Steel window frames must be galvanized or primed and painted for corrosion resistance.

Because aluminum is susceptible to galvanic action, anchoring materials and flashing should be aluminum or a material compatible with aluminum, such as stainless steel or galvanized steel. Dissimilar materials, such as copper, should be insulated from direct contact with the aluminum by a waterproof, nonconductive material, such as neoprene or coated felt.

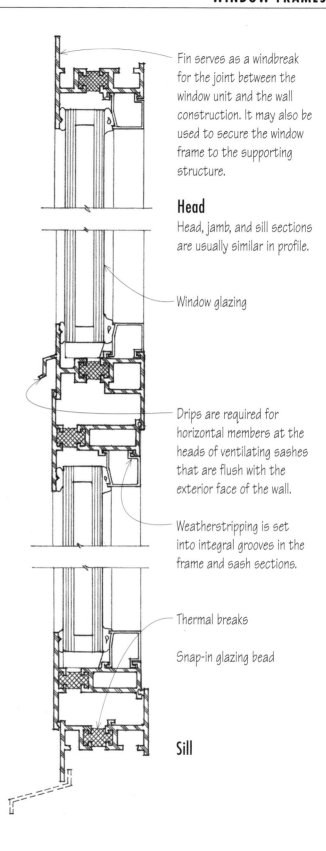

Fin serves as a windbreak for the joint between the window unit and the wall construction. It may also be used to secure the window frame to the supporting structure.

### Head
Head, jamb, and sill sections are usually similar in profile.

Window glazing

Drips are required for horizontal members at the heads of ventilating sashes that are flush with the exterior face of the wall.

Weatherstripping is set into integral grooves in the frame and sash sections.

Thermal breaks

Snap-in glazing bead

### Sill

**Typical Metal Window**

179

Views from windows become an integral part of the fabric of interior space. They not only provide an outward focus from within a room; they also convey visual information to us about where we are. They form a connection between inside and outside.

In determining the size, shape, and placement of windows in a room, consideration should be given to what can be seen through the window openings (both from inside and outside), how these views are framed, and how the visual scenes shift as we move about the room.

Windows do more than simply frame views. In
daylighting a space and providing for its ventilation,
a window may also expose a less than desirable
view. In such a case, the treatment of a window
can fragment, filter, or divert our view. Exterior
landscaping can also aid in shielding an interior space
from an undesirable view or even create a pleasant
outlook where none exists.

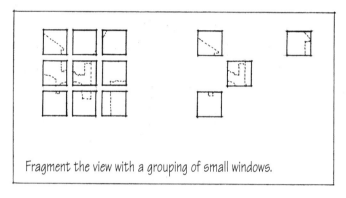

Fragment the view with a grouping of small windows.

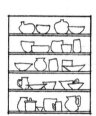

Filter the view by setting a collection of objects within the
window opening.

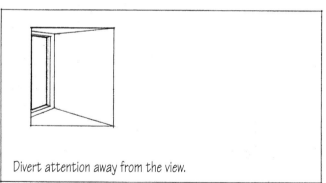

Divert attention away from the view.

Where no view exists, create a garden or courtyard view.

## Ways to Deal with an Unsightly View

The size and orientation of windows and skylights control the quantity and quality of natural light that penetrates and illuminates an interior space. Window size is obviously related to quantity of light. The quality of light—its intensity and color—is determined by a window's orientation and placement in a room. See Chapter 6, pages 242–245 for more information on daylighting.

Building codes regulate the minimum size of windows that provide natural lighting and ventilation for habitable spaces.

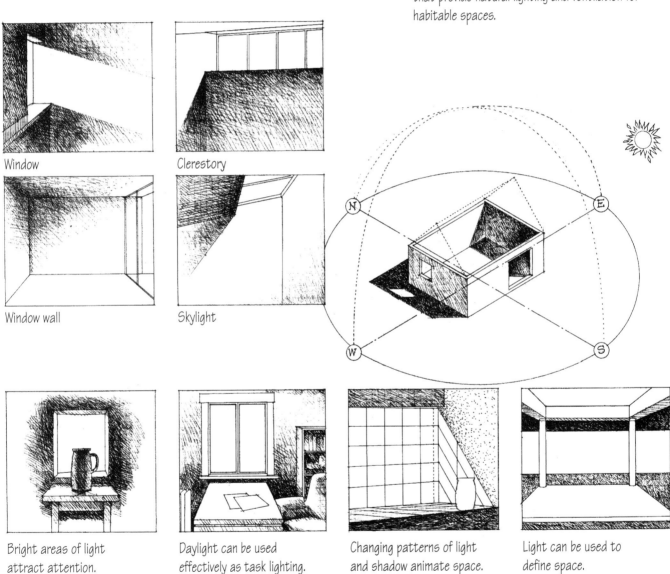

Window

Clerestory

Window wall

Skylight

Bright areas of light attract attention.

Daylight can be used effectively as task lighting.

Changing patterns of light and shadow animate space.

Light can be used to define space.

Wind velocity, temperature, and direction are
important site considerations in locating windows in
all climatic regions. During hot periods, wind-induced
ventilation is desirable for cooling by evaporation or
conduction. In cold weather, wind should be avoided
or screened from windows to minimize the infiltration
of cold air into a building. At all times, some degree
of ventilation is desirable for good health and the
removal of stale air and odors from interior spaces.

Natural ventilation in the interior spaces is generated
by differences in air pressure as well as temperature.
Air flow patterns induced by these forces are
affected more by building geometry than air speed.

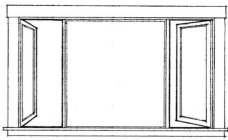

Natural ventilation requires the use of operable windows.

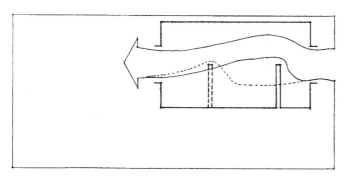

High inlets and outlets produce air movement above our body
level. Lowering the outlets does not ameliorate this condition.

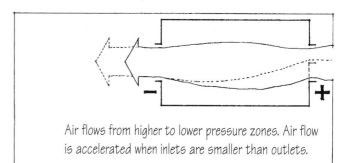

Air flows from higher to lower pressure zones. Air flow
is accelerated when inlets are smaller than outlets.

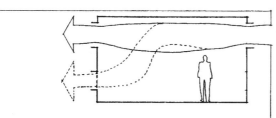

Interior partitions and tall furnishings can adversely
affect the pattern of air flow.

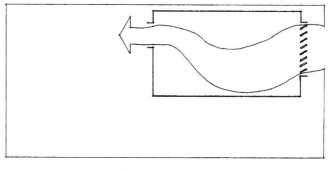

Louvers can help direct air flow.

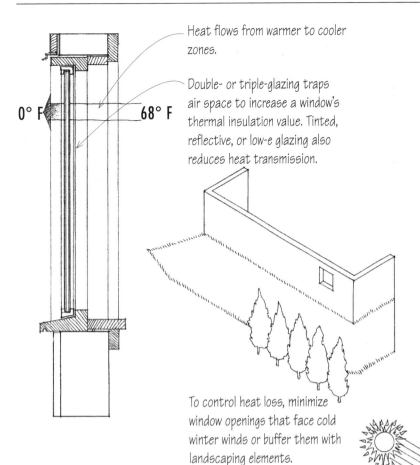

Heat flows from warmer to cooler zones.

0° F    68° F

Double- or triple-glazing traps air space to increase a window's thermal insulation value. Tinted, reflective, or low-e glazing also reduces heat transmission.

To control heat loss, minimize window openings that face cold winter winds or buffer them with landscaping elements.

Ventilation is provided by window openings. Even when closed, windows are sources of heat gain and loss. Heat gain, desirable in cold winter months and undesirable in hot summer months, is due to solar radiation through a window's glazing. Heat loss through a window, undesirable in cold weather, is due to the temperature differential between a heated interior space and the colder outside air.

Glass is a poor thermal insulator. To increase its resistance to heat flow, a window can be double- or triple-glazed, so that the trapped air space between the glass panes can be used as insulation. For improved thermal efficiency, tinted, reflective, or low-emissivity (low-e) glazing can also be used.

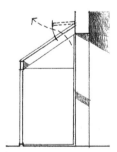

A window's orientation is a more cost-effective factor in controlling solar radiation than is its construction.

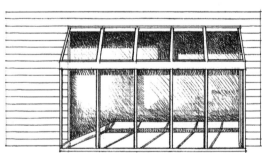

One passive solar heating method utilizes a sun space glazed and oriented to admit large amounts of sunlight. Masonry elements store the thermal energy for later release. Provision for some operable glazing is necessary so that the space can be ventilated in warm weather.

In addition to their aesthetic impact on the interior environment, windows also influence the physical arrangement of furnishings within a room. Their brightness during daylight hours and the views they offer attract our attention and often persuade us to gather about or orient a furniture grouping toward them.

Windows occupy wall space. When locating windows, one planning consideration is how much wall area remains between window openings and whether the size and proportion of these wall segments can accommodate the furnishings placed in front of them. If wall space is at a premium, clerestory windows and skylights can be considered as alternatives.

The sill height of a window also affects what can be placed below it. A low sill height may dictate that the floor area in front of the window be left open, thereby reducing the amount of usable floor space in a room. This is especially pertinent when window walls extend down to the floor to promote visual continuity between interior and exterior space.

Another consideration in the placement of windows is the adverse effect direct sunlight can have on a room's occupants (heat and glare) and on the finishes of its carpet and furnishings (fading and deterioration.)

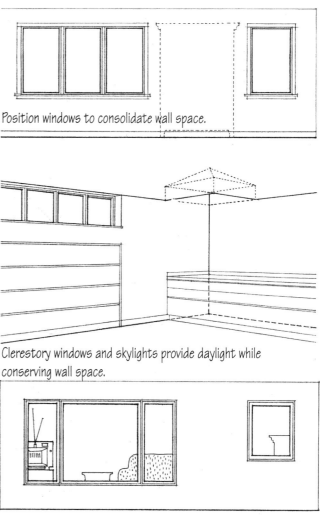

Position windows to consolidate wall space.

Clerestory windows and skylights provide daylight while conserving wall space.

Windows expose the backs of furniture placed against them.

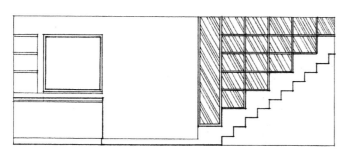

Windows should be coordinated with built-in elements, such as countertops and stairways.

Window walls that extend to the floor inhibit the placement of furniture against them.

Doors and doorways allow physical access for ourselves, our furnishings, and our goods in and out of a building and from room to room within it. Through their design, construction, and location, doors and doorways can control the use of a room, the views from one space to the next, and the passage of light, sound, warmth, and air.

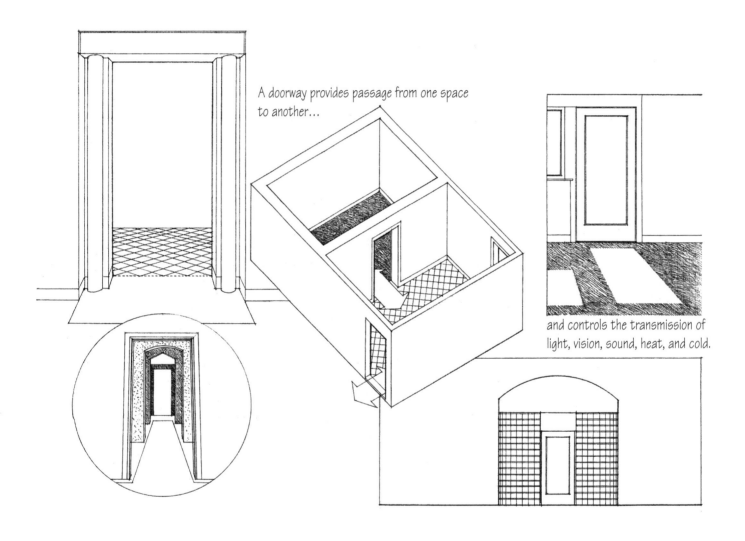

A doorway provides passage from one space to another...

and controls the transmission of light, vision, sound, heat, and cold.

Doors may have wood or metal frames surfaced with wood, metal, or a specialty material such as plastic laminate. They may be prepainted, factory-primed for painting, or clad in various materials. They may be glazed for transparency or contain louvers for ventilation.

Glass doors are generally constructed of ¹/₂ or ³/₄ inch (13 or 19 mm) tempered glass, with fittings to hold pivots and other hardware. Jamb frames are not necessary, and the door can be butted directly against the wall or partition.

Special doors include those constructed to have a fire-resistance rating, an acoustical rating, or a thermal insulation value.

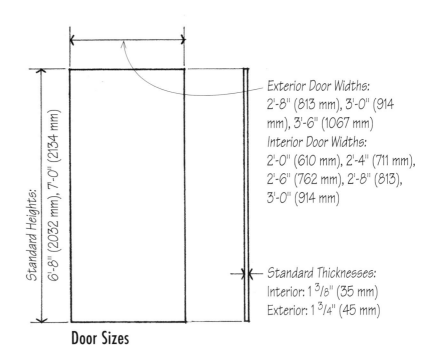

*Standard Heights:*
6'-8" (2032 mm), 7'-0" (2134 mm)

*Exterior Door Widths:*
2'-8" (813 mm), 3'-0" (914 mm), 3'-6" (1067 mm)
*Interior Door Widths:*
2'-0" (610 mm), 2'-4" (711 mm), 2'-6" (762 mm), 2'-8" (813), 3'-0" (914 mm)

*Standard Thicknesses:*
Interior: 1 ³/₈" (35 mm)
Exterior: 1 ³/₄" (45 mm)

**Door Sizes**

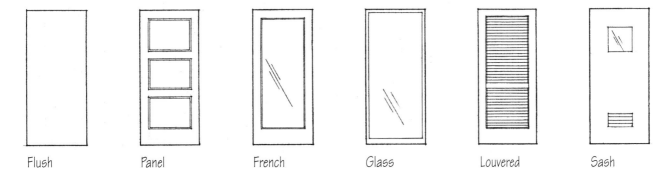

Flush          Panel          French          Glass          Louvered          Sash

**Door Designs**

In addition to how they are designed and constructed, doors may be categorized according to how they operate.

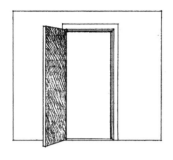

### Swinging

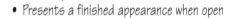

- Hinged on side jamb
- Heavy or wide doors may pivot at head and sill
- Most convenient for entry and passage
- Most effective type for isolating sound and for weather-tightness
- For exterior and interior use
- Requires space for swing

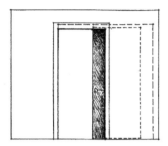

### Pocket Sliding

- Door is hung on a track and slides into pocket within width of wall
- Used where normal door swing would interfere with use of space
- Presents a finished appearance when open
- For interior use only

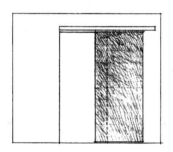

### Surface Sliding

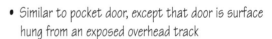
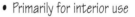

- Similar to pocket door, except that door is surface hung from an exposed overhead track
- Primarily for interior use
- Difficult to weatherproof, but can be used on the exterior in warm climates

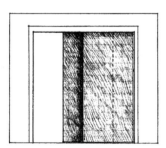

### By-Pass Sliding

- Doors slide along an overhead track and along guides or a track on the floor
- Opens only to 50% of doorway
- Used indoors primarily for visual screening
- Used on the exterior as sliding glass doors

- Consists of hinged door panels that slide on an overhead track
- For interior use only
- Commonly used as a visual screen to close off storage and closet spaces

### Bifold

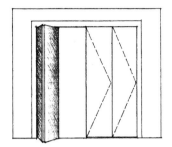

- Similar to bi-fold doors except that panels are smaller
- For interior use only
- Used to subdivide large spaces into smaller rooms

### Accordion Folding

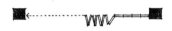

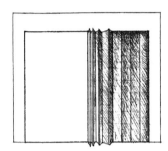

- Door panels slide on overhead tracks
- Tracks can be configured to follow a curvilinear path
- Panels can be stored in pocket or recess
- For interior use

### Special Folding

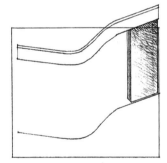

- Consist of hinged door sections that roll upward on an overhead track
- Capable of closing off unusually tall or wide openings for exterior or interior use
- Not for frequent use

### Overhead Doors

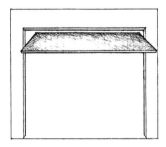

Hollow metal doors have steel face sheets bonded to a steel channel frame and reinforced with channels; a kraft, honeycomb structure; or a rigid plastic-foam core. They are available as flush doors and with full glass, small vision panels, narrow lights, or louvers. Metal doors may be primed or galvanized for painting. They may have a baked enamel finish, be clad in vinyl, or have stainless steel or aluminum skins in polished or textured finishes.

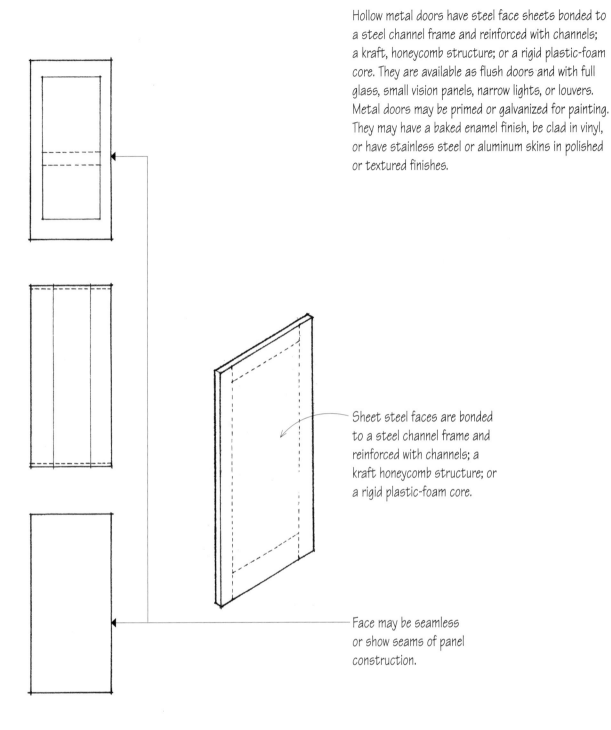

Sheet steel faces are bonded to a steel channel frame and reinforced with channels; a kraft honeycomb structure; or a rigid plastic-foam core.

Face may be seamless or show seams of panel construction.

## Hollow Metal Doors

Wood flush doors may have glass inserts or louvers. Hollow core doors have a framework encasing a corrugated fiberboard core or a grid of wood strips. They are lightweight but have little inherent thermal or acoustic insulation value. They are intended primarily for interior use.

Solid core doors have a core of bonded lumber blocks, particleboard, or a mineral composition. Solid core doors are used primarily as exterior doors, but they may also be used wherever increased fire resistance, sound insulation, or dimensional stability is desired.

Wood doors come in three hardwood veneer grades: premium, which is suitable for natural, transparent finishes; good, which is used for transparent or paint finishes; and sound, which requires two coats of paint to cover surface defects.

Wood rail-and-stile doors consist of a framework of vertical stiles and horizontal rails that hold solid wood or plywood panels, glass lights, or louvers in place. Various panel designs are available, including full-louvered and French door styles.

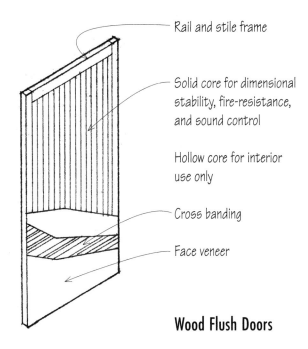

Rail and stile frame

Solid core for dimensional stability, fire-resistance, and sound control

Hollow core for interior use only

Cross banding

Face veneer

**Wood Flush Doors**

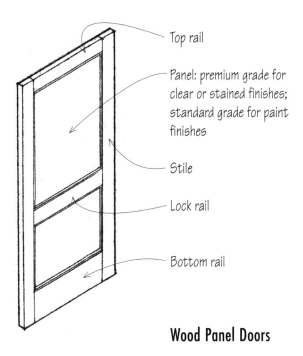

Top rail

Panel: premium grade for clear or stained finishes; standard grade for paint finishes

Stile

Lock rail

Bottom rail

**Wood Panel Doors**

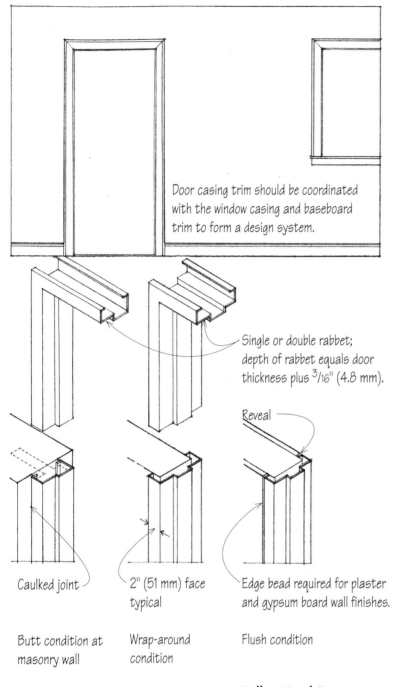

Door casing trim should be coordinated with the window casing and baseboard trim to form a design system.

Single or double rabbet; depth of rabbet equals door thickness plus $3/16"$ (4.8 mm).

Reveal

Caulked joint

2" (51 mm) face typical

Edge bead required for plaster and gypsum board wall finishes.

Butt condition at masonry wall

Wrap-around condition

Flush condition

**Hollow Metal Frames**

Because most doors are manufactured in a number of standard sizes and styles, the treatment of the opening and the design of the casing trim are the areas where the designer can manipulate the scale and character of a doorway.

Like doors, door frames are standard items. Hollow metal doors are hung in hollow metal frames. These may have single or double rabbets and may either butt up against or wrap around the wall thickness. In addition to the standard flat face, various trim style moldings are available.

Wood doors use wood or hollow metal frames. Exterior door frames usually have integral stops, while interior frames may have applied stops. Casing trim is used to conceal the gap between the door frame and the wall surface. Casing trim can be omitted if the wall material can be finished neatly and butt up against the door frame.

Door casing trim, through its form and color, can accentuate a doorway and articulate the door as a distinct visual element in a space. The doorway opening itself can also be enlarged physically with sidelights and transoms above or visually with color and trimwork.

Conversely, a door frame and trim can, if desired, be minimized visually to reduce the scale of a doorway or to have it appear as a simple void in a wall.

If flush with the surrounding wall, a door can be finished to merge with and become part of the wall surface.

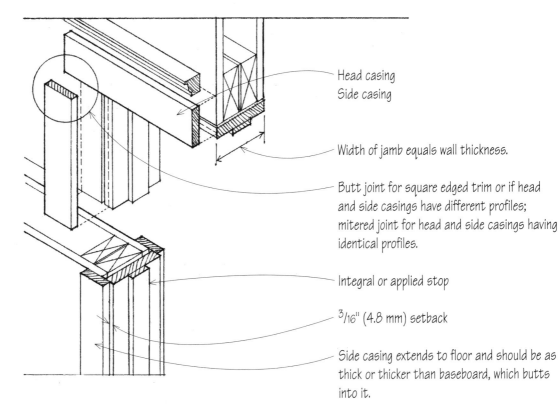

Head casing
Side casing

Width of jamb equals wall thickness.

Butt joint for square edged trim or if head and side casings have different profiles; mitered joint for head and side casings having identical profiles.

Integral or applied stop

$^3/_{16}$" (4.8 mm) setback

Side casing extends to floor and should be as thick or thicker than baseboard, which butts into it.

## Wood Frames

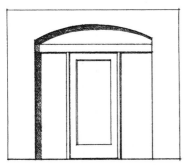

Sidelights and a transom enlarge the scale of the doorway opening.

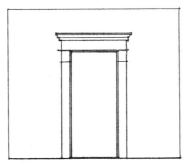

Trimwork elaborates the doorway and can give a hint as to what lies beyond.

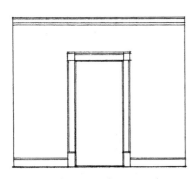

Even simple trimwork can emphasize the opening of a doorway.

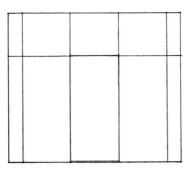

A doorway can merge with the surrounding wall surface.

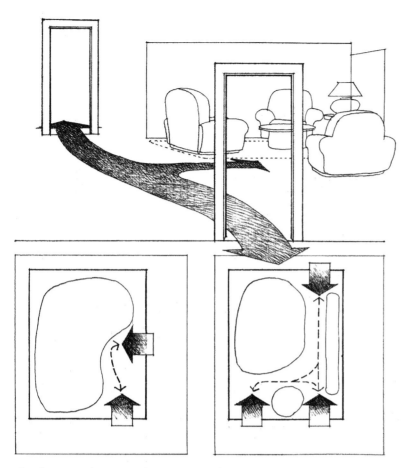

In linking the interior spaces of a building, doorways connect pathways. Their locations influence our patterns of movement from space to space as well as within a space. The nature of these patterns should be appropriate to the uses and activities housed within the interior spaces.

Space must be provided for our comfortable movement and the operation of doors. At the same time, there must also be sufficient and appropriately proportioned space remaining for the arrangement of furnishings and activities.

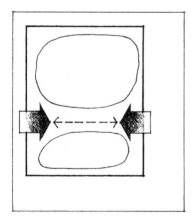

Two doorways close to each other define a short path that leaves a maximum amount of usable floor space.

Doorways situated at or near corners can define paths that run along a wall of a room. Locating the doorways away from the corners allows furnishings, such as storage units, to be placed along the wall.

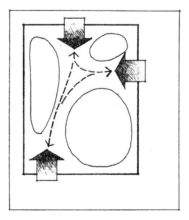

Opposing doorways define a straight path that subdivides a room into two zones.

Three doorways on three walls can present a problem if the possible pathways take up much of the floor area and leave a fragmented series of usable spaces.

Another consideration in determining the location of a doorway is the view seen through its opening both from the adjacent space and upon entering. When visual privacy for a room is desired, a doorway, even when open, should not permit a direct view into the private zone of the space.

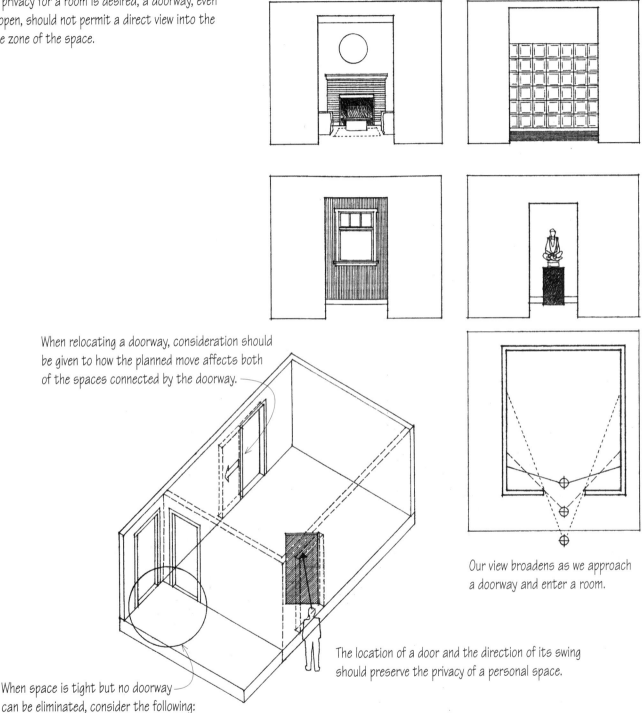

When relocating a doorway, consideration should be given to how the planned move affects both of the spaces connected by the doorway.

Our view broadens as we approach a doorway and enter a room.

The location of a door and the direction of its swing should preserve the privacy of a personal space.

When space is tight but no doorway can be eliminated, consider the following:
- Change the swing of one or both doors.
- Change to a bifold or sliding door.
- If a door is not necessary, remove it and keep the doorway.

Stairs allow us to move vertically between the various floor levels of a building. The two most important functional criteria in the design of stairs are safety and ease of ascent and descent. The dimensions of a stair's risers and treads should be proportioned to fit our body movement. Their pitch, if steep, can make ascent physically tiring as well as psychologically forbidding and can make descent precarious. If shallow, a stair must have treads deep enough to fit our stride.

Building codes regulate the maximum and minimum dimensions of risers and treads. Risers and treads should be uniform in dimension with a tolerance of 3/8" (9.5 mm) between the smallest and the largest within any flight.

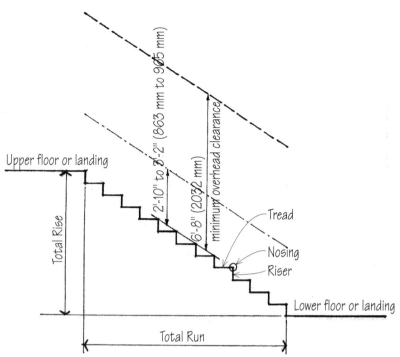

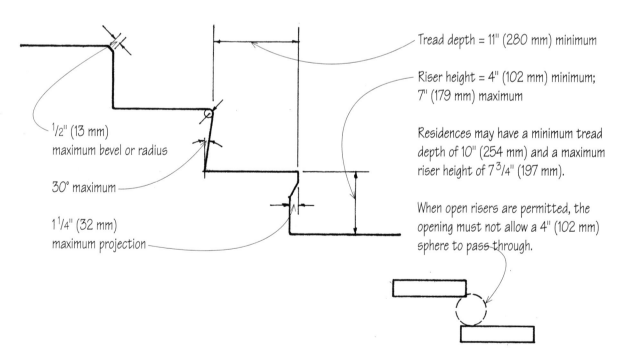

Tread depth = 11" (280 mm) minimum

Riser height = 4" (102 mm) minimum; 7" (179 mm) maximum

Residences may have a minimum tread depth of 10" (254 mm) and a maximum riser height of 7 3/4" (197 mm).

When open risers are permitted, the opening must not allow a 4" (102 mm) sphere to pass through.

**Stair Risers and Treads**

A stairway should be wide enough to comfortably accommodate our passage tas well as any furnishings and equipment that must be moved up or down the steps. Building codes specify minimum widths based on use and occupant loads. Beyond these minimums, however, the width of a stairway also provides a visual clue to the public or private quality of the stairway.

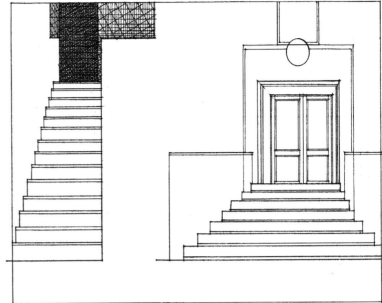

The width and angle of ascent are the variables that determine a stair's accessibility.

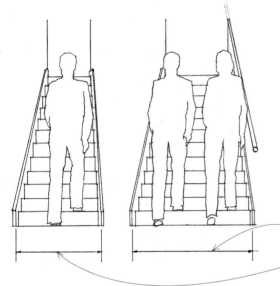

44" (1118 mm) minimum clear width

36" (914 mm) for an occupant load of 49 or less.

Handrails may project a maximum of 3 1/2" (89 mm) into the required width.

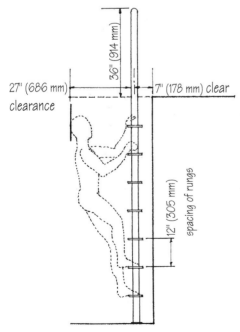

27" (686 mm) clearance

36" (914 mm)

7" (178 mm) clear

12" (305 mm) spacing of rungs

**Ladders**

7'-4" (2235 mm) clearance

35" (889 mm)

12" (305 mm)

50°–60°

**Ship's Ladders**

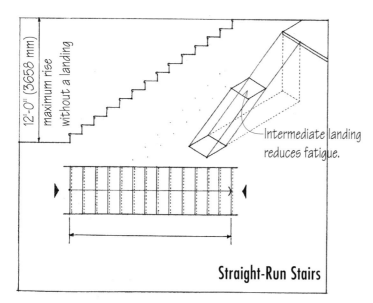

12'-0" (3658 mm) maximum rise without a landing

Intermediate landing reduces fatigue.

### Straight-Run Stairs

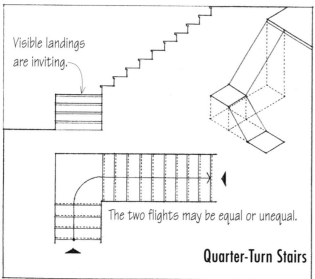

Visible landings are inviting.

The two flights may be equal or unequal.

### Quarter-Turn Stairs

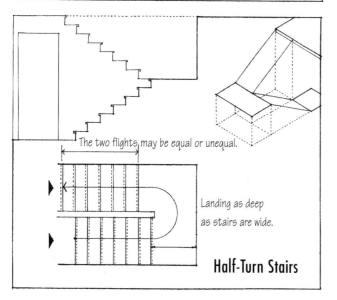

The two flights may be equal or unequal.

Landing as deep as stairs are wide.

### Half-Turn Stairs

The configuration of a stairway determines the direction of our path as we ascend or descend its steps. There are several basic ways in which to configure the runs of a stairway. These variations result from the use of landings, which interrupt a stair run and enable it to change direction. Landings also provide opportunities for rest and possibilities for access and outlook from the stairway. Together with the pitch of a stair, the locations of landings determine the rhythm of our movement up or down a stair.

An important consideration in the planning of any stairway is how it links the paths of movement at each floor level. Another is the amount of space the stair requires. Each basic stair type has inherent proportions that will affect its possible location relative to other spaces around it. These proportions can be altered to some degree by adjusting the location of landings in the pattern. In each case, space should be provided at both the top and bottom of a stairway for safe and comfortable access and egress.

Landings should be as least as wide as the stairway width and have a length of at least 44" (1118 mm) in the direction of travel. Landings in dwelling units may have a length of 36" (914 mm).

Winders refer to the tapered treads used in circular and spiral stairs. Quarter-turn and half-turn stairways may also use winders rather than a landing to conserve space when changing direction.

Winders can be hazardous because they offer little foothold at their interior corners. Building codes generally restrict their use to private stairs within individual dwelling units.

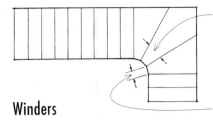

**Winders**

11" (279 mm) minimum at a point 12" (305 mm) in from the narrow end of the tread.

10" (254 mm) minimum at narrow end of tread; 6" (152 mm) minimum allowable in residences.

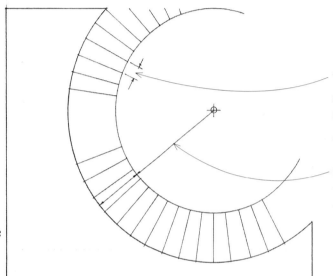

10" (254 mm) minimum at narrow end of tread; 6" (152 mm) minimum allowable in residences.

Smaller radius no less than twice the width of the stairway.

Circular stairs may be used for emergency egress if its inner radius is at least twice the width of the stairway; consult the building code for detailed requirements.

**Circular Stairs**

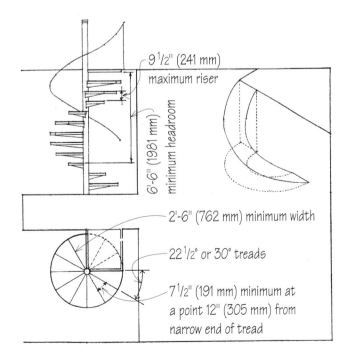

9 1/2" (241 mm) maximum riser

6'-6" (1981 mm) minimum headroom

Building codes restrict the use of spiral stairs to private use in individual dwelling units.

2'-6" (762 mm) minimum width

22 1/2° or 30° treads

7 1/2" (191 mm) minimum at a point 12" (305 mm) from narrow end of tread

**Spiral Stairs**

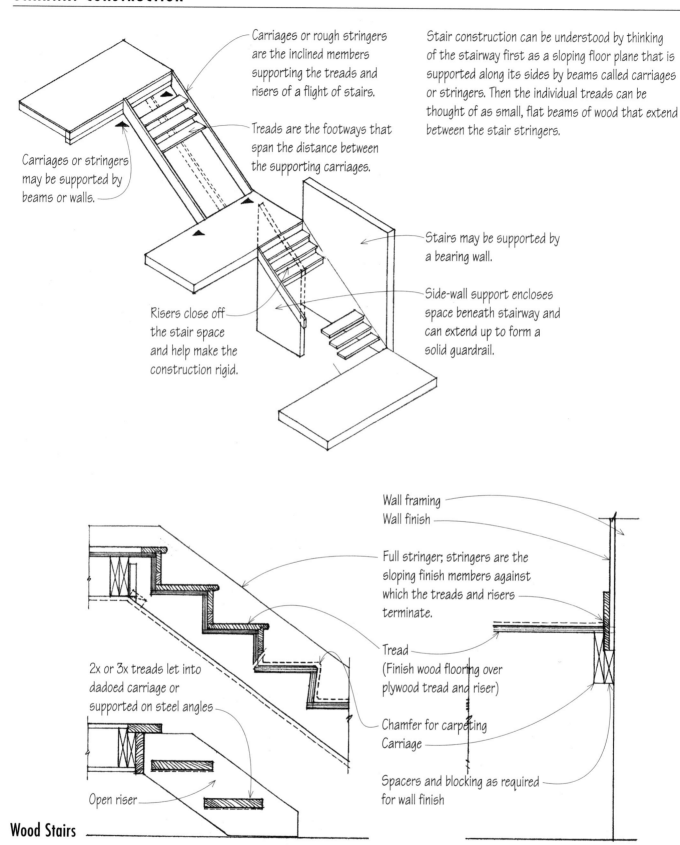

Carriages or rough stringers are the inclined members supporting the treads and risers of a flight of stairs.

Treads are the footways that span the distance between the supporting carriages.

Carriages or stringers may be supported by beams or walls.

Stair construction can be understood by thinking of the stairway first as a sloping floor plane that is supported along its sides by beams called carriages or stringers. Then the individual treads can be thought of as small, flat beams of wood that extend between the stair stringers.

Stairs may be supported by a bearing wall.

Side-wall support encloses space beneath stairway and can extend up to form a solid guardrail.

Risers close off the stair space and help make the construction rigid.

Wall framing
Wall finish

Full stringer; stringers are the sloping finish members against which the treads and risers terminate.

Tread
(Finish wood flooring over plywood tread and riser)

2x or 3x treads let into dadoed carriage or supported on steel angles

Chamfer for carpeting
Carriage

Open riser

Spacers and blocking as required for wall finish

**Wood Stairs**

Steel stairs are analogous in form to wood stairs. Steel channel sections serve as carriages and stringers. Stair treads span the distance between the stringers. The treads may consist of concrete-filled steel pans, bar grating, or flat plates with a textured top surface. Steel stairways are typically pre-engineered and prefabricated for a particular job.

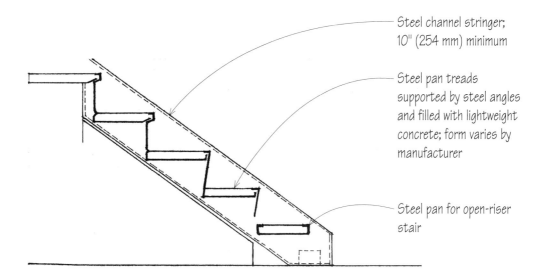

Steel channel stringer; 10" (254 mm) minimum

Steel pan treads supported by steel angles and filled with lightweight concrete; form varies by manufacturer

Steel pan for open-riser stair

**Steel Stairs**

A concrete stair is designed as an inclined, one-way reinforced slab with steps formed along its upper surface. Concrete stairs require careful analysis of load, span, and support conditions.

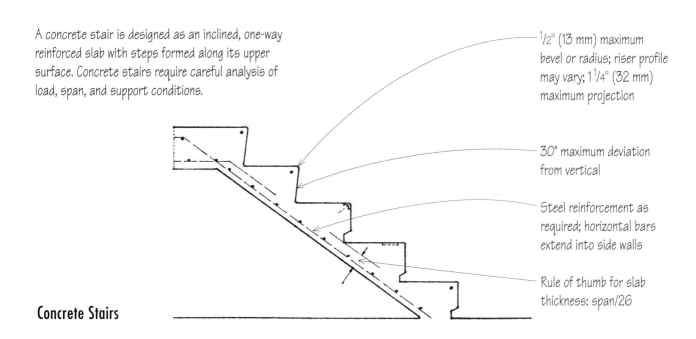

1/2" (13 mm) maximum bevel or radius; riser profile may vary; 1 1/4" (32 mm) maximum projection

30° maximum deviation from vertical

Steel reinforcement as required; horizontal bars extend into side walls

Rule of thumb for slab thickness: span/26

**Concrete Stairs**

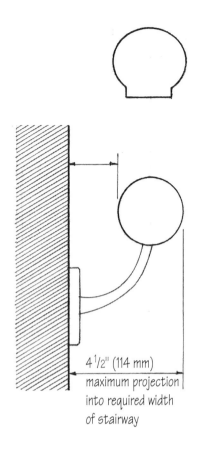

4 1/2" (114 mm)
maximum projection
into required width
of stairway

ADA guidelines regulate the minimum and maximum dimensions and the profiles of handrails to ensure their graspability.

Handrails should be free of sharp or abrasive elements; they should have a circular cross section and a diameter from 1 1/4" to 2" (32 mm to 51 mm); other shapes are allowable if they provide equivalent graspability and have a perimeter of from 4" to 6 1/4" (102 mm to 159 mm) and a maximum cross section dimension of 2 1/4" (57 mm).

1 1/2" (38 mm) minimum clearance

Building codes regulate the minimum height of guardrails and the maximum size of openings within the railings that protect the open sides of stairways, balconies, and decks.

Extend handrails at least 12" (305 mm) horizontally beyond the top and bottom of each flight.

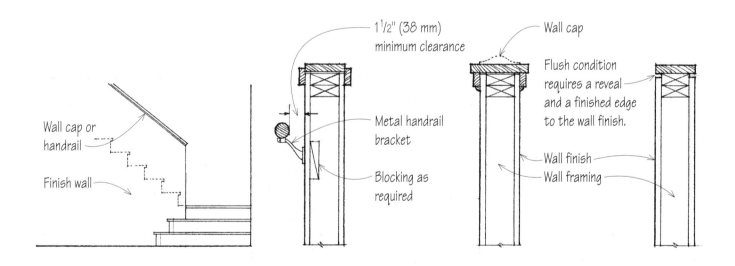

Wall cap or handrail

Finish wall

1 1/2" (38 mm) minimum clearance

Metal handrail bracket

Blocking as required

Wall cap

Flush condition requires a reveal and a finished edge to the wall finish.

Wall finish

Wall framing

## Solid Rail

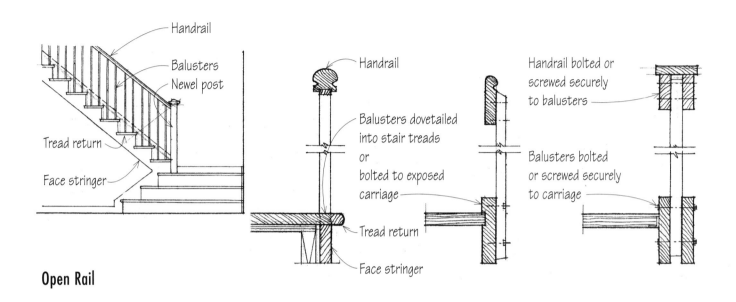

Handrail

Balusters

Newel post

Tread return

Face stringer

Handrail

Balusters dovetailed
into stair treads
or
bolted to exposed
carriage

Tread return

Face stringer

Handrail bolted or
screwed securely
to balusters

Balusters bolted
or screwed securely
to carriage

**Open Rail**

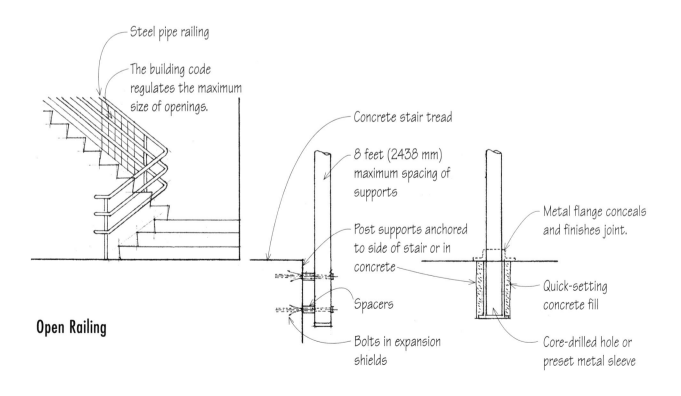

Steel pipe railing

The building code
regulates the maximum
size of openings.

Concrete stair tread

8 feet (2438 mm)
maximum spacing of
supports

Post supports anchored
to side of stair or in
concrete

Spacers

Bolts in expansion
shields

Metal flange conceals
and finishes joint.

Quick-setting
concrete fill

Core-drilled hole or
preset metal sleeve

**Open Railing**

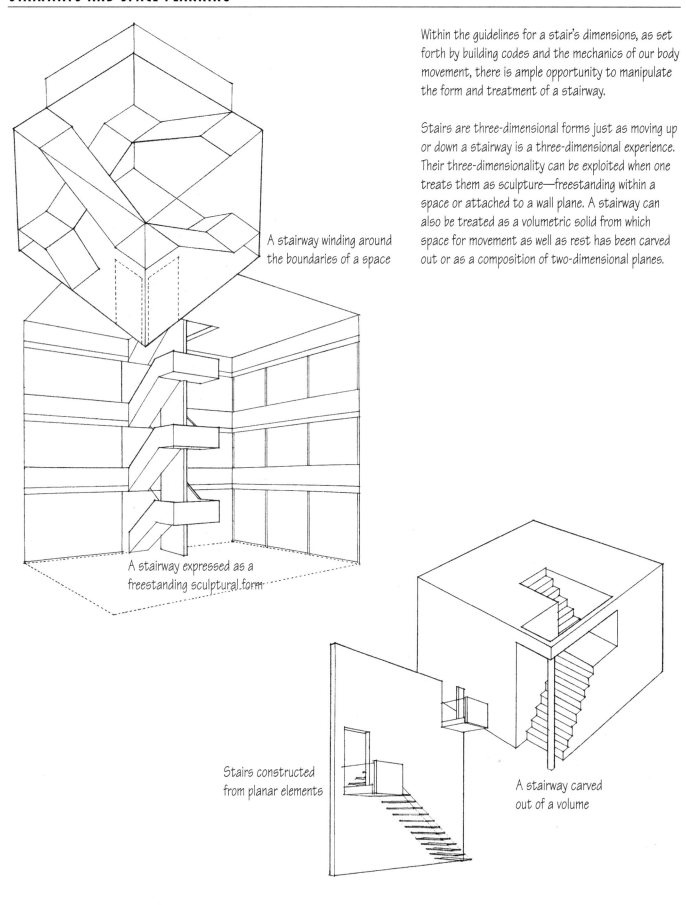

Within the guidelines for a stair's dimensions, as set forth by building codes and the mechanics of our body movement, there is ample opportunity to manipulate the form and treatment of a stairway.

Stairs are three-dimensional forms just as moving up or down a stairway is a three-dimensional experience. Their three-dimensionality can be exploited when one treats them as sculpture—freestanding within a space or attached to a wall plane. A stairway can also be treated as a volumetric solid from which space for movement as well as rest has been carved out or as a composition of two-dimensional planes.

A stairway winding around the boundaries of a space

A stairway expressed as a freestanding sculptural form

Stairs constructed from planar elements

A stairway carved out of a volume

A stair may interrupt a path or meet it at an angle. In a similar manner, the run of the stair may be parallel, perpendicular, or oblique to the path's direction.

A stair can be an organizing element and knit together a series of spaces at different levels of a building.

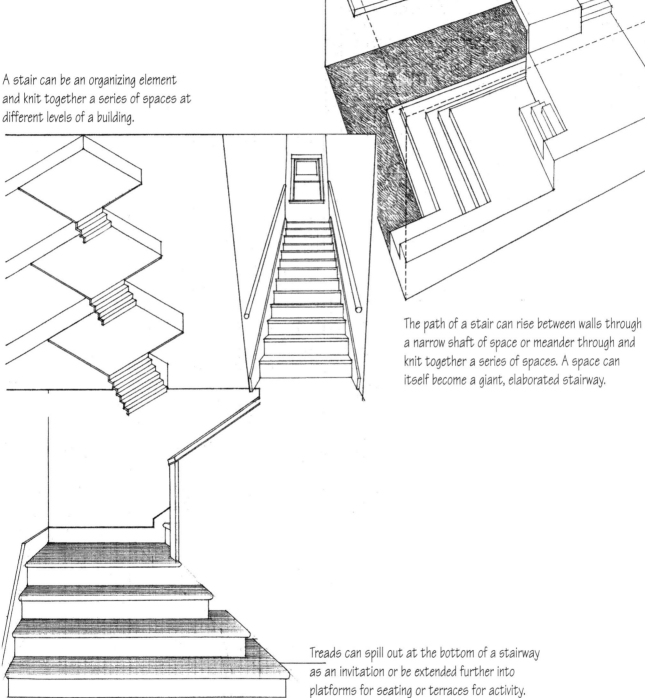

The path of a stair can rise between walls through a narrow shaft of space or meander through and knit together a series of spaces. A space can itself become a giant, elaborated stairway.

Treads can spill out at the bottom of a stairway as an invitation or be extended further into platforms for seating or terraces for activity.

Ramps provide smooth transitions between the floor levels of a building. To have comfortably low slopes, they require relatively long runs. They are typically used to accommodate a change in level along an accessible route or to provide access for wheeled equipment.

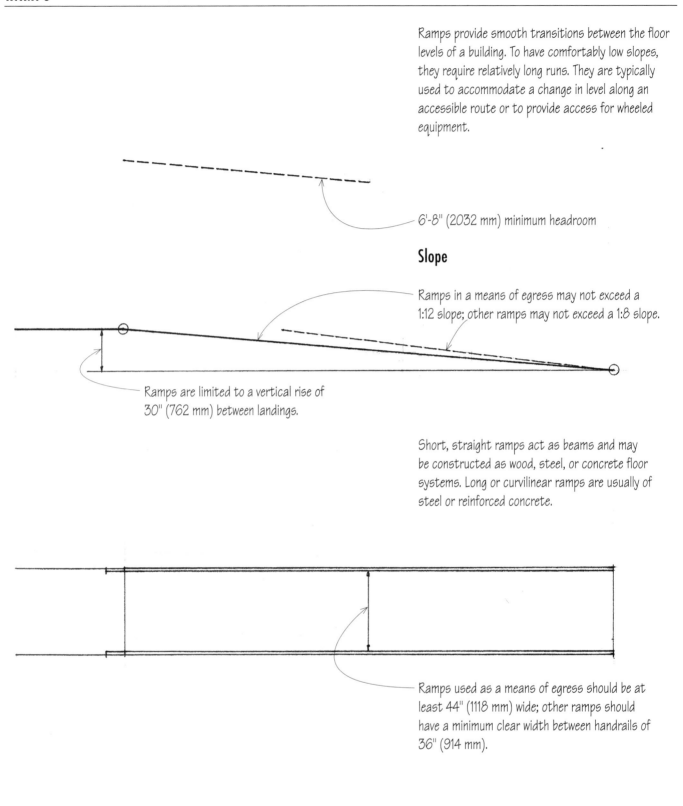

6'-8" (2032 mm) minimum headroom

### Slope

Ramps in a means of egress may not exceed a 1:12 slope; other ramps may not exceed a 1:8 slope.

Ramps are limited to a vertical rise of 30" (762 mm) between landings.

Short, straight ramps act as beams and may be constructed as wood, steel, or concrete floor systems. Long or curvilinear ramps are usually of steel or reinforced concrete.

Ramps used as a means of egress should be at least 44" (1118 mm) wide; other ramps should have a minimum clear width between handrails of 36" (914 mm).

## Guardrails and Handrails

Ramps having a rise greater than 6"
(152 mm) or a run greater than 72"
(1829 mm) should have guardrails
along both sides.

Handrails should be from 34" to 38"
(864 mm to 965 mm) above the ramp
surface.

Extend handrails at least 12" (305
mm) horizontally beyond the top and
bottom of the ramp runs.

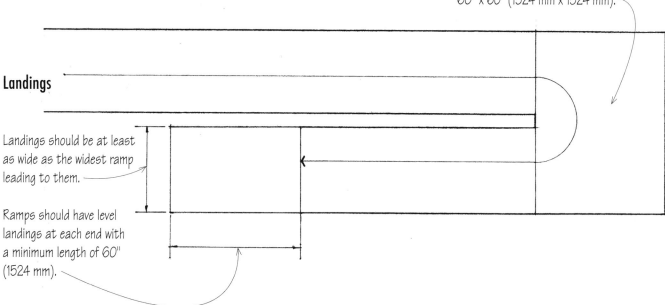

Landings that occur where a ramp
changes direction should be at least
60" x 60" (1524 mm x 1524 mm).

## Landings

Landings should be at least
as wide as the widest ramp
leading to them.

Ramps should have level
landings at each end with
a minimum length of 60"
(1524 mm).

# ELEVATORS

Elevators travel vertically to carry passengers, equipment, and freight from one level of a building to another. The two most common types are electric elevators and hydraulic elevators.

Electric elevators consist of a car that is mounted on guide rails, supported by hoisting cables, and driven by electric hoisting machinery in a penthouse.

Hydraulic elevators consist of a car supported by a piston that is moved by or moves against a fluid under pressure. A penthouse is not required, but the hydraulic elevator's lower speed and piston length limit its use to buildings up to six stories in height.

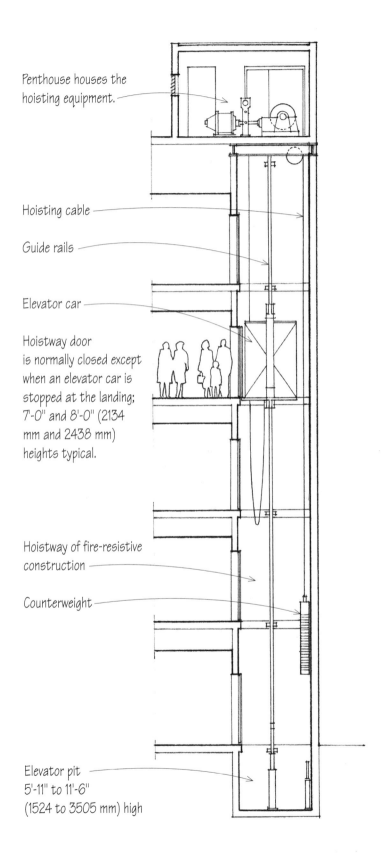

Penthouse houses the hoisting equipment.

Hoisting cable

Guide rails

Elevator car

Hoistway door is normally closed except when an elevator car is stopped at the landing; 7'-0" and 8'-0" (2134 mm and 2438 mm) heights typical.

Hoistway of fire-resistive construction

Counterweight

Elevator pit 5'-11" to 11'-6" (1524 to 3505 mm) high

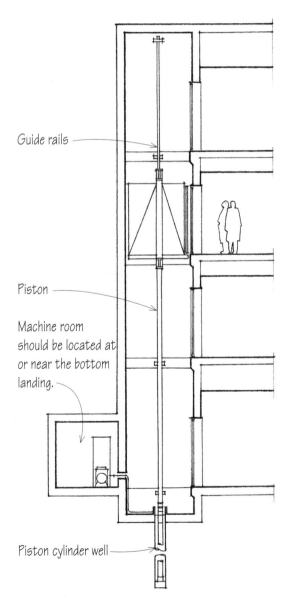

Guide rails

Piston

Machine room should be located at or near the bottom landing.

Piston cylinder well

ADA accessibility guidelines for passenger elevators cover the type and location of call signals, lanterns, floor designations, call buttons, and cab controls. Elevator doors should be provided with an automatic reopening device that is activated if the door becomes obstructed by an object or person. Elevator cars should be sized to allow wheelchair users to enter the car, maneuver within reach of controls, and exit from the car.

Interior cab finishes must consider dimensions permitted by cab construction, durability, tamper resistance, and ease of maintenance. Elevator interiors should be fabricated by experienced craftspeople.

## Escalators

Escalators are power-driven stairways consisting of steps attached to a continuously circulating belt. They can move a large number of people efficiently and comfortably among a limited number of floors; six floors are a practical limit. Because escalators move at a constant speed, there is practically no waiting period, but there should be adequate queuing space at each loading and discharge point.

Both elevators and escalators may not be used as required fire exits.

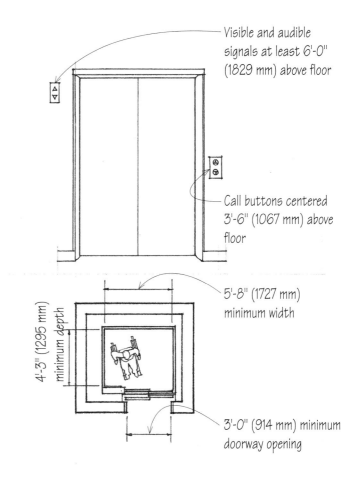

Visible and audible signals at least 6'-0" (1829 mm) above floor

Call buttons centered 3'-6" (1067 mm) above floor

5'-8" (1727 mm) minimum width

4'-3" (1295 mm) minimum depth

3'-0" (914 mm) minimum doorway opening

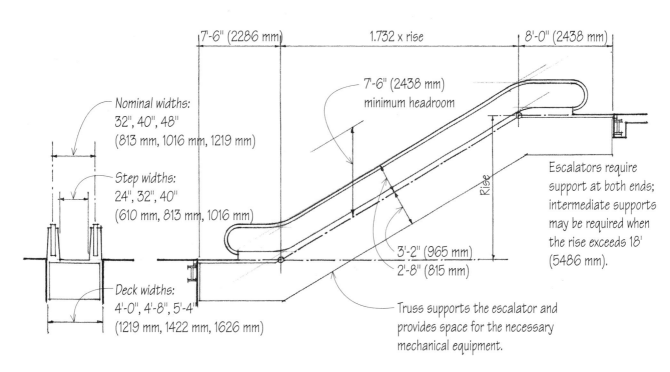

7'-6" (2286 mm)

1.732 x rise

8'-0" (2438 mm)

7'-6" (2438 mm) minimum headroom

Nominal widths: 32", 40", 48" (813 mm, 1016 mm, 1219 mm)

Step widths: 24", 32", 40" (610 mm, 813 mm, 1016 mm)

Deck widths: 4'-0", 4'-8", 5'-4" (1219 mm, 1422 mm, 1626 mm)

Rise

3'-2" (965 mm)
2'-8" (815 mm)

Escalators require support at both ends; intermediate supports may be required when the rise exceeds 18' (5486 mm).

Truss supports the escalator and provides space for the necessary mechanical equipment.

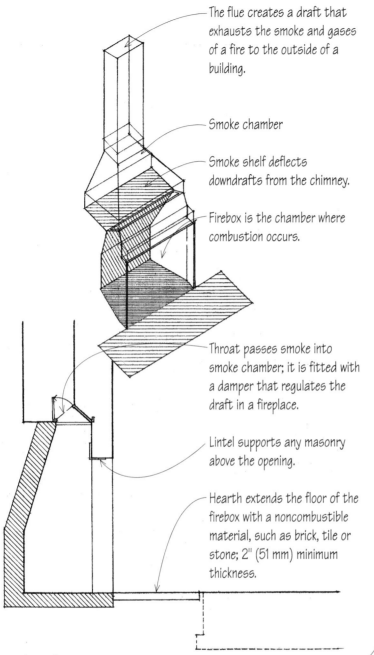

The flue creates a draft that exhausts the smoke and gases of a fire to the outside of a building.

Smoke chamber

Smoke shelf deflects downdrafts from the chimney.

Firebox is the chamber where combustion occurs.

Throat passes smoke into smoke chamber; it is fitted with a damper that regulates the draft in a fireplace.

Lintel supports any masonry above the opening.

Hearth extends the floor of the firebox with a noncombustible material, such as brick, tile or stone; 2" (51 mm) minimum thickness.

While a traditional fireplace is not as efficient for heating an interior space as a wood stove, few would dispute the special attraction it holds for people. The warmth and flames of an open fire are like a magnet, enticing people to gather around a fireplace. Even without a fire, a fireplace can be a unique center of interest, and serve as the focal point about which a room can be arranged.

A fireplace must be designed to draw properly, to sustain combustion safely, and to carry smoke away efficiently. Thus the proportions of a fireplace and the arrangement of its components are subject to both the laws of nature and the local building code.

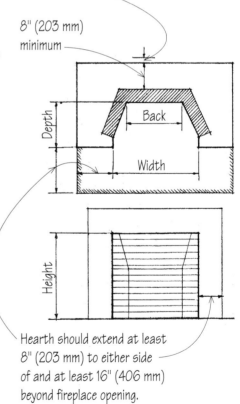

4" (102 mm) minimum to wood framing

8" (203 mm) minimum

Depth

Back

Width

Height

Hearth should extend at least 8" (203 mm) to either side of and at least 16" (406 mm) beyond fireplace opening.

## Typical Fireplace Dimensions in Inches (millimeters)

| Width | Height | Depth | Back |
|---|---|---|---|
| 24 (610) | 24 (610) | 16–18 (406–457) | 14 (356) |
| 28 (711) | 24 (610) | 16–18 (406–457) | 14 (356) |
| 30 (762) | 28–30 (711–762) | 16–18 (406–457) | 16 (406) |
| 36 (914) | 28–30 (711–762) | 16–18 (406–457) | 22 (559) |
| 42 (1069) | 28–30 (711–762) | 16–18 (406–457) | 28 (711) |
| 48 (1219) | 32 (813) | 18–20 (457–508) | 32 (813) |

When considering the location of a fireplace, evaluate its effect on a room's proportions and the space required if furniture is to be arranged about it.

It is important for the interior designer to note the amount of space a fireplace requires and how the face—the opening, surround, and hearth—can be treated. The treatment of the surround visually enlarges the fireplace opening, enhances it as a focal point, and integrates it with the rest of a room's trimwork.

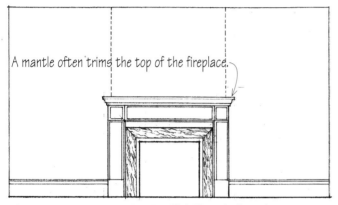

A mantle often trims the top of the fireplace.

No woodwork is permitted within 6" (152 mm) of the fireplace opening.

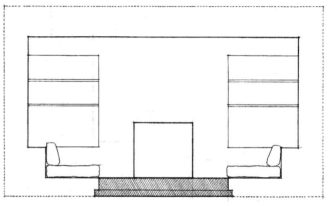

The raised hearth of a fireplace can be extended to form a platform for seating. This platform along with the fireplace can begin to define an alcove space.

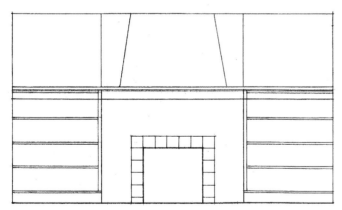

On the wall of the room, the chimney breast often projects a few inches into the room. When projecting into a room, a fireplace also forms recesses to either side that can be used for storage.

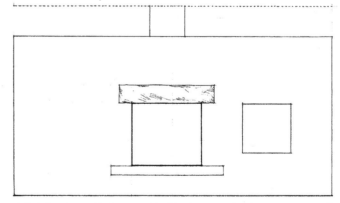

A lintel or beam that spans the fireplace opening in a masonry wall can be exposed and embellished as a visual design element.

Prefabricated fireplaces and woodburning stoves should be certified by the Environmental Protection Agency (EPA) for burning efficiency and allowable particulate emissions.

Woodburning stoves must be located at safe distances from combustible surfaces, with noncombustible materials below and around the stove.

The stove's location affects furniture arrangements and circulation paths, with areas with a view of the stove getting most of the radiant heat.

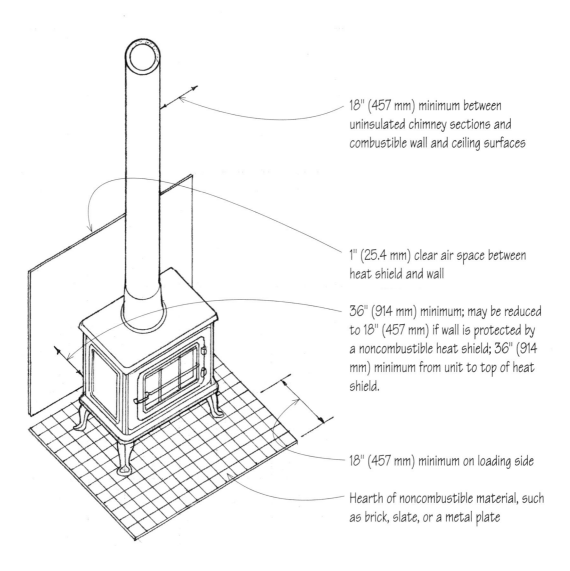

18" (457 mm) minimum between uninsulated chimney sections and combustible wall and ceiling surfaces

1" (25.4 mm) clear air space between heat shield and wall

36" (914 mm) minimum; may be reduced to 18" (457 mm) if wall is protected by a noncombustible heat shield; 36" (914 mm) minimum from unit to top of heat shield.

18" (457 mm) minimum on loading side

Hearth of noncombustible material, such as brick, slate, or a metal plate

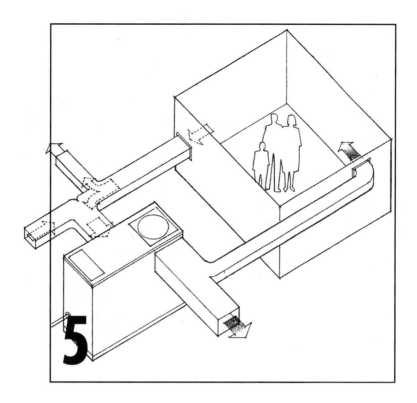

# 5

# Interior Environmental Systems

Heating, Ventilating, and
Air-Conditioning

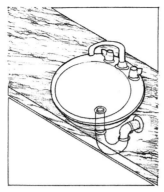

Water Supply and
Sanitary Drainage

Interior environmental systems are essential
components of any building. They provide the thermal,
visual, auditory, and sanitary conditions necessary
for the comfort and convenience of the building's
occupants. These systems must be designed and
laid out well to function properly. They must also be
coordinated with a building's structural system. This
requires the knowledge and expertise of professional
engineers and architects. The interior designer,
nevertheless, should be aware that these systems
exist and know how they affect the quality of the
interior environment.

## INTERIOR ENVIRONMENTAL SYSTEMS

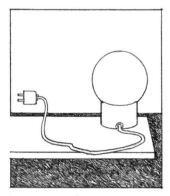

Electric Power and
Lighting

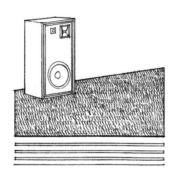

Room Acoustics and
Noise Control

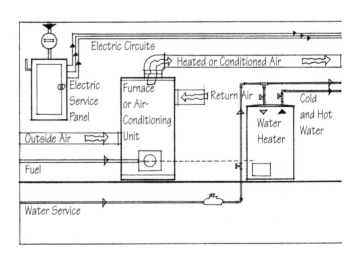

Sources

While the nature of a building's structural system can manifest itself in its interior spaces, the often complex networks of its mechanical and electrical systems are normally hidden from view. Interior designers, however, should be aware of the visible items that directly affect the interior environment—light fixtures, electrical outlets, plumbing fixtures, and air supply registers and return grills. Also of interest are the space requirements for horizontal and vertical runs of air ducts and electrical and plumbing lines.

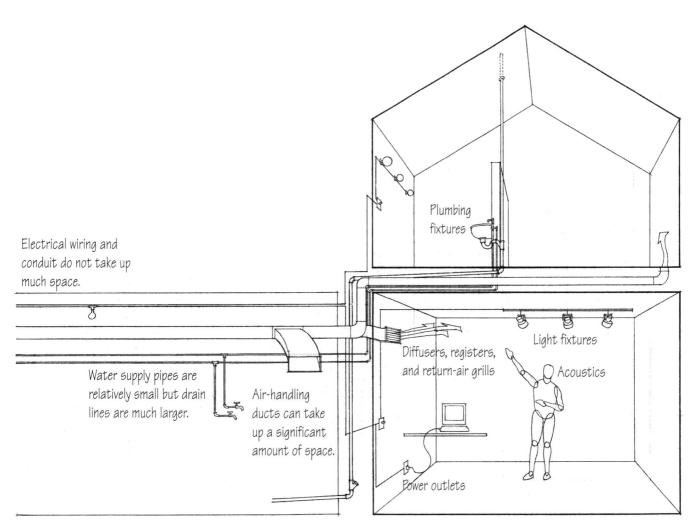

Electrical wiring and conduit do not take up much space.

Water supply pipes are relatively small but drain lines are much larger.

Air-handling ducts can take up a significant amount of space.

Plumbing fixtures

Diffusers, registers, and return-air grills

Light fixtures

Acoustics

Power outlets

**Transmission**

**Control and Output Devices**

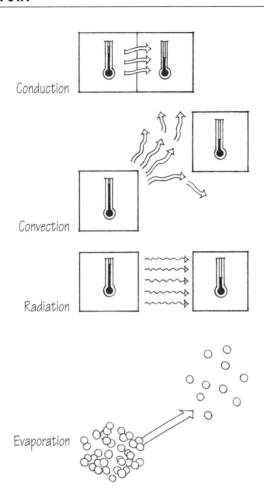

Conduction

Convection

Radiation

Evaporation

Thermal comfort is achieved when the human body is able to dissipate the heat and moisture it produces by metabolic action to maintain a stable, normal body temperature.

## Modes of Heat Transfer

Radiation: Heat energy is emitted by a warm body, transmitted through an intervening space, and absorbed by a cooler body; radiant heat is not affected by air motion or temperature.

Convection: Transfer due to the circulatory motion of the heated parts of a liquid or gas.

Conduction: Direct transfer from the warmer to the cooler particles of a medium or of two bodies in direct contact.

Evaporation: Heat loss due to the process of converting moisture into a vapor.

Thermal comfort is dependent not only on air temperature but also on relative air humidity, the radiant temperature of surrounding surfaces, air motion, and air purity. To achieve and maintain thermal comfort, a reasonable balance must be reached among these factors.

• The higher the mean radiant temperature of a room's surfaces, the cooler the air temperature should be.
• The higher the relative humidity of a space, the lower the air temperature should be.
• The cooler the moving air stream, the less velocity it should have.

Radiation gain from light fixtures and other heated equipment

Solar radiation gain

Loss by convection of cool air or by evaporation

Radiation gain from heater

Radiation loss to cooler surfaces

Conductive loss to a cold floor

## Indoor Air Quality

Indoor air quality considerations affect the type of heating, ventilating, and air-conditioning (HVAC) equipment chosen to control air pressure and provide fresh and conditioned air to the interior spaces of a building. Equipment maintenance also affects the quality of air delivered. Molds and viruses thrive in warm, moist equipment. Filters must be changed often.

Some interior design materials may release volatile organic chemicals (VOCs) that may irritate eyes, skin, and respiratory systems. Examples include pressed wood products such as particleboard; carpet and carpet pads and adhesives; vinyl sheet flooring and wall coverings; paints, stains and other coatings; treated fabrics; and modular office partitions. The interior designer should specify materials with low VOC emission levels or take steps to seal them or allow them to outgas to safe levels before the space is occupied.

## Ventilation

Buildings need a source of fresh air to replenish the oxygen used by the people and equipment inside and to remove carbon dioxide and other wastes from the air. Buildings designed without operable windows limit the intake of fresh air. Increasing ventilation and air distribution is the best and most cost-effective way to freshen the air inside most buildings.

Air flows through a building because it moves from higher pressure to lower pressure areas. Mechanical systems incorporate controls for regulating the volume, velocity, and direction of air flow.

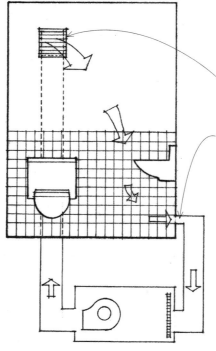

Blowers and fans move the air through ductwork that delivers it to the building's rooms.

Registers control the flow of air into interior spaces.

Return air grilles take in contaminated air to be cleaned and reused or exhausted from the building.

*Natural ventilation requires:*
• A source of air having an acceptable temperature, moisture content, and cleanliness and
• A force—usually wind or thermal convection—to move the air through the inhabited spaces of the building.

The primary objective of a heating system is to replace the heat lost within an interior space. The basic heating system consists of a heat-producing medium, equipment to convert the medium to heat, a means to deliver the heat to a space, and finally a method for discharging the heat within the space.

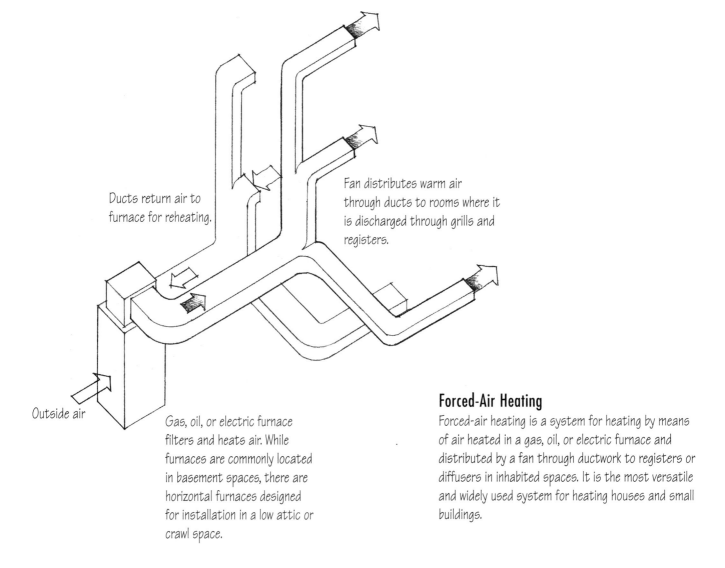

Ducts return air to furnace for reheating.

Fan distributes warm air through ducts to rooms where it is discharged through grills and registers.

Outside air

Gas, oil, or electric furnace filters and heats air. While furnaces are commonly located in basement spaces, there are horizontal furnaces designed for installation in a low attic or crawl space.

## Forced-Air Heating

Forced-air heating is a system for heating by means of air heated in a gas, oil, or electric furnace and distributed by a fan through ductwork to registers or diffusers in inhabited spaces. It is the most versatile and widely used system for heating houses and small buildings.

## Hot-Water Heating

Hot-water or hydronic heating is a system for heating by means of water heated in a boiler and circulated by a pump through pipes to radiators or convectors. Steam heating is similar in principle, utilizing steam generated in a boiler and circulating it through piping to radiators. In large cities and building complexes, hot water or steam generated at a central boiler plant may be available via underground pipelines. This availability would eliminate the need for an on-site boiler.

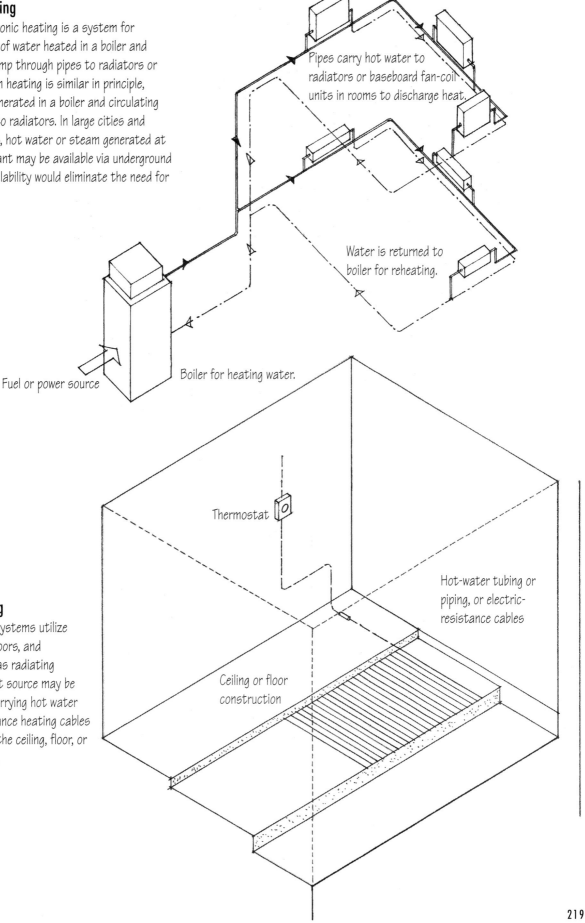

Pipes carry hot water to radiators or baseboard fan-coil units in rooms to discharge heat.

Water is returned to boiler for reheating.

Fuel or power source

Boiler for heating water.

Thermostat

Hot-water tubing or piping, or electric-resistance cables

Ceiling or floor construction

## Radiant Heating

Radiant heating systems utilize heated ceilings, floors, and sometimes walls as radiating surfaces. The heat source may be pipes or tubing carrying hot water or electric-resistance heating cables embedded within the ceiling, floor, or wall construction.

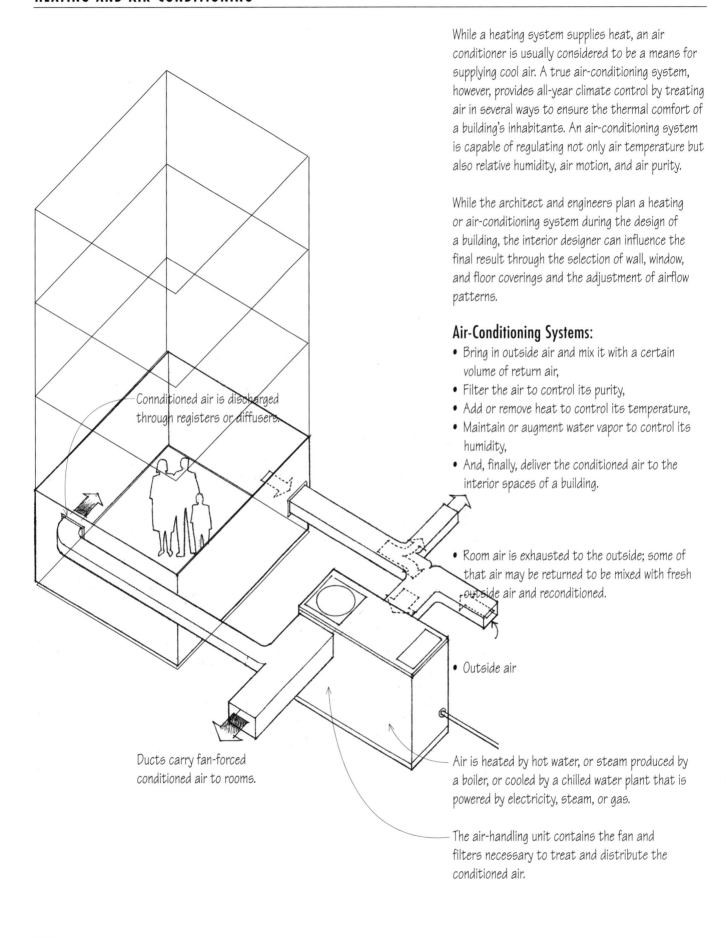

Connditioned air is disoharged through registers or diffusers.

Ducts carry fan-forced conditioned air to rooms.

While a heating system supplies heat, an air conditioner is usually considered to be a means for supplying cool air. A true air-conditioning system, however, provides all-year climate control by treating air in several ways to ensure the thermal comfort of a building's inhabitants. An air-conditioning system is capable of regulating not only air temperature but also relative humidity, air motion, and air purity.

While the architect and engineers plan a heating or air-conditioning system during the design of a building, the interior designer can influence the final result through the selection of wall, window, and floor coverings and the adjustment of airflow patterns.

## Air-Conditioning Systems:
- Bring in outside air and mix it with a certain volume of return air,
- Filter the air to control its purity,
- Add or remove heat to control its temperature,
- Maintain or augment water vapor to control its humidity,
- And, finally, deliver the conditioned air to the interior spaces of a building.

- Room air is exhausted to the outside; some of that air may be returned to be mixed with fresh outside air and reconditioned.

- Outside air

Air is heated by hot water, or steam produced by a boiler, or cooled by a chilled water plant that is powered by electricity, steam, or gas.

The air-handling unit contains the fan and filters necessary to treat and distribute the conditioned air.

There are two separate but parallel networks in a water system. One supplies potable water for human use and consumption as well as use by mechanical and fire-protection systems. The other disposes of waterborne waste material once the water has been used.

Water is typically supplied to a building under pressure from a water main. The water supply system must overcome the forces of gravity and friction to deliver water up to the various points of use. The pressure required to upfeed water may come from the water main or from pumps within the building. When this pressure is insufficient, water can be pumped to an elevated storage tank for gravity downfeed.

A separate supply subsystem common to all buildings is the hot water supply system, leading from the heater or boiler to each required fixture. To conserve energy, the hot water supply can be a closed and constantly circulating system.

A series of valves is required to control the flow of water at each fixture as well as to isolate one or more fixtures from the water supply system for repair and maintenance.

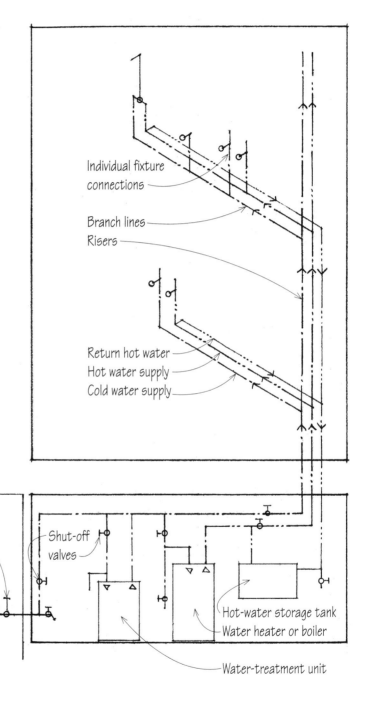

Individual fixture connections

Branch lines

Risers

Return hot water

Hot water supply

Cold water supply

Outside shut-off valve

Meter

Street main

Shut-off valves

Hot-water storage tank

Water heater or boiler

Water-treatment unit

Plumbing fixtures receive water from a supply system and discharge the liquid waste into a sanitary drainage system. Some building codes mandate the use of water-efficient fixtures and valves to conserve water resources.

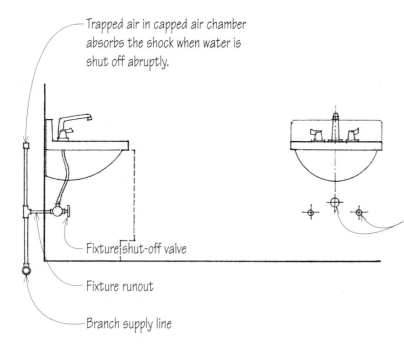

Trapped air in capped air chamber absorbs the shock when water is shut off abruptly.

Access to shut-off valves must be maintained in any interior construction.

Sizes and locations of supply and draingage lines are supplied by the fixture manufacturer.

Fixture shut-off valve

Fixture runout

Branch supply line

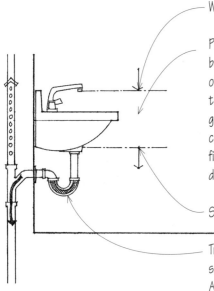

Water supply system ends.

Plumbing fixtures have an air gap between the spout of a faucet or other outlet of a supply pipe and the flood level of a receptacle. Air gaps are required to prevent used or contaminated water from a plumbing fixture being siphoned into a supply pipe due to negative pressure in the pipe.

Sanitary drainage system begins.

Traps are an essential feature of the sanitary drains from plumbing fixtures. A trap is a U-shaped or S-shaped section of drainpipe in which wastewater remains, forming a seal that prevents the passage of sewer gas without affecting the flow of water or sewage through it.

Plumbing fixtures may be made of the following materials.

- Water closets, urinals, and bidets: vitreous china

| | Water Closet | Urinal | Bidet |
|---|---|---|---|
| Width | 20"–24" (510–610 mm) | 18" (455 mm) | 14" (355 mm) |
| Depth | 22"–29" (560–735 mm) | 12"–24" (305–610 mm) | 30" (760 mm) |
| Height | 20"–28" (510–710 mm) | 24" (610 mm) | 14" (355 mm) |

- Lavatories and utility sinks: hard, smooth, scrubbable materials like vitreous china, resin-based solid surfacing materials, enameled cast iron, enameled steel

| | Lavatory | Lavatory | Lavatory |
|---|---|---|---|
| Width | 30"–36" (7600 to 915 mm) | 18–24" (455–610 mm) | 18–24" (455–610 mm) |
| Depth | 21" (535 mm) | 16"–21" (405–535 mm) | 16"–21" (405–535 mm) |
| Height | 31" (785 mm) rim height | 31" (785 mm) rim height | 31" (785 mm) rim height |

- Shower receptacles: terrazzo, enameled steel, fiberglass, acrylic plastic
- Shower enclosures: enameled steel, stainless steel, ceramic tile, fiberglass, acrylic, glass

 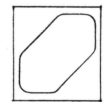

**Shower**

| Width | 30"–42" (760–1065 mm) |
|---|---|
| Depth | 30"–42" (760–1065 mm) |
| Height | 74"–80" (1880–2030 mm) |

**Square Bathtub**

44"–50" (1120–1270 mm)
44"–50" (1120–1270 mm)
12"–16" (305–405 mm)

- Bathtubs: acrylic, fiberglass, enameled cast iron, cultured marble

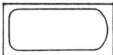 

**Bathtub**

| Width | 42"–72" (1065–1830 mm) |
|---|---|
| Depth | 30"–32" (760–815 mm) |
| Height | 12"–20" (305–510 mm) |

- Kitchen sinks: enameled cast iron, enameled steel, stainless steel

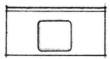  

| | Sink with Drainboards | Double Bowl Sink | Utility Sink |
|---|---|---|---|
| Width | 54"–84" (1370–2135 mm) | 28"–46" (710–1170 mm) | 22"–48" (560–1220 mm) |
| Depth | 21"–25" (535–635 mm) | 16"–21" (405–535 mm) | 18"–22" (455–560 mm) |
| Height | 8" (205 mm) | 8"–10" (205–255 mm) | 27"–29" (685–735 mm) |
| | | | rim height |

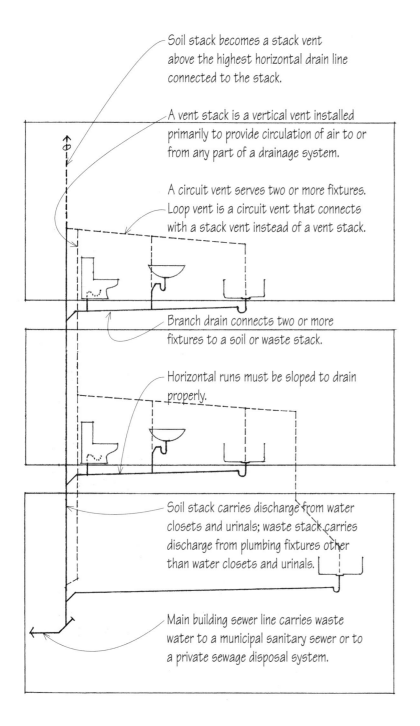

Soil stack becomes a stack vent above the highest horizontal drain line connected to the stack.

A vent stack is a vertical vent installed primarily to provide circulation of air to or from any part of a drainage system.

A circuit vent serves two or more fixtures. Loop vent is a circuit vent that connects with a stack vent instead of a vent stack.

Branch drain connects two or more fixtures to a soil or waste stack.

Horizontal runs must be sloped to drain properly.

Soil stack carries discharge from water closets and urinals; waste stack carries discharge from plumbing fixtures other than water closets and urinals.

Main building sewer line carries waste water to a municipal sanitary sewer or to a private sewage disposal system.

The water supply system terminates at each plumbing fixture. After the water has been drawn and used, it enters the sanitary drainage system. The primary objective of this drainage system is to dispose of fluid waste and organic matter as quickly and efficiently as possible.

Because a sanitary drainage system relies on gravity for its discharge, its pipes are much larger than water supply lines, which are under pressure. In addition, there are restrictions on the length and slope of horizontal runs and on the types and number of turns.

Gases are formed in drainage pipes by the decomposition of the waste matter. To prevent these gases from entering the interior spaces of a building, traps or water seals are required at each fixture.

In addition, the entire sanitary drainage system must be vented to outside air. Venting prevents water seals in traps from being siphoned out and allows air to circulate within the system.

The electrical power system of a building supplies power for lighting, heating, and the operation of electrical equipment and appliances. This system should be installed to operate safely, reliably, and efficiently. A second system of wiring provides connections for data, communications and control equipment, and for security systems.

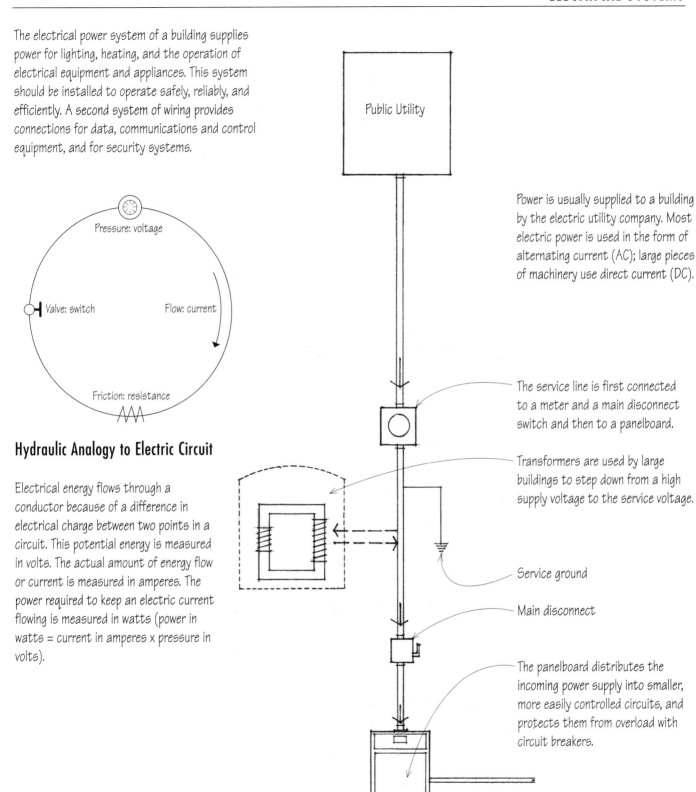

Pressure: voltage

Valve: switch

Flow: current

Friction: resistance

## Hydraulic Analogy to Electric Circuit

Electrical energy flows through a conductor because of a difference in electrical charge between two points in a circuit. This potential energy is measured in volts. The actual amount of energy flow or current is measured in amperes. The power required to keep an electric current flowing is measured in watts (power in watts = current in amperes x pressure in volts).

Public Utility

Power is usually supplied to a building by the electric utility company. Most electric power is used in the form of alternating current (AC); large pieces of machinery use direct current (DC).

The service line is first connected to a meter and a main disconnect switch and then to a panelboard.

Transformers are used by large buildings to step down from a high supply voltage to the service voltage.

Service ground

Main disconnect

The panelboard distributes the incoming power supply into smaller, more easily controlled circuits, and protects them from overload with circuit breakers.

For electric current to flow, a circuit must be complete. Switches control current flow by introducing breaks in a circuit until power is required.

Branch circuits distribute electric power to the interior spaces of a building. The wiring in a circuit is sized according to the amount of current it must carry. A fuse or circuit breaker in the distribution panel disconnects a circuit when too much current is drawn for its wiring. The continuous load on a circuit should not exceed 80% of its rated capacity. For example, a 15 amp circuit should have a continuous load rating of 12 amperes. On a 110 volt line, the circuit could then be assumed to handle 12 amperes multiplied by 110 volts or 1320 watts. Because room should be allowed for expansion, the safe capacity of a 15 amp circuit on a 110 Volt line is 1200 watts.

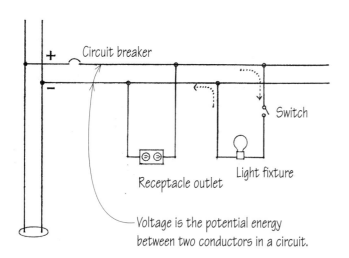

Circuit breaker

Switch

Receptacle outlet

Light fixture

Voltage is the potential energy between two conductors in a circuit.

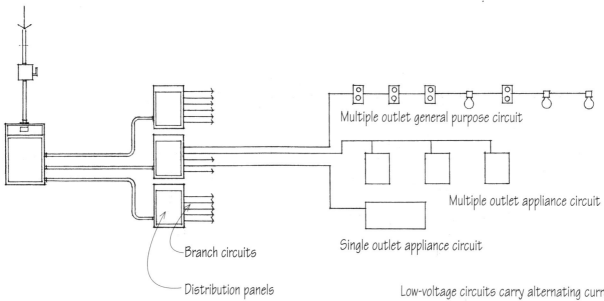

Multiple outlet general purpose circuit

Multiple outlet appliance circuit

Single outlet appliance circuit

Branch circuits

Distribution panels

Low-voltage circuits carry alternating current below 50V, supplied by a step-down transformer from the normal line voltage. These circuits are used in residential systems to control doorbells, intercoms, heating and cooling systems, and remote lighting fixtures. Low-voltage wiring does not require a protective raceway such as conduit.

Electrical systems are designed by electrical engineers. The interior designer often provides information on the location of lighting fixtures, power outlets, and switches to control their operation. The designer should also be aware of the power requirements of an electrical installation so that they can be coordinated with the existing or planned circuits.

Load requirements for lighting fixtures and electrically powered equipment are specified by their manufacturer. The design load for a general purpose circuit, however, depends on the number of receptacles served by the circuit and how they are used. The National Electrical Code should be consulted for these requirements.

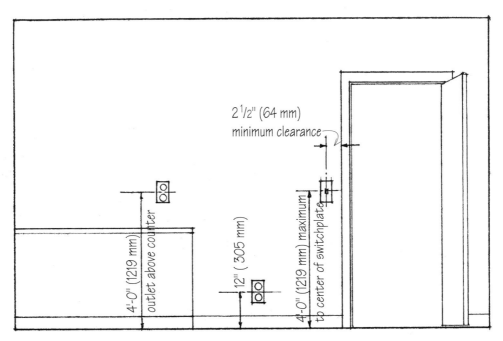

2¹⁄₂" (64 mm) minimum clearance

4'-0" (1219 mm) outlet above counter

12" (305 mm)

4'-0" (1219 mm) maximum to center of switchplate

**Heights of Switches and Outlets**

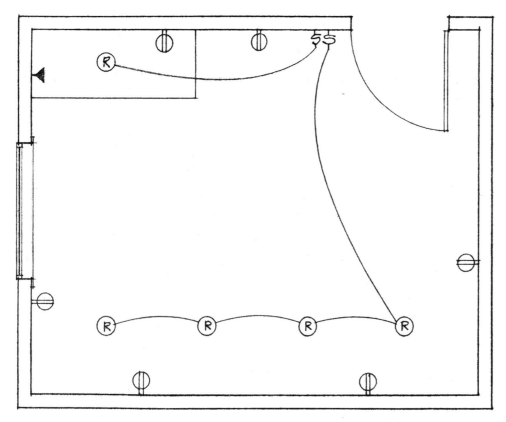

## Typical Electrical and Lighting Plan

## Common Electrical Symbols

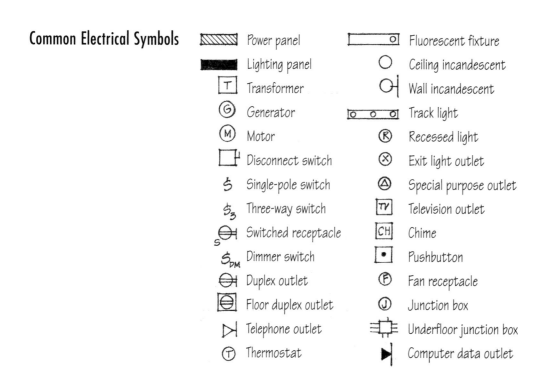

| | | | |
|---|---|---|---|
| ▨ | Power panel | ▭○ | Fluorescent fixture |
| ▬ | Lighting panel | ○ | Ceiling incandescent |
| T | Transformer | ○⊢ | Wall incandescent |
| G | Generator | ▭○○○▭ | Track light |
| M | Motor | R | Recessed light |
| ⊏ | Disconnect switch | X | Exit light outlet |
| S | Single-pole switch | ▲ | Special purpose outlet |
| S₃ | Three-way switch | TV | Television outlet |
| ⊖⊢ₛ | Switched receptacle | CH | Chime |
| S_DM | Dimmer switch | ▪ | Pushbutton |
| ⊖⊢ | Duplex outlet | F | Fan receptacle |
| ⊖ | Floor duplex outlet | J | Junction box |
| ▷ | Telephone outlet | ⊣⊢ | Underfloor junction box |
| T | Thermostat | ▶ | Computer data outlet |

Fire alarm and suppression systems connect electrical sensing and annunciation devices to a system that carries water to the location of a fire. Many parts of these systems are highly visible within the finished interior space and must, therefore, be integrated into the interior design while remaining unblocked.

Automatic sprinkler systems are fed from very large pipes that branch out to supply water to grids of sprinkler heads. When the system detects a fire, water sprays out of the closest sprinkler heads to drown the fire. Sprinkler heads are available in upright, pendant, and sidewall types, and can be recessed or concealed in finished ceilings. Their locations are dictated by code, and they must not be painted once installed. The interior designer should coordinate ceiling design elements, including lighting fixtures, with the location of sprinkler heads.

Many buildings have standpipe and hose systems that supply large quantities of water to hoses housed in wall cabinets throughout the building. These hoses are intended for use by firefighters, as they are very powerful and hard to control.

Fire alarms usually include both a flashing light and an audible alarm. Usually, these fire alarms are bright red and conspicuously mounted on walls or ceilings. They are intended to be seen easily by building occupants and may not be concealed or camouflaged.

Annunciator panels are located at building entrances and other strategic sites to help firefighters identify the location of fires. They are sometimes quite large, bright red, and very conspicuous.

Many buildings are supplied with communications systems designed to alert occupants of conditions during an emergency and to allow firefighters to keep in touch while fighting a fire. Some buildings have a central emergency desk with controls as well.

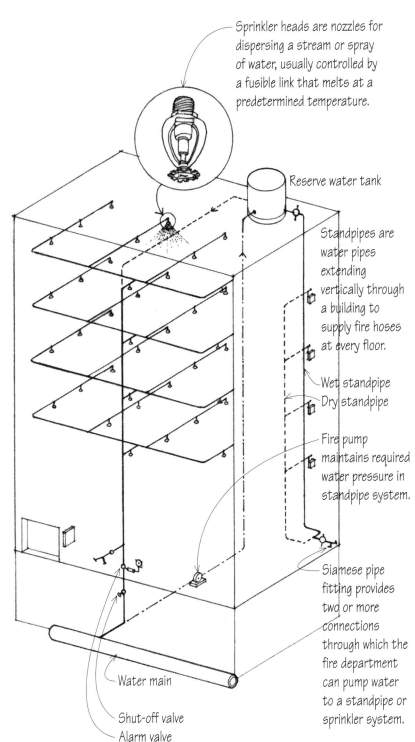

Sprinkler heads are nozzles for dispersing a stream or spray of water, usually controlled by a fusible link that melts at a predetermined temperature.

Reserve water tank

Standpipes are water pipes extending vertically through a building to supply fire hoses at every floor.

Wet standpipe
Dry standpipe

Fire pump maintains required water pressure in standpipe system.

Siamese pipe fitting provides two or more connections through which the fire department can pump water to a standpipe or sprinkler system.

Water main

Shut-off valve
Alarm valve

## Building Codes

This section outlines some considerations of a system that, while not immediately visible, affects the design of a building and its interior spaces. This system consists of a variety of laws and regulations enacted by federal, state, and local governments in an effort to protect the public health, safety, and general welfare.

Zoning regulations control the size, location, and use of buildings. Building codes regulate how a building is constructed and occupied. Many of these regulations incorporate standards established by governmental or independent testing agencies.

While architects and engineers bear the primary responsibility for complying with code requirements, the interior designer should be aware of these regulatory devices and be sensitive to how they affect the design of interior spaces. It should also be remembered that codes often set minimum standards, and mere compliance will not ensure that a building will be efficient, comfortable, or well designed.

The applicable building code usually specifies minimum standards for the structural stability of a building and the quality and design of its materials and construction. When planning the interior of a new building or the remodeling of an existing one, an architect or engineer should be consulted if any alterations to a building's structural elements are anticipated.

## Model Codes and Sponsoring Organizations

Building Officials and Code Administrators International, Inc. (BOCA)
    BOCA National Building Code
    National Plumbing Code
    National Mechanical Code

International Code Council, Inc. (ICC)
    2000 International Building Code
    International Residential Code
    International Energy Conservation Code

International Conference of Building Officials (ICBO)
    Uniform Building Code
    Uniform National Plumbing Code
    Uniform National Mechanical Code

National Fire Protection Association (NFPA)
    National Electrical Code
    Life Safety Code

Southern Building Code Congress International (SBCC)
    Standard Building Code
    Standard National Plumbing Code
    Standard National Mechanical Code

## Organizations that Issue Standards

| | |
|---|---|
| ANSI | American National Standards Institute |
| ASTM | American Society for Testing and Materials |
| FHA | Federal Housing Administration |
| GSA | General Services Administration |
| HUD | Department of Housing and Urban Development |
| NFPA | National Fire Protection Association |
| NIST | National Institute of Standards and Technology |
| UL | Underwriters' Laboratories Inc.. |

## Fire Safety Codes

Fire safety is a prime area of concern in building codes. Requirements for the noncombustibility or fire-resistance of a building's structural elements and exterior walls are specified according to the building's occupancy, floor area, height, and location. In addition, fire-resistant walls and doors may be required to subdivide a building into separate areas and prevent a fire in one area from spreading to others.

Even when a building's structure would not support combustion, a fire can occur because of its finish materials and contents. This is of particular significance for interior designers when specifying such wall, floor, and ceiling finishes and furnishings such as carpeting, draperies, and upholstery. Regulations may prohibit the use of materials with a low flash point or set standards for the degree of flame spread and smoke emission allowed.

Sprinkler systems are increasingly being relied on to control a fire that does start. In addition, a type of fire/smoke detector and alarm system is usually required to warn of fire.

## Means of Egress

The means of egress requirements of building and fire codes provide for the safe and efficient evacuation of a building in case of fire or other emergency. These requirements are usually based on a building's size, construction, and type of occupancy. In principle, there should be at least two alternate ways of exiting a building from any space in case one route is cut off by fire or smoke. Exit passages, stairs, ramps, and doorways should be clearly marked, well lit, and wide enough to accommodate the appropriate number of occupants. Exit doors should swing outward in the direction of travel and, in places of public assembly, be equipped with fire exit hardware that will unlatch under pressure.

## Health and Safety Codes

In addition to structural and fire safety, general areas of health and safety are dealt with in building codes. These include the design of stairways in terms of allowable riser-to-tread ratios, minimum widths based on occupancy, the use of landings, and requirements for handrails.

For habitable spaces, natural light must be provided by exterior glazed openings and natural ventilation by means of operable windows. These requirements are usually based on a percentage of a room's floor area. For some types of occupancy, artificial light and a mechanically operated ventilating system can be substituted.

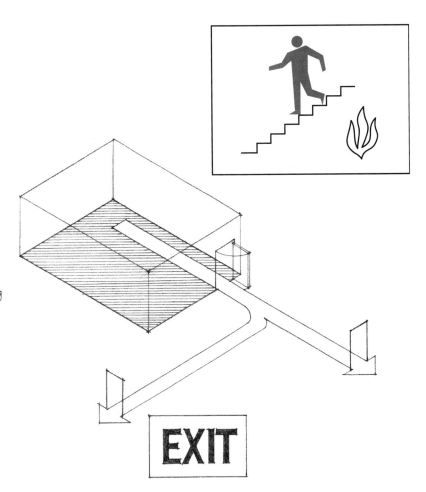

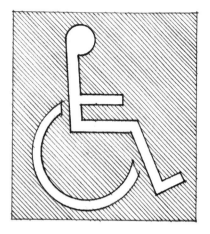

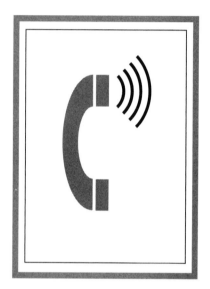

## Accessibility

The Americans with Disabilities Act (ADA) of 1990 is the federal legislation that requires buildings be made accessible to persons with physical and certain defined mental disabilities as a civil right. Access is to be provided for all disabilities, not just for people with mobility impairments. These include hearing, vision, speech, and cognitive impairments as well as persons of short stature and with limited mobility not necessarily requiring the use of a wheelchair. The ADA also requires that barriers to access be removed from existing buildings where such work is readily achievable.

Specific concerns include the use of ramps and elevators or lifts for access to the various levels of a building; adequate space and uncluttered layouts for ease of movement; provision of usable restrooms and other facilities; accessibility of hardware such as door handles, light switches, and elevator controls; and nonvisual means of orientation for the sight-impaired.

Designers should first concentrate on complying with codes and standards adopted locally and also keep national statutory requirements such as the ADA in mind. It is prudent to review design work against ADA Accessibility Guidelines (ADAAG) at the same time as the model code review.

## Energy Conservation Codes

The International Energy Conservation Code (IECC) contains requirements for energy-efficient design. Many states and local jurisdictions have adopted their own energy conservation codes that may have quite different standards than this model code. Energy conservation codes limit a building's total energy use, including lighting and electrical power and mechanical systems, and require documentation of the design and calculation of the energy loads to assure compliance. Limits for lighting use are integrated into the total building energy design and can strongly affect the interior designer's work.

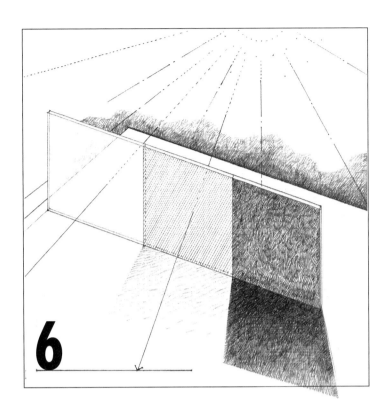

# 6

# Lighting and Acoustics

Light is radiant energy. It radiates equally in all directions and spreads over a larger area as it emanates from its source. As it spreads, it also diminishes in intensity according to the square of its distance from the source.

As it moves, light reveals to our eyes the surfaces and forms of objects in space. An object in its path will reflect, absorb, or allow the light striking its surface to pass through.

# LIGHTING

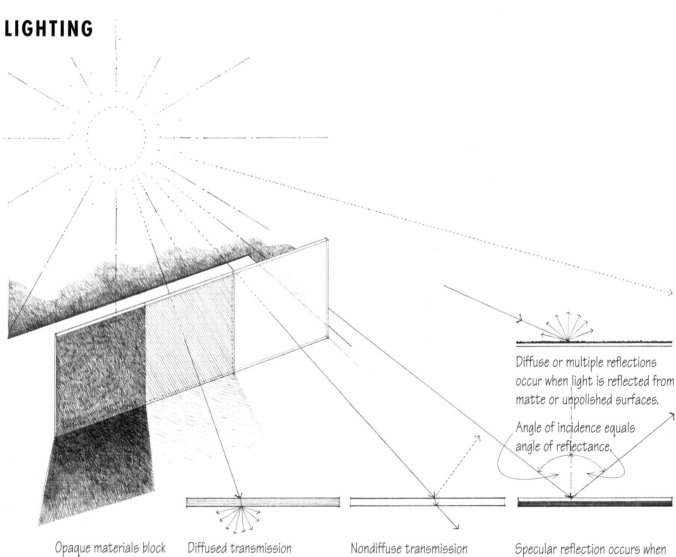

Diffuse or multiple reflections occur when light is reflected from matte or unpolished surfaces.

Angle of incidence equals angle of reflectance.

Opaque materials block the transmission of light and cast shadows.

Diffused transmission occurs through translucent materials, such as frosted glass. The light source is not clearly visible.

Nondiffuse transmission occurs through clear, transparent materials, such as glass and some plastics.

Specular reflection occurs when light is reflected from a shiny, opaque surface.

The sun, stars, and electric lamps are visible to us because of the light they generate. Most of what we see, however, is visible because of the light that is reflected from the surfaces of objects. Our ability to see well—that is, to discern shape, color, and texture, and to differentiate one object from another—is affected not only by the amount of light available for illumination but also by the following factors:

- Brightness
- Contrast
- Glare
- Diffusion
- Color

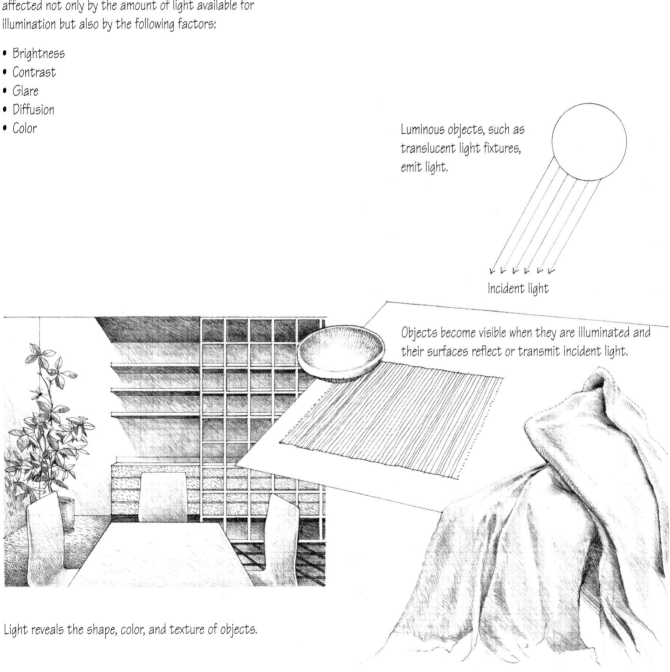

Luminous objects, such as translucent light fixtures, emit light.

Incident light

Objects become visible when they are illuminated and their surfaces reflect or transmit incident light.

Light reveals the shape, color, and texture of objects.

Brightness refers to how much light energy is reflected by a surface. The degree of brightness of an object, in turn, depends on the color value and texture of its surface. A shiny, light-colored surface will reflect more light than a dark, matte, or rough-textured surface, even though both surfaces are lit with the same amount of illumination.

Generally speaking, visual acuity increases with object brightness. Of equal importance is the relative brightness between the object being viewed and its surroundings. To discern its shape, form, and texture, some degree of contrast or brightness ratio is required. For example, a white object on an equally bright white background would be difficult to see, as would a dark object seen against a dark background.

Even though these objects may be uniformly illuminated, their surfaces differ in brightness according to their color value and texture and, consequently, their ability to reflect light.

Brightness = illumination x reflectance

Contrast in brightness aids our perception of shape and form.

Contrast between an object and its background is especially critical for visual tasks that require the discrimination of shape and contour. An obvious example of this need for contrast is the printed page where dark letters can best be read when printed on light paper.

For seeing tasks requiring discrimination of surface texture and detail, less contrast between the surface and its background is desirable because our eyes adjust automatically to the average brightness of a scene. Someone seen against a brightly illuminated background would be silhouetted well, but it would be difficult to discern that person's facial features.

The surface brightness of a task area should be the same as its background or be just a bit brighter. A maximum brightness ratio of 3:1 between the task surface and its background is generally recommended. Between the task area and the darkest part of the surrounding room, the brightness ratio should not exceed 5:1. Higher brightness ratios can lead to glare and associated problems of eye fatigue and loss in visual performance.

High background brightness is helpful in delineating shape and outline.

To aid in discriminating surface detail, surface brightness must be increased.

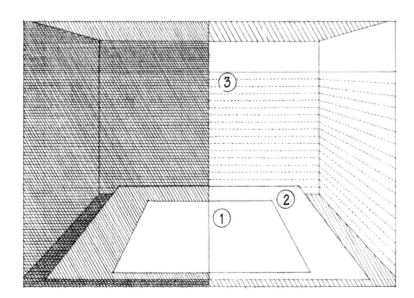

Surrounding area (3) should range from $1/5$ to 5 times the brightness of the task area (1).

3:1 is the maximum recommended brightness ratio between the visual task area (1) and its immediate background (2).

Contrasting brightness levels can be desirable in certain situations.

Direct glare is caused by the brightness of light sources within a person's normal field of vision.

Even though our eyes prefer even lighting, particularly between a task surface and its background, our eyes are able to adapt to a wide range of brightness levels. We can respond to a minimum brightness ratio of 2:1 as well as to a maximum of 100:1 or more, but only over a period of time. Our eyes cannot respond immediately to extreme changes in lighting levels. Once our eyes have adjusted to a certain lighting level, any significant increase in brightness can lead to glare, eyestrain, and impairment of visual performance.

There are two types of glare, direct and indirect. Direct glare is caused by the brightness of light sources within our normal field of vision. The brighter the light source, the greater the glare potential. Possible solutions to problems of direct glare include the following:

• Locate the sources of brightness out of the direct line of vision.
• If this is not possible, use properly shielded or baffled lighting fixtures.
• In addition, raise the background brightness of the light sources and reduce the brightness ratio.

1. Reduce the brightness ratio between the light source and its background.

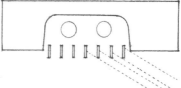

2. Use well-shielded or baffled light fixtures that minimize a direct view of bulbs or lamps.

## Possible Solutions to Glare

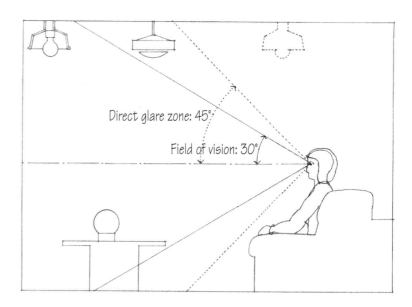

Direct glare zone: 45°

Field of vision: 30°

3. Locate light fixtures out of the direct-glare zone.

Indirect or reflected glare is caused by a task or viewing surface reflecting light from a light source into the viewer's eyes. The term *veiling reflection* is sometimes used to describe this type of glare because the reflection of the light source creates a veiling of the image on the task surface and a resultant loss of contrast necessary for seeing the image.

Indirect glare is most severe when the task or viewing surface is shiny and has a high, specular reflectance value. Using a dull, matte task surface can help alleviate but will not eliminate veiling reflections.

Possible solutions to problems of reflected glare include the following:
- Locate the light source so that the incident light rays will be reflected away from the viewer.
- Use lighting fixtures with diffusers or lenses that lower their brightness levels.
- Lower the level of general overhead lighting and supplement it with localized task lighting closer to the work surface.

To minimize veiling reflections when the task locations are unknown, use low-brightness lighting fixtures or rely on a low level of ambient lighting.

Glitter and sparkle are desirable types of glare.

Reflected glare affects our ability to perform critical seeing tasks, such as reading or drafting.

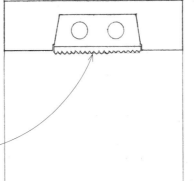

Low-level ambient lighting supplemented by individual task lighting, which is adjustable by the user, is a good general purpose solution.

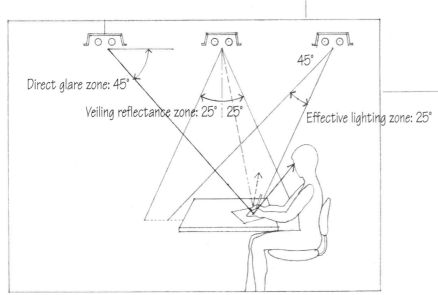

Direct glare zone: 45°

Veiling reflectance zone: 25° | 25°

45°

Effective lighting zone: 25°

Bright, concentrated light sources above and forward of the task surface present the ideal condition for veiling reflectances.

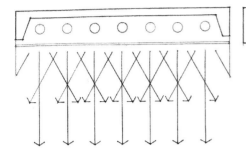

Broad sources of light produce diffused illumination.

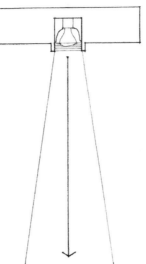

Concentrated light sources produce directional lighting.

Diffuseness is a measure of a light's direction and dispersion as it emanates from its source. This quality of light affects both the visual atmosphere of a room and the appearance of objects within it. A broad source of light, such as evenly spaced 2-feet x 4-feet (610 mm x 1219 mm) fluorescent fixtures with diffusing grids, produces diffused illumination that is flat, fairly uniform, and generally glare-free. The soft light provided minimizes contrast and shadows and can make the reading of surface textures difficult.

On the other hand, a concentrated source of light, such as an incandescent downlight, produces a directional light with little diffusion. Directional lighting enhances our perception of shape, form, and surface texture by producing shadows and brightness variations on the objects it illuminates.

While diffused lighting is useful for general vision, it can be monotonous. Some directional lighting can help relieve this dullness by providing visual accents, introducing brightness variations, and brightening task surfaces. A mix of both diffused and directional lighting is often desirable and beneficial, especially when a variety of tasks are to be performed in a room.

Diffused illumination minimizes contrast and shadows.

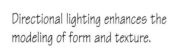

Directional lighting enhances the modeling of form and texture.

Another important quality of light is its color and how it affects the coloration of objects and surfaces in a room. While we assume most light to be white, the spectral distribution of light varies according to the nature of its source. The most evenly balanced white light is noon daylight. But in the early morning hours, daylight can range from purple to red. As the day progresses, it will cycle through a range of oranges and yellows to blue-white at noon, and then back again through the oranges and reds of sunset.

The spectral distribution of electric light sources varies with the type of lamp. For example, an incandescent bulb produces a yellow-white light while a cool-white fluorescent produces a blue-white light.

The apparent color of a surface is a result of its reflection of its predominant hue and its absorption of the other colors of the light illuminating it. The spectral distribution of a light source is important because if certain wavelengths of color are missing, then those colors cannot be reflected and will appear to be missing or grayed in any surface illuminated by that light.

| ° Kelvin | Light Source |
|---|---|
| 10000° | Clear blue sky (up to 25,000°) |
| 9000° | |
| 8000° | North light |
| 7000° | |
| | Daylight fluorescent |
| 6000° | Overcast sky |
| 5000° | Noon sunlight |
| | Cool-white fluorescent |
| 4000° | Daylight incandescent |
| | Warm-white fluorescent |
| 3000° | |
| | Incandescent lamp |
| 2000° | Sunrise |

## Color Temperature Scale

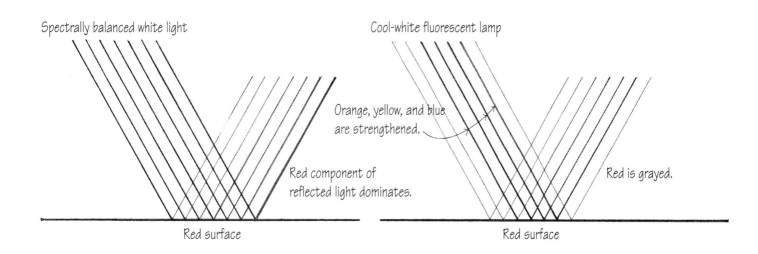

Spectrally balanced white light

Red component of reflected light dominates.

Red surface

Cool-white fluorescent lamp

Orange, yellow, and blue are strengthened.

Red is grayed.

Red surface

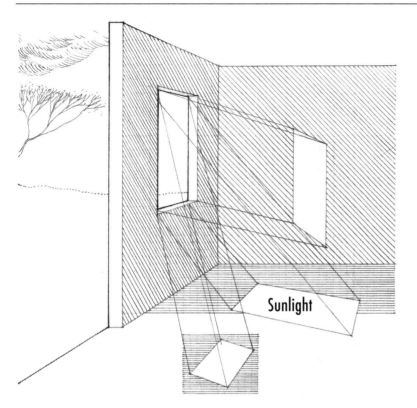

Sunlight

The source of all natural daylight is the sun. Its light is intense but will vary with the time of day, from season to season, and from place to place. It can also be diffused by cloud cover, haze, precipitation, or any pollution that may be present in the air.

In addition to direct sunlight, two other conditions must be considered when designing the daylighting of a space—reflected light from a clear sky and light from an overcast sky. While direct sunlight emphasizes hot, bright colors, skylight is more diffuse and enhances cool colors.

Introducing sunlight into a building can decrease dependence on electric lighting, which in turn reduces energy use. Sunlight will also bring solar heat into the building, which may result in energy savings in cold weather, but will increase air-conditioning costs in warmer months.

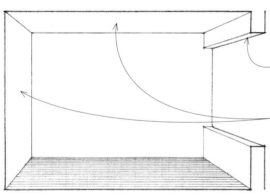

The larger and higher a window, the more daylight will enter a room.

The ceiling and rear wall of a room are generally more effective than the side walls or the floor in reflecting and distributing daylight.

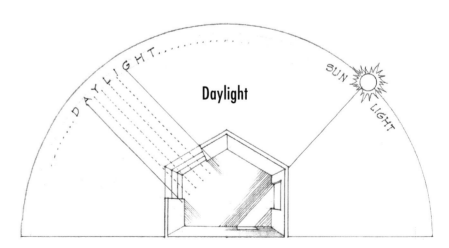

Daylight

A problem associated with daylighting is glare, which is caused by excessive contrast between the brightness of a window opening and the darker wall surfaces or cast shadows adjacent to it. When one deals with glare, the placement of windows is as important as their size. The optimum condition is balanced lighting from at least two directions—from two walls or a wall and the ceiling. Skylights, in particular, can help soften the harshness of direct sunlight.

In rooms with windows close to the floor, glare can be caused by the light reflected off of the exterior ground surface. This ground glare can be reduced through the use of shade trees or a vertical screen of horizontal louvers.

Locating a window adjacent to a perpendicular wall or ceiling surface maximizes the light entering the window. The perpendicular surface is illuminated by the entering light and becomes itself a broad source of reflected light.

Glare results when our eyes cannot adjust simultaneously to widely contrasting areas of brightness. Our eyes adjust to the brightest light in our field of vision, reducing our ability to discern less brightly lit areas.

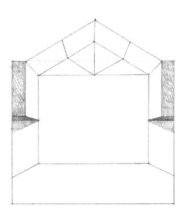 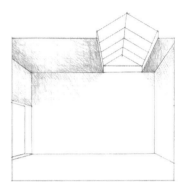

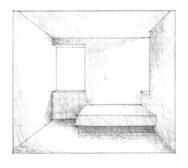 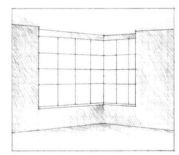

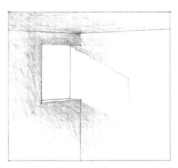 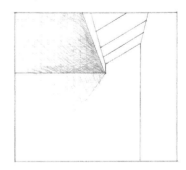

Bidirectional lighting—lighting from two directions—raises the level of diffused light in a space and reduces the possibility of glare.

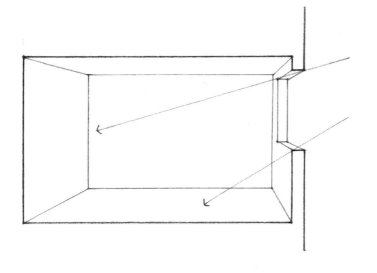

High window openings allow daylight to penetrate more deeply into an interior space and help to reduce glare.

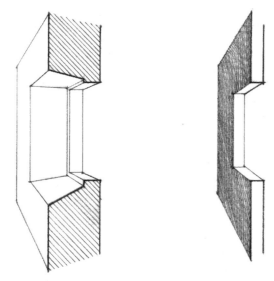

Windows set flush in a wall or ceiling accentuate contrasts between the bright exterior and darker interior surfaces. Deep-set windows, splayed jambs, and rounded jambs can soften this contrast.

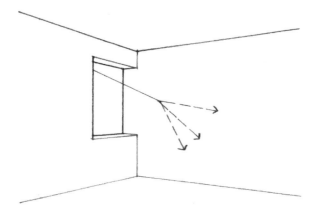

Locating a window adjacent to a perpendicular wall or ceiling surface maximizes the light entering the window. The perpendicular surface is illuminated by the entering light and becomes itself a broad source of reflected light.

A light shelf is an exterior horizontal construction located below the head of a window opening and typically just above eye level. The light shelf shades the lower portion of the window from direct sunlight and reflects daylight onto the ceiling of the room, which becomes a light-reflecting surface and diffuses light deeper into the space.

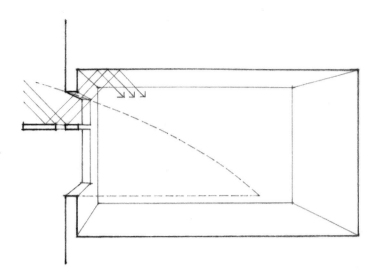

Skylights are glazed with clear, patterned, or translucent glass or with clear, gray-tinted, or milk-white acrylics.

Flat skylights are prone to leaks and dirt accumulation.

Domed or slanted skylights stay cleaner and leak less.

Tubular skylights (light tubes) collect sunlight through a small, clear acrylic dome on the roof, transmit it though a cylindrical shaft, and disperse it through a translucent diffuser lens into interior spaces.

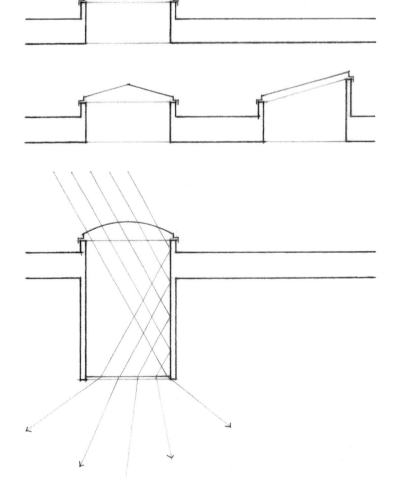

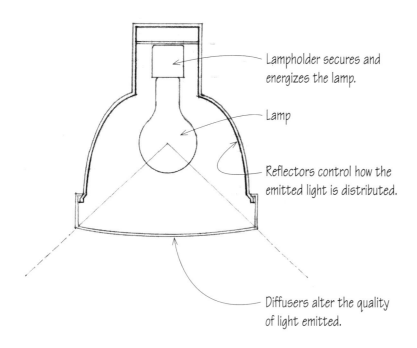

Lampholder secures and energizes the lamp.

Lamp

Reflectors control how the emitted light is distributed.

Diffusers alter the quality of light emitted.

The electric light sources used in lighting fixtures are called lamps. The two major types in common use are *incandescent* and *discharge* lamps. The quantity and quality of light produced differ according to the specific type of lamp used. The light is further modified by the housing that holds and energizes the lamp and any reflector, lens, or baffle used to control how the light is distributed, diffused, or shielded.

How a specific light source appears when lighted is called its *color temperature*, which is measured in degrees kelvin (K). For example, an incandescent bulb produces light with a color temperature of 2700°K to 3000°K; the light from a cool-white fluorescent lamp operates at a color temperature of about 4250°K. Generally speaking, the lower the color temperature of a light source, the warmer it will appear.

The color rendering index (CRI), which is usually published in lamp manufacturers' product catalogs, should be considered when selecting and specifying lamps. The CRI rating is a measure of a lamp's ability to render color accurately when compared with a reference light source of similar color temperature. A tungsten lamp operating at a color temperature of 3200°K, noon sunlight having a color temperature of 4800°K, and average daylight having a color temperature of 7000°K all have a CRI of 100 and are considered to render color perfectly. Fluorescent lamps have CRIs from 50 to 90; high-intensity discharge (HID) lamps have CRI ratings from 60 to 85.

| CRI | Light Source |
|-----|--------------|
| 100 | Noon sunlight; average daylight |
| 93 | 500-watt incandescent |
| 89 | Cool-white deluxe fluorescent |
| 78 | Warm-white deluxe fluorescent |
| 62 | Cool-white fluorescent |
| 52 | Warm-white fluorescent |

## Color Rendering Index (CRI) of various light sources

Incandescent lamps consist of material filaments that are heated within a glass enclosure until they glow. They are generally less expensive, easier to dim with rheostats, and warmer in color than discharge lamps. Their relatively small size and compact shape allow them to be used as point sources of light that emphasize the form and texture of objects.

Incandescent lamps are available from 6 to 1,500 watts and have a low efficacy rating of from 4 to 24.5 lumens/watt. Only about 12% of the wattage used goes toward the production of light; the remainder is heat. They also have a comparatively short life of from 750 to 4,000 hours.

Tungsten-halogen lamps, also known as halogen or quartz lamps, are incandescent lamps with a small amount of halogen gas sealed inside the bulb. They maintain close to their full output over time. Available from 5 to 1,500 watts, they produce 10 to 22 lumens per watt.

While standard incandescent lamps operate on standard-voltage circuits, low-voltage lamps are incandescent, including tungsten-halogen, lamps that operate between 6 and 75 volts. Their design offers:
- More precise beam control
- Higher efficacy
- Energy savings where focused light is needed
- 1,000–6,000 hours life

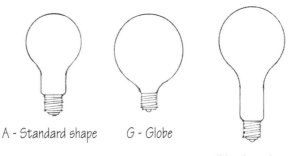

A - Standard shape    G - Globe

PS - Pear shape

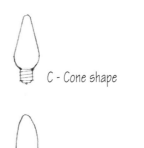

C - Cone shape

F - Flame shape

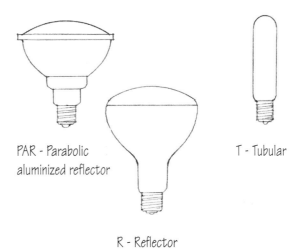

PAR - Parabolic aluminized reflector

T - Tubular

R - Reflector

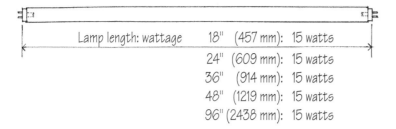

| Lamp length: wattage | 18" | (457 mm): | 15 watts |
| | 24" | (609 mm): | 15 watts |
| | 36" | (914 mm): | 15 watts |
| | 48" | (1219 mm): | 15 watts |
| | 96" | (2438 mm): | 15 watts |

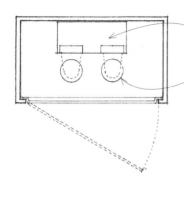

Ballast limits current and provides starting and operating lamp voltage.

Tubular lamp or bulb

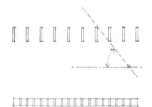

Glass or plastic lenses serve as diffusers, redirecting the light and reducing the fixture brightness.

One-way baffling can be provided by slats that should shield the length of the tubes.

Egg-crate louvers provide two-way baffling and also diffuse the light.

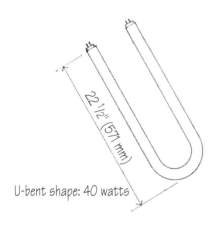

22 1/2" (571 mm)

U-bent shape: 40 watts

| 8 1/4" | (210mm): | 22 watts |
| 12" | (304 mm): | 32 watts |
| 16" | (406 mm): | 40 watts |

Circline shape

Compact fluorescent: 9 watts

Discharge lamps produce light by the discharge of electricity between electrodes in a gas-filled glass enclosure. A common type is the fluorescent lamp.

Fluorescent lamps are tubular, low-intensity, discharge lamps. They produce light by generating an electric arc that passes through the mercury vapor sealed within their tubes. This produces ultraviolet light that energizes the phosphors that coat the tubes' inner walls thus emitting visible light.

Fluorescent lamps are more efficient (efficacy of 10–104.5 lumens per watt) and have a longer life (6,000–24,000+ hours) than incandescent lamps. They produce little heat and are available from 4 to 215 watts. Fluorescent lamps require a ballast to regulate electric current through the lamp.

Manufacturers control the output and color of fluorescent lamps by changing the phosphors that coat the inner wall of the tube. There are, therefore, many types of "white" light produced by the various types of fluorescent lamps.

Standard T12 Lamp:
- Linear light source that produces diffused light
- Light can be difficult to control optically and the resulting flat light can be monotonous.
- Circular and U-shaped lamps are available to fit compact fixture housings.

T8 and T5 Lamps:
- Good color rendering
- Increased lighting efficiency
- Smaller tube diameters
- Increased luminance requires better shielding from glare.

Compact Fluorescent Lamps:
- Available from 5 to 80 watts
- High efficacy (28–76 lumens per watt)
- Good color rendering
- Very long lives (6,000–14,000 hours)
- Some are available with a built-in ballast for direct replacement of incandescent lamps.

High-intensity discharge (HID) lamps—mercury vapor, high-pressure sodium, and metal halide lamps—produce light by passing an electrical current through a gas or vapor under high pressure. These lamps have a long life expectancy and consume little energy to produce a great amount of light from a relatively small source. They take several minutes to warm up.

HID lamps were originally used primarily for lighting streets, sidewalks, and large industrial spaces. Despite their efficiency, they had uneven spectral distributions and acutely distorted the color of objects they illuminated. Because of improvements in their rendition of color, however, HID lamps are increasingly being used in large commercial and public interior spaces. Lamp technology is rapidly evolving, and new lamp types continue to come onto the market.

Mercury-vapor lamps produce light when an arc is struck in a quartz tube containing vaporized mercury. Available in 40W to 1,000W sizes, they produce twice as much light as a comparable incandescent lamp and have about the same efficacy (19–59 lumens/watt) as fluorescent lamps. Because they have a life of 12,000–24,000+ hours, they are often used when burning hours are long and service is difficult. Clear mercury lamps cast a definite blue-green light. Phosphor-coated lamps have improved efficiency and color quality, making them usable for interior lighting.

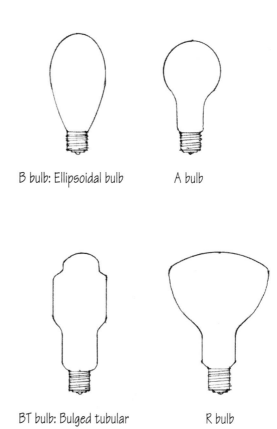

B bulb: Ellipsoidal bulb     A bulb

BT bulb: Bulged tubular     R bulb

**Mercury-Vapor Lamp Shapes**

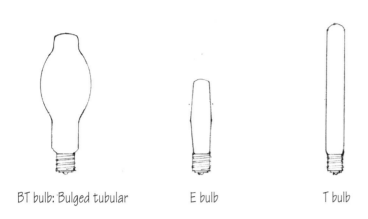

BT bulb: Bulged tubular      E bulb      T bulb

**Metal-Halide and High-Pressure Sodium Lamp Shapes**

Metal-halide lamps are similar to mercury-vapor lamps except that metal halide is added to provide more light (efficacy of 35–100 lumens/watt) and better color. They are available from 32W to 1,500W sizes and have a life of 3,000–20,000 hours. Because of their compact shape, their light can be more easily controlled optically. And because they render color fairly well, they can be used for both outdoor and interior applications.

High-pressure sodium (HPS) lamps are among the most efficient sources of light. Available in 33–1,000W sizes, they have an efficacy of 31–127 lumens/watt and a life of 7,500–24,000+ hours. Their light has an orange-tinted cast often seen in street lighting. White HPS lamps offer color-rendering properties similar to incandescent lamps, but they tend to have shorter lives and lower light levels.

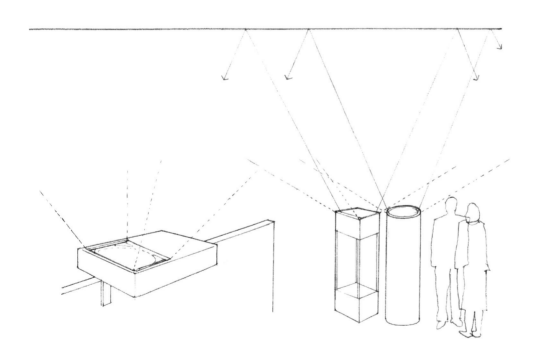

HID lights are an alternative to conventional overhead lighting in commercial interior spaces. They are often installed to provide indirect, ambient lighting by using the ceiling surface to reflect and diffuse their light.

The optical glass or plastic fibers in fiber optic lighting transmit light from one end to the other by reflecting light rays back and forth inside the fiber's core in a zigzag pattern. Each fiber is protected by a transparent sheath. Small diameter fibers are combined into flexible bundles.

A typical fiber-optic lighting system includes:
- A light projector, which may have a color wheel
- A tungsten-halogen or metal halide light source
- An optical-fiber harness
- Bundles of optical fibers and their fittings

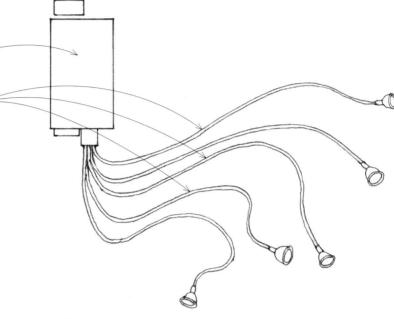

Light-emitting diode lamps (LEDs) are rated for around 100,000 hours of life. LEDs are typically very low in light output and are available in cool white, amber, green, red, and blue. The tiny $1/8$ inch (3 mm) lamps can be combined into larger groups to mix colors. They have potential as decorative lighting and are commonly used for auditorium steps and exit-sign lights.

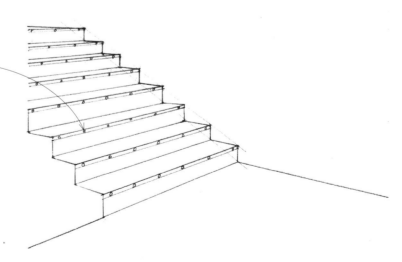

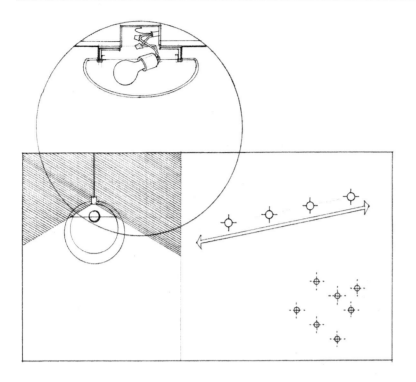

Light fixtures are integral parts of a building's electrical system, transforming energy into usable illumination. Light fixtures require an electrical connection or power supply, a housing assembly, and a lamp.

We are concerned not only with the shape and form of the fixture but also with the form of the illumination it provides. Point sources give focus to a space since the area of greatest brightness in a space tends to attract our attention. They can be used to highlight an area or an object of interest. A number of point sources can be arranged to describe rhythm and sequence. Small point sources, when grouped, can provide glitter and sparkle.

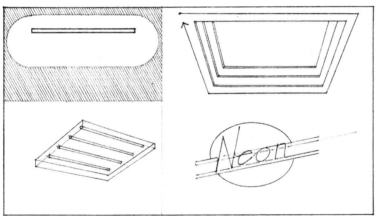

Linear sources can be used to give direction, emphasize the edges of planes, or outline an area. A parallel series of linear sources can form a plane of illumination that is effective for the general, diffused illumination of an area.

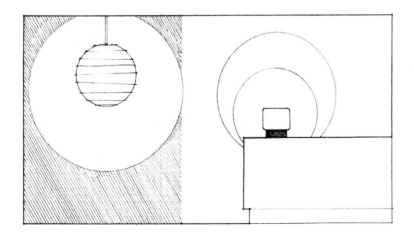

Volumetric sources are point sources expanded by the use of translucent materials into spheres, globes, or other three-dimensional forms.

A light fixture consists of one or more electric lamps with all of the necessary parts and wiring for supporting, positioning, and protecting the lamps, connecting the lamps to a power supply, and distributing the light.

Light fixtures can provide direct and/or indirect illumination. The form of distribution depends on the design of the fixture as well as its placement and orientation in a space. Some light sources serve primarily as decorative focal points. Others provide needed light while the fixtures themselves are de-emphasized or hidden.

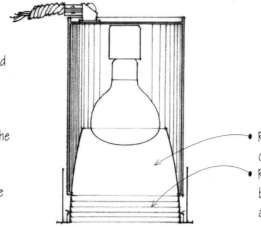

- Reflectors control the distribution of the light emitted by a lamp.
- Ridged baffles reduce the brightness of a light source at the aperture of the housing.

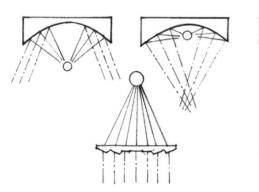

- Baffles, such as louvers and eggcrates, redirect the emitted light and/or shield the light source from view at certain angles.

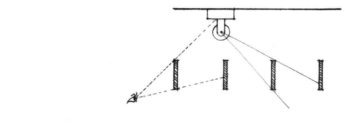
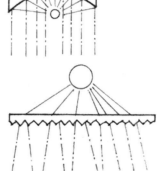

- Parabolic reflectors spread, focus, or collimate (make parallel) the rays from a light source.

- Lens are used to focus or disperse the emitted light.

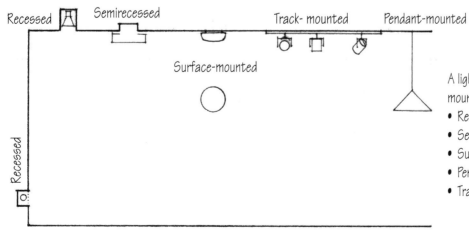

Recessed    Semirecessed    Track- mounted    Pendant-mounted

Surface-mounted

Recessed

A light fixture's housing may be mounted on a ceiling or wall and be:
- Recessed
- Semirecessed
- Surface-mounted
- Pendant-mounted
- Track-mounted

253

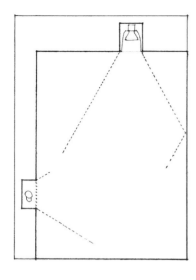

Lighting fixtures may be recessed in the ceiling or a wall.

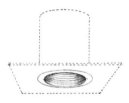

Baffled downlight

Adjustable eyeball

Pinhole downlight

Baffled wall washer

Recessed lighting fixtures are hidden above the finished ceiling and shine light through an aperture in the ceiling plane. They preserve the flat plane of the ceiling. When lit, their brightness can be discretely de-emphasized against a bright ceiling. However, some recessed fixtures appear as black holes in a light ceiling when they are turned off.

Recessed lighting fixtures offer an unobtrusive way to bring light to circulation paths within a larger space or to provide increased light levels in a specific area. When used indiscriminately throughout a space, however, they can create a monotonously even pattern on the ceiling and a uniform but dull level of illumination.

Downlights are used in multiple arrangements to provide ambient light for a large space or to offer a focal glow on a floor or work surface. The lamps for recessed incandescent downlights are available as floods, spots, and pinpoints, allowing the designer a range of effects. They are usually mounted in a reflector to control the brightness and distribution of the emitted light.

Downlights located too close to a wall can create an unattractive scalloped pattern. Wall washers are designed to illuminate a matte vertical surface in a more uniform manner. Individual wall washers can be placed one-third of the wall height away from the wall and an equal distance from each other.

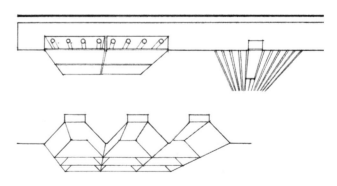

Recessed lighting fixtures often form part of suspended ceiling systems.

The housings of some light fixtures are partially
recessed into the ceiling or wall construction while
part of their housing, reflectors, or lenses project
beyond the ceiling or wall surface.

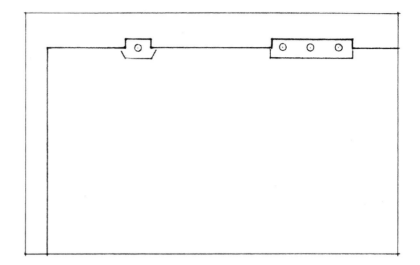

Fixtures that shine down from above can cause glare
on computer screens, especially if the lamps are
visible or if the fixture creates a bright area in the
darker field of the ceiling.

Diffusers provide some protection, but suspended
fixtures that bounce light off the ceiling and filter
light downward as well may do a better job of
minimizing glare.

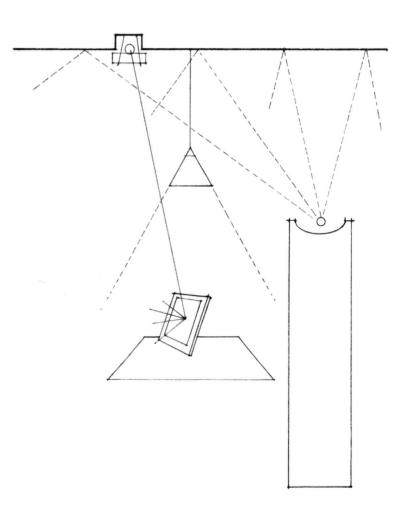

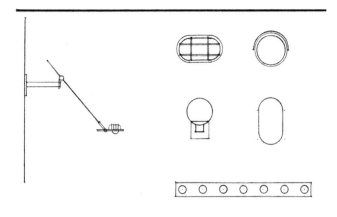

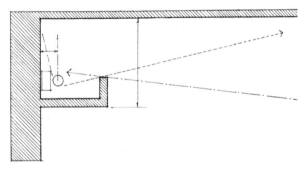

Surface-mounted light fixtures are mounted on the finished ceiling or wall and are usually attached to a recessed junction box. Light fixtures that are mounted directly on a ceiling are generally positioned above the people and furnishings in the room and can spread their light over a broad area.

Wall-mounted light fixtures are often decorative and help to create the ambience of the space. Wall sconces can shine light upward, downward or sideways, as well as produce a gentle glow from the fixture itself.

Wall-mounted fixtures can provide task lighting, their illumination focused on the task area. When shining on a wall or ceiling, they add to the general illumination of the space. Their horizontal and vertical positions must be carefully coordinated with windows and with furnishings.

Cove, valance, and cornice lighting are all methods for illuminating a space indirectly from within an architectural detail or a manufactured fixture. They give a soft, indirect glow to the area they illuminate and are often used to highlight ceiling details or wall textures.

Cove lighting directs the light upward from an interior cornice at the edge of a ceiling

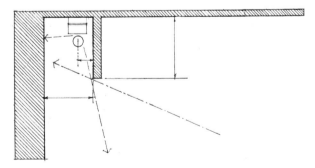

Cornice lighting directs the light downward from an interior cornice at the edge of a ceiling.

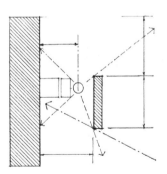

Valance lighting directs the light upward or downward from a light source concealed by a horizontal board or band.

Pendant-mounted light fixtures are attached to either a recessed or surface-mounted junction box concealed by a canopy and hang below the ceiling on a stem, chain, or cord. The fixtures may throw light up, down, or at an adjustable angle.

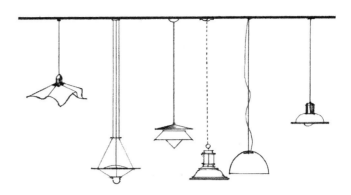

Chandeliers often provide more sparkle than illumination and become a focal point in the space.

Uplights or indirect lighting fixtures wash the ceiling in light. Some also provide downlight. They may be:
• Suspended from the ceiling
• Mounted on top of tall furniture
• Attached to walls, columns, or floor stands

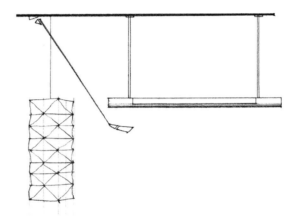

## Track-Mounted Fixtures

Track-mounted light fixtures consist of adjustable spotlights or floodlights mounted on a recessed, surface-mounted, or pendant-mounted track through which current is conducted. The light fixtures can be moved along the track and adjusted to shed light in multiple directions.

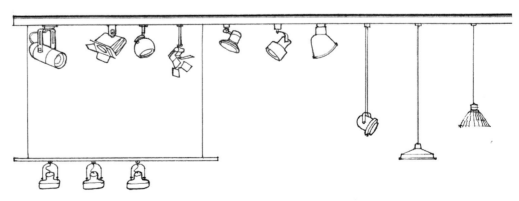

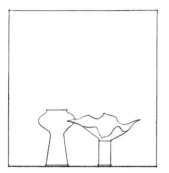

Decorative lights serve as accents within the space. The light they produce may be secondary to the appearance of the fixture, whose glowing surface draws the eye.

Desk and task lamps are found in both residential and work spaces. Many are adjustable to accommodate varied tasks and individual preferences.

Table lamps often serve both decorative and practical functions. They become part of a room's décor, while providing either general illumination or task light.

Floor lamps may shine up (torchières), down, or at adjustable angles. Like table lamps, they become part of the décor and can provide either task or general lighting.

Portable lamps help to bring human scale to architectural spaces by creating decorative detail and localized light. They also are usually easily controlled at the fixture itself, giving users easy control over their environment.

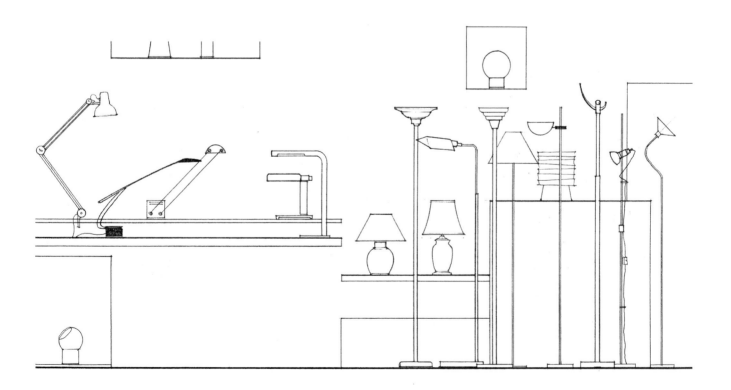

The layout of lighting fixtures and the pattern of light they radiate should be coordinated with the architectural features of a space and the pattern of its use. Since our eyes seek the brightest objects and the strongest tonal contrasts in their fields of vision, this coordination is particularly important in the planning of localized or task lighting.

For the purpose of planning the visual composition of a lighting design, a light source can be considered to have the form of a point, a line, a plane, or a volume. If the light source is shielded from view, then the form of the light emitted and the shape of surface illumination produced should be considered. Whether the pattern of light sources is regular or varied, a lighting design should be balanced in its composition, provide an appropriate sense of rhythm, and give emphasis to what is important.

Lighting design manipulates the fundamental elements and qualities of ambient and focal lighting as well as sparkle.

• *Ambient lighting* provides a basic, shadowless light level that is restful and minimizes interest in objects and people.

• *Focal lighting* offers a contrast in brightness that is directive and creates a sense of depth. Examples include spotlights, beacon sunburst, and reading lamps.

• *Sparkle*—such as highlights, scintillating sequins, crystal chandeliers, and twinkling stars— is stimulating and can heighten sensations. Sparkle may be distracting, but it is also often entertaining.

Light animates space and reveals forms and textures.

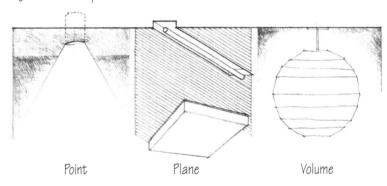

Point   Plane   Volume

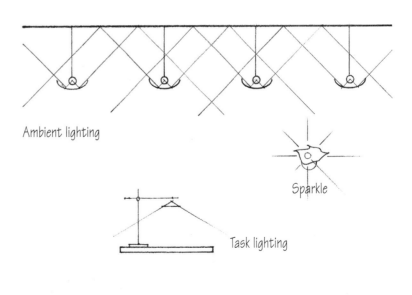

Ambient lighting

Sparkle

Task lighting

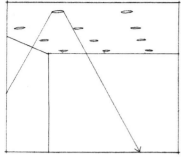

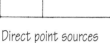

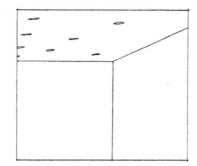

Direct point sources

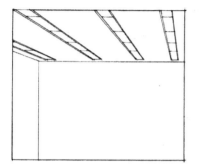

Direct linear sources

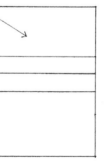

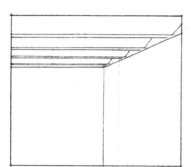

Direct/indirect linear sources

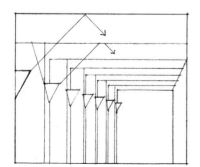

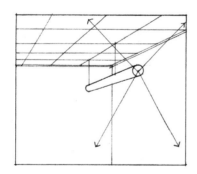

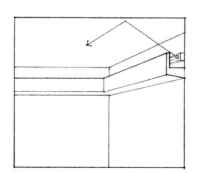

Indirect point sources

Indirect linear sources

Ambient or general lighting illuminates a room in a fairly uniform, generally diffuse manner. The dispersed quality of the illumination can effectively reduce the contrast between task lighting and the surrounding surfaces of a room. Ambient lighting can also be used to soften shadows, smooth out and expand the corners of a room, and provide a comfortable level of illumination for safe movement and general maintenance.

General-ambient systems are appropriate for frequently reconfigured spaces and where the location of tasks varies widely.

Task-ambient systems provide higher-level focal lighting for task areas, with surrounding areas illuminated at a lower level. Task-ambient lighting saves energy and improves the quality of lighting.

Focal lighting creates brighter areas within the ambient light levels of a space through the use of task lighting and accent lighting.

Task or local lighting illuminates specific areas of a space for the performance of visual tasks or activities. The light sources are usually placed close to—either above or beside—the task surface, enabling the available wattage to be used more efficiently than with ambient lighting. The lighting fixtures are normally of the direct type, and adjustability with dimmers in terms of brightness and direction is always desirable.

To minimize the risk of an unacceptable brightness ratio between task and surroundings, task lighting is often combined with ambient lighting. Depending on the types of lighting fixtures used, local lighting can also contribute to the general illumination of a space.

In addition to making a visual task easier to see, local lighting can also create variety and interest, partition a space into a number of areas, encompass a furniture grouping, or reinforce the social character of a room.

## Accent Lighting

Accent lighting is a form of focal lighting that creates focal points or rhythmic patterns of light and dark within a space. Instead of serving simply to illuminate a task or activity, accent lighting can be used to relieve the monotony of ambient lighting, emphasize a room's features, or highlight art objects or prized possessions.

Lighting can bring out the highlights in the objects that it shines on or introduce sparkle in the brilliance of the fixture itself. Small, tightly focused tungsten-halogen lamps reflect dancing bits of light off reflective surfaces. Chandeliers often produce little ambient light; they are all about sparkle.

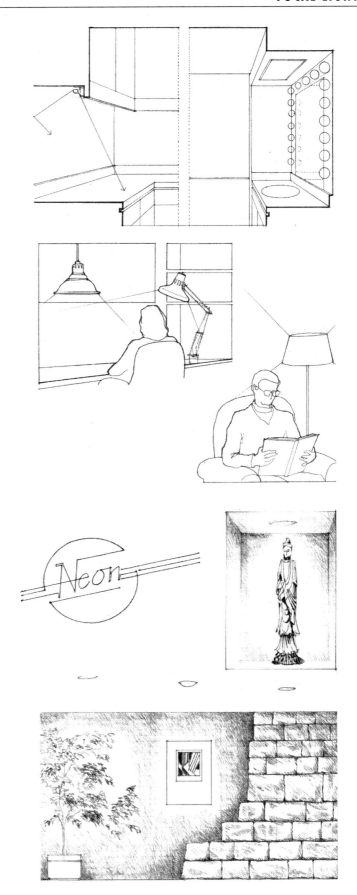

The properties of light, especially luminous intensity, is measured by the science of photometry.

Luminous intensity refers to the amount of luminous flux emitted in a specific direction by a source, expressed in candelas. The term candlepower is often used to describe the relative intensity of a light source.

Luminous flux is the rate of flow of visible light, expressed in lumens. One lumen is equivalent to the quantity of light, emitted from a point source of one candela, which passes through a one square-foot area of a one-foot diameter sphere surrounding the point source.

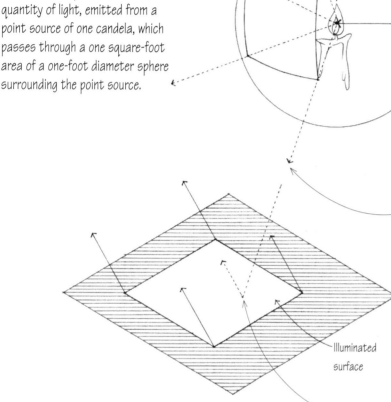

Illuminated surface

Illuminance is the intensity of light falling at any given place on a lighted surface, equal to the luminous flux incident per unit area and expressed in lumens per unit of area.

One footcandle is a unit of illuminance equal to one lumen spread evenly over an area of one square foot. Illuminance calculations overlook the aesthetic, psychological, and physiological variables of vision, including the ability of the eye to adapt to varying light levels over time. ESI (Equivalent Sphere Illumination) footcandle is a measure of density at a given location in a room. It is a better measure of lighting performance since it takes into account the ability of a fixture to control glare and reflections.

Brightness is our subjective perception of varying degrees of light intensity. Since the majority of what we see is due to the light reflected from the surfaces in a room, brightness is measured by the total quantity of light emitted, reflected, or transmitted in all directions from a surface.

Luminance is a quantitative measure of brightness of a light source or an illuminated surface, equal to the luminous intensity per unit projected area of the source or surface viewed from a given direction and expressed in foot-lamberts. One foot-lambert is equal to 0.32 candela per square foot. Luminance is probably the best measure of how we perceive light.

A successful lighting design is determined by the balance of relative luminances, rather than by the quantity of illuminance striking the surfaces of a room. Measurements of Illuminance, however, are used to select lamps and lighting fixtures and to evaluate a lighting design. The photometric data to be considered includes:

- The Luminous-Intensity Distribution Curve (LIDC) represents the light pattern produced by a lamp or light fixture in a given direction from the center of the light source. This information is usually available from lighting fixture manufacturers.

- The Coefficient of Utilization (CU) indicates the efficiency of a light fixture. The CU is expressed as the ratio of the luminous flux reaching a specified work plane to the total lumen output of a light fixture.

- The Light Loss Factor (LLF) is used in calculating the effective illumination provided by a lighting system after a given period of time and under given conditions. The LLF reflects the decrease in luminous output that occurs due to such factors as the loss of lumen output over the operating life of a lamp, the accumulation of dirt on the surfaces of a light fixture, and the effects of temperature.

**Direct-Concentrating**
*0%–10% upward*
*90%–100% downward*

**Direct-Spread**
*0%–10% upward*
*90%–100% downward*

**Semidirect**
*10%–40% upward*
*60%–90% downward*

**General Diffuse**
*40%–60% upward*
*40%–60% downward*

**Semi-Indirect**
*60%–90% upward*
*10%–40% downward*

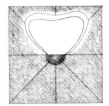

**Indirect**
*90%–100% upward*
*0%–10% downward*

**Direct-Indirect**
*40%–60% upward*
*40%–60% downward*

Light fixtures may be classified according to how they distribute the light emitted by their lamps. The basic types listed here are based on the percentage of light emitted above and below the horizontal.

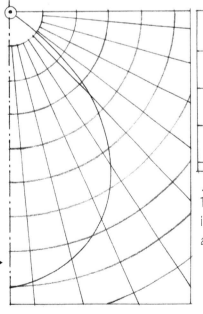

An example of a Luminous-Intensity Distribution Curve of a light fixture. ►

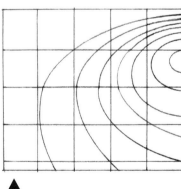

▲
The isochart plots the pattern of illumination produced on a surface by a lamp or light fixture.

The lumen or zonal cavity method calculates the number and types of lamps and light fixtures required to provide a uniform level of illuminance on a work plane, taking into account both direct and reflected luminous flux, the room's size, proportions and reflectances, and the manufacturer's photometric test reports.

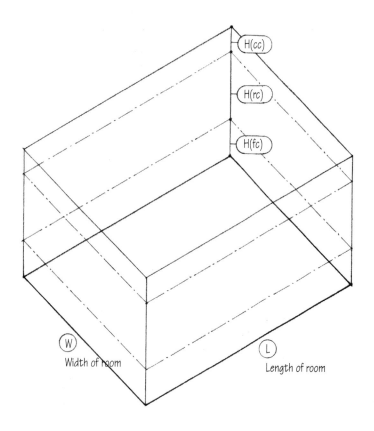

H(cc): Height of the ceiling cavity, measured from the ceiling to a horizontal luminaire plane.

H(rc): Height of the room cavity, measured from the luminaire plane to a horizontal work plane across the task surfaces.

H(fc): Height of the floor cavity, measured from the work plane to the floor.

W — Width of room

L — Length of room

Illuminance values are typically listed in footcandles and usually represent the amount of light striking a horizontal plane 30 inches (762 mm) above the floor. They have limited use when applied to actual interior conditions, since they do not take into account wall lighting, brightness, accents, shadow, sparkle, or color. Illuminance requirements vary with the visual difficulty of the work task, the age and condition of the viewers' eyes, and the importance of speed and accuracy.

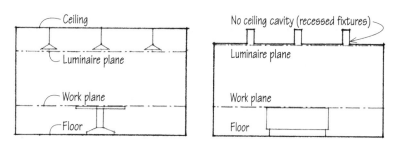

Ceiling
Luminaire plane
Work plane
Floor

No ceiling cavity (recessed fixtures)
Luminaire plane
Work plane
Floor

Computer programs offer the most accurate means of determining the number and locations of lighting fixtures for an application.

Light is the prime animator of interior space. Without light, there would be no visible form, color, or texture nor any visible enclosure of interior space. The first function of lighting design, therefore, is to illuminate the forms and space of an interior environment and enable users to undertake activities and perform tasks with appropriate speed, accuracy, and comfort. Interior lighting can effectively guide the viewer through a space or series of spaces and direct the viewer's gaze to points of interest. Lighting also provides security through the illumination of spaces and the potential hazards that may exist.

Interior lighting enables us to:
• See forms
• Navigate space
• Perform tasks

Lighting design is a process of integrating light with:
• The physical structure of the building
• The designer's concept for the interior space
• The functional uses of the space

## Lighting Patterns

Poorly placed or irregularly scattered lighting fixtures contribute to distracting visual clutter.

• Carefully organized lighting patterns emphasize architectural features, provide cues to the use and orientation of the space, and support the designer's intent.
• Lighting layout drawings coordinate lighting fixture locations with sprinkler heads, air diffusers, return grilles, smoke detectors, loudspeakers, and other ceiling elements.

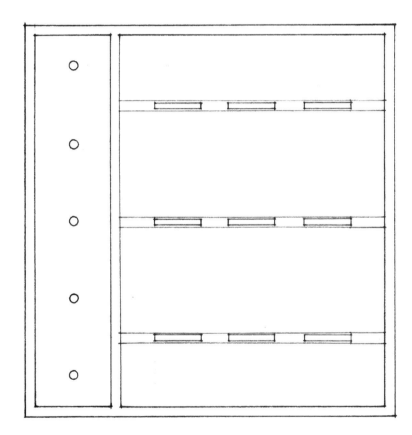

## Brightness Balance

Vertical surfaces are the most visually conspicuous features in a space. Lighting should preserve the integrity of vertical planes, highlight special features or finishes, and avoid spatial distortions such as scallops on walls.

- Light opposite walls of a space.
- Wall washers on one wall can be mixed with nonuniform lighting on the other.
- Balance perimeter illumination of a space with its center and adding downlights in the center if necessary.
- Lighting horizontal surfaces within a space emphasizes detail, people and movement, and de-emphasizes the architecture.
- Illuminate vertical and overhead surfaces to emphasize the architectural envelope.

## Luminance Ratios

Luminance differences are specified as a ratio between one luminance and another.

- Vary luminances at some points in the space to increase visual interest and prevent eye fatigue.
- Computer visual display terminals (VDTs) tend to reflect surrounding walls, ceilings, windows, and lighting fixtures, causing visual fatigue in the user. Use lighting fixtures with luminance matching the ceiling and any indirect lighting systems.

## Shadows

Patterns of light and shade create visual interest by rendering the texture and three-dimensional form of objects.

## Energy Efficiency

Building codes limit the number of watts available for lighting.

- Use available watts to supply light where and when needed; limit unwanted light.
- Use daylight as much as possible.
- Choose light sources carefully and locate them with discretion.
- Control lighting with dimmers, timers, and occupancy sensors when possible.

Acoustics is the branch of physics that deals with the production, control, transmission, reception, and effects of sound. In interior design, we are concerned with the control of sound in interior spaces. More specifically, we want to preserve and enhance desired sounds and reduce or eliminate sounds that would interfere with our activities.

Sound is the sensation stimulated by mechanical radiant energy transmitted as longitudinal pressure waves through the air or other elastic medium. A sound wave travels outward spherically from its source until it encounters an obstacle in its path.

In a room, we first hear a sound directly from its source and then a series of reflections of that sound. Reflective surfaces are useful when they reinforce desirable sounds by directing and distributing their paths in a room. The continued presence of reflected sounds, however, can also cause problems of echo, flutter, or reverberation.

Echoes can occur in large spaces when parallel reflective surfaces spaced more than 60 feet (18 m) apart reflect sound waves that are loud enough and received late enough to be perceived as distinct from the source. In smaller rooms, parallel reflective surfaces can cause a rapid succession of echoes we call flutter.

Reverberation refers to the persistence of a sound within a space, caused by multiple reflections of the sound after its source has stopped. While some music is enhanced by long reverberation times, speech can become muddled in such an acoustic environment. To ensure the clarity of sound, it may be necessary to alter the shape and orientation of a room's surfaces or adjust the ratio of reflective and absorbent materials.

The requirements for sound level, reverberation time, and resonance vary with the nature of the activity and the types of sounds generated. An acoustical engineer, given stated criteria, can determine the acoustical requirements for a space. The interior designer should be aware of how the selection and disposition of reflective and absorbent materials affect the acoustical qualities of a room.

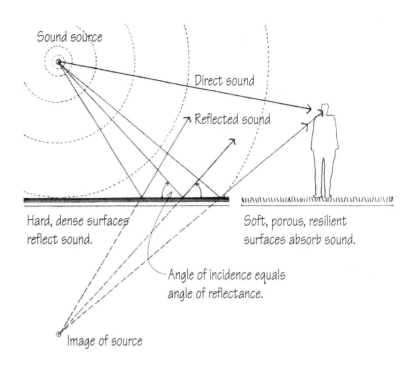

Sound source

Direct sound

Reflected sound

Hard, dense surfaces reflect sound.

Soft, porous, resilient surfaces absorb sound.

Angle of incidence equals angle of reflectance.

Image of source

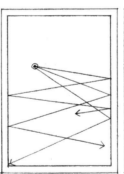
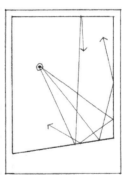
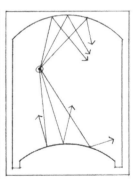

Parallel reflective surfaces can cause echoes and flutter.

Splayed surfaces can fragment sound.

Concave surfaces focus sound; convex surfaces diffuse sound.

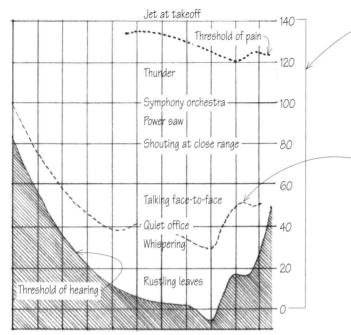

Audio frequency from 15 Hz to 16,000 Hz

Decibel (dB) is a unit for expressing the relative pressure or intensity of sounds on a uniform scale from 0 for the least perceptible sound to about 130 for the average threshold of pain. Because decibel measurement is based on a logarithmic scale, the decibel levels of two sound sources cannot be added mathematically: e.g., 60 dB + 60 dB = 63 dB, not 120 dB.

An equal loudness contour is a curve that represents the sound pressure level at which sounds of different frequencies are judged by a group of listeners to be equally loud.

## Noise

We refer to unwanted, annoying, or discordant sounds as noise. Noise can be controlled in three ways.
- Isolate the noise at its source.
- Locate noisy areas as far away as possible from quiet areas.
- Reduce the transmission of sound from one space to another.

## Isolating Sound

Sound can be transmitted through the air as well as through the solid materials of a building's structure. Because structure-borne sounds are difficult to control, they should, whenever possible, be isolated at their source.

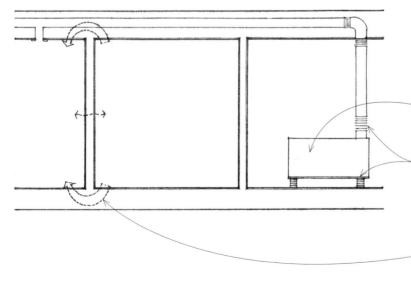

- Select mechanical equipment with low sone ratings. Sone is a unit for measuring the apparent loudness of a sound.
- Use resilient mountings and flexible connections to isolate equipment vibrations from the building structure.
- Inertia blocks increase the mass of equipment and decrease the potential for vibratory movement.
- Eliminate flanking paths along interconnecting ductwork or piping that the noise can take from its source to the space.

## Reducing Noise

Noise reduction, expressed in decibels, refers to the perceived difference in sound pressure levels between two enclosed spaces, due to:

- The transmission loss through the wall, floor, and ceiling construction
- The absorptive qualities of the receiving space
- The level of masking or background sound, which increases the threshold of audibility for other sounds in its presence

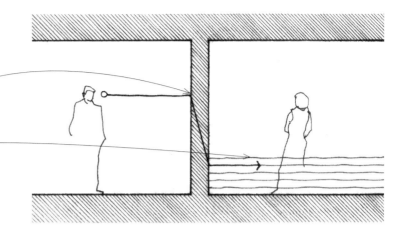

Background or ambient sound is normally present in an environment, comprising both exterior and interior sources, none of which is distinctly identifiable by the listener. A type of background sound called white noise is sometimes deliberately introduced into a space to mask or obliterate unwanted sound.

The required noise reduction from one space to another depends on the level of the sound source and the level of the sound's intrusion that may be acceptable to the listener.

The Noise Criteria Curve is one of several curves representing the sound pressure level across the frequency spectrum for background noise that should not be exceeded in various environments. Higher noise levels are permitted at the lower frequencies because the human ear is less sensitive to sounds in this frequency region.

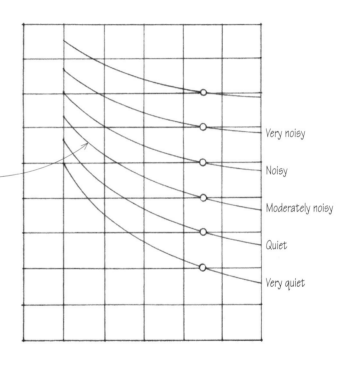

Very noisy

Noisy

Moderately noisy

Quiet

Very quiet

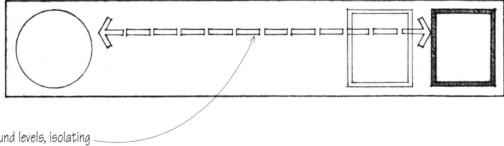

## Organizing the Plan

- Zone activities according to sound levels, isolating quiet areas from noisier ones or separating them with mass or distance.

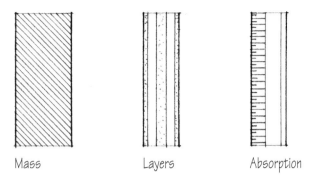

Mass           Layers           Absorption

Transmission Loss (TL) is a measure of the performance of a building material or construction assembly in preventing the transmission of airborne sound as it passes through the material or assembly. Three factors enhance the TL rating of a construction assembly:

- *Mass.* In general, the heavier and more dense a body, the greater its resistance to sound transmission.
- *Separation into layers.* Introducing discontinuity in the construction assembly disrupts the path through which structure-borne sound may be transmitted from one space to another.
- *Absorptive capacity.* Absorptive materials help to dissipate both reflected and transmitted sound in a room.

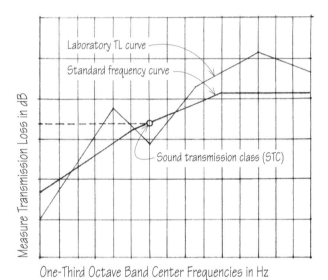

Measure Transmission Loss in dB

Laboratory TL curve

Standard frequency curve

Sound transmission class (STC)

One-Third Octave Band Center Frequencies in Hz

Comparing the laboratory TL curve of a building material or construction assembly to a standard frequency curve results in a single-number rating of the sound-isolating performance of the material or assembly called the Sound Transmission Class (STC). The higher the STC rating, the greater the sound-isolating value of the material or construction. An open doorway has an STC rating of 10; normal construction has STC ratings from 30 to 60; special construction is required for STC ratings above 60.

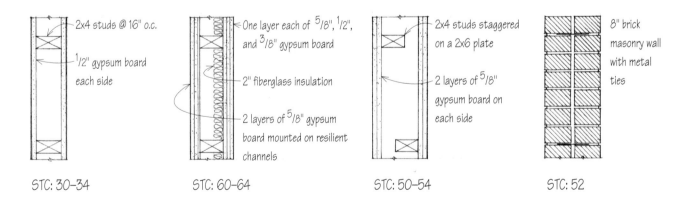

2x4 studs @ 16" o.c.

1/2" gypsum board each side

STC: 30–34

One layer each of $^5/8$", $^1/2$", and $^3/8$" gypsum board

2" fiberglass insulation

2 layers of $^5/8$" gypsum board mounted on resilient channels

STC: 60–64

2x4 studs staggered on a 2x6 plate

2 layers of $^5/8$" gypsum board on each side

STC: 50–54

8" brick masonry wall with metal ties

STC: 52

Staggering the studs of a wall or partition—forming two separate rows of studs arranged in a zigzag fashion—breaks the continuity of the path through which structure-borne sound can be transmitted.

Installing a fiberglass blanket in between the two rows of studs increases the transmission loss.

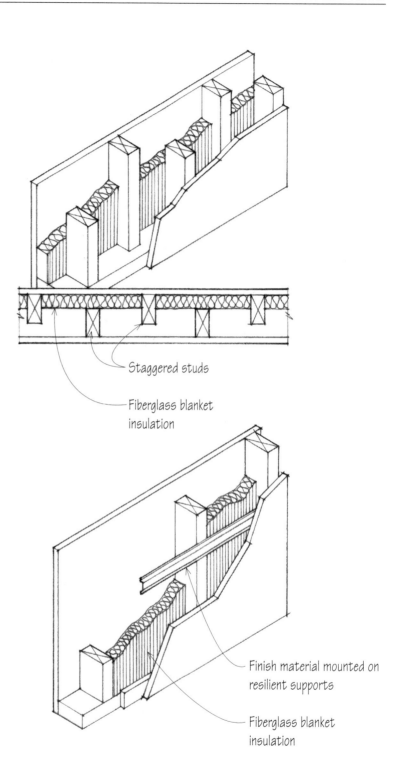

Staggered studs

Fiberglass blanket insulation

Mounting the finish material on flexible or resilient attachments or supports permits the surface to vibrate normally without transmitting the vibratory motions and associated noise to the supporting structure.

Finish material mounted on resilient supports

Fiberglass blanket insulation

Sound can be transmitted through any clear air path, even the tiniest cracks around doors, windows, and electrical outlets. Careful sealing of these openings can help prevent airborne noise from entering a room.

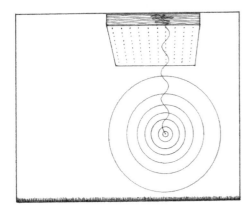

The sound-absorptive qualities of a material depend on its thickness, density, porosity, and resistance to airflow. Fibrous materials allow the passage of air while trapping sound energy and are, therefore, often used in acoustic materials such as batts and blankets of fiberglass or mineral fiber.

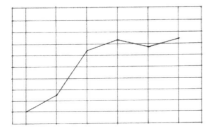

The Absorption Coefficient measures how efficiently a material absorbs sound. When all of the sound energy striking the material is absorbed and none of it is reflected, the absorption coefficient is 1.0. Because different materials reflect and absorb different sound frequencies, the absorption coefficients at 250, 500, 1,000, and 2,000 Hz are averaged together to arrive at the Noise Reduction Coefficient (NRC), which is useful for measuring the effectiveness of a porous sound absorber at midrange frequencies.

In a normally constructed room without acoustical treatment, sound waves strike the wall, ceiling, and floor surfaces, which then transmit a small portion of the sound to adjacent spaces. The surfaces absorb another small amount, but most of the sound is reflected back into the room.

Absorptive materials can change the reverberation characteristics of a room by dissipating some of the incident sound energy and reducing the portion of the sound transmitted. This is particularly helpful in spaces with distributed noise sources, like offices, schools, and restaurants.

Reducing reverberation from the ceiling plane is usually the most effective approach to sound control in a room. Acoustical ceiling tiles are excellent absorbers of sound. They absorb more sound when mounted in a suspended ceiling system than when attached directly to a surface. Perforated metal ceiling panels with acoustic backing and acoustical ceiling panels made of bonded wood fibers also work well to control noise.

Treating walls and floors also helps to control sound. Acoustical wall panels usually have fire-rated fabric coverings.

Carpet is the only floor finish that absorbs sound. In addition, it can cushion footfalls and the sounds of furniture movement, thus limiting sound transmission to the space below.

Interior designers are often faced with the need to provide speech privacy in offices. Combining ceiling and wall treatments with careful siting of furnishings helps to keep sounds from spreading. Electronic sound-masking systems can also help to reduce the intelligibility of overheard speech.

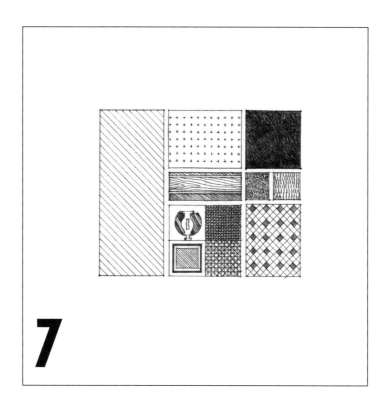

**7**

# Finish Materials

Finish materials may be an integral part of the architectural assemblies that define an interior space, or they may be added as an additional layer or coating to the constructed walls, ceilings, and floors of a room. In either case, they should be selected with the architectural context in mind. Together with furnishings, finish materials play a significant role in creating the desired atmosphere in an interior space.

In specifying finish materials, there are functional, aesthetic, and economic factors to consider.

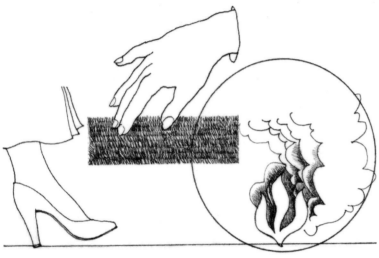

# FINISH MATERIALS

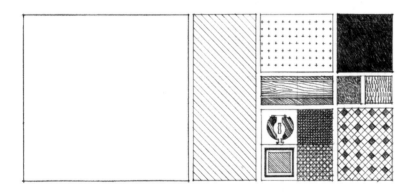

## Functional Criteria

- Safety and comfort
- Durability in anticipated use
- Ease of cleaning, maintenance and repair
- Required degree of fire-resistance
- Appropriate acoustic properties

## Aesthetic Criteria

- Color, natural or applied
- Texture
- Pattern

## Economic Criteria

- Initial cost of acquisition and installation
- Lifetime cost, the expected durability of the material and the costs for cleaning, maintenance, and repair over the anticipated life of the material as well as the cost of replacing the material when necessary.

Finish flooring is the final layer of the floor structure. Because flooring is subject to direct wear and represents a major portion of a room's surface area, it should be selected with both functional and aesthetic criteria in mind.

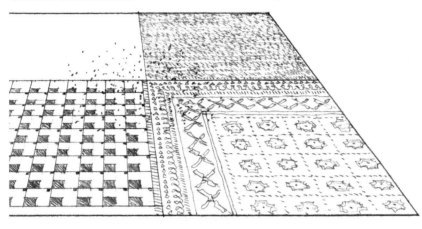

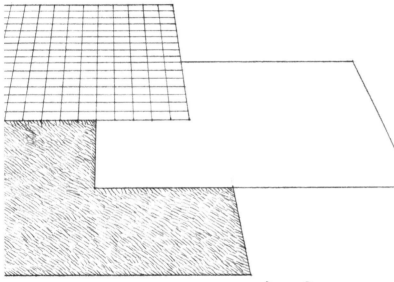

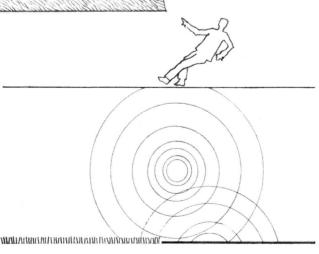

- Durability is of utmost importance because of the wear and use a flooring material must withstand from our feet as well as the occasional moving of furniture and equipment. The flooring material should be resistant to physical abrasion, denting, and scuffing.
- Directly related to a flooring's durability is the ease with which it can be maintained in good condition. For durability as well as ease of maintenance, a flooring material should be resistant to dirt, moisture, grease, and staining, especially in work and high-traffic areas.
- There are several strategies for disguising the dirt that normally collects on a floor. One is to use a mixture of neutral colors of middle value. Another is to use a pattern that camouflages any dirt and surface marks. Still another is to use a material whose natural color and texture is attractive and more noticeable than any dirt on the floor.
- Foot comfort is related to the degree of resilience a flooring material has and, to a lesser degree, its warmth.
- The warmth of a floor may be real or apparent. A flooring material may be warmed by radiant heat and kept warm by its own thermal mass or by insulating the floor. The flooring may also appear warm if it has a soft texture, a middle to dark value, or a warm hue. Of course, in warm climates, a cool floor surface would be more comfortable than a warm one.
- In areas susceptible to wetting, it is advisable to avoid using hard, slick flooring materials.
- Hard floor surfaces reflect airborne sound originating from within a room, and amplify impact noise caused by our footwear or the moving of equipment. Resilient flooring can cushion some of this impact noise. Soft, plush, or porous flooring materials reduce impact noise as well as help muffle airborne sound reaching their surfaces.

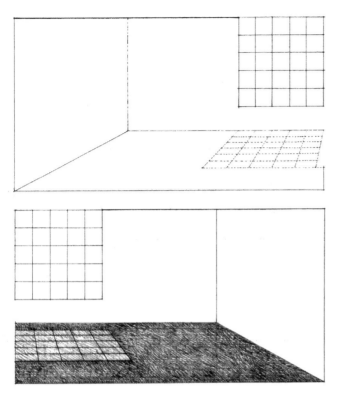

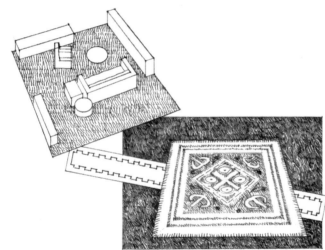

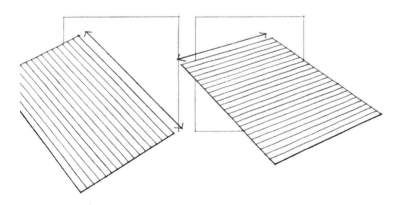

Although generally considered to be a utilitarian surface and a visual background for an interior space, the floor can, through its color, pattern, and texture, play an active role in determining the character of a space.

• A light-colored floor will enhance the light level within a room, while a dark floor will absorb much of the light falling on its surface. A warm, light color has an elevating effect on a floor, while a warm, dark floor conveys a sense of security. A cool, light color suggests spaciousness and emphasizes the smoothness of polished floors. A cool, dark color gives a floor plane depth and weight.

• Unlike the wall and ceiling surfaces of a room, a floor transmits its tactile qualities—its texture and density—directly to us as we walk across its surface.

• The physical texture of a flooring material and how the material is laid are directly related to the visual pattern created. It is this visual texture that communicates to us the nature of the flooring material and the character of a space.

• While a neutral, patternless floor can serve as a simple background for a room's occupants and furnishings, a floor can also become, through the use of pattern, a dominant element in an interior space. The pattern can be used to define areas, suggest paths of movement, or simply provide textural interest.

• Our perception of a flooring pattern is affected by the laws of perspective. Thus a small-scale pattern may often be seen as a fine texture or a blended tone rather than as a composition of individual design elements.

• In addition, any continuous linear elements in a flooring pattern will dominate. Directional patterns can often affect the apparent proportion of a floor, either exaggerating or foreshortening one of its dimensions.

Finish flooring is usually separated into two groups: hard flooring, such as wood, stone, tile, and resilient flooring, and soft floor coverings, which consist primarily of carpets and rugs. Of the hard floor coverings, wood flooring is admired for its warm, natural appearance and its attractive blend of comfort, resilience, and durability. It is also fairly easy to maintain under moderate use and, if damaged, can be refinished or replaced.

Durable, close-grained species of hardwoods (white and red oak, maple, birch, beech, and pecan) and soft woods (Southern pine, Douglas fir, Western larch, hemlock, and others) are used for wood flooring. Of these, oak, Southern pine, and Douglas fir are the most common. The best grades are clear or select and will minimize or exclude defects, such as knots, streaks, checks, and torn grain.

Other types of wood used for floor include bamboo and antique wood flooring. Bamboo is technically a grass and Its ability to regrow quickly after harvesting has earned it a reputation as a sustainable material. Antique wood flooring, retrieved from buildings that are about to be demolished, offers a distinctive character and patina.

Wood flooring is available in boards or manufactured blocks and panels.

Wood flooring is most often finished with a clear polyurethane, varnish, or a penetrating sealer; the finishes can range from high gloss to satin or a dull sheen. Ideally, the finish should enhance the durability of the wood and its resistance to water, dirt, and staining without concealing the wood's natural beauty. Stains are used to add some color to the natural color of the wood without obscuring the wood grain. Wood flooring can also be waxed, painted, or even stenciled, but painted surfaces require more maintenance.

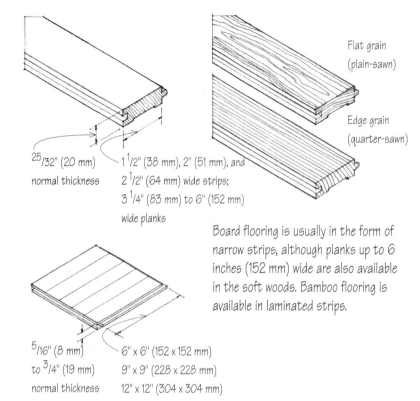

Flat grain (plain-sawn)

Edge grain (quarter-sawn)

25/32" (20 mm) normal thickness

1 1/2" (38 mm), 2" (51 mm), and 2 1/2" (64 mm) wide strips; 3 1/4" (83 mm) to 6" (152 mm) wide planks

Board flooring is usually in the form of narrow strips, although planks up to 6 inches (152 mm) wide are also available in the soft woods. Bamboo flooring is available in laminated strips.

5/16" (8 mm) to 3/4" (19 mm) normal thickness

6" x 6" (152 x 152 mm) 9" x 9" (228 x 228 mm) 12" x 12" (304 x 304 mm)

Parquet blocks consist of strip flooring, factory-assembled into squares with various geometric patterns.

Prefinished panels that have the appearance of traditional strip flooring are another type of factory-made flooring. Engineered hardwood flooring is impregnated with acrylic or sealed with urethane or vinyl. Laminated flooring assembles high-pressure laminates, including wood veneers, into durable, acrylic-urethane sealed panels. Bamboo is also laminated under high pressure, milled into planks, immersed in polyurethane, and coated with acrylic polyurethane.

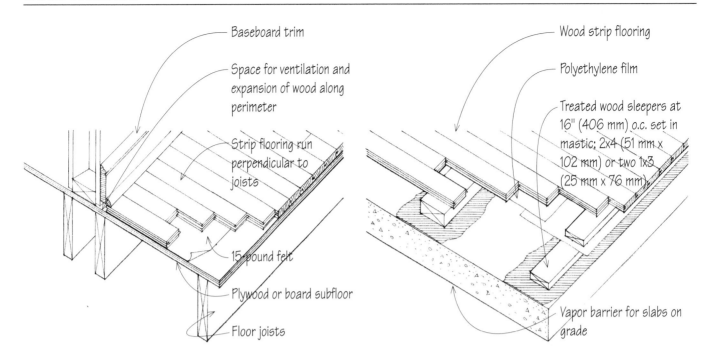

Baseboard trim

Space for ventilation and expansion of wood along perimeter

Strip flooring run perpendicular to joists

15-pound felt

Plywood or board subfloor

Floor joists

Wood strip flooring

Polyethylene film

Treated wood sleepers at 16" (406 mm) o.c. set in mastic; 2x4 (51 mm x 102 mm) or two 1x3 (25 mm x 76 mm)

Vapor barrier for slabs on grade

**Wood Flooring over a Subfloor and Joists**

**Wood Flooring over a Concrete Slab**

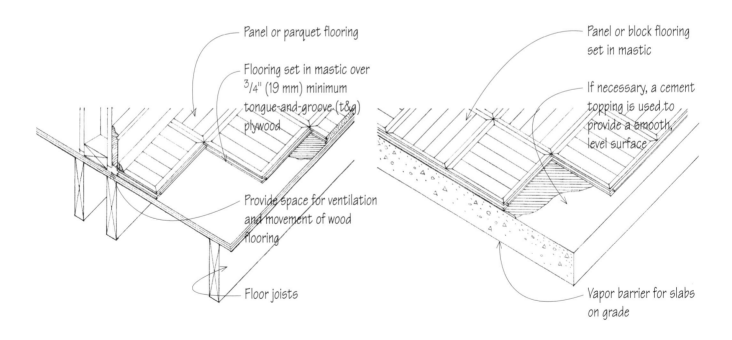

Panel or parquet flooring

Flooring set in mastic over ³/₄" (19 mm) minimum tongue-and-groove (t&g) plywood

Provide space for ventilation and movement of wood flooring

Floor joists

Panel or block flooring set in mastic

If necessary, a cement topping is used to provide a smooth, level surface

Vapor barrier for slabs on grade

**Wood Flooring over a Subfloor and Joists**

**Wood Flooring over a Concrete Slab**

Tile and stone flooring materials are solid and durable. Depending on the shape of the individual pieces and the pattern in which they are laid, these flooring materials can have a cool, formal appearance or convey an informal feeling to a room.

Ceramic mosaic tiles —small, modular units of natural clay or porcelain— are widely used for flooring. The natural clay type is unglazed, with muted earth colors; the porcelains can have bright colors and are vitreous (made dense and impervious).

Quarry tiles and pavers are larger modular flooring materials. Quarry tiles are unglazed units of heat-hardened clay. Larger-sized ceramic tile are available in a range of sizes and patterns, some of which mimic natural stone, and are practically impervious to moisture, dirt, and stains.

Stone flooring materials provide a solid, permanent, highly durable floor surface. Colors range from the tans, beiges, and reddish browns of flagstone to the grays, greens, and blacks of slate. A random pattern of flagstone conveys an informal feeling. Slate, available in square or irregular shapes, can be formal or informal. Marble lends itself to formal elegance.

Tile or stone flooring is set with grout. Grout is available in a variety of colors and can be selected to blend or contrast with the flooring material.

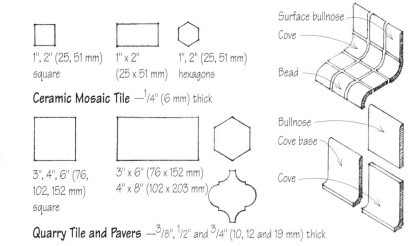

1", 2" (25, 51 mm) square    1" x 2" (25 x 51 mm)    1", 2" (25, 51 mm) hexagons

**Ceramic Mosaic Tile** —1/4" (6 mm) thick

3", 4", 6" (76, 102, 152 mm) square    3" x 6" (76 x 152 mm) 4" x 8" (102 x 203 mm)

**Quarry Tile and Pavers** —3/8", 1/2" and 3/4" (10, 12 and 19 mm) thick

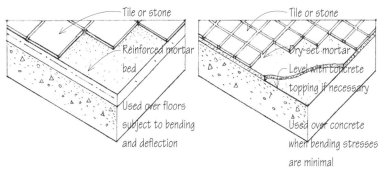

**Installation over a Concrete Slab**

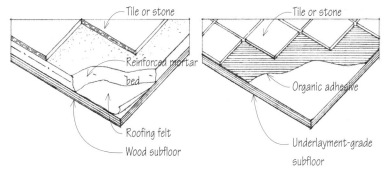

**Installation over a Wood Floor**

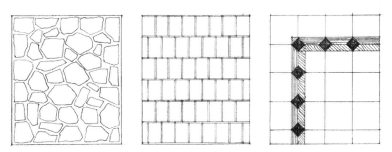

**Stone Flooring Patterns**

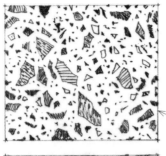

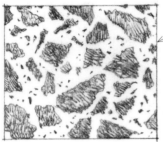

Concrete can also be used as a finish flooring surface if smooth and level enough. It should be sealed against stains and grease. It can be painted, stained, or integrally colored when cast. An exposed aggregate finish can provide textural interest.

Terrazzo is a special type of exposed aggregate finish with mosaic-like patterns created by the marble chips used and is available in poured or tile forms.

- Standard terrazzo is a ground and polished finish that consists mainly of relatively small stone chips.
- Venetian terrazzo consists mainly of large stone chips, with smaller chips filling the spaces between.

Seamless, durable, fluid-applied flooring materials are poured over concrete or other rigid substrates. Seamless quartz flooring consists of colored quartz aggregates in clear epoxy.

### Thinset Terrazzo
$1/4$" to $1/2$" (6 to 13 mm) resinous terrazzo topping is placed over a wood, metal, or concrete subfloor.

### Monolithic Terrazzo
$5/8$" (16 mm) or thicker portland cement terrazzo topping is laid over a rough-finished concrete slab.

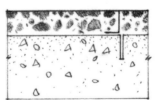

### Chemically Bonded Terrazzo
A chemical bonding agent is used if the concrete surface is too smooth for a mechanical bond.

### Bonded Terrazzo
$5/8$" (16 mm) or thicker portland cement terrazzo topping and a mortar underbed is mechanically bonded to a rough-finished concrete slab.

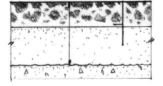

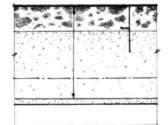

### Sand-Cushion Terrazzo
$5/8$" (16 mm) or thicker portland cement terrazzo topping is installed over a reinforced mortar underbed and an isolation membrane of sand to control cracking when structural movement is expected.

Resilient flooring materials provide an economical, dense, nonabsorbent flooring surface with relatively good durability and ease of maintenance. Their degree of resilience enables such flooring materials to resist permanent indentation while contributing to their quietness and comfort underfoot. The degree of comfort provided will depend not only on the material's resilience but also on the type of backing used and the hardness of the supporting substrate.

Linoleum and vinyl sheets come in rolls 6 feet (1829 mm) to 15 feet (4572 mm) wide. They can be cut into patterns in the factory or the field. Other resilient flooring materials are available as tiles, typically 9 inches (228 mm) and 12 inches (304 mm) square. While sheet goods provide a seamless floor, tiles are easier to install if the floor outline is irregular. Individual resilient tiles can also be replaced if damaged.

None of the resilient flooring types is superior in all respects.
• Rubber tile, vinyl sheet, linoleum, and cork products offer the best resilience.
• Vinyl sheets and tiles and linoleum resist staining, grease, and cigarette burns well.
• Vinyl products, especially sheet materials, pollute during manufacture, give off volatile organic chemicals (VOCs), and are difficult to dispose of.
• Natural linoleum and cork are made of renewable natural materials and have lower VOC levels.
• The pattern on vinyl tiles and sheets can wear off, whereas linoleum and cork have consistent color throughout. Linoleum looks and performs best when waxed.
• Vinyl flooring is available in static dissipative and electrostatic conductive forms suitable for use in computer rooms and clean rooms.
• Leather tiles, which are relatively expensive, develop an attractive patina with time and use.

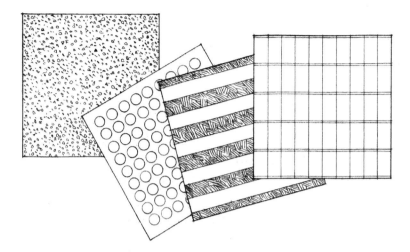

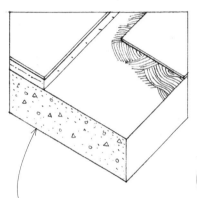

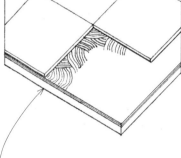

2" to 3" (51 mm to 76 mm) of reinforced concrete topping is required over precast concrete planks.

Linoleum and cork tiles should be laid only over slabs that are suspended above grade.

Hardboard or underlayment-grade plywood

The wood or concrete substrate for resilient flooring should be clean, dry, flat, and smooth because any irregularities in the base material will show through.

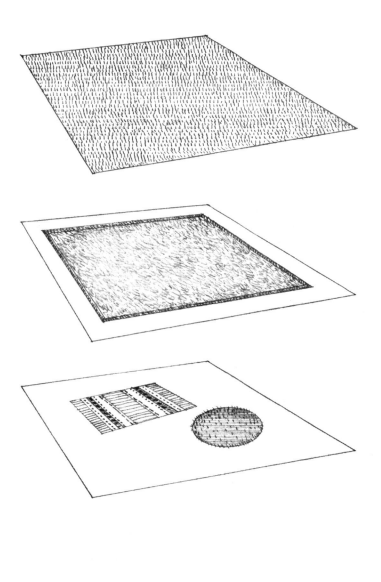

There are two major categories of soft floor coverings—carpeting and rugs. These coverings provide floors with both visual and textural softness, resilience, and warmth in a wide range of colors and patterns. These qualities, in turn, enable carpeting and rugs to absorb sound, reduce impact noise, and provide a comfortable and safe surface to walk on. As a group, carpeting is easier to install than hard floor coverings, is fairly easy to maintain, and is often the most economical floor covering.

Carpeting is most often manufactured in 12-foot (3658 mm) wide swaths, referred to as broadloom. Some specialty carpet comes in widths up to 18-feet (5486 mm) wide. Woven carpet is also manufactured in 27- to 36-inch (6858 to 9144 mm) widths referred to as narrow goods or runners and typically used in high-end residential installations.

Broadloom carpet is sold by the square foot, cut to fit, and installed over cushion using tackless strips, or glued down using an adhesive in commercial installations. Carpeting normally is installed wall-to-wall, covering the entire floor of a room. It can be laid directly over a subfloor and underlayment pad, obviating the need for a finish floor. It can also be laid over an existing floor.

Because carpet is usually fastened to a floor, it must be cleaned in place and cannot be turned to equalize wear. The location of seams, the type of backing, and the technique used to seam carpet can have a substantial effect on the useful lifespan of a broadloom carpet. Fraying seams result from improper installation and failure to seal the edges properly. The installation of carpeting should therefore be specified to meet the standards set by the Carpet and Rug Institute (CRI)—CRI 104 for commercial installation and CRI 105 for residential installation.

Carpet tiles are modular pieces of carpet that can be laid to resemble a seamless wall-to-wall installation or be arranged in subtle or bold patterns. They are constructed by tufting or by fusion bonding, which is more expensive. They offer the following advantages:

• They can be easily cut to fit odd-shaped contours with a minimum of waste.

• Individual tiles can be replaced if worn or damaged.

• Carpet tiles can be moved easily and reused.

• In commercial installations, the tiles can be removed for access to underfloor utilities or used with flat wire run under the carpet.

Residential carpet tiles are 9 or 12 inches (229 to 305 mm) square with a rubber backing and self-stick adhesive. Commercial-grade carpet tiles are 18 inches (457 mm) square with a backing strong enough to prevent shrinkage or expansion of the tile and to protect the carpet edges from unraveling. Some commercial-grade carpet tiles are intended to be glued down, while others are laid loosely with only enough adhesive to prevent the tiles from shifting along the edges of the installation and in high-traffic areas.

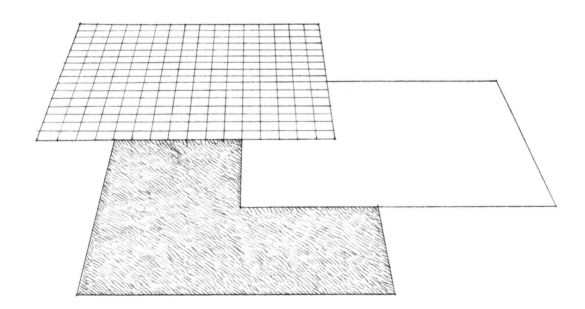

The performance of a carpet depends upon several factors, particularly the type of fiber used. Each carpet manufacturer offers blends of generic face fibers that improve on specific characteristics, such as durability, soil resistance, cleaning ability, color, and luster.

## Synthetic Fibers

**Nylon** is the predominant face fiber today. It has excellent strength and wearing ability, is soil-, mold-, and mildew-resistant, and dries quickly. Antistatic properties can be achieved through the use of conductive filaments. Solution-dyed nylon resists fading from sunlight and chemicals. Type 6.6 nylon has superior structure, hardiness, and resiliency. Newer soft nylons have increased nylon's desirability for residential use.

**Polyester** lacks the durability of nylon but has the texture and feel of wool. It resists soiling, abrasion, stains, and fading; it is also low in cost and is often used for residential carpeting.

**Olefin** (Polypropylene) is colorfast and resistant to abrasion, soil, and mildew. It lacks nylon's resiliency and crush-resistance but is less expensive than other synthetics. Olefin is used in both commercial and residential carpets.

## Natural Fibers

**Wool** is a protein fiber that sets the standard for fiber quality. It is the most expensive and desirable of fibers with excellent resilience and warmth as well as good soil-, flame-, and solvent-resistance. Wool has an outstanding ability to absorb color. It cleans and maintains well, has superior long-term appearance retention, and ages gracefully.

**Jute** is a harsh, brittle plant fiber that becomes very soft and pliable when used for decorative rugs. This fiber is also used for carpet and linoleum backing. It is available in neutral colors from cream to brown. However, jute becomes slippery with wear.

**Sisal**, made from the agave plant, is the most popular of natural plant fibers. More durable than jute, sisal also hides foot soiling. It is susceptible to liquid stains, however, and its use on stairs should be avoided.

**Coir**, the short fibers from coconut husks, cannot be tightly woven; yet it dries quickly. Coir is used for enclosed porches and mats.

**Seagrass** is harvested from reeds in saltwater marshes. Smoothest and most water-resistant of plant fibers, seagrass is durable and inexpensive, with a beautiful heathery texture.

**Cotton** is not as durable as other face fibers, but its softness and acceptance of colors can be used to advantage in flat-woven rugs. Cotton is not easily cleanable.

## Types of Dyes

**Reactive dyes** react with a fiber to form a new compound or chemical bond. These dyes produce excellent colorfast properties and bright colors.

**Acid dyes** are of two types. Original natural acid dyes were derived from plants. Synthetic acid dye is linked to a molecule of chromium for colorfastness and is commonly used for coloring nylon.

**Chrome dyes** are similar to acid dyes, but they are more sensitive to oxidizing bleaches. Chrome dyes work very quickly and are used extensively on wool and nylon.

**Dispersed dyes** utilize dye particles that are held to the surface of the fiber by friction and by strong electrical forces.

## Dye Techniques

**Yarn or skein dyeing** consists of spinning yarn and then dyeing the yarn in small batches. This process produces expensive, hard-to-match dye lots.

**Stock dyeing** is the dyeing of large quantities of fiber stock before spinning the fiber into yarn.

**Solution dyeing** consists of adding dye to synthetic carpet before the yarn is extruded. This technique is the most colorfast and resistant to chemicals, gasses, bleaches, and sunlight.

**Continuous dyeing** involves applying dye to the open face of a carpet and setting it by steam injection. This is the least expensive dyeing method, but it is less colorfast and uniform.

**Piece or beck dyeing** is currently the most popular dyeing method. White carpet, with a primary backing called greige goods, is run through the dye beck before the secondary backing is applied.

**Print or contact dyeing** can be used on almost any type of pile. This technique produces good colorfastness and penetration.

## Tufted Carpet

Lengths of yarn are inserted into a woven or nonwoven fabric called the primary backing. The tufts of yarn are stitched into the backing using hundreds of rows of equally spaced needles (needlebar). A secondary backing may be added for greater dimensional stability.

Tufted carpet

## Woven Carpet

Made on looms, woven carpet is a much slower and more expensive process than tufting. Axminster carpets, which are generally made of 100% wool or 80% wool and 20% nylon, are the most durable and long-wearing carpet type. It is often used in hospitality and residential applications. Wilton carpet is a decorative wool carpet used in homes. Both carpet types are woven through the back of the fabric and do not require a secondary backing.

Woven carpet

## Fusion-Bonded Carpet

Fusion bonding is a method wherein face yarns are heat-fused to a vinyl backing that is supported by other materials.

Fusion-bonded carpet

## Needle-punched Carpet

Short fibers are densely punched into a backing. Needle-punched carpet is used with polypropylene fibers for indoor-outdoor carpeting.

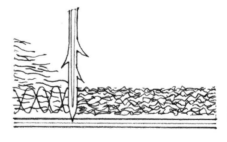

Needle-punched carpet

## Handmade Carpet

Knotted, hooked, braided, and hand-tufted techniques produce various styles of looped and/or cut yarns that are commonly used for area rugs. Oriental rugs are hand-knotted.

After color, texture is a carpet's prime visual characteristic. The various carpet textures available are a result of the pile construction, pile height, and the manner in which the carpet is cut. There are three major groups of carpet textures.

- **Cut pile** results when every yarn loop is cut. It can be produced in tufted, woven, or bonded constructions. Saxony pile has a smooth, soft appearance. Textured saxony has more casual textured surface that hides footprints well. Velvets are more formal, finely sheared cut piles. Frieze is a fine textured cut pile with the look of bouclé.

- **Loop or uncut pile** is tougher and more easily maintained than cut pile, and computer-aided-design programs now offer much more variety in the patterns that can be achieved. Loop pile also lacks the softness of cut pile since light tends to reflect off the carpet surface. Loop pile can be produced through tufted, woven, and knitted techniques.

- **Combination cut-and-uncut pile** adds a degree of warmth to all-loop pile. It can be produced in tufted and woven constructions.

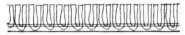

**Plush**
Smooth-cut pile

**Saxony Plush**
Utilizes thicker yarn

**Twist or Frieze**
Twists are set into yarn to create a heavier, rougher texture.

**Shag**
Textured surface is created with long, twisted yarns.

**Level Loop**
Looped tufts of the same height

**Ribbed Loop**
Directional or corrugated texture

**Hi-Lo Loop**
Loops of different heights

**Multi-Level Loop**
Capable of creating sculptured patterns

**Cut and Loop**
Alternating cut and uncut loops

**Cut and Loop**
Mostly loop pile with symmetrical, geometric figures created by cut rows

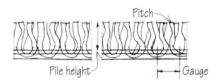

### Some Useful Terms

- Density is a measure of the amount of pile fiber by weight in a given area of carpet. Increased density generally results in better performance.

$$\text{Density} = \frac{\text{Average pile weight } (^{oz.}/\text{sq. yd.})}{\text{Average pile height in inches}}$$

- Pitch refers to the number of ends of yarn in 27 inches (685 mm) of width of woven carpet.
- Gauge refers to the needle spacing across the width of a tufting machine, expressed in fractions of an inch.
- Face weight is the total weight of face yarns measured in ounces per square yard.

Rugs are single pieces of floor coverings manufactured or cut to standard sizes, often with a finished border. They are not intended to cover the entire floor of a room and are therefore simply laid over another finish flooring material.

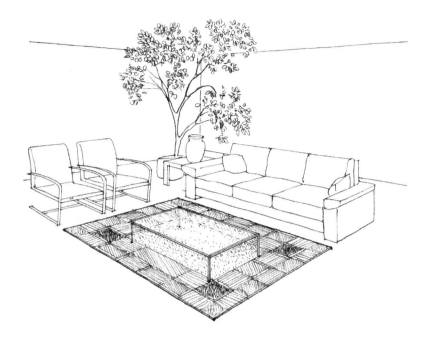

Room-sized rugs cover most of a room's floor, leaving a strip of finish flooring exposed along the room's edges. They approximate the appearance of wall-to-wall carpeting but can be moved if desired, removed for cleaning when necessary, and turned for more even distribution of wear.

Area rugs cover a smaller portion of a room's floor and can be used to define an area, unify a furniture grouping, or delineate a path. Decorative rugs, especially handmade ones, can also serve as a dominant design element and provide a focal point for a room's arrangement.

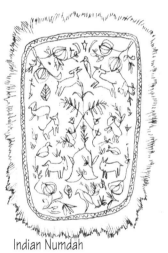

Indian Numdah

Navajo Rug

Afghanistan Bokhara

Chinese Bengali

Some wall finishes are an integral part of a wall's material structure, while others are separate layers attached to the frame of a wall. Still other wall finishes are thin coatings or coverings that are applied over a wall surface. In addition to aesthetic factors such as color, texture, and pattern, there are functional and economic considerations in selecting a wall material and finish.

• If the finish is an applied material, what type of support or base is required?
• What type of finish, coating, or covering will a wall accept?
• How durable must the material or finish be, and how easy is it to maintain?
• What degree of sound absorption, light reflectance, and fire-resistance is required?
• How much does it cost to purchase and to install or apply?

The major types of wall materials and finishes and their general characteristics are detailed on the following pages.

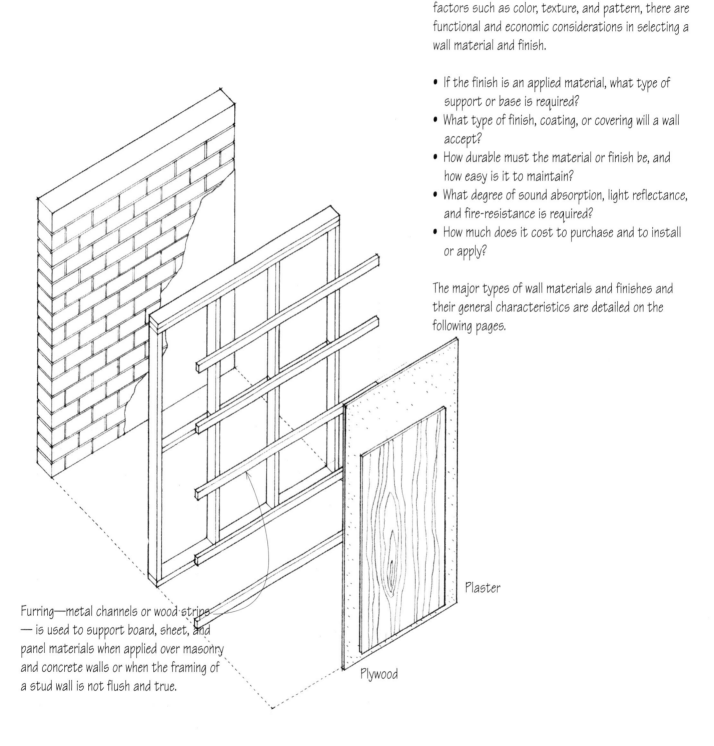

Plaster

Plywood

Furring—metal channels or wood strips—is used to support board, sheet, and panel materials when applied over masonry and concrete walls or when the framing of a stud wall is not flush and true.

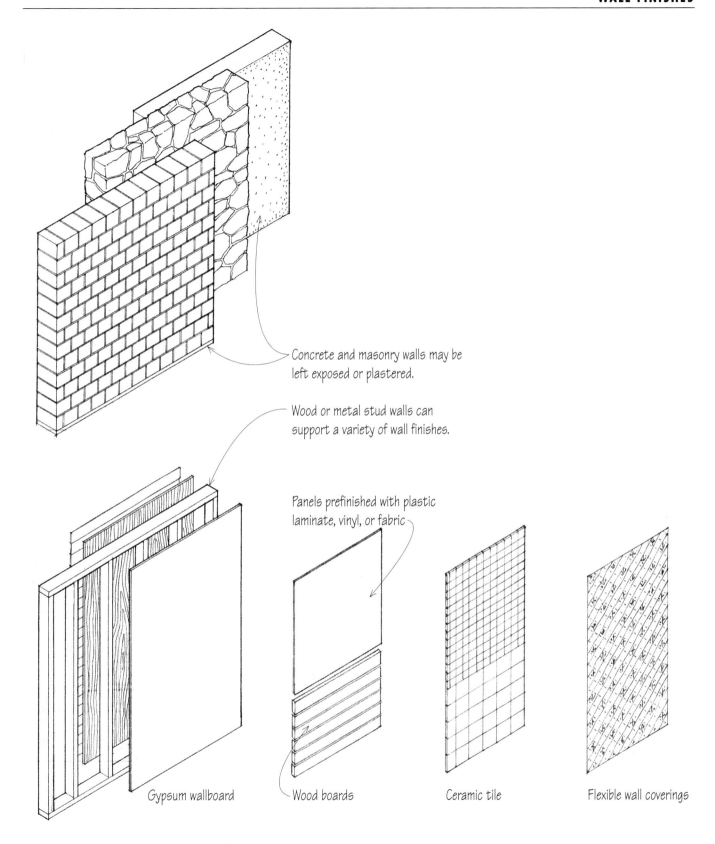

Concrete and masonry walls may be left exposed or plastered.

Wood or metal stud walls can support a variety of wall finishes.

Panels prefinished with plastic laminate, vinyl, or fabric

Gypsum wallboard

Wood boards

Ceramic tile

Flexible wall coverings

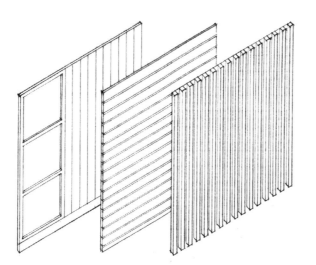

## Wood Boards

Wall pattern and texture depend on the width, orientation, and spacing of the boards as well as on the joint details.

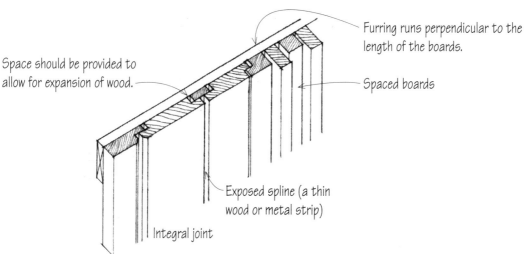

Furring runs perpendicular to the length of the boards.

Space should be provided to allow for expansion of wood.

Spaced boards

Exposed spline (a thin wood or metal strip)

Integral joint

**Examples of Joints**

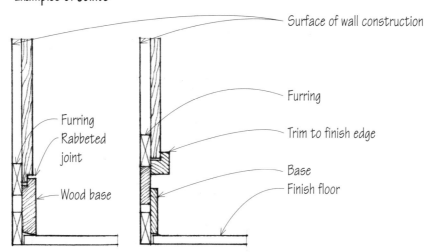

Surface of wall construction

Furring
Rabbeted
joint

Wood base

Furring

Trim to finish edge

Base
Finish floor

**Examples of Base Details**   Details at ceiling can be treated in a similar manner.

# Plywood

Plywood is a wood panel product made by bonding veneers together under heat and pressure, usually with the grain of adjacent plies at right angles to each other. High-density overlay (HDO) is a wood panel product that has a resin-fiber overlay on both sides, providing a smooth, hard, abrasion-resistant surface.

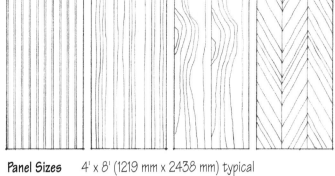

**Panel Sizes**　4' x 8' (1219 mm x 2438 mm) typical
⅟4" to ³/4" (6 mm to 9 mm) thick

## Plywood Appearance Grades

*Softwood Panels:*

N　For natural finishes
A　Smooth face suitable for painting
B　Utility panel

*Hardwood Panels:*

Premium (A)　Slight imperfections only
Good (1)　　For natural finishes
Sound (2)　　Smooth for painting

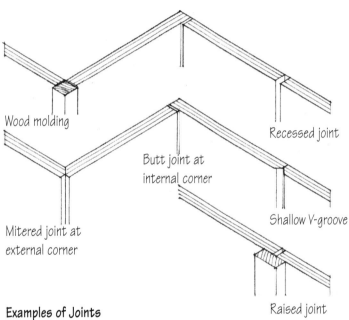

Wood molding

Mitered joint at external corner

Butt joint at internal corner

Recessed joint

Shallow V-groove

Raised joint

## Examples of Joints

Exposed edges of plywood panels must be finished with a hardwood strip or concealed with trim molding.

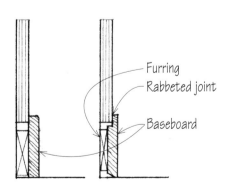

Furring
Rabbeted joint
Baseboard

## Examples of Base Details

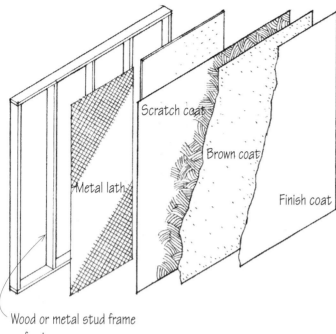

Scratch coat

Brown coat

Finish coat

Metal lath

Wood or metal stud frame
or furring over masonry or
concrete wall

Plaster is a composition of gypsum or lime, water,
sand, and sometimes hair or other fiber that is
applied in a pasty form to the surfaces of walls
or ceilings and allowed to harden and dry. Gypsum
plaster is a durable, relatively lightweight, and fire-
resistant material that can be used on any wall or
ceiling surface that is not subject to moist or wet
conditions. Portland cement plaster, also known as
stucco, is used on exterior walls and in areas subject
to wet or moist conditions. Veneer or thin-coat
plaster is a ready-mixed gypsum plaster applied as a
very thin, one- or two-coat finish over a veneer base.

Plaster is applied in either two or three layers, the
number of which depends on the type and strength of
base used.

- The scratch coat is the first coat in three-coat
  plaster. It must adhere firmly to lath and provide a
  better bond for the second, or brown, coat.
- The brown coat is a roughly finished, leveling coat
  of plaster—either the second coat in three-coat
  plaster or the base coat applied over a gypsum
  lath or masonry.
- The finish coat of plaster serves as the finished
  surface or as a base for decoration.
- The total thickness of a plaster finish is from $1/2$ to
  $3/4$ of an inch (12 mm to 19 mm).

The final appearance of a plaster surface depends
on both its texture and its finish. It may be troweled
to produce a smooth, nonporous finish, floated to
a sandy, lightly textured finish, or sprayed on for a
rougher finish. The finish may be painted; smooth
finishes will accept textile or paper wall coverings.

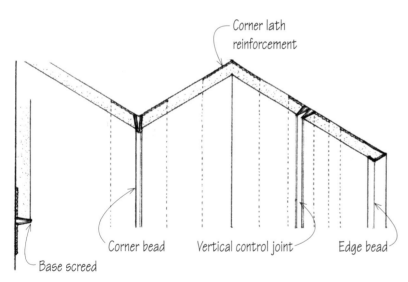

Corner lath
reinforcement

Corner bead        Vertical control joint        Edge bead

Base screed

Metal accessories are required to
finish and protect the edges and
corners of plaster surfaces.

Gypsum board—often called drywall or plasterboard—consists of a gypsum core surfaced with paper or other covering material. It may be finished by painting or by the application of ceramic tile or a flexible wall covering.

Major types of gypsum board include:

• Regular gypsum board for interior walls and ceilings
• Moisture-resistant gypsum board used as a backing for ceramic tile in high-moisture conditions
• Fire-resistant (Type-X) gypsum board used in fire-resistant construction

Prefinished panels are also available in a variety of colors, textures, and patterns.

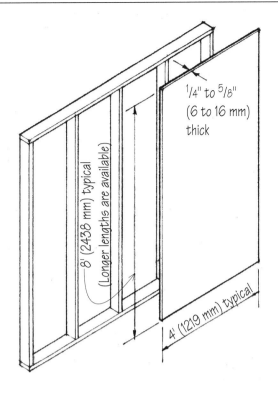

1/4" to 5/8" (6 to 16 mm) thick

8' (2438 mm) typical (Longer lengths are available)

4' (1219 mm) typical

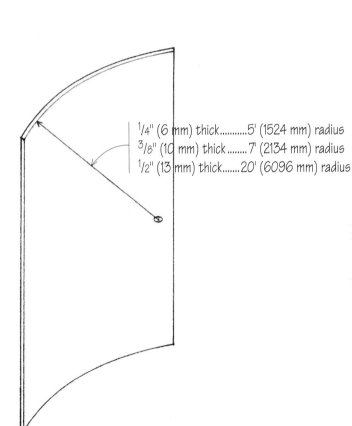

1/4" (6 mm) thick............5' (1524 mm) radius
3/8" (10 mm) thick........7' (2134 mm) radius
1/2" (13 mm) thick.......20' (6096 mm) radius

Gypsum board may be bent, depending on its thickness.

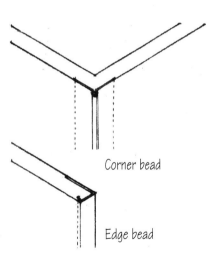

Corner bead

Edge bead

Metal trim shapes are required to finish and protect the edges and corners of gypsum board surfaces.

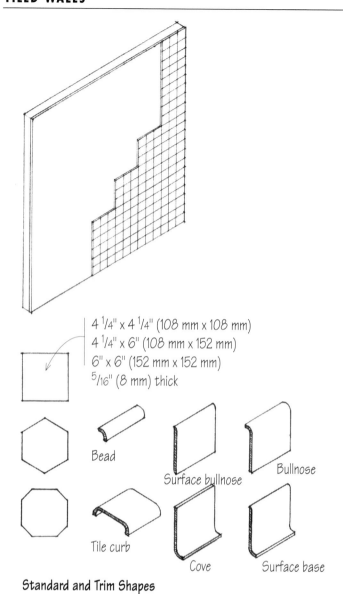

4 1/4" x 4 1/4" (108 mm x 108 mm)
4 1/4" x 6" (108 mm x 152 mm)
6" x 6" (152 mm x 152 mm)
5/16" (8 mm) thick

Bead

Surface bullnose

Bullnose

Tile curb

Cove

Surface base

**Standard and Trim Shapes**

## Ceramic Tile

Ceramic tiles are modular surfacing units of fired clay and other ceramic materials. They provide a permanent, durable, waterproof surface for interior walls. They are available in bright or matte glazes in a wide range of colors and surface designs. Specialty tiles include glass tiles, handmade and custom tiles, special sizes, and trim pieces. Grouts for wall tiles are available in a wide variety of colors. Avoid using highly pigmented grouts with contrasting colored tiles, as they may bleed.

Ceramic tile may be applied with either the thinset or the thickset process.

- In the *thinset process*, ceramic tile is bonded to a continuous, stable backing of gypsum plaster, gypsum board, or plywood, using a thin coat of dry-set mortar, latex-portland cement mortar, epoxy mortar, or an organic adhesive.
- In the *thickset process*, ceramic tile is applied over a bed of portland cement mortar. The relatively thick bed ( 1/2 to 3/4 of an inch; 13 mm to 19 mm) allows for accurate slopes and true planes in the finished work. Suitable backings include metal lath over concrete, masonry, plywood, gypsum plaster and gypsum board, and metal lath over stud framing.

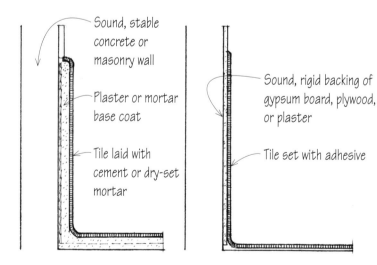

Sound, stable concrete or masonry wall

Plaster or mortar base coat

Tile laid with cement or dry-set mortar

Sound, rigid backing of gypsum board, plywood, or plaster

Tile set with adhesive

In addition to being painted, smooth plaster and gypsum board surfaces can be finished with a variety of flexible wall coverings that are available in an almost infinite range of colors, patterns, and designs.

Wallpaper, however, is subject to soiling, abrasion, and fading and is not tested for flame resistance.

Cloth or paper backed vinyl are designed for serviceability and durability, as well as tested for flame resistance. They are easily cleaned and resistant to fading and abrasion. But environmental problems exist in their manufacture, use, and disposal. They are classified into three types:
• Type I: light duty
• Type II: medium duty
• Type III: heavy duty

Foils conduct electricity and are subject to abrasion and scratches. They may create glare due to high levels of reflectance. Foils are also difficult to install.

Fabrics (wool, linen, cotton, burlap, grass cloth) can be installed over varied surfaces but may require extra backing. They should be treated for soil-resistance and may require flame-retardant treatment.

Cork obtained from the renewable bark of the cork oak tree is both durable and resilient. It accepts either wax or polyurethane finishes, possesses excellent acoustical and thermal ratings, but moisture may cause problems.

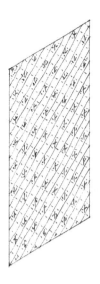

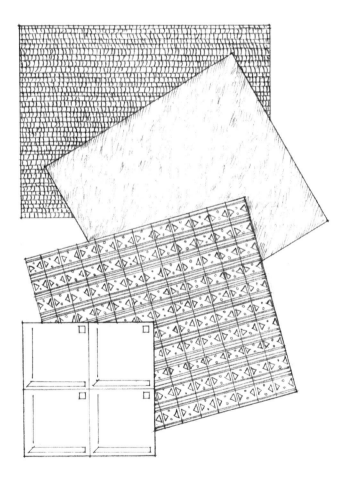

### Paint

Paint is a mixture of a solid pigment suspended in a vehicle and applied as a thin, usually opaque coating. Paints can decorate, protect, and modify the surface to which they are applied.

Pigment is a finely ground, insoluble substance suspended in a liquid vehicle to impart color and opacity to a coating.

**+**

Binder is the nonvolatile part of a paint vehicle that bonds particles of pigment into a cohesive film during the drying process.

The solvent is the volatile part of a paint vehicle that ensures the desired consistency for application by brush, roller, or spray.

Vehicle is a liquid in which pigment is dispersed before being applied to a surface to control consistency, adhesion, gloss, and durability.

- Alkyd paints are solvent-thinned resins that utilize any of several oil-modified polyesters as a vehicle. These paints are faster-drying, harder, more durable, more colorfast, easier to apply, and give off less odor than oil-based paints.

- Oil-based paints are solvent-thinned resins that utilize one of several natural drying oils as a vehicle.

- Latex paints are water-based. They are fast drying, porous, and easy to clean up with water.

- Primers improve the adhesion of subsequent coatings. They may also provide color and serve as a moisture barrier or a rust inhibitor.

- Catalyzed epoxy coatings cure to form dense, hard films that are resistant to chemicals, solvents, stains and abrasions. They usually consist of two-parts, a resin and a catalyst mixed just prior to use.

- Multicolor coatings are durable, scratch-resistant spray-on coatings that use beads of various colors.

### Stain

Stains are translucent or transparent solutions of dyes or pigments applied to penetrate and color a wood surface without obscuring the grain.

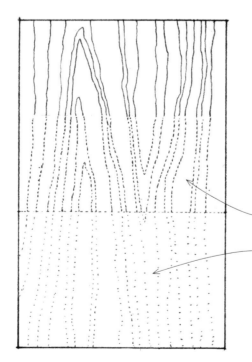

- Penetrating stains permeate a wood surface, leaving a vey thin film on the surface.
- Pigmented or opaque stains are oil stains that contain pigments capable of obscuring the grain and texture of a wood surface.

The underside of the floor or roof structure above can be left exposed and serve as the ceiling. More often, however, a separate ceiling material is attached to or hung from a supporting structure. The range of ceiling materials is similar to that for walls except for those that are too heavy to be hung from an overhead structure.

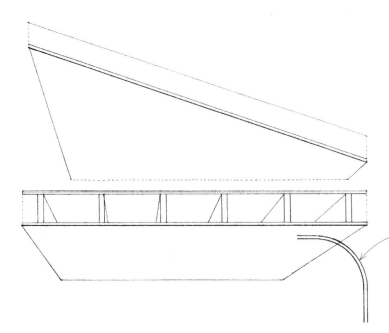

## Plaster and Gypsum Board

Plaster and gypsum board provide uninterrupted ceiling surfaces that can be finished smooth, textured, painted, or wallpapered.

Plaster also affords the opportunity for merging ceiling and wall planes with curved surfaces called coves.

Both plaster and gypsum board require a supporting framework of wood or metal that is attached to or suspended from the roof or floor framing.

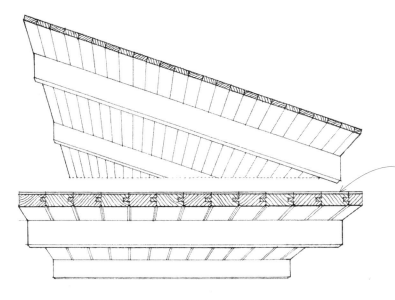

## Wood

Wood decking or planks span the spaces between beams to form the structural platform of a floor or roof. The underside of the planks may be left exposed as the finish ceiling.

Wood planks are normally 5 1/4 inches (133 mm) wide and typically have V-groove, tongue-and-groove joints. Channel groove, striated, and other machined patterns are available.

With this structural system, there is no concealed ceiling space.

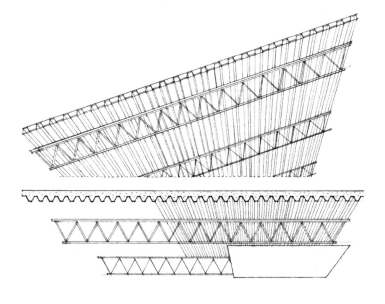

## Metal

On roofs, corrugated steel decking forms the structural platform for thermal insulation and the roofing material. Cellular or corrugated steel decking also provides permanent formwork and reinforcement for concrete when forming composite floor slabs.

The underside of steel decking can be left exposed as the ceiling surface. Together with open-web steel joists, steel decking defines ceilings with a linear, textural quality.

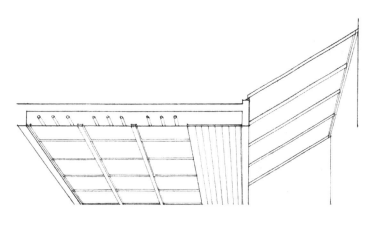

## Modular

Illuminated ceilings may consist of a modular lighting grid or, during daylight hours, comprise skylights that open up a space to the sky.

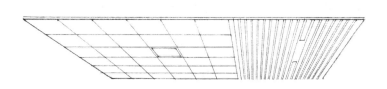

Modular ceiling materials are normally supported on a metal grid suspended from a roof or floor structure. Acoustical ceiling tiles form a square or rectangular grid pattern that may be strong or subtle, depending on the tile design. In contrast to this, long, narrow metal panels form a linear pattern on ceilings. In both cases, light fixtures, air diffusers, and other mechanical fixtures can be integrated into the modular system.

In commercial spaces, a modular suspended ceiling system is often used to integrate and provide flexibility in the layout of lighting fixtures and air distribution outlets. The typical system consists of modular ceiling tiles supported by a metal grid suspended from the overhead structure. The tiles are usually removable for access to the ceiling space.

Acoustical tiles are modular units of glass or mineral fiber. They are available in a variety of square and rectangular styles. Some may have aluminum, vinyl, ceramic, or mineral faces. Their edges may be square, beveled, rabbeted, or tongue-and-grooved. Acoustical tiles come in perforated, patterned, textured, or fissured faces.

Acoustical tiles are excellent absorbers of sound within a room. Some tiles are fire-rated, and some are rated for use in high-humidity areas.

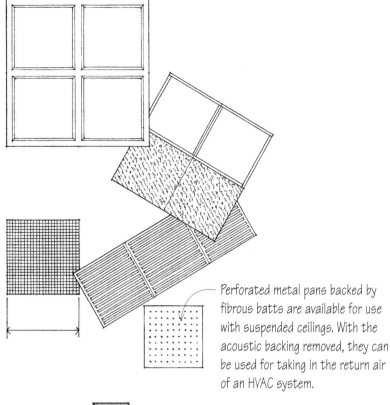

Perforated metal pans backed by fibrous batts are available for use with suspended ceilings. With the acoustic backing removed, they can be used for taking in the return air of an HVAC system.

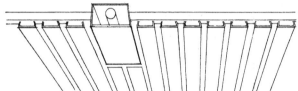

Linear metal ceilings use steel, aluminum, or stainless steel panels. Open slots permit sound to be absorbed by backing of batt insulation.

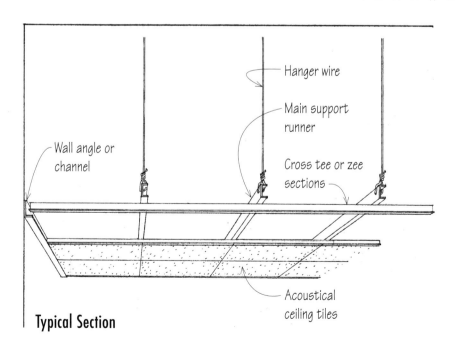

Hanger wire

Main support runner

Cross tee or zee sections

Wall angle or channel

Acoustical ceiling tiles

**Typical Section**

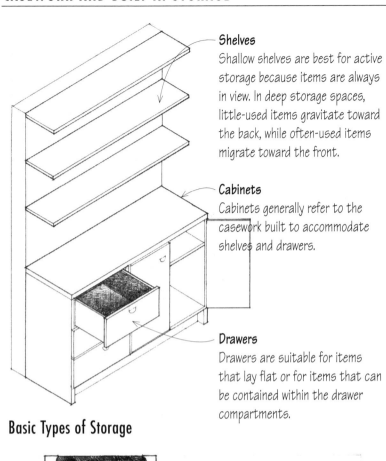

**Shelves**

Shallow shelves are best for active storage because items are always in view. In deep storage spaces, little-used items gravitate toward the back, while often-used items migrate toward the front.

**Cabinets**

Cabinets generally refer to the casework built to accommodate shelves and drawers.

**Drawers**

Drawers are suitable for items that lay flat or for items that can be contained within the drawer compartments.

## Basic Types of Storage

• Unit furniture; see Chapter 8, pages 326–327, for information on storage furniture.

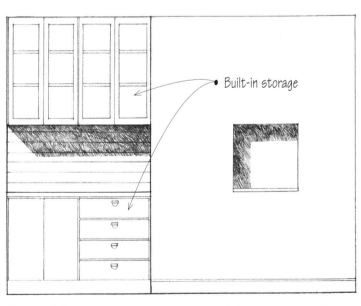

• Built-in storage

## Forms of Storage

• Built-in architectural features, such as wall niches

Providing adequate and properly designed storage is an important concern in the planning of interior spaces, particularly where space is tight or where an uncluttered appearance is desired. To determine storage requirements, analyze the following:

**Accessibility:** Where is storage needed?

**Convenience:** What type of storage should be provided? What sizes and shapes of items are to be stored? What is the frequency of use?

**Visibility:** Are items to be on display, or concealed?

Storage should be distributed where needed. How far we can reach while we are seated, standing, or kneeling should govern the means of access to the storage area. Active storage of often-used items should be readily accessible while dead storage of little-used or seasonal items can be hidden away.

The size, proportion, and type of storage units used depend on the type and amount of items to be stored, the frequency of use, and the degree of visibility desired. Basic types of storage units are shelves, drawers, and cabinets. These may be suspended from the ceiling, mounted on a wall, or simply placed on the floor as a piece of furniture. Storage units can also be built into the thickness of a wall, occupy a niche, or utilize otherwise unusable space such as under a stairway.

In a residence, built-in storage and cabinetry are most common in kitchens, pantries, and bathroom spaces but can effectively be extended into other spaces as well. Standard-sized bases and wall cabinets are fitted into the kitchen layouts of most homes.

Countertop options include:

- *Plastic laminates*: Moderate cost; dark edge requires trim; waterproof, stain-resistant, easily cleaned. Not heat-resistant; joints may be damaged; scratches not repairable.

- *Granite*: Durable, water- and heat-resistant; expensive installation.
- *Slate*: Water- and heat-resistant, stainproof, antibacterial, expensive.
- *Soapstone*: Water-, heat-, and stain-resistant; pleasant feel; expensive; bimonthly oil treatment required.

- *Solid surfacing*: Water- and stain-resistant; light stains, scratches, scorch marks can be buffed out; integral sinks available; may water spot.
- *Epoxy resin*: Durable, poured surface over painted or other surfaces.
- *Engineered composite stone*: Nonporous; abrasion, stain and impact resistant; resinous feel and appearance.
- *Concrete*: Durable, tactile surface, acquires patina from use. May stain and crack; sealer recommended.

- *Tile, ceramic*: Heat- and stain-resistant; durable; costly to install; grout requires maintenance.

- *Wood*: Water may damage surface; requires monthly application of mineral oil. Light damage can be sanded off.

- *Zinc*: Warm metal appearance; easy maintenance; many finishes available.

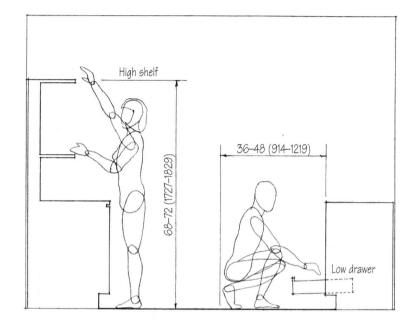

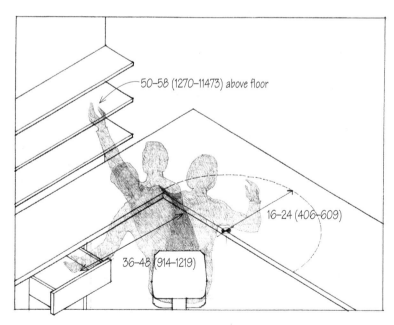

**Dimensional Criteria**   All dimensions are in inches, with their metric equivalents in millimeters (shown in parentheses).

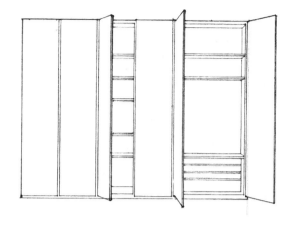

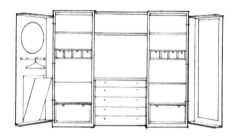

In commercial buildings, the varying demands of offices, schools, research facilities, libraries, retail stores, and other facilities are met by a wide variety of manufactured casework and custom-built pieces.

Offices often feature bookcases and credenzas for storage and display.

Reception desks may be custom-designed to project corporate image.

Retail display cases may be stock design, corporate standard pieces, or custom designs.

Food service counters and server lines must accommodate equipment and work flow.

Hospital nurses' stations and patient room cabinetry must accommodate equipment.

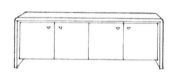

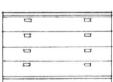

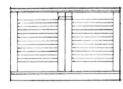

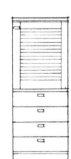

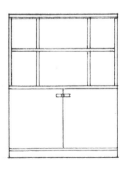

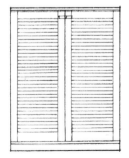

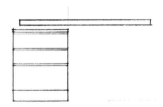

# 8

# Furnishings

# FURNISHINGS

Furnishings are the one category of design elements that lies almost wholly within the realm of interior design. While walls, floors, ceilings, windows, and doors are established in the architectural design of a building, the selection and arrangement of moveable interior elements—furniture, window treatments, and accessories—within the building's spaces are major tasks of interior design.

Furnishings mediate between architecture and people. They offer a transition in form and scale between an interior space and the individual. Furnishings make interiors habitable by providing comfort and utility in the tasks and activities we undertake.

Interior designers commonly differentiate between residential and commercial furnishings. Furnishings for offices—modular partition systems, chairs, desks—are sometimes referred to as "contract furnishings." The distinction may be one of style, durability or fire resistance. Some pieces serve equally well in either residential or business settings. With the advent of home offices, many crossover pieces are now on the market.

Spaces open to use by the public usually have more stringent requirements for fire safety. Requirements for accessibility also affect furnishings in public spaces and at work. Facilities that receive intensive use like classrooms, healthcare facilities, and restaurants require very durable and well-constructed furnishings.

In addition to fulfilling specific functions, furniture contributes to the visual character of interior settings. The form, lines, color, texture, and scale of individual pieces, as well as their spatial organization, play a major role in establishing the expressive qualities of a room.

The pieces can be linear, planar, or volumetric in form; their lines may be rectilinear or curvilinear, angular or free flowing. They can have horizontal or vertical proportions; they can be light and airy or sturdy and solid. Their texture can be slick and shiny, smooth and satiny, warm and plush, or rough and heavy; their color can be natural or transparent in quality, warm or cool in temperature, light or dark in value.

Today many designs mix furniture from different historical periods with contemporary pieces. Most designers do not seek to design period rooms, although these are appropriate in historic settings or for a client with a collection of antiques. Historical and cultural references extend to furniture arrangements and the selection of finishes and accessories as well as to pieces of furniture. The designs of the past that endure today are still in production, although many reproductions lack the quality of the originals in material, craftsmanship, or durability.

Antique furniture is generally recognized as being at least one hundred years old. Antiques are often identified with major cultures, periods, countries, or individuals. Authentic pieces in good condition are usually expensive.

*Modern furniture* includes pieces produced in the late nineteenth and early twentieth century by designers such as Michael Thonet, Charles Rennie Mackintosh, and the craftsmen of the Bauhaus movement.

*Contemporary furniture* encompasses pieces produced today by working designers.

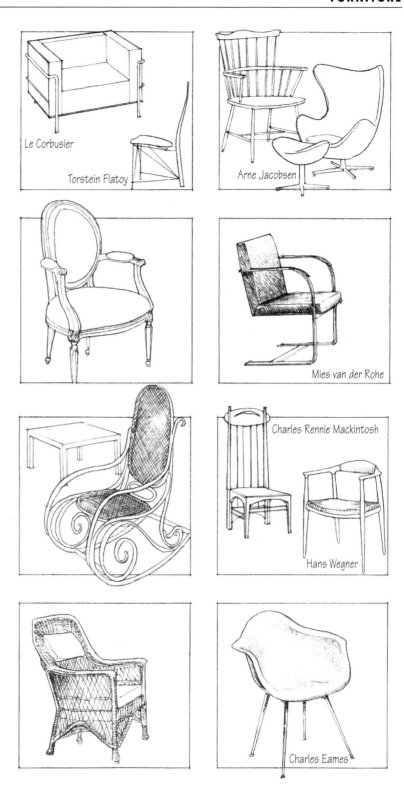

Le Corbusier

Torstein Flatoy

Arne Jacobsen

Mies van der Rohe

Charles Rennie Mackintosh

Hans Wegner

Charles Eames

Furniture can, depending on the quality of its design, either offer or limit physical comfort in a real and tangible way. Our bodies will tell us if a chair is uncomfortable or if a table is too high or too low for our use. There is definite feedback that tells us whether a piece of furniture is appropriate for its intended use.

Human factors, therefore, are a major influence on the form, proportion, and scale of furniture. To provide utility and comfort in the execution of our tasks, furniture should be designed first to respond or correspond to our dimensions, the clearances required by our patterns of movement, and the nature of the activity we are engaged in.

Our perception of comfort is, of course, conditioned by the nature of the task or activity being performed, its duration, and other circumstantial factors such as the quality of lighting and even our state of mind. At times, the effectiveness of a furniture element may depend on its correct use—on our learning how to use it.

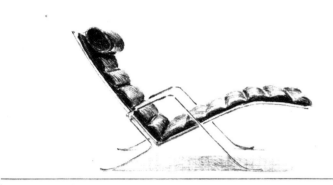

Knoll International, Inc.

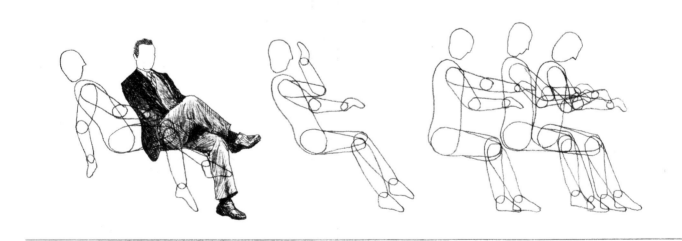

The way furniture is arranged in a room will affect how the space is used and perceived. Furniture can simply be placed as sculptural objects in space. More often, however, furniture is organized into functional groupings. These groupings, in turn, can be arranged to organize and structure space.

Most furniture consists of individual or unit pieces that allow for flexibility in their arrangement. The pieces are movable and may consist of various specialized elements as well as a mix of forms and styles.

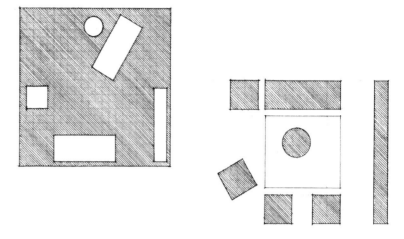

Built-in arrangements of furniture, on the other hand, allow for the flexible use of more space. There is generally more continuity of form among the furniture elements with fewer gaps between them.

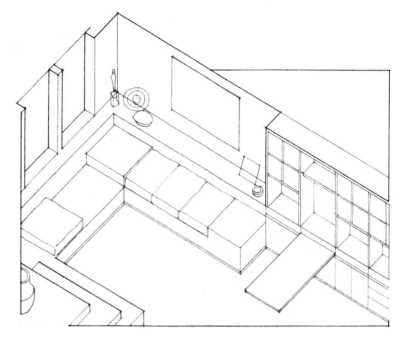

Modular units combine the unified appearance of built-in furniture with the flexibility and movability of individual unit pieces.

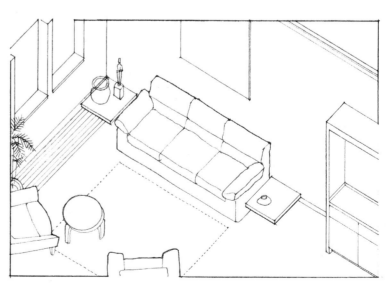

Furniture may be constructed of wood, metal, or plastic and other synthetic materials. Each material has strengths and weaknesses that should be recognized in furniture design and construction if a piece is to be strong, stable, and durable in use.

## Wood

Wood is the standard furniture material. A primary consideration in how wood is used and joined is the direction of its grain. Wood is strong when compressed with the grain but can be dented or crushed when loaded perpendicular to the grain. In tension, wood can be pulled in the direction of its grain, but it will split when pulled at a right angle to the grain. Wood is weakest in shear along its grain. Another important consideration is the expansion and contraction of wood across its grain with changes in moisture content. All these factors bear on the way wood is configured and joined in furniture construction.

Plywood is a sheet material that consists of an odd number of plies (thin sheets) layered at right angles in grain direction to each other. Thus, a plywood panel has strength in two directions. In addition, the quality and appearance of the face veneer can be controlled.

Particleboard is made by bonding small wood particles under heat and pressure. It is commonly used as a core material for decorative panels and cabinetwork.

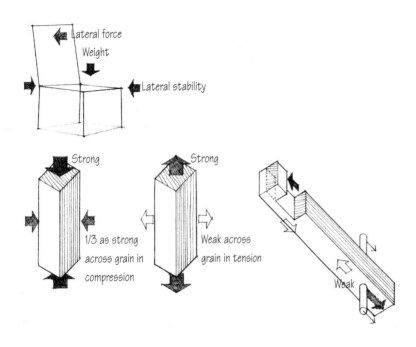

**Wood Strength Relative to Grain Direction**

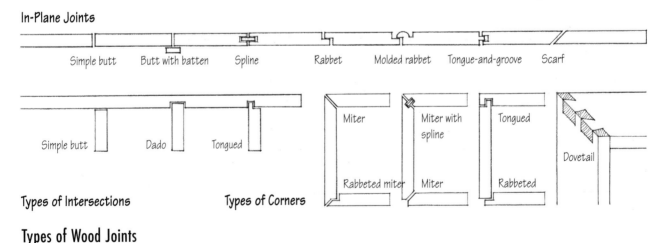

In-Plane Joints

Simple butt    Butt with batten    Spline    Rabbet    Molded rabbet    Tongue-and-groove    Scarf

Simple butt    Dado    Tongued

Miter    Miter with spline    Tongued

Rabbeted miter    Miter    Rabbeted    Dovetail

**Types of Intersections**    **Types of Corners**

**Types of Wood Joints**

## Metal

Like wood, metal is strong both in compression and tension, but it does not have a strong grain direction. Metal is also ductile (capable of being drawn into wire and hammered thin). These factors, along with a high strength-to-weight ratio, enable metal to have relatively thin cross sections and to be curved or bent in furniture construction. Methods for joining metal are analogous to those for wood. Instead of being nailed, metal can be screwed, bolted, or riveted; instead of being glued, metal can be welded.

## Plastic

Plastic is a unique material in the way it can be shaped, formed, textured, colored, and used. This is due to the numerous types and variations of plastic materials available and under development today. While not as strong as wood or metal, plastic can be strengthened with glass fiber. More significantly, it can be easily shaped into structurally stable and rigid forms. For this reason, plastic furniture almost always consists of a single piece without joints or connections.

New synthetic materials that combine strength with flexibility and have the property of returning to their original shape after being stretched are stimulating the design of furniture that supports the body without compressing tissues and nerves.

Many pieces of furniture combine a variety of materials, including chairs with wood or metal frames and fabric or plastic seats and backs and dressers and tables with glass mirrors or tops. Upholstered furniture adds a layer of cushioning covered by a fabric to a firmer frame for comfort and appearance.

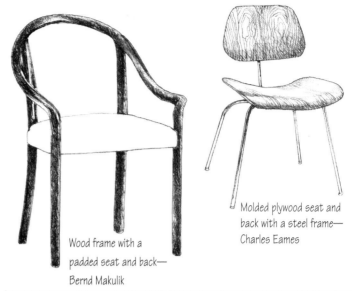

Wood frame with a padded seat and back— Bernd Makulik

Molded plywood seat and back with a steel frame— Charles Eames

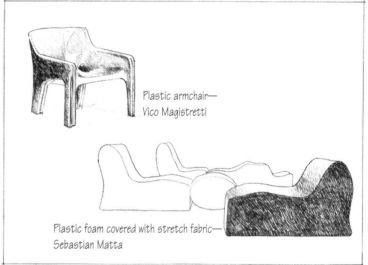

Plastic armchair— Vico Magistretti

Plastic foam covered with stretch fabric— Sebastian Matta

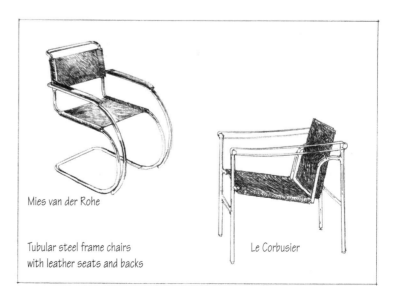

Mies van der Rohe

Tubular steel frame chairs with leather seats and backs

Le Corbusier

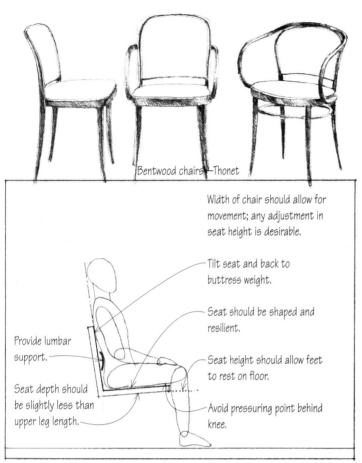

Bentwood chairs—Thonet

Width of chair should allow for movement; any adjustment in seat height is desirable.

Tilt seat and back to buttress weight.

Seat should be shaped and resilient.

Provide lumbar support.

Seat height should allow feet to rest on floor.

Seat depth should be slightly less than upper leg length.

Avoid pressuring point behind knee.

**General Considerations**

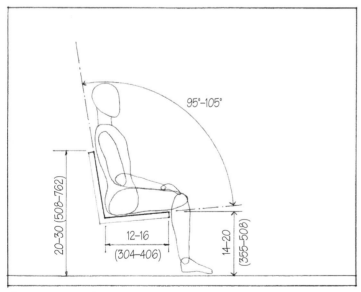

95°–105°

20–30 (508–762)

12–16 (304–406)

14–20 (355–508)

**General Purpose Chair**

Seating should be designed to support comfortably the weight and shape of the user. Because of the great variation in body sizes, however, and the danger of designing too precisely for the specific conditions that would result in a comfortable seating device, what is illustrated on these two pages are the factors that affect our personal judgment of comfort and a range of dimensions that should serve only as guidelines.

The appropriate dimensions for a chair are determined not only by the dimensions of the human body and the chair's proposed user but also by cultural factors and matters of scale and style. A relatively uncomfortable, small, hard chair may encourage the customers in a fast-food restaurant to move on. A deeply upholstered lounge chair invites the user to relax.

The comfort factor is also affected by the nature of the activity the user might be engaged in at the time. There are different types of chairs and seating for different uses. Ergonomic design principles are especially important for chairs intended for long periods of use, such as computer desk chairs. Adjustable heights and back supports allow different users to customize their chair's fit. Poorly designed seating is a major cause of health problems among sedentary workers.

Chairs for older users and people with mobility problems should have sturdy arms, relatively high seats, and stable bases. Children's furniture has its own dimensional constraints.

All dimensions are in inches, with their metric equivalents in millimeters (shown in parentheses).

Upholstery fabrics should be selected to withstand the normal wear of their intended use. Commercial-grade fabrics are labeled for wear, sun, and fire resistance. Upholstery materials include:

| | |
|---|---|
| Cotton | Plant fiber with low elasticity and resiliency. Combustible and wrinkles easily. |
| Linen | Derived from stalk of the flax plant. Extremely strong, tends to be brittle, wrinkles easily. More mildew resistant than cotton. |
| Ramie | Very strong, lustrous natural fiber. Stiff, brittle, nonelastic. Often blended with linen and cotton. |
| Silk | Produced by silk moths; strongest natural fiber. Resistant to solvents but degenerates in sunlight. |
| Rayon | Manufactured from wood pulp. Viscose rayon blends well with other fibers and takes dyes well. |
| Acetate | Poor resiliency, flexible, drapes well, wrinkles easily. |
| Triacetate | Good resiliency, stable, abrasion resistant, permanent pleats. |
| Acrylic | Mimics silk or wool, accepts dyes well, may pill. |
| Modacrylic | Withstands high temperatures; good for draperies. |
| Vinyl | Durable, easy to clean; simulates leather or suede. |
| Polyester | Wrinkle resistant, abrasion resistant, dimensional stability, crease resistant. |
| Elastomeric fibers (spandex) | Rubber-like fabrics that return to their original shapes. |

Knoll International, Inc.

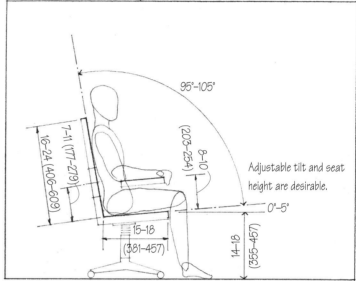

**Office Chair**

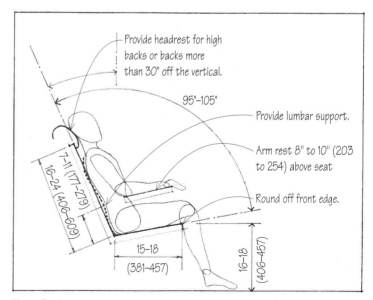

**Easy Chair**

## Chairs

| | |
|---|---|
| Armchairs | Intended for relaxing, conversation, or reading; fully upholstered; constructed of wood, plastic, steel, or a combination of materials. |
| Side chairs | Usually lighter and smaller than armchairs; upright backs for dining and studying. |
| Lounge chairs | For relaxing in a semireclining position; often adjustable; should be easy to get into and out of, neither too low nor too soft; should provide proper back support. |

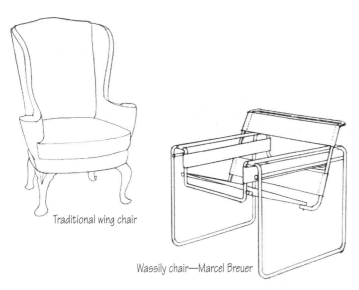

Traditional wing chair

Wassily chair—Marcel Breuer

Arne Jacobsen

Alvar Aalto

Shaker ladderback chair

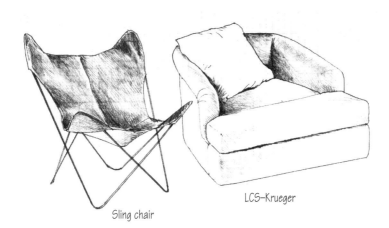

Sling chair

LCS–Krueger

| | |
|---|---|
| *Sofas* | Designed for seating of two or more people; generally upholstered; curved, straight, or angled; with or without arms. |
| *Couch* | A long upholstered unit with a low, raised back for reclining. |
| *Loveseat* | A small sofa with only two seating positions. |

Four sofas—Ward Bennett Designs/Brickel Associates

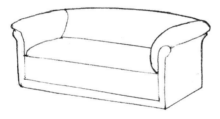 

Pier Luigi Molinari

Alessandro Mendini

Mauro Lipparini–Roberto Tapinassi

Burkhard Vogtherr

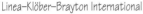

Linea–Klöber–Brayton International

Wilkhahn Seating–Vecta Contract

Arne Jacobsen

Eero Saarinen

Commercial seating must be durably constructed to support workers without stress throughout the work day. Seating should not be selected solely on the basis of the user's status within the company or enterprise but rather selected to accommodate the size of the individual user and to provide proper support for the type of activity envisioned.

| | |
|---|---|
| Desk chairs | Designed to be flexible and mobile; swivel mechanism; rolling casters; arms. |
| Executive chairs | Often designed as status symbols; allow the user to lean back from the desk; swivel; not appropriate for extended computer use. |
| Side chairs | Intended for office visitors or short term use; usually small in scale and often armless. |
| Stacking and folding chairs | Used for large gatherings of people or as auxiliary seating; lightweight and modular; often made of steel, aluminum, or plastic; some available with arms and lightly upholstered, with padded seats and backs; some have coupling devices for use in rows. |
| Restaurant chairs | Available in many styles and materials; must be durably constructed; comfort level is usually selected to match intended service style. Chairs with arms must be coordinated with tabletop heights; chair size affects seating patterns. |
| Stools | Should be selected for stability and ease of movement as well as for appearance. |

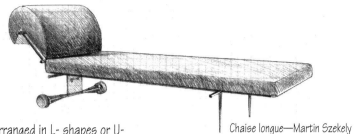

Chaise longue—Martin Szekely

| | |
|---|---|
| Sofas | Can be arranged in L- shapes or U-shapes for conversation groups in lobbies, large private offices, waiting areas; strangers generally sit at opposite ends, leaving center seat empty. |
| Loveseats | Intimate style tends to discourage use by two strangers; but they are useful in smaller private offices where they can be used for naps. |

Modular or sectional seating

Single seating units that can be arranged in a variety of ways; available armless, with left or right arm only, or as corner piece. Modular seating also refers to seating with a continuous base to which individual seats are attached.

| | |
|---|---|
| Booths | Seating arrangement consisting of a table with seats on two sides, the backs of which often serve as partitions; commonly designed for two to four persons; larger booths and U-shaped or circular configurations present access problems for central seats; usually upholstered. |
| Banquettes | Long, usually upholstered seats facing multiple tables with chairs opposite; allow tables to be moved along the length of the banquette and clustered to accommodate varying sizes of groups. |

Auditorium seating

Provides acoustic absorption as well as seating; fire safety requirements for materials and arrangements.

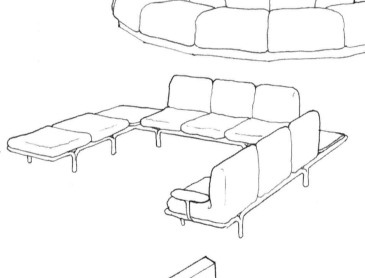

315

Tables are essentially flat, horizontal surfaces, supported off the floor, and used for dining, working, storage, and display. They should have the following attributes:

• Strength and stability to support items in use
• Correct size, shape, and height off floor for intended use
• Construction of durable materials

Tabletops can be of wood, glass, plastic, stone, metal, tile, or concrete. The surface finish should be durable and have good wearing qualities. The surface color and texture should have the proper light reflectance for the visual task.

Tabletops can be supported with legs, trestles, solid bases, or cabinets. They can also swing out or down from wall storage units and be supported by folding legs or brackets. Table bases should relate in scale and size to the tabletop to provide adequate support and stability.

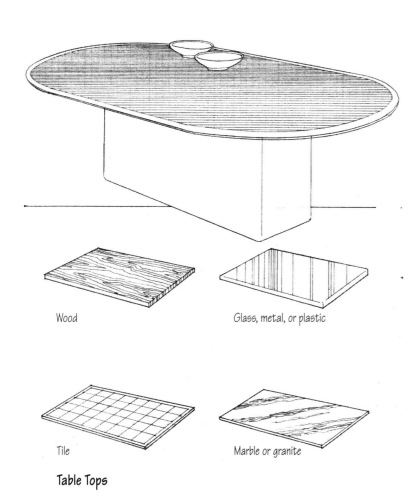

Wood

Glass, metal, or plastic

Tile

Marble or granite

**Table Tops**

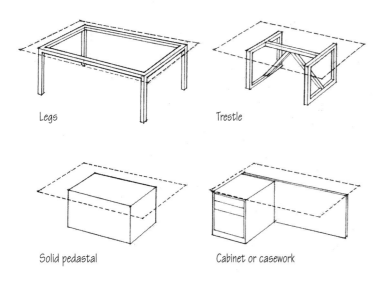

Legs

Trestle

Solid pedastal

Cabinet or casework

**Table Supports**

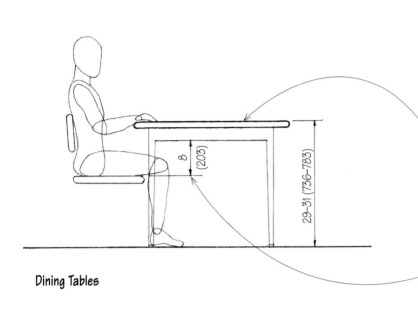

**Dining Tables**

See also Chapter 2, page 51, for plan dimensions of dining tables and page 53 for dimensions of work stations.

A minimum of 24" (609 mm) should be provided for each person around the perimeter of a dining table.

Table shape should be compatible with the shape of the room.

Surface finish should provide an attractive background for table settings.

For flexibility in accommodating both small and large groups, tables that extend with leaves are desirable.

Table supports should not reduce the space for users' knees and legs.

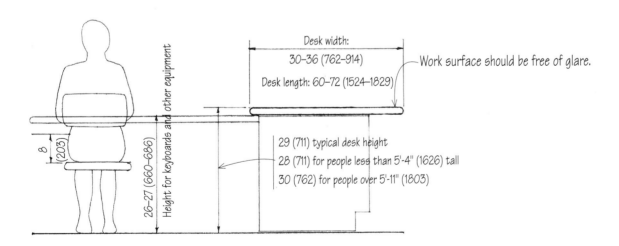

Desk width:
30–36 (762–914)
Desk length: 60–72 (1524–1829)

Work surface should be free of glare.

29 (711) typical desk height
28 (711) for people less than 5'-4" (1626) tall
30 (762) for people over 5'-11" (1803)

**Desks and Work Surfaces**

All dimensions are in inches, with their metric equivalents in millimeters (shown in parentheses).

Marble top and lacquered
wood base—Ignazio Gardella

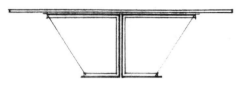

Glass top and lacquered metal
base—R. Carta Mantiglia

Glass top and encaustic painted
metal base—Lella e Massimo

Marble and wood top with metal
legs—Daniela Puppa

Wood top and chromed iron
tubing—Arne Jacobsen

Granite top and metal
base—Laura Griziotti

**Dining tables**   Selected for style, number of seats (with optional leaves for expansion), fit in room; custom designs as well as manufactured.

**Occasional tables**

Coffee tables are designed to hold books, magazines, and beverages in front of a sofa. End tables provide surfaces for a lamp and other accessories next to a seat. Other small tables hold accessories and help to balance décor.

Glass top and painted metal
base—Michele de Luchi

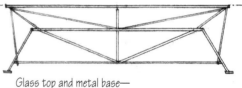

Glass top and metal base—
Kurt Ziehmer

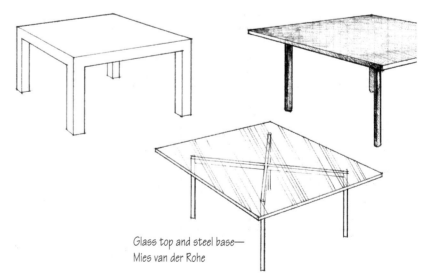

Glass top and steel base—
Mies van der Rohe

Restaurant tables

Selected for durability, style, number of seats, and fit in space; center post support; tabletops can be custom or stock. Rectangular "deuces" (tables for two) can be combined for larger parties; circular tables often used for large groups; square tables can be oriented on diagonal.

Conference tables

Large single tables with many seats or smaller tables designed to be reconfigured for conference and seminar rooms; selected for capacity, flexibility, and appearance.

Boardroom tables

Large tables designed for prestige, style; may have built-in data and communications equipment.

Hotel tables and desks

Similar to residential pieces in style but commercial quality for durability.

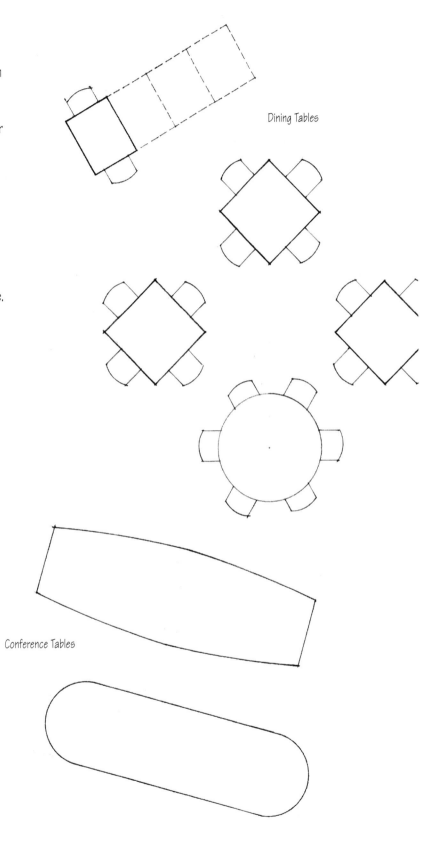

Dining Tables

Conference Tables

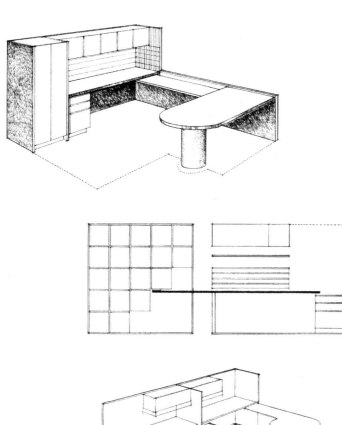

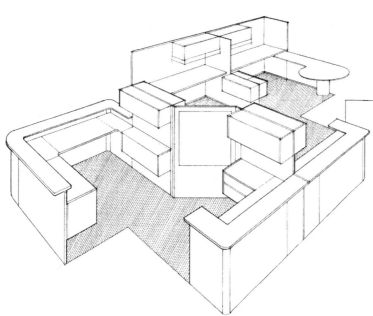

Integrated work station

Designers often refer to an individual's work area—comprising a desk, chair, computer and related equipment, as well as storage—as a workstation. The desk and adjacent horizontal surfaces are called worksurfaces.

Desks vary in style and function. The traditional desk incorporates drawers and storage into its base. A desk may also consist simply of a freestanding table or a work surface supported on a pedestal base with storage. This basic workstation can be extended with additional work surfaces to the side or behind the user.

The selection of a desk should consider how it would be used as well as issues of style and status. The size and configuration of the desk should respond to the need to accommodate storage and equipment, including computers and peripherals.

See page 317 for recommended dimensions for desks and work surfaces.

While the private office encloses a workstation within a room, open office environments utilize modular work surfaces and storage units to integrate multiple workstations and enhance user communication and productivity.

Open office systems offer flexibility in plan arrangements, efficiency in space utilization, and the ability to tailor a workstation to suit individual needs and specific tasks. The details of office systems vary with each manufacturer. They also vary from systems comprising modular panels, work surfaces, and storage units to freestanding and mobile units designed for maximum communication and flexibility.

Modular panels can be configured for stability and support the required work surfaces, storage units, lighting, and accessories. These partially enclosed areas can be located within a private office or in an open office layout. The panels are available in a variety of heights, widths, and finishes; some include glazing. Wiring for power, lighting, and telecommunications is often incorporated into the panel frames.

Freestanding systems function like floor-supported desks and frequently include mobile units.

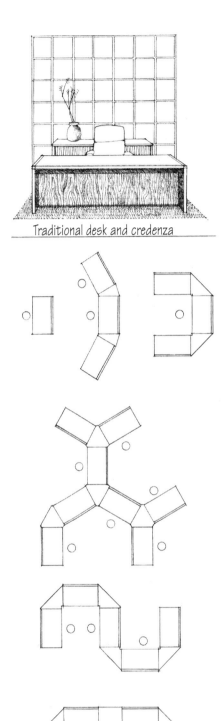

Traditional desk and credenza

Possible work station configurations

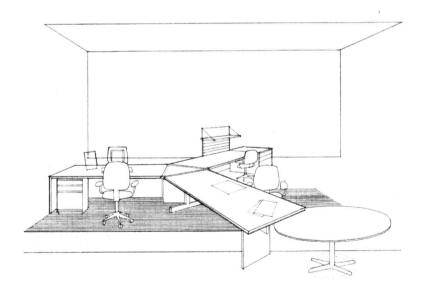

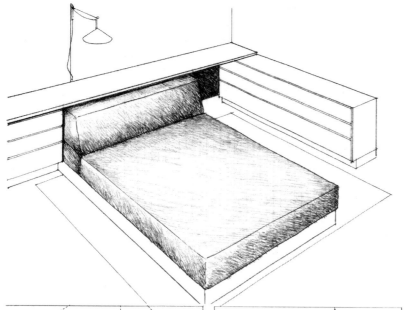

Beds consist of two basic components: the mattress or mattress set and the base or support frame. There are various types of mattresses, each made in its own way to respond to and support one's body shape and weight. Personal judgment and choice, therefore, are required in the selection of a mattress.

Interior designers are involved in the selection of the base or bed frame, headboard, footboard, canopy, associated tables, storage pieces, lighting, and electronic controls. The designer may also specify bed linens and covers and other room finishes.

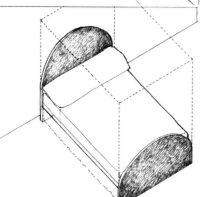

Headboards, footboards, and canopies define the volume of space occupied by a bed.

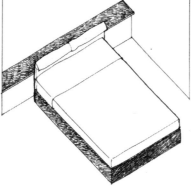

A bed can rest on a platform base, emphasizing the horizontality of the setting.

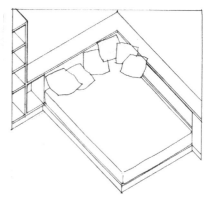

A bed built into a corner or alcove takes up less floor space, but it may be difficult to make.

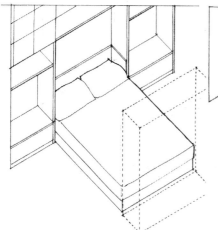

A bed can be integrated into a wall storage system at the head, the foot of the bed, or both.

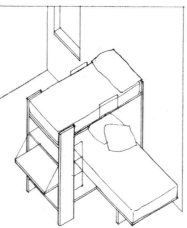

Bunk beds utilize vertical space to stack sleeping levels. Storage and desk surfaces can also be integrated into the system.

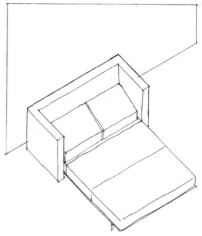

Sofas and armchairs that convert into beds offer convenient short-term sleeping arrangements.

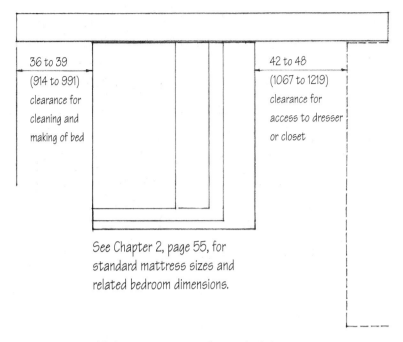

36 to 39
(914 to 991)
clearance for
cleaning and
making of bed

42 to 48
(1067 to 1219)
clearance for
access to dresser
or closet

See Chapter 2, page 55, for
standard mattress sizes and
related bedroom dimensions.

All dimensions are in inches, with their
metric equivalents in millimeters (shown
in parentheses).

For reading in bed, the headboard should
support the back and head comfortably. An
adjustable reading lamp, able to be focused
on reading matter, should be provided.

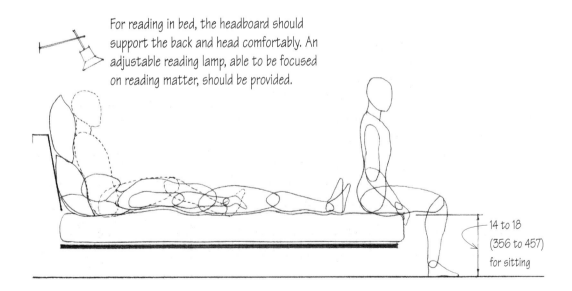

14 to 18
(356 to 457)
for sitting

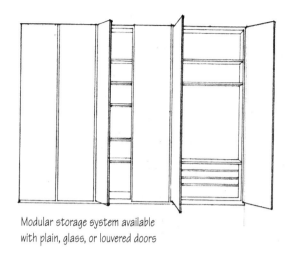

Modular storage system available
with plain, glass, or louvered doors

The amount and type of furniture in a bedroom depends upon the size of the room, the style of the project, and the needs of the intended user. A bedroom with a separate walk-in closet or dressing room may need fewer pieces of unit furniture for storage. A child's bedroom may double as a playroom or study area, while guest bedrooms may have alternate lives as home offices, sewing rooms, or storage rooms. Bedrooms may include extensive video and audio equipment or computer equipment, requiring special provisions for wiring.

Built-in storage can help to keep the lines of the room clean and avoid clutter. Individual pieces can balance the size and scale of the bed and add style, detail, and useful surfaces.

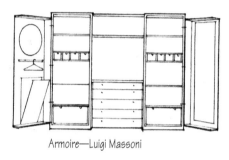

Armoire—Luigi Massoni

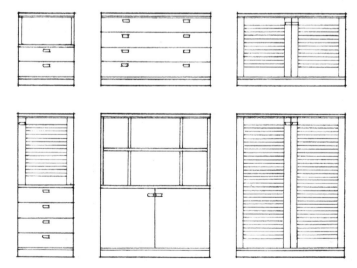

Modular set of chests of drawers and cupboards that
can be used singly or in stacked or tandem groupings

Armoires are freestanding closets with doors covering the front, often with drawers inside at the bottom.

Chests for bedcovers and clothing storage range from simple wood boxes opening at the top to more elaborate pieces with drawers below.

Antique-style court cupboards and press cupboards have drawers or doors in both its upper and lower sections.

Secretaries or escritoires and highboys have slanting fronts that drop down to create a writing surface with drawers below. They sometimes have bookcases or display cases above.

Dressing tables are designed for the user to sit facing a mirror while applying makeup or jewelry. Dressers hold smaller items of clothing and often include a mirror.

Night tables and nightstands are designed to hold items that may be needed during the night.

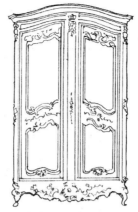

French Provincial armoire

American block front secretary

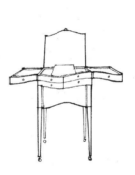

English dressing table

Early American dresser

English naval captain's chest

Chinese chest

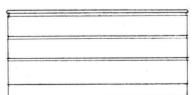

Chest of drawers

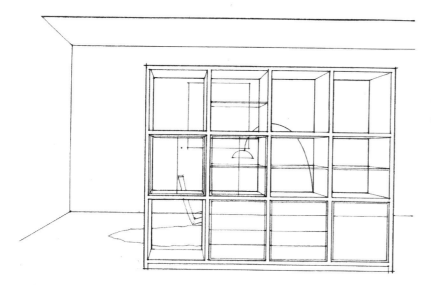

Wall storage systems consist of modular shelving, drawer, and cabinet units that can be combined in various ways to form self-supporting assemblies. The units may have open fronts or be fitted with solid, glass, or louvered doors. Some systems integrate display lighting into their construction.

A wall system can serve effectively as a freestanding room divider.

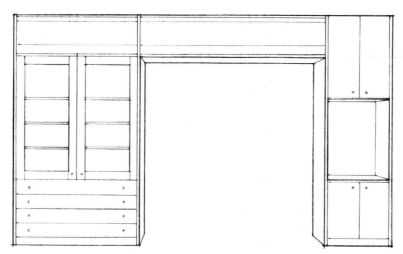

A wall storage system can form a shallow alcove space.

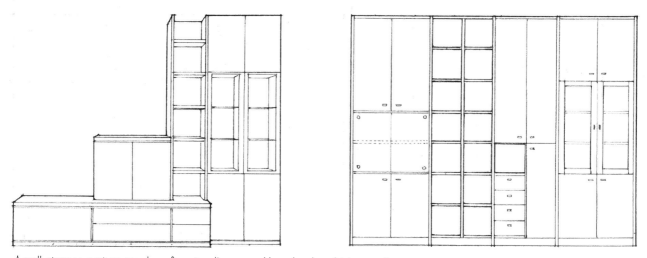

A wall storage system may be a freestanding assembly or be placed into a wall recess.

# Offices

Back storage units or credenzas are designed for storing documents, supporting equipment, and displaying work in progress. They eliminate clutter on the desk itself by containing box drawers, file drawers, doors with shelves, pullout equipment shelves, or bar units.

- 29" (737 mm) high
- 18" to 20" (457 mm to 508 mm) deep

Filing system should be selected for the client's filing needs, space availability, and quality of workmanship. Vertical files have two to five drawers, usually 15" (381 mm) or 18" (457 mm) wide and 18" to 29" (457 mm to 737 mm) deep.

Lateral files are two to five drawers high and are usually 30", 36", or 42" (762 mm, 914 mm, or 1067 mm) wide and 15" or 18" (381 mm or 457 mm) deep.

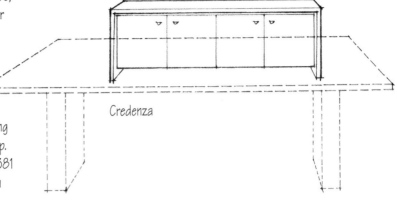

Credenza

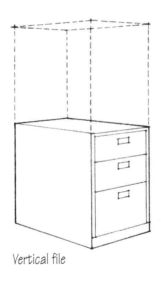

Vertical file

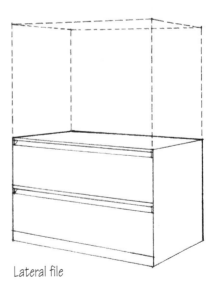

Lateral file

See pages 320–21 for workstations and office systems furniture.

Shutter

Awning

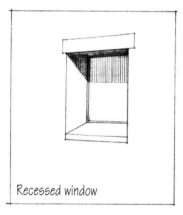

Recessed window

Trellis

In the broad category of window treatments are included devices that provide additional control of light, available views, and the passage of air, heat, and cold.

## Exterior Window Treatments

Exterior treatments are normally designed as integral elements of a building's architecture. If added to an existing building, such alterations should respect the existing architectural style.

| | |
|---|---|
| Shutters | Traditionally used to moderate light, heat, and cold. True shutters are seldom used today. |
| Awnings | Weatherproof, sometimes translucent, fabric stretched over a frame to provide shade. Some are retractable. |
| Overhangs and recessed windows | Provide protection from sun and rain. |
| Trellises | Open framework filters light and provides support for vines. |

## Interior Window Treatments

Interior window treatments vary according to how they temper the light, how they ventilate and provide a view, and how they alter a window's form and appearance. They play a role in absorbing sound, conserving energy, and enhancing fire safety. They also differ in how they open and close; a window treatment should not interfere with a window's operation or restrict access to its hardware.

### Shutters

- Rigid panels, usually of wood, are hinged to open and close like miniature doors.
- Panels usually have adjustable louvers so that filtering of light and view can be controlled.
- Shutters provide a clean, precise, uncluttered appearance.
- When closed, shutters enhance a sense of enclosure.

### Grills

- Grills are decorative screens of wood or metal that can be used to mask views, filter light, or diffuse ventilation.
- The degree of masking, filtration, or diffusion depends on the spacing and orientation of the spaced members.
- Grill may be fixed or adjustable.
- Design of grill pattern can be important visual element.

### Blinds

- Horizontal blinds consist of thin or wide slats of wood or metal.
- The spacing and adjustability of slats provide good control of light and air flow; thin slats obstruct view less than wide slats.
- Blinds are difficult to clean.
- Thin horizontal blinds are available inserted between the panes of thermal glazing in a window.
- Vertical blinds have slats, generally of opaque or translucent fabric, that pivot at the top and bottom. Vertical blinds enhance the height of a room, gather less dust, and can be made to fit odd-shaped openings.
- Manual or automatic controls are available.

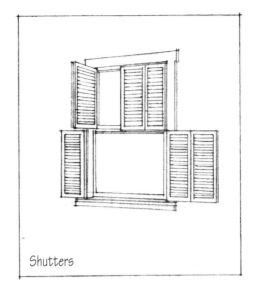

Shutters

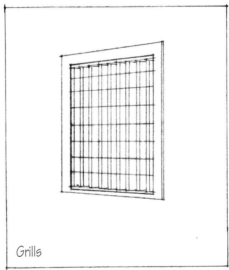

Grills

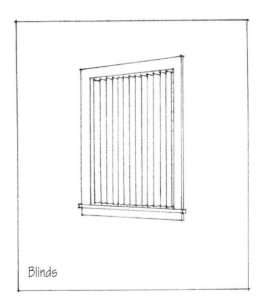

Blinds

Window treatments made of soft fabrics soften the lines of an interior space and add visual stimulation and detail. They can adjust for privacy needs and varying light levels, absorb sound, and provide thermal insulation. Sheer fabric softens and diffuses light, filters the view, and provides daytime privacy. Synthetic drapery fabrics including acetates, modacrylics, polyester, and glass fibers offer better resistance to sun and flame.

## Draperies

* Fabric panels are made of heavy opaque, partially opaque, or translucent fabrics that are generally pleated, hung on a rod, and pulled to one or both sides of the window.
* Types of drapery pleats include pinch, French, and spring-rod pleats.
* Draperies can be full and hung straight, tied back, or poufed.
* Draperies should start at the ceiling or slightly above the top of the frame and end slightly below the bottom of the frame or near the floor.

## Curtains

* Curtains are less formal than draperies. They may be stationary or hand-operated. Their tops can be looped, shirred, scalloped, or pleated. There may be a valance at the top.
* Curtains can be hung within the window frame or hang outside the frame to unify a group of windows.
* Shirred or sash curtains are gathered directly on rods across the sash of a window, and either hang straight down or are fastened to another rod at the bottom.
* Café curtains are either made in tiers to cover the whole window or only the bottom half.
* Ruffled curtains often have a ruffled valance and tiebacks.

Drapes

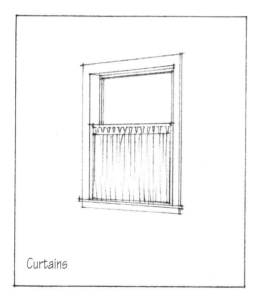

Curtains

### Shades

- Shades are made of translucent, opaque, or blackout fabric. Vinyl, fiberglass mesh, bamboo, or wooden slatted shades are also available.
- Shades usually operate from the top down to cover part or all of a window opening. Manual and automatic controls and skylight mountings are available.
- Roller shades have a spring mechanism attached to a length of flexible material.
- Translucent, transparent, or opaque pleated shades fold into a compact accordion shape.
- Cellular or honeycomb blinds offer both thermal insulating properties and varying degrees of translucence by bonding two layers of polyester fabrics with an insulating layer of air. They stack compactly.
- Roman shades are pulled up into horizontal pleats when raised by cords and hang flat when extended. They can be made of insulating materials and mounted to thwart drafts.
- Austrian shades are made of sheer or semi-sheer fabric gathered vertically into soft horizontal scallops by cords.
- Balloon, pouf, or cloud shades form balloonlike poufs when pulled up with vertical cords.

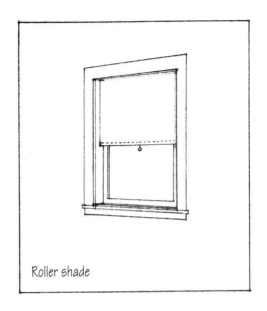

Roller shade

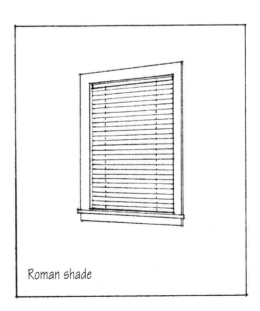

Roman shade

Accessories in interior design refer to those items that provide a space with aesthetic enrichment and embellishment. These items may provide visual delight for the eye, textural interest for the hand, or stimulation for the mind. Ultimately, accessories—individually or collectively—are the inevitable evidence of habitation.

Accessories help relate architectural interiors to human scale and to differentiate personal, social, and public zones around the human body. They help to identify the intended use of a space and the character of its users.

Accessories should be selected to support the design concept of the space and to reinforce design principles such as rhythm, balance, texture, pattern, and color. They can serve to tie design elements together or function as a focal point.

Accessories that add visual and tactile richness to an interior setting may be utilitarian, incidental, or decorative.

Utilitarian  Useful tools and objects
Incidental  Architectural elements and furnishings
Decorative  Artwork, collections, and plants

## Utilitarian Accessories

Utilitarian accessories come in a range of designs and their selection over time is often a reflection of the personality of those who inhabit the space. In work settings, office accessories are often specified in standardized sets to establish uniformity and hierarchy.

## Incidental Accessories

Incidental accessories enrich a space while simultaneously serving other functions. Architectural elements and the details that express the way materials are joined are an example of a dual purpose accessory. Other examples are the forms, colors, and textures of interior furnishings.

## Decorative Accessories

Decorative accessories delight the eye, the hand, or the intellect without necessarily being utilitarian in purpose. Decorative accessories and artwork should be included in the project budget and provisions must be made for display and lighting. Decorative accessories may include:

Artwork    Enriching a space with art follows an age-old tradition of decorating objects and surfaces. Many utilitarian and incidental items can be considered art. The selection and placement of artwork can emphasize strong design elements or alter the perception of the proportions of the space. Artwork may be selected from a client's collection, acquired to start a collection, or commissioned especially for a given project. Art consultants help designers and clients find and acquire appropriate pieces. In addition to paintings, prints, and photos, designers may include sculpture and crafts such as ceramics, glass, metal, and textiles.

Collections    Collections of objects may be serious or not so serious, but they almost always have personal meaning. Collections often create an opportunity for repetition of form, color, texture, or pattern. Individual pieces may be featured as focal elements.

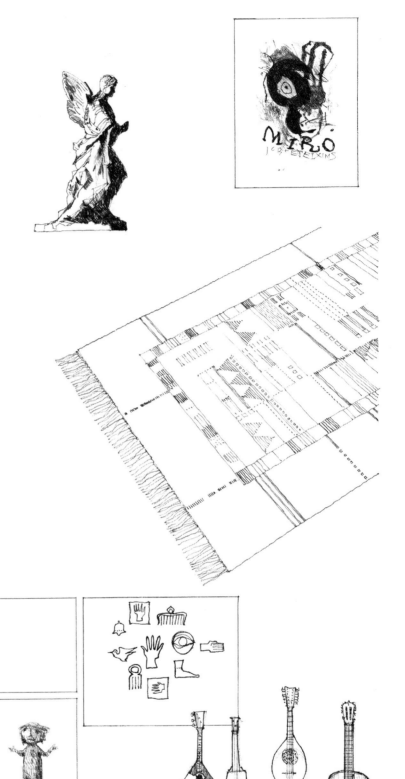

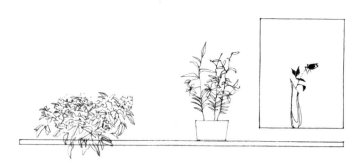

## Plants

Plants and flowers, as visible signs of nature, bring their expression of life and growth to interior spaces. Plants improve air quality and raise indoor humidity levels. However, plants may shelter insects and other pests and can harbor molds. Plants must be carefully selected for their required levels of light and maintenance, as well as for scale, form, and color. Some businesses hire companies to select, place, maintain, and replace plants on a schedule.

Artificial plants can closely resemble living plants and can substitute for them where the use of live plants is limited by lack of light or pest control concerns. Artificial plants and floral arrangements are prone to brittleness and dust collection and require maintenance as well.

# BIBLIOGRAPHY

Albers, Anni. *On Weaving*. New York: Dover Publications, 2003.

Allen, Edward. *How Buildings Work*. 3rd Ed. New York: Oxford University Press, 1995.

Allen, Phyllis Sloan, Miriam F. Stimpson, and Lynn M. Jones. *Beginnings of Interior Environment*. 9th Ed. Upper Saddle River, N.J.: Pearson Prentice Hall, 2004.

Arnheim, Rudolph. *Art and Visual Perception: A Psychology of the Creative Eye*. Berkeley: University of California Press, 1983.

Bevlin, Marjorie Elliott. *Design Through Discovery: The Elements and Principles*. 2nd Ed. New York: International Thomson Publishing, 1997.

Binggeli, Corky. *Building Systems for Interior Designers*. New York: John Wiley and Sons, 2003.

Birren, Faber. *Light, Color, and Environment*. 2nd Ed. West Chester, P.: Schiffer Publishing, Ltd., 1988.

Birren, Faber. *Principles of Color: A Review of Past Traditions and Modern Theories of Color Harmony*. Rev. Ed. Atglen, P.: Schiffer Publishing, Ltd., 1987.

Ching, Francis D.K. *Architectural Graphics*. 4th Ed. Hoboken, N.J.: John Wiley and Sons, 2003.

Ching, Francis D.K. *Building Construction Illustrated*. 3rd Ed. New York: John Wiley and Sons, 2001.

Doyle, Michael E. *Color Drawing*. 2nd Ed. New York: John Wiley and Sons, 1999.

Faulkner, Ray, and Sarah Faulkner. *Inside Today's Home*. 6th Ed. Fort Worth, Tex.: International Thomson Publishing, 1994.

Gordon, Gary. *Interior Lighting for Designers*. 4th Ed. Hoboken, N.J.: John Wiley and Sons, 2003.

Hall, Edward T. *The Hidden Dimension*. Reissued Ed. New York: Anchor, 1990.

Illuminating Engineering Society of North America. *IES Lighting Handbook*. Edited by Mark S. Rea. 9th Ed. New York: Illuminating Engineering Society of North America, 2000.

Itten, Johannes. *The Elements of Color*. New York: Van Nostrand Reinhold Co., 1970.

Karlen, Mark. *Space Planning Basics*. 2nd Ed. Hoboken, N.J.: John Wiley and Sons, 2003.

Kilmer, Rosemary, and W. Otie Kilmer. *Designing Interiors*. 1st Ed. New York: International Thomson Publishing, 1994.

McGowan, Maryrose, and Kelsey Kruse. *Interior Graphic Standards*. Hoboken, N.J.: John Wiley and Sons, 2003.

Panero, Julius, and Martin Zelnick. *Human Dimension and Interior Space*. New York: Watson-Guptill Publications, 1989.

Pile, John F. *Interior Design*. 3rd Ed. Upper Saddle River, N.J.: Prentice Hall Press, 2003.

Pile, John F. *Perspective for Interior Designers*. Reprint Ed. New York: Whitney Library of Design, 1989.

Piotrowski, Christine M., and Elizabeth A. Rogers. *Designing Commercial Interiors*. New York: John Wiley and Sons, 1999.

Ramsey, C., and H. Sleeper, *Architectural Graphic Standards*, 10th Ed. New York: John Wiley and Sons, 2000.

Rasmussen, Steen Eiler. *Experiencing Architecture*. 2nd Ed. Cambridge, Mass.: MIT Press, Massachusetts Institute of Technology, 1964.

Tilley, Alvin R., and Dreyfuss Associates. *Measure of Man and Woman: Human Factors in Design*. Revised Ed. New York: John Wiley and Sons, 2002.

Whiton, Sherrill and Stanley Abercrombie. *Interior Design & Decoration*. 5th Ed. Upper Saddle River, N.J.: Prentice Hall, 2002.

Other important sources of information for the interior designer include current periodicals such as **Architecture, Architectural Record, Case Da Abitare, Contract, Domus, Interior Design, Interiors,** and **Interiors and Sources**.

For information on current materials and product offerings, always consult manufacturers' catalogs or sales representatives.

# INDEX

## A

Aalto, Alvar, 312
Absorption Coefficient, sound, 272
accent lighting, 261
accessibility. See also Americans with Disabilities Act
     (ADA) of 1990; standards and codes
     bathing, human functional dimensions, 54
     fitting to space, 62–63
     standards and codes, 232
     accessories, 332–334
     decorative, 333
     incidental, 332
     plants, 334
     utilitarian, 332
accordion folding doors, 189
acoustical ceiling tiles, 165, 299
acoustics, 267–272
     ceilings, 171
     construction materials/assembly, 270–271
     environmental systems, 214
     generally, 267
     interior space shaping, 17
     noise reduction, 268–269
     sound, 268
     sound absorption, 272
     transmission loss (TL), 270
activity requirements, programming, 57
aesthetics, plan arrangements, 65
air conditioning, environmental systems, 218. See
     also HVAC (heating, ventilation, and air
     conditioning)
air movement, ceilings, 171. See also ventilation
air quality, environmental systems, 217
alarms, fire suppression systems, 229
alterations, interior space, 32–34
alternatives, interior design process, 42
ambient lighting, 259, 260
Americans with Disabilities Act (ADA) of 1990. See
     also accessibility; standards and codes;
     wheelchairs
     accessibility, 232
     elevators, 209
     stair railings, 202
analysis, interior design process, 40
antique furniture, 305, 325
architecture, interior space, 3, 6–7
area rugs, 287. See also carpeting and rugs
armchairs, 312
armoire, 324–325
articulation, of walls, 159
artwork, decorative accessories, 333
asymmetrical balance, 133–134
auditorium seating, 315
automatic sprinklers,, 229, 231
awnings, window treatments, 328

awning windows, 175
axonometric projections
     isometrics, 75
     paraline drawings, 74

## B

baffles, lighting fixtures, 253
balance, 129–134
     asymmetrical, 133–134
     elements in, 129
     radial, 132
     symmetrical, 131
     visual, 130
banquette seating, 315
bathing, human functional dimensions, 54
bathtub, 223
bay windows, 175
beams, structural systems, linear elements, 10–11
bedroom furniture, 324–325
beds, 322–323
Bengali rug, 287
bidet, 223
bidirectional daylighting, 243
bi-fold doors, 189
Birren, Peter, 117
black, color, simultaneous contrast, 113
blinds, window treatments, 329
boardroom tables, 319
body dimensions, human factors, 47–48
Bokhara rug, 287
booth seating, 315
Breuer, Marcel, 312
brightness
     light, 236
     light measurement, 262
brightness balance, lighting design, 266
building elements, 145–212. See also ceilings; doors;
     stairs; walls; windows
     ceilings, 162–171
     doors, 186–195
     elevators, 208–209
     escalators, 209
     fireplaces, 210–211
     floors, 148–149
     overview, 146–147
     ramps, 206–207
     stairs, 196–205
     walls, 150–161
     windows, 172–185
     woodburning stoves, 212
building envelope, structural system, 9
building section drawing, graphic representation, 72
built-in furniture, 307
built-in storage, 300–302
by-pass sliding doors, 188

## C

cabinets, finish materials, 300–302
carpeting and rugs, 282–287
    construction, 285
    fibers, 284
    rugs, 287
    sound absorption, 272
    textures, 286
carriages, stair construction, 200
casement windows, 174
casework, built-in storage, 300–302
ceilings, 162–171. See also building elements
    acoustics, 171
    finish materials, 297–299
    form, 168–169
    generally, 162–163
    height, dimensional elements, 26–27
    height and scale, 166–167
    interior space delimitation, 6–7
    lighting, 170
    suspended, 164–165
    wall articulation, 159
ceramic mosaic tile flooring materials, 279
ceramic tile wall materials, 294
chairs. See also seating
    dimensional requirements, 311
    office, 314
    residential seating, 312
chandeliers, sparkle, 261
chests, 325
Chinese Bengali rug, 287
chromatic distribution, 118
circle, shape, 94
circular stair plan, 199
clerestory windows, 185
climate, live loads, 8
coatings and paints, wall finish materials, 296
codes. See standards and codes
Coefficient of Utilization (CU), illumination
    measurement, 263
coffee tables, 318
coir carpeting fibers, 284
collections, decorative accessories, 333
color, 105–119
    chromatic distribution, 118
    dimensions of, 107
    light, 105–106, 111, 241
    pigments, 110
    schemes of, 116–117
    simultaneous contrast, 112–113
    space, 114–115
    systems of, 108–109
    tonal distribution, 119
    walls, 159, 161
color rendering index (CRI), light sources, 246

color temperature scale, 241
column, structural systems, linear elements, 10–11
column-and-beam construction, nonbearing walls, 155
comfort, furniture, 306
commercial seating, 311, 314–315. See also office
    furniture; seating
commercial tables, 319
Commission Internationale l'Eclairage (CIE), color
    system, 109
communication systems, fire suppression, 229
computer programs
    illumination measurement, 264
    3D modeling programs, 77
concept development, interior design process, 41
concrete flooring materials, 280
concrete slab construction
    floor construction, 149
    wood flooring materials, 278
concrete stair construction, 201
concrete wall construction, 153
conference tables, 319
construction materials/assembly. See also structural
    systems
    acoustics, 270–271
    carpeting and rugs, 285
    doors, 190–191
    floors, 149, 278
    stairs, 200–201
    walls, 151–155
        generally, 151–153
        load-bearing, 154
        nonbearing walls, 155
    windows, 176–177
contemporary furniture, 305
continuation, interior space delimitation, 7
contrast
    daylighting, 243
    interior space delimitation, 7
    light, 237
    simultaneous, color, 112–113
    texture, 100
cork
    flooring materials, 281
    wall coverings, 295
cornice lighting, 256
cotton carpeting fibers, 284
couch, residential seating, 313
counterpoint, interior space delimitation, 7
coved ceiling, 169
cove lighting, 256
credenza, office storage units, 327
cupboards, 325
curtains, window treatments, 330
curved line, form, 88
curvilinear space, dimensional elements, 24–25

## D

daylighting, 242–245. See also lighting
    ceilings, 170
    color, 111
    examples, 244–245
    fitting to space, 63
    interior space shaping, 16–17
    principles of, 243
    sunlight, 242
    windows, 182
dead loads, structural systems, 8
decibel (dB), sound measurement, 268
decision making, interior design process, 42
decorative accessories, 333
degree, proportion, 121
design principles
    balance, 129–134
    elements of, 120
    emphasis, 142–143
    harmony, 135–136
    proportion, 121–124
    rhythm, 138–141
    scale, 125–128
    unity and variety, 137
desk chairs, 311, 314
desks, dimensional requirements, 317
diagonal line, form, 88
diffused light transmission, 234
diffusers, lighting fixtures, 255
diffusion, light, 240
dimensional elements
    curvilinear, 24–25
    height, 26–27
    rectangles, 22–23
    squares, 20–21, 23
dimensional requirements. See also human factors
    beds, 323
    casework and built-in storage, 301
    chairs, 311
    electrical system, 227
    fireplaces, 210
    human scale, 127
    programming, 58–59
    stairs, 197
    tables, 317
dining, human functional dimensions, 51
dining tables, 317, 318
directional lighting, 240
discharge lamp, electric light source, 246, 248–250
domed ceiling, 169
doors, 186–195
    construction, 190–191
    design types, 187
    exterior/interior interface, 5
    frames, 192–193

generally, 186–187
operation, 188–189
space planning, 194–195
doorways
fitting to space, 62–63
interior space transitions, 29
double bowl sink, 223
double-hung windows, 174
downlights, 254–255
drainage, environmental systems, 214–215, 224
draperies, window treatments, 330
drawers, finish materials, 300–302
drawing systems, graphic representation, 69. See also
graphic representation
dressing tables, 325
drywall materials, 293
dyes, carpeting fibers, 284
dynamic loads, structural systems, 8

**E**

Eames, Charles, 305, 309
earthquake, dynamic loads, 8
easy chair, dimensional requirements, 311
echoes, defined, 267
economy, interior design criteria, 45
eggcrates, lighting fixtures, 253
egress, standards and codes, 231
electrical systems, environmental systems, 214–215,
225–228
electric light sources, 246–251. See also lighting
color rendering index (CRI), 246
fiber optic, 251
fluorescent lamp, 248
generally, 246
high-intensity discharge lamps, 249–250
incandescent lamps, 247
light-emitting diode lamps (LEDs), 251
elevations, interior, graphic representation, 73
elevators, 208–209
emphasis, 142–143
achievement of, 142
degrees of, 143
energy conservation
ambient lighting, 260
codes for, 232, 266
lighting design, 266
entries, fitting to space, 62–63
Environmental Protection Agency (EPA), 212
environmental systems, 213–232
air quality, 217
electrical circuits, 226–227
electrical outlets, 228
electrical systems, 225
fire suppression, 229
generally, 214–215

HVAC, 218–220
plumbing, 221–224
plumbing fixtures, 222–223
sanitary drainage, 224
standards and codes, 230–232
thermal comfort, 216
water supply, 221
Equivalent Sphere Illumination (ESI) footcandle, 262
escalators, 209
escritoires, 325
Euclid, 122
evaluation, interior design process, 42
executive chairs, 311, 314. See also office furniture
exits, standards and codes, 231
exterior space
delimiting of, 4–5
interior space interface, 5
exterior window treatments, 328
external outlook. See views
eye
lighting and, 235–241
perception, 82–84

**F**

fabric wall coverings, 295
fiber optic light sources, 251
Fibonacci series, proportion system, 122
figure-ground relationship
interior space, 18–19
perception, 83–84
files, office storage units, 327. See also office furniture
filtering views, windows, 181
finish materials, 273–302. See also flooring finish
materials; wall finish materials
acoustics, 271, 272
casework and built-in storage, 300–302
ceilings, 297–299
floor construction, 149
flooring, 274–287
selection criteria, 274
walls, 288–296
fire exits, elevators/escalators, 209
fireplaces, 210–211
fire safety, standards and codes, 231
fire suppression systems, 229
fit, human factors, 46
fitting to space, interior design, 62–63
fixed windows, 174
fixtures. See lighting fixtures; plumbing fixtures
Flatoy, Torstein, 305
flexible wall coverings, 295
flooring finish materials, 274–287. See also carpeting
and rugs
carpeting and rugs, 282–287
resilient, 281

selection criteria, 275–276
terrazzo, 280
tile and stone, 279
wood, 277–278
floor plans, graphic representation, 71
floors, 148–149
construction of, 149
interior space delimitation, 6–7
loads, 148
flowers, accessories, 334
fluorescent lamp
color, 241
electric light source, 246, 248
flush doors, 187, 191
flutter, ceiling acoustics, 171
focal lighting, 259, 261
foil wall coverings, 295
folding chairs, 314
folding doors, 189
footcandle, light measurement, 262
forced-air heating, 218
form
ceilings, 168–169
elements of, 85
figure-ground relationship, interior space, 18–19
interior design criteria, 45
interior space delimitation, 6–7
line, 87–88
linear elements, 89
linear forms, 90
planar form, 92
plane, 91
point, 86
shape, 93–96
volume, 103–104
walls, 157
foundation, structural system, 8
frames
doors, 192–193
windows, 178–179
freeform ceiling, 169
freehand sketching, graphic representation, 80
freestanding partitions, 156
French doors, 187
function
interior design criteria, 45
interior space shaping, 17
plan arrangement criteria, 64
functional dimensions, 50–55. See also dimensional
requirements; human factors
bathing, 54
dining, 51
heights, 55
kitchen activities, 52
seating, 50

functional dimensions (continued)
sleeping, 55
work stations, 53
furnishings and furniture, 303–334. See also office
furniture
accessories, 332–334
arrangement, 307
bedroom, 324–325
beds, 322–323
generally, 304–305
human factors, 306
interior space shaping, 16–17
materials, 308–309
programming requirements, 57, 58
seating, 310–315
commercial, 311, 314–315
generally, 310
residential, 312–313
upholstery, 311
storage units, 326–327
systems furniture, 321
tables, 316–319
dimensions, 317
generally, 316
styles and uses, 318–319
window treatments, 328–331
generally, 328
hard, 329
soft, 330–331
workstations, 320
furring, wall finish materials, 288
fusion-bonded carpet construction, 285

**G**

gabled ceiling, 168
Gardella, Ignazio, 318
glare
daylighting, 243
light, 238–239
lighting fixtures, 255
glass doors, 187
glitter
lighting fixtures, 252
reflected glare, 239
golden section, proportion system, 122–123
graphic representation, 68–80
drawing systems, 69
freehand sketching, 80
interior elevations, 73
isometrics, 75
multiview drawings, 70
paraline drawings, 74
perspective drawing, 77–79
one-point perspective, 78
two-point perspective, 79

plan obliques, 76
plans, 71
section drawing, 72
grid layout, linear structural system, 11
grills, window treatments, 329
Griziotti, Laura, 318
grouting, tile and stone flooring materials, 279
gypsum board materials
ceilings, 297
walls, 293

**H**

half-turn stair plan, 198
halogen lamps, 247
handmade punched carpet construction, 285
handrails
ramps, 207
stairs, 202–203
hard window treatments, 329
harmony
creation of, 136
defined, 135
health and safety codes, 231. See also standards and
codes
heat gain/loss, windows, 184
heating, ventilation, and air conditioning (HVAC),
environmental systems, 214–215, 218–220.
See also ventilation
heat transfer, thermal comfort, 216
height
ceilings, 166–167
human functional dimensions, 55
highboys, 325
high-intensity discharge lamps, 249–250
high-pressure sodium discharge lamps, 249, 250
hollow metal door, 190
hollow metal door frame, 192
hopper windows, 175
horizontal slab, planar structural systems, 12–13
hose systems, fire suppression, 229
hotel tables and desks, 319
hot-water heating, 219
hue. See also color
color, 107
lighting, 111
mixing of, 110
human factors, 46–55. See also dimensional
requirements
body dimensions, 47–48
fit, 46
functional dimensions, 50–55
bathing, 54
dining, 51
heights, 55
kitchen activities, 52

seating, 50
sleeping, 55
workstations, 53
furniture, 306
personal space requirements, 49
scale, 125, 127
senses, 46
HVAC (heating, ventilation, and air conditioning),
environmental systems, 214–215, 218–220.
See also ventilation

**I**

illuminance, light measurement, 262
illumination
measurement of, 263–264
reflectance and, brightness, 236
image, interior design criteria, 45
implementation, interior design process, 43
incandescent lamps, electric light sources, 247
incidental accessories, 332
Indian Numdah rug, 287
indirect glare, light, 239
indirect lighting, lighting fixtures, 257
indoor air quality, environmental systems, 217
integration, of requirements and spaces, 59–61
interior building elements. See building elements
interior design, 35–80
criteria in, 45
defined, 36
design and construction team, 38
elements of, interior space shaping, 16–17
fitting to space, 62–63
graphic representation, 68–80
drawing systems, 69
freehand sketching, 80
interior elevations, 73
isometrics, 75
multiview drawings, 70
paraline drawings, 74
perspective drawing, 77–79
plan obliques, 76
plans, 71
section drawing, 72
human factors, 46–55
body dimensions, 47–48
fit, 46
functional dimensions, 50–55
personal space requirements, 49
senses, 46
interior space modifications, 34
plan arrangements, 64–67
aesthetics, 65
functional criteria, 64
loose fit, 67
tight fit, 66

process of, 39–43
    analysis, 40
    evaluation, 42
    implementation, 43
    problem statement, 39
    synthesis, 41
programming, 56–61
    activity requirements, 57
    dimensional requirements, 58–59
    furnishing requirements, 57, 58
    integration, 59–61
    space analysis, 58
    user requirements, 56
purpose of, 36–37
value judgments, 44
interior elevations, graphic representation, 73
interior environmental systems. See environmental
    systems
interior space, 1–34. See also space
    architectural space, 3
    delimiting of, 6–7
    dimensional elements, 20–27
        curvilinear, 24–25
        height, 26–27
        rectangles, 22–23
        squares, 20–21, 23
    doors and doorways, 194–195
    exterior space interface, 5
    figure-ground relationship, 18–19
    fireplaces, 211
    modification, 32–34
    shaping of, 16–17
    site elements, 4
    space, defined, 2
    stairs, 204–205
    structural systems, 8–15
        building envelope, 9
        composite systems, 15
        linear elements, 10–11
        loads, 8
        mechanical systems, 9
        planar elements, 12–13
        volumetric, 14
    transitions, 28–31
        doorways, 29
        stairways, 31
        windows, 30
    windows, 185
interior window treatments, 328
internal focus, fitting to space, 62–63
International Energy Conservation Code (IECC), 232
International Metric System, 125
intimate space, personal space requirements, 49
isometrics, graphic representation, 75

**J**
Jacobsen, Arne, 305, 312, 314, 318
jalousie windows, 175
jute carpeting fibers, 284

**K**
kitchen activities, human functional dimensions, 52
kitchen sink, 223
Knoll International, 306

**L**
ladders, dimensional requirements, 197
lamps, portable, 258. See also electric light sources
landings
    ramps, 207
    stairs, 198–199
lavatory, 223
LCS-Krueger chair, 312
leather tile flooring materials, 281
Le Corbusier, 305, 309
Lella e Massimo, 318
lens, lighting fixtures, 253
light. See also daylighting; electric light sources;
    lighting; lighting fixtures
    brightness, 236
    color, 105–106, 111, 241
    color rendering index (CRI) of sources, 246
    contrast, 237
    diffusion, 240
    glare, 238–239
    illumination measurement, 263–264
    interior space delimitation, 6–7
    lighting and, 234
    measurement of, 262
    texture, 99
light-emitting diode lamps (LEDs), 251
lighting, 234–266. See also daylighting; electric light
    sources; lighting fixtures
    ceilings, 170
    color, 111
    color rendering index (CRI), 246
    daylighting, 242–245
    design considerations, 265–266
    electric sources, 246–251
    environmental systems, 214–215
    fixtures, 252–258
    flooring finish materials, 276
    health and safety codes, 231
    illumination measurement, 263–264
    interior space shaping, 16–17
    light and, 234
    programming integration, 61
    types of, 259–261
    vision and, 235–241
    windows, 182

lighting fixtures, 252–258. See also daylighting;
    electric light sources; lighting
    generally, 252
    pendant-mounted, 257
    portable lamps, 258
    recessed, 254
    semirecessed, 255
    surface-mounted, 256
    track-mounted, 257
    types of, 253
Light Loss Factor (LLF), illumination measurement,
    263
line, form, 85, 87–88
Linea-Klöber-Brayton International, 314
linear elements
    composite systems, 15
    form, 89
    structural systems, 10–11
linear forms, 90
linoleum flooring materials, 281
Lipparini, Mauro, 313
live loads, structural systems, 8
load(s)
    electrical circuits, 227
    floors, 148
    structural systems, 8
load-bearing wall(s), 150–151
    construction of, 154
    planar structural systems, 12–13
loose fit, plan arrangements, 67
lounge chairs, 312
louvered doors, 187
louvers, lighting fixtures, 253
loveseat
    commercial seating, 315
    residential seating, 313
Luchi, Michelle de, 318
luminance, defined, 262
luminance ratio, lighting design, 266
luminous flux, light measurement, 262
luminous intensity, light measurement, 262
Luminous-Intensity Distribution Curve (LIDC), 263

**M**
Mackintosh, Charles Rennie, 305
Magistretti, Vico, 309
magnitude, proportion, 121
Makulik, Bernd, 309
Mantiglia, R. Carta, 318
masonry wall construction, 153
Massoni, Luigi, 324
mathematical systems, proportion, 122–123
Matta, Sebastian, 309
meaning, interior design criteria, 45
measurement, scale, 125

mechanical systems
    structural systems, 9
    suspended ceilings, 165
Mendini, Alessandro, 313
mercury-vapor discharge lamps, 249
metal(s)
    ceiling materials, 298
    furniture materials, 309
    window frames, 179
metal halide discharge lamps, 249, 250
Mies van der Rohe, Ludwig, 305, 309, 318
modern furniture, 305
modification, interior space, 32–34
modular bedroom furniture, 324
modular ceiling materials, 298
modular furniture arrangements, 307
modular seating, 315
moldings, wall articulation, 159
Molinari, Pier Luigi, 313
movement, fitting to space, 62–63
multiview drawings, 70
Munsell color system, 108–109

**N**

National Electrical Code, 227
Navajo rug, 287
needle-punched carpet construction, 285
night tables and nightstands, 325
noise control. See also acoustics
    acoustics, 268–269
    environmental systems, 214
Noise Reduction Coefficient (NRC), sound absorption,
    272
nonbearing walls, 155
nondiffused light transmission, 234
nonload-bearing walls, 150–151
nylon carpeting fibers, 284

**O**

oblique projections, 74
occasional tables, 318
off-center pyramid ceiling, 168
office furniture. See also furnishings and furniture
    chairs, 311, 314
    desks and work surfaces, 317
    storage units, 327
    systems furniture, 321
    tables, 319
    workstations, 320
olefin carpeting fibers, 284
one-point perspective drawing, 78
opaque materials, light, 234
openings, within or between walls, 158
open stair railings, 202
organizational standards, model codes, 230

outlook, interior space delimitation, 6–7
overhead doors, 189

**P**

paints and coatings, wall finish materials, 296
panel doors, 187
Pantone color system, 109
parabolic reflectors, lighting fixtures, 253
paraline drawings, 74
particleboard furniture materials, 308
passive solar heating, windows, 184
pattern, texture, 101
paver flooring materials, 279
pendant-mounted lighting fixtures, 257
perception, 82–84. See also light; lighting; vision
personal space requirements, human factors, 49
perspective drawing, 77–79
    one-point perspective, 78
    two-point perspective, 79
pigments, color, 110
plan(s), graphic representation, 71
planar elements
    composite systems, 15
    structural systems, 12–13
planar form, 92
plan arrangements, 64–67
    aesthetics, 65
    functional criteria, 64
    loose fit, 67
    tight fit, 66
plane, form, 85, 91
plan obliques, graphic representation, 76
plants, accessories, 334
plaster, wall materials, 292
plasterboard materials
    ceilings, 297
    walls, 293
plastic furniture materials, 309
plumbing
    environmental systems, 214–215, 221–224
    wall construction, 152
plumbing fixtures, 222–223
plywood
    furniture materials, 308
    wall materials, 291
pocket sliding doors, 188
point, form, 85, 86
polyester carpeting fibers, 284
porch, exterior/interior interface, 5
portable lamps, 258. See also electric light sources
primary hues, 107
privacy, sound absorption, 272
programming, 56–61
    activity requirements, 57
    dimensional requirements, 58–59

    furnishing requirements, 57, 58
    integration, 59–61
    space analysis, 58
    user requirements, 56
proportion, 121–124
    defined, 121
    mathematical systems, 122–123
    proportional relationships, 124
    scale, 125
public zone, personal space requirements, 49
Puppa, Daniela, 318
purpose. See function
pyramid ceiling, 168

**Q**

quantity, proportion, 121
quarry tile flooring materials, 279
quarter-turn stair plan, 198
quartz lamps, 247

**R**

radial balance, 132
radiant heating, 219
railings
    ramps, 207
    stairs, 202–203
ramps, 206–207
ratio, proportion system, 122–123
recessed lighting fixtures, 254–255
rectangles, dimensional elements, 22–23
reevaluation, interior design process, 43
reflectance, illumination and, brightness, 236
reflected glare, light, 239
reflection, light, 234
reflectors, lighting fixtures, 253
remodeling, interior space, 32–34
repetition, rhythm, 138–139
residential seating, 312–313. See also seating
resilient flooring materials, 281
restaurant chairs, 314
restaurant tables, 319
reveal, wall articulation, 159
reverberation
    defined, 267
    sound absorption, 272
rhythm, 138–141
    repetition, 138–139
    spatial, 141
    visual, 140
ridged baffles, lighting fixtures, 253
risers, stairs, 196, 200, 201
roller shade, window treatments, 331
Roman shade, window treatments, 331
rubber flooring materials, 281
rugs, 287. See also carpeting and rugs

## S

Saarinen, Eero, 314

safety and health codes, 231. See also standards and codes

sanitary drainage, environmental systems, 214–215, 224

sash doors, 187

saturation, color, 107

scale
ceilings, 166–167
human, 127
interior space delimitation, 6–7
measurement, 125
relationships among, 128
texture, 98
visual, 126

seagrass carpeting fibers, 284

seating
commercial, 311, 314–315
generally, 310
human functional dimensions, 50
residential, 312–313
upholstery, 311

secondary hues, 107

secretaries, 325

sectional seating, 315

section drawing, graphic representation, 72

semirecessed lighting fixtures, 255

shades, window treatments, 331

shadows, lighting design, 266

Shaker ladderback chair, 312

shape, form, 93–96

shelving, finish materials, 300–302

ship's ladders, dimensional requirements, 197

showers, 223

shutters, window treatments, 328, 329

side chairs, 312, 314

simultaneous contrast, color, 112–113

single-slope ceiling, 168

sinks, 223

sisal carpeting fibers, 284

site elements, exterior space, 4

skylights
daylighting, 182, 243, 245
space planning, 185
window construction, 175

slabs, planar structural systems, 12–13

sleeping, human functional dimensions, 55

sliding doors, 188

sliding windows, 174

slope, ramps, 206

social zone, personal space requirements, 49

sodium discharge lamps, 249, 250

sofas
commercial seating, 315

residential seating, 313

soft window treatments, 330–331

solar heat gain
thermal comfort, 216
windows, 184

solid core door construction, 191

solids, volume, 103–104

solid stair railings, 202

sound. See also acoustics
acoustics, 268
defined, 267

sound absorption, acoustics, 272

space. See also interior space
color, 114–115
defined, 2
exterior space, 4–5
form, 104
texture, 102
wall forms, 157

space analysis, programming, 58

sparkle
ambient lighting, 259
chandeliers, 261
lighting fixtures, 252
reflected glare, 239

spatial rhythm, 141

special folding doors, 189

specular reflection, light, 234

speech privacy, sound absorption, 272

spiral stair plan, 199

sprinkler systems, fire suppression, 229, 231

square(s)
dimensional elements, 20–21, 23
shape, 96

square bathtub, 223

stacking chairs, 314

stains, wall finish materials, 296

stairs and stairways, 196–205
construction, 200–201
dimensions, 197
generally, 196
interior space transitions, 31
plan types, 198–199
railings, 202–203
space planning, 204–205

standards and codes. See also accessibility; Americans with Disabilities Act (ADA) of 1990
accessibility, 232
building codes, 230
electrical circuits, 227
elevators/escalators, 209
energy conservation, 232
exits, 231
fire safety, 231

health and safety, 231
model codes, 230
stair railings, 202
stairs, 196, 199
windows, 175

standpipes, fire suppression systems, 229

steel stair construction, 201

stone flooring materials, 279

stools, 314

storage
bedroom furniture, 324–325
casework and, finish materials, 300–302
office furniture, 327
wall systems, 326

straight line, form, 88

straight-run stair plan, 198

stringers, stair construction, 200, 201

structural systems, 8–15. See also construction materials/assembly
building envelope, 9
composite systems, 15
interior space modifications, 32–34
linear elements, 10–11
loads, 8
mechanical systems, 9
planar elements, 12–13
volumetric, 14

stud-framed wall construction, 152

style, interior design criteria, 45

subfloor/joist construction, wood flooring materials, 278

sunlight, daylighting, 242. See also daylighting

superstructure, structural system, 8

surface-mounted lighting fixtures, 256

surface sliding doors, 188

suspended ceilings, 164–165, 299

swinging doors, 188

symbols, electrical systems, 228

symmetrical balance, 131

synthesis, interior design process, 41

synthetic carpeting fibers, 284

systems furniture, office furniture, 321

## T

tables, 316–319
dimensions, 317
generally, 316
styles and uses, 318–319

tactile texture, 97

Tapinassi, Roberto, 313

task lighting
ambient lighting, 259, 260
focal lighting, 261
glare, 239

terrazzo flooring materials, 280

texture, 97–102
    carpeting and rugs, 286
    contrast, 100
    defined, 97
    flooring finish materials, 276
    light, 99, 237
    pattern, 101
    scale, 98
    space, 102
    walls, 159, 160, 161
thermal comfort, environmental systems, 216
3D computer modeling programs, 77
tight fit, plan arrangements, 66
tile
    flooring materials, 279
    wall materials, 294
tonal distribution, color, 119
track-mounted lighting fixtures, 257
transitional spaces
    exterior/interior interface, 5
    interior space, 28–31
        doorways, 29
        stairways, 31
        windows, 30
transmission loss (TL), acoustics, 270
treads, stairs, 196, 200, 201
trellis, window treatments, 328
triangle, shape, 95
trim
    door frames, 192–193
    wall articulation, 159
    window construction, 177
tufted carpet construction, 285
tungsten-halogen lamps, 247
two-point perspective drawing, 79

## U

U.S. Customary System, 125
unity, variety and, 137
upholstery, seating, 311
uplights, lighting fixtures, 257
urinal, 223
user requirements, programming, 56
utilitarian accessories, 332
utility, interior design criteria, 45
utility sink, 223

## V

valance lighting, 256
value, color, 107
value judgments, interior design, 44
variety, unity and, 137
vaulted ceiling, 169
ventilation. See also heating, ventilation, and air
    conditioning (HVAC), environmental systems;
    windows
    ceilings, 171
    environmental systems, 217
    health and safety codes, 231
    programming integration, 61
    walls, 150
    windows, 174–175, 183, 184
views
    doors and doorways, 195
    fitting to space, 62–63
    windows, 180–181
vinyl flooring materials, 281
vision
    lighting and, 235–241
    perception, 82–84
visual balance, 130
visual rhythm, 140
visual scale, 126
visual texture, 97
Vogtherr, Burkhardt, 313
voids, volume, 104
volume, form, 85, 103–104
volumetric structural systems, 14, 15

## W

wainscots, wall articulation, 159
wall finish materials, 288–296
    flexible wall coverings, 295
    generally, 288–289
    gypsum board, 293
    paints and coatings, 296
    plaster, 292
    tile, 294
    wood, 290–291
wall-mounted lighting fixtures, 256
wallpaper, 295
walls, 150–161. See also building elements
    articulation of, 159
    color, 161
    construction of, 152–153
    exterior/interior interface, 5
    forms, 157
    freestanding partitions, 156
    generally, 150–151
    interior space delimitation, 6–7
    load-bearing, 154
    nonbearing, 155
    openings within or between, 158
    planar structural systems, 12–13
    texture, 160
    windows, 172–173
wall systems, storage, 326
Ward Bennett Designs/Brickel Associates, 313

Wassily chair (Marcel Breuer), 312
water closet, 223
water supply
    environmental systems, 214–215, 221
    fire suppression systems, 229
Wegner, Hans, 305
wheelchairs. See also accessibility; Americans with
        Disabilities Act (ADA) of 1990; standards
        and codes
    body dimensions, 48
    elevators, 209
    functional activities, 52
    ramps, 206
white, color, simultaneous contrast, 113
Wilkhahn Seating-Vecta Contract, 314
winders, stair plan, 199
windows, 172–185. See also building elements
    construction, 176–177
    daylighting, 182, 243–245
    exterior/interior interface, 5
    fitting to space, 63
    frames, 178–179
    generally, 172–173
    interior space transitions, 30
    operational categories, 174–175
    solar heat gain, 184
    space planning, 185
    ventilation, 183
    view framing, 180–181
window treatments, 328–331
    generally, 328
    hard, 329
    soft, 330–331
winds, dynamic loads, 8
woodburning stoves, 212
wood ceiling materials, 297
wood door construction, 191
wood door frames, 192–193
wood flooring materials, 277–278
wood furniture materials, 308
wood stair construction, 200
wood wall materials, 290–291
wood window frame, 178
wool carpeting fibers, 284
work areas, lighting, 239
workstations
    dimensional requirements, 317
    furniture, 320
    human functional dimensions, 53
woven carpet construction, 285

## Z

Ziehmer, Kurt, 318